EMPIRICAL POVERTY RESEARCH IN A COMPARATIVE PERSPECTIVE

Empirical Poverty Research in a Comparative Perspective

Edited by
Hans-Jürgen Andreß
University of Bielefeld

Routledge
Taylor & Francis Group
LONDON AND NEW YORK

First published 1998 by Ashgate Publishing

Reissued 2018 by Routledge
2 Park Square, Milton Park, Abingdon, Oxon, OX14 4RN
711 Third Avenue, New York, NY I 0017, USA

Routledge is an imprint of the Taylor & Francis Group, an informa business

A Library of Congress record exists under LC control number: 97076950

ISBN 13: 978-1-138-31351-4 (hbk)
ISBN 13: 978-1-138-33800-5 (pbk)
ISBN 13: 978-0-429-44200-1 (ebk)

Contents

Empirical poverty research in a comparative perspective: Basic orientations and outline of the book

Hans-Jürgen Andreß

1 Introduction

It is astonishing. In the social science literature one finds a large number of publications discussing how to define poverty. The term itself, however, is taken for granted. Apparently it has become so common in our daily life that it appears unnecessary to explain it. What is meant therefore by the term 'poverty'? Before answering this question, we need to clarify which units or phenomena the term should describe. Since most of the studies collected in this book study individuals in different countries, poverty in this context is first of all understood as an individual characteristic and not as a collective phenomenon of a whole society. As an individual characteristic we define poverty as a condition of individual scarcity which frequently takes extreme forms. According to Simmel 'individual' poverty exists for those people 'whose means are not sufficient for their aims' (1908, p. 369; transl. by H.J.A.). Somewhat differently formulated one could say: Poor is that person whose resources do not satisfy their needs. This asks the question of how to define resources and needs and how far both have to differ from each other to raise the issue of poverty.

Let us begin first of all with the term 'needs' (a definition of the term 'resources' follows in section 2). The term 'needs' quite generally comprises all those goods and services that an individual needs for living at a given point in time. Depending on the individual preferences of the person, however, this quantity of goods and services is in principal unlimited. Therefore, one usually talks about a minimum amount of needs, because otherwise (almost) all persons would be poor.

For centuries the debate on poverty was occupied with the question whether minimum standards and thus poverty should be defined in absolute or relative terms. 'An absolute definition of needs assumes that there is a firm scale which does not change over time. If the level of prices changes, the money equivalent will rise that is necessary to satisfy certain needs; however, with an absolute standard the needs themselves remain always unchanged' (Piachaud 1992, p. 64; transl. by H.J.A.). As a rule the absolute standard is equated with those goods which are necessary for the physical existence of a person. 'This is a definition of material poverty which starts from situations of scarcity that refer to nutrition, clothing, housing, and health care' (Hauser/Neumann 1992, p. 245; transl. by H.J.A.). A relative definition, in contrast, refers to the average and generally accepted standard of living at a certain point of time in a given society, relative to which a minimum standard is determined, which includes not only material but also immaterial goods. In contrast to the physical minimum standard a relative definition of poverty refers to a socio-cultural minimum standard.

Both definitions have been criticized for different reasons. For reasons of space we do not repeat this debate here (for an overview cf. e.g. Piachaud 1992; Schäuble 1984; Zimmermann 1993). However, there exists a broad consensus that it is difficult if not impossible to talk about poverty without refering to the historically given living standard of a society. If one looks for instance at the change in living conditions in Western industrial societies in this century, the assumption of a time-invariant minimum standard is hard to maintain. This is even true for such basic material goods like nutrition and housing: 'All together it can be ascertained that a clear and objective physical minimum standard does not exist. At best such a standard can be determined approximately with reference to the natural, social, and economic general conditions and taking into consideration subjective appraisals' (Scheurle 1992, p. 6; transl. by H.J.A.). Thus, in our opinion poverty can be understood only in relation to the historically given living standard of a society. We concede, however, that there is a subsistance minimum in each society beyond which the physical survival of a person is no longer guaranteed. Thus, in (underdeveloped) societies with huge nutrition problems it can very well be meaningful to examine the physical survival of their citizens in terms of food baskets, a measure developed by nutritionists and other experts. In developed Western industrial societies, however, in which these problems have been largely solved, poverty research concentrates on the analysis of situations of scarcity compared to an average and generally accepted standard of living.

A direct consequence of this procedure is that value judgements are unavoidable when selecting the standard of comparison. Which persons are classified as poor is a question of definition so to speak. However, similar value judgements are necessary when using an absolute definition of poverty based on nutrition standards. The differences between both concepts are, therefore, more of a gradual than a principal nature. Today it is widely accepted that an objective definition of poverty is impossible and poverty is thus a normative concept. As Piachaud puts it: 'A definition and measurement of poverty is [only] in that sense objective that it is explicit, clear, and verifiable and uses the best available measurement methods. The necessity to apply value judgements will always exist' (Piachaud 1992, p. 66, transl. by H.J.A.).

Given this observation the question emerges of who makes these value judgements. First of all, the poverty researchers themselves have to be mentioned. They conceptually define the phenomena to be analyzed empirically, decide about the methods of data collection, and finally use certain methods of analysis to arrive at results. In doing so they very often use judgements of other experts (e.g. nutritionists), politically motivated definitions (e.g. minimum income standards of different social security and welfare systems), or simply statistical criteria (e.g. average incomes in a society). But with the increasing application of survey methods we observe a tendency to replace a part of these value judgements with public opinion. Following corresponding surveys in the United States (summarized e.g. by Rainwater 1974) it was asked, for instance, what minimum income the household of the interviewed person should have to make ends meet (Goedhart et al. 1977). Similarly, attempts have been made to ground the classical approach of poverty analysis by Townsend (1979) on a broader empirical basis by asking a representatively selected sample, which goods and services of daily life in their opinion should belong to the absolutely necessary standard of living (Mack and Lansley 1985). These kinds of approaches are called subjective or consensual poverty definitions.

Finally, there remains the question of how to observe the individual state of scarcity termed poverty. In this connection a distinction, which was introduced by Ringen (1988), is interesting: The distinction is between indirect and direct poverty measures (cf. Figure 1). In the first case, one observes poverty indirectly and considers the access of individuals to different resources. Therefore, this approach is sometimes also called the resources approach. In the second case one observes poverty directly and considers the results of individual behaviour after individuals have employed the resources available to them. In other words: One studies the living standard actually available to the individual.

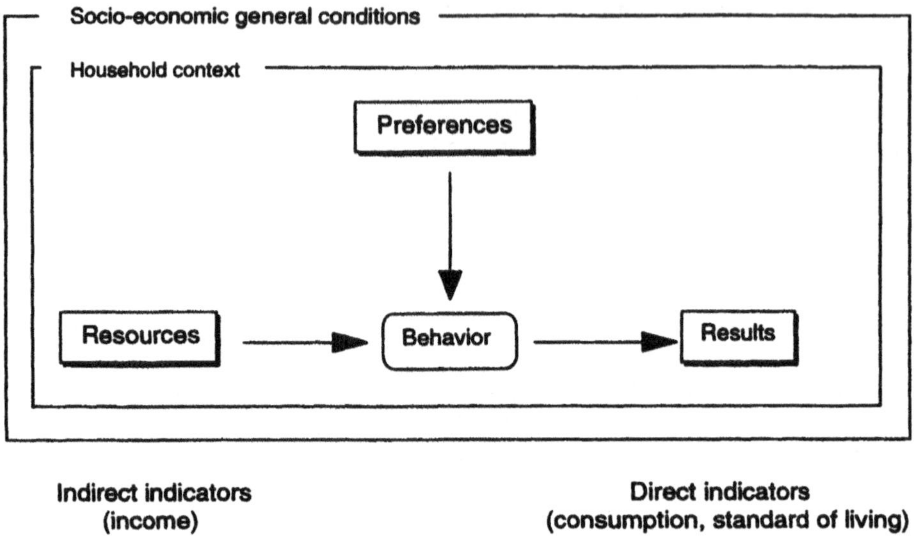

Figure 1 Indirect and direct poverty measures

When looking at the results of individual behaviour one has to consider, as Figure 1 suggests, that the living standard actually achieved depends not only on resources which are available to the person, but also on his or her individual preferences and the socio-economic general conditions. Indirect and direct poverty measures are discussed in greater detail in the following two sections.

2 Indirect poverty measures

The term resource is central to indirect poverty measures. Taking the aforementioned poverty definition by Simmel one could define resources as the means that a person uses to achieve certain aims. Resources per sé do not have an intrinsic value. Only if one uses them for certain purposes that have a certain value are they useful. A somewhat more general definition is given by Coleman. For him resources are things over which individuals (he speaks more generally about actors) 'have control and in which they have some interest' (1990, p. 28).

Both definitions are functional definitions. When thinking of empirical examples it is, however, much more difficult to formulate a classification of concrete resources which is clear, exclusive, and complete. 'The resources each actor has which are of interest to others include a wide variety of things. The most obvious of these are what economists call private goods. Neoclassical economic theory describes the functioning of systems in which each actor has control of certain private divisible goods that are of interest to other actors in the system. But private divisible goods are only one of several kinds of things over which actors have control and in which they are interested' states Coleman (1990, p. 33). Therefore public goods, e.g. the social infrastructure, are also important resources that the individual relies upon. Kindergartens, for instance, allow parents to be employed for part of the time during which they normally would be responsible for their children. And when Coleman (1990, p. 33) counts individual characteristics like skills and beauty as resources then it becomes evident that not only material things are implied. Some examples from the literature may illustrate the term 'resource' in greater detail.

Bryant in his book about the economic organization of the household (1990, p. 6) distinguishes between human and physical resources. Human resources include time, abilities, and the energy of each household member. While the time that is available to an individual is in principal limited, abilities and energy are variable and renewable. The later two are usually called the human capital of the individual (Becker 1975). Among the physical resources of the household, Bryan includes different kinds of financial resources, which can be distinguished according to their liquidity and durability. In their survey of data collection techniques and methods of analysis for empirical household research, Galler and Ott (1993, p. 23) distinguish between human resources (number of household members, education, health), material resources (money, financial assets, tangible property, social wealth), and social resources (the availability of market, public, and private infrastructure). Similar classifications are used in family research (cf. e.g. McCubbin et al. 1980; Walper 1988). They distinguish between external resources (e.g. social and financial support in connection with social networks and social institutions), resources of households (e.g. characteristics of the familiy system like household size, completeness, alternative roles of each household member) and individual resources of each household member. The later are decomposed into different components: financial resources, education/knowledge/abilities, health, psychological resources as well as values and norms.

Poverty research, however, limits itself very often to financial resources of which current incomes from work or public and private transfers stand in the foreground, whereas financial assets and private property (including the incomes derived from them) go unheeded, not to mention transfers in kind, money-like privileges at the workplace (e.g. a car or a telephone), etc. A person is poor according to this definition if he or she earns a smaller income than is necessary to insure a minimum standard of living. Of course the restriction to financial resources in general and to current incomes in particular has a certain plausibility in market economies since many goods included in the aforementioned minimum needs (nutrition, housing, health care etc.) can be bought for money on the market. However, even the designation resource, for e.g. current income from work, is problematic because income from work is a result of employing the resources 'time' and 'human capital'. Also following Figure 1 one could say: Income from work is a result of individual behaviour - namely: to go to work - after employing the resources available to the individual. Therefore, the income from work is really an indicator of the resource 'human capital'. It is only a resource in itself, when it exists in accumulated form as private property or financial assets that make up an additional source of income besides the person's labour power. Since the resource 'human capital' is, however, not easily observed and since it is not completely used in times of low labour demand it is meaningful to use the results of this resource - namely: the income gained from work - as an indirect indicator of human capital resources.

The frequent use of income as a resource indicator can also be explained on pragmatic grounds. Representative income data are available in all developed Western industrial societies in arbitrary social differentiation, and the universal medium 'money' makes easy a comparison of different resources within as well as between different societies. If one wanted to use the resource 'human capital' instead then one faces, for instance, the problem of comparing different school certificates, skills, and knowledge. By using income, the individual human capital, so to speak, is evaluated externally, i.e. by the market, in terms of money units. It should be mentioned, however, that it is difficult to collect valid and reliable income data, especially when it comes to household (and not personal) incomes that are formed from different sources and by different persons in the household. Additionally, incomes are subject to seasonal and cyclical variations so that a temporary income position of a person ascertained at one point in time can deviate considerably from the permanent income position that applies to a longer time period (cf. Hauser and Berntsen 1992; Berntsen and Rendtel 1991 for an estimate of the permanent income component with German longitudinal data).

The distinction between transitory and permanent income components once more demonstrates the importance of private property and financial assets. Assets can be used to equalize temporary losses of current earnings. Assets also increase creditworthiness so that loans can be transacted on the basis of future earnings. Besides that, not only the financial capital, but also the human capital plays an important role in the creditworthiness of the person: A well educated person, who can expect large income increases in the future, is considerably more financially sound than a person without a school certificate. Generally one may say: The smaller the incomes and wealth an individual can rely on the more difficult it is to stretch resources over time and the more pressing is the daily need (Piachaud 1992, p. 81).

Several attempts have been made to use human capital as well as wealth as indirect poverty indicators. Representative data about human capital indicators are easily available with high reliability. This is, however, not true for financial assets and private property. The concept of earnings capacity developed by Garfinkel et al. tries to capture both components: 'Earnings capacity is defined as the income stream that would be generated if a household unit employed its human and physical assets to capacity' (1977, p. 8). More specifically, a multiple regression is used with personal incomes as the dependent, and several human capital indicators as well as working time as the independent variables. The earnings capacity of a person equals the income that results when including all values of the independent variables for the person into the estimated regression equation and setting the working time variable to its maximum value, irrespective of whether the person works full time, part-time, or does not work at all. Therefore, the earnings capacity equals the income that is expected when the person works full time given his or her human capital. Finally, capital incomes of the person are added to the expected earnings variable. '[The earnings capacity] purges the income measure from tastes (by in effect placing a value on the time devoted to leisure when work is deliberately less than full time), reflects the potential rates of return to both physical and human capital, and is close to a permanent-income notion in that transitory, year-to-year fluctuations in actual income are not reflected in the measure' (Haveman 1987, p. 61; insertion by H.J.A.).

With the concept of earnings capacity several incompatibilities can be excluded that result when poverty measurement is restricted to simple current incomes of persons and households: e.g. the wealthy family that is classified as poor, because current incomes at the time of the interview are too low, or the student of business administration who has a low income in the last year of his studies but expects a considerable larger income in the near future. However, besides the advantages of this concept it should not be forgotten that the estimation of earnings capacities also needs to consider far reaching assumptions such as the fact that persons are not able to work full time because of individual or social restrictions (e.g. health, handicaps, child care, low labour demand).

3 Direct poverty measures

As already mentioned, direct poverty measures refer to the results of individual behaviour after employing the available resources. Direct measures consider the living standards that persons, at a certain point in time, actually have in a given society. Based on the last section, in which we discussed the importance of income as an indicator of resources, one might also say: Direct poverty measures concern income consumption. However, the term income consumption is not general enough because it considers only the consumption of private income resources. Public resources, such as the social infrastructure of a municipality or non-monetary resources like the social network of a person, are equally important components of the living standard of individuals and households.

Peter Townsend's study about 'Poverty in the United Kingdom' from the year 1979 was groundbreaking for the direct approach of poverty measurement. In his study Townsend starts from the observable standard of living of the population ('community's style of living'), and investigates which groups of the population can participate in it. Poverty starts for him at that point where people are disproportionally deprived of participation in the community's style of living because of poor income (Townsend 1979, p. 249). Disproportional, in this context, means an exclusion from the community's style of living that is greater than expected because of the low income of the individual. We call this involuntary exclusion, from large parts of a general accepted standard of living, *deprivation*. Poverty indicators based on this concept are also called deprivation-based poverty measures. Townsend additionally uses the adjective 'relative' and talks about relative deprivation to make clear that he is using a relative poverty concept (a living standard relative to a community's style of living).

This approach is attractive for various reasons. The one-sided fixation of poverty research on the measurement of incomes is broken up, and the general living situation of the persons affected by poverty stands in the center of the analysis. Accordingly, the poverty concept used is multidimensional and more directly connected to the real living conditions of the people under study. Nevertheless, this poverty measure brings at least as many problems as indirect poverty measures. The problems start with the multidimensionality of the concept: Which relevant dimensions constitute the standard of living? Should only the already mentioned basic needs be considered, i.e. nutrition, household equipment, housing, etc., or do subjective well-being, participation in social and political life (including the employment system) also belong to a necessary standard of living? And most importantly: Who decides which dimensions to consider and which not?

Let us assume for the moment that it is possible to name a number of dimensions that constitute the standard of living and that there exist for each of these dimensions several indicators. Then one could observe the existence, as well as the lack of, certain indicators within a household. From this a further difficulty emerges: The lack of a certain indicator is not necessarily sufficient evidence of the deprivation of the household because persons have individual preferences and may voluntarily do without certain things that others consider important (e.g. the vegetarian not eating meat or the ecologically conscious person not using a car). Additionally, if one thinks about resources not only in terms of personal incomes but also in terms of public infrastructure, social networks, work places, schools, etc., then it is evident that the use of these resources depends not only on individual preferences but also on external factors. Whether a person uses a certain work place or has a certain dwelling of a given quality, depends not only on his or her work orientation or housing preferences, but also on the question whether these resources are available at all (cf. the socio-economic general conditions in Figure 1). It is well-known, that the supply of work places and adequate housing can be little influenced by job seekers and people looking for good housing. Therefore, the control of individual preferences only makes sense with those resources that are largely subject to the control of the individuals. This is certainly true for the consumption of private incomes, less however for public resources.

The term 'relative deprivation' used by Townsend was introduced for the first time in the classical study 'The American Soldier' by Stouffer et al. (1949). A formal definition of relative deprivation was given by Runciman (1966). And this definition mentions a third difficulty: '[A person]... is relatively deprived of X when (i) he does not have X, (ii) sees some other person or persons, which may include himself at some previous or expected time, as having X (whether or not this is or will in fact be the case), (iii) he wants X, and (iv) he sees it as feasible that he should have X' (1966, p. 10). The criteria (i), (iii), and (iv) repeat again what we have already mentioned: An indicator of the standard of living must be missing (i), but it must not be a voluntary renunciation. The person must want to have the indicator (iii), and this wish must be feasible (iv). Criterium (ii) points to the additional fact that the evaluation of the missing indicator by the individual is based on processes of social comparision: '... relative deprivation means that the sense of deprivation is such as to involve a comparison with the imagined situation of some other person or group. This other person or group is the "reference group", or more accurately the "comparative reference group"' (Townsend 1979, p. 11). Two conclusions can be drawn from this quotation for poverty research:

1. Preferences are formed through processes of social comparison.[1] Therefore, the assumption of a generally accepted standard of living ('community's style of living') including its significance for individual behavior has to be examined very carefully.
2. One has not only to consider the objective fact that certain indicators of the standard of living are missing, but also the fact how individuals evaluate this absence subjectively.

Some researchers, e.g. Muffels (1993), think that this aspect is so important that they explicitly talk about *subjective* rather than relative deprivation. Townsend (1979) on the other hand makes clear stand against the second interpretation: 'The term "relative deprivation" was coined originally by Stouffer and his colleagues, and elaborated valuably first by Merton and Runciman, to denote *feelings* of deprivation relative to others and not conditions of deprivation relative to others. Yet the latter would be a preferable usage since differences in conditions between men underlie social structure and values are not as easy to define and measure, and may in fact be obscured by social belief' (Townsend 1979, p.47; emphasis by Townsend).

However, it would be an illusion to believe that similar problems do not exist with indirect, income-based poverty measures. Income is, as already mentioned, only one indicator of resources and under closer scrutiny as multidimensional as direct poverty indicators (cf. e.g. the distinction between transitory and permanent income components, or between current incomes, financial assets, and private property). Earning incomes is likewise dependent on individual preferences, i.e. a low income can be chosen in a similar manner like a low standard of living. Which income a person considers to be necessary depends as well on his or her comparative reference group, personal demands, and possibilities. Goedhart et al. (1977) ascertain, for instance, that the necessary minimum income, as estimated by the interviewees, increases with the actual household income of the respondents (cf. as well the analysis about income satisfaction by Glatzer 1988). Finally, it is a common fact of social survey research that subjective evaluations of the standard of living (e.g. the evaluation of incomes) do not correspond with the objective standard of living.

4 Poverty research in practice: An outline of this book

4.1 General remarks

Given these general remarks on the concept of poverty and its definition in the literature, we now want to give an overview of the empirical analyses collected in this book. Empirical poverty studies vary, among other things, according to their basic methodological orientation. Generally one can distinguish between qualitatively oriented field research on the one hand and quantitatively oriented population-wide surveys on the other. The first group mostly uses case studies, while the latter group wants to make representative statements about the incidence of poverty in a given population. Whereas the first group of studies can assume that most of the investigated individuals are in fact poor by selecting a suitable research field (e.g. a poverty ghetto, a shelter for the homeless, typical poverty groups), the latter group of studies has to develop specific criteria defining how to identify poor individuals within a representative cross-section of the population. Independently of their methodological orientation and concrete definition of poverty, however, all empirical studies basically face the same methodological problems:

1. What are suitable empirical indicators for a given poverty definition?
2. Who or what should be the units of analysis and what time frame should be used for data collection?
3. How do we select the units of analysis and which methods of data collection should be employed?
4. How do we account for individual preferences and subjective evaluations during both the phase of data collection and that of data analysis?
5. How do we consider the fact that individuals join in groups (families, households) in order to share and use resources more efficiently?
6. Is it useful to combine the information from different poverty indicators into one index and if so: What is a suitable threshold on this index to distinguish poor and non-poor units of analysis?

The reader will find different answers to these questions in the following chapters that either consist of direct analyses of empirical data or that discuss results from such research. Therefore, besides the substantive results from major European countries (including Belgium, Finland, France, Germany, Great Britain, Italy, The Netherlands, Russia, and Sweden) this book also illustrates the different possibilities for operationalizing concepts of poverty in a sound empirical way.

If there is a consensus among these analyses then it is the understanding that one single concept of poverty is not sufficient to describe the poverty phenomena in modern industrialized countries. Therefore, all the following fourteen chapters stress the point that poverty is a multidimensional phenomenon and, with different emphases, they discuss conceptual, methodological, and practical issues in implementing such a view. Four chapters (by Walker, Kronauer, Friedrichs, and van Oorschot) focus mainly on *conceptual questions*, like the dynamic approach to poverty analysis, the 'new' debate on 'social exclusion' and 'underclass', the impact of regional contexts on poverty incidence, and the effectiveness of welfare programs. Three chapters concentrate on the *metho-dological prerequisites* of a multidimensional analysis of poverty using survey methods. Bosch investigates whether there is a public consensus on a minimum standard of living. Kangas and Ritakallio adress the question of poverty measurement using different poverty indicators and the fact that these indicators classify different groups as poor. Similarly, Jeandidier and Kop test the convergence of these different measures both in a static and a dynamic perspective.

The main part of the book consists of *substantive applications* of these methods. The chapters by Muffels and Dirven about the effects of different pension systems, by Dirven and Fouarge about the similarity of the Dutch and the Belgian welfare regime, and by Halleröd about the determinants of deprivation in Sweden and Great Britain clearly demonstrate that indeed much can be learned by using different poverty indicators. Explicit applications of the *dynamic approach* can be found in the chapters by Buhr and Weber using quantitative and by Andreß and Schulte using interpretative methods, although many of the other chapters also use panel data and test dynamic hypotheses (e.g. Muffels and Dirven, Bosch, Dirven and Fouarge, Jeandidier and Kop). Finally, the chapters by Kazepov and Mikhalev illustrate the *difficulties of poverty measurement* in societies that are either undergoing rapid socio-economic change or that are characterized by large regional disparities. Russia and Italy, the two countries studied, face specific problems that separate them clearly from many other European welfare states.

4.2 Conceptual issues

Walker starts with some well-known results based on cross-sectional studies of poverty risks in different European countries. Although important - both from a substantive as well as from a political point of view - these data do not reveal very much about either the nature or the distribution of poverty. According to

Walker, simple questions like 'What is the nature of poverty? What does it mean to the people who experience it?', 'How many experience it?', 'How long does it last?', and 'How severe is it?' cannot be answered with these kinds of data, not to speak of questions like 'What causes poverty?' and 'What can be done about it?'. He then argues that much can be learned by rethinking poverty in a dynamic perspective. He illustrates his argument with various empirical studies from different European countries and the United States. The income distribution, for instance, is much more egalitarian when using lifetime instead of annual incomes, and therefore poverty risks show a different picture when changing the accounting period and studying the distribution of economic resources over time. Looking at all individuals experiencing a poverty spell within a given observation period instead of those individuals being poor at a certain point in time, reveals the fact that some poverty risks are rather short-term and singular, while others are long-term and recurrent. The distribution of entry risks into and exit chances out of poverty varies considerably between European countries, and thereby constitutes a specific national poverty pattern. Besides duration, the scarcity of economic resources is another important dimension of severity of poverty, and again the shortfall in resources is not independent of the length of poverty spells. What this all means for the afflicted individuals can be learned from qualitative case studies, and Walker summarizes some of the British ones. Time is not only the medium in which poverty occurs, it also helps to forge the different experiences. In re-reading all this empirical knowledge, Walker convincingly shows that the nature of poverty is a function of its distribution, not only within a population, but also over time. Moreover, the patterning of poverty over time suggests, as he says, 'that there may be more than one kind of poverty, each experienced in a different way, with a unique aetiology and, perhaps, demanding a different policy response.'

Kronauer starts from the observation that mass unemployment has introduced new cleavages into all Western capitalistic countries. He then asks what new insights can be gained from the terms 'social exclusion' and 'underclass' for this and other forms of social divisions, like e.g. poverty. Both terms are contested both theoretically and empirically. Kronauer, referring to Katz, sees them as 'metaphors of social transformation' that can be used to direct our attention to new societal divisions and make our research questions more precise. From a theoretical point of view, both terms have certain similarities with concepts of 'center' and 'periphery'. They point to the fact that social divisions exist that are not captured by the traditional system of social class and status which is mostly related to differences in the employment system. Kronauer then reviews present empirical research from the United States and various European countries to answer the following four questions: Firstly, who is at risk of social exclusion by current mass unemployment, secondly, what does social exclusion mean for the society, thirdly, what does it mean for the afflicted individuals, and finally, how sharp is the divide between 'in' and 'out'? The third question, of course, is the most interesting one in this context. Kronauer names six dimensions of social exclusion that warrant further empirical investigation: exclusion at the labour market, economic exclusion, cultural exclusion, exclusion by social isolation, spatial exclusion, and institutional exclusion. This conceptualisation resembles a multi-dimensional concept of poverty, but as Kronauer insists, 'both concepts - social exclusion and underclass - are *relational* categories and in this respect both of them focus much more on the society as a whole. It only makes sense to talk about exclusion, if the excluding institutions themselves are at the center of analysis.'

Friedrichs deals with context effects of poverty neighborhoods on their residents: Do poor neighborhoods make their residents poorer? To address the problem, he takes William J. Wilson's publication on 'The Truly Disadvantaged' (1987) as an example and explicates the implicit hypotheses of Wilson's theory. If Wilson's hypotheses were true, poverty neighborhoods should have dramatic consequences for their residents. Friedrichs then continues and investigates the theoretical and methodological foundations of this conclusion: How can we define and delineate contexts and what kind of general theories support the assumption that context has an effect? He discusses models of interaction and social learning, both of which are empirically hard to test. He also notes that social networks and action spaces of the residents are not necessarily coincident with the neighborhood. After reviewing the empirical literature from the United States and several European countries, he concludes that in general neighborhood has only low or negligible effects. Much more can be explained by individual characteristics of the resident or by institutional variables (like e.g. school composition). With respect to poverty, 'poor neighborhoods do indeed aggravate the poverty of its residents. But this conclusion only holds under specific conditions.' The restriction of the individual's social network to the neighborhood is a crucial prerequisite, effects of the independent variables are highly non-linear, and the impact of the neighborhood may differ among social groups.

As one means of alleviating poverty welfare states usually provide a number of means-tested benefits targeted at the poor. Participation in such programs (e.g. social assistance recipiency) is very often used as a poverty indicator. However, the effectiveness of such selective measures tends to be rather low, because many poor do not receive the benefits to which they are entitled. This questions the validity of poverty indicators like welfare recipiency. Since the extent of non-take-up is often underestimated, and the dominant ideas about its causes are not adequately reflecting reality either, *van Oorschot* presents the main theoretical and some empirical results of a study in which research on non-take-up of social security benefits was reviewed internationally, and in which new perspectives on the causes of non-take-up were developed and applied in empirical research. Van Oorschot's review of the empirical literature on non-take-up in different countries, like e.g. Britain, Belgium, (the former) West Germany, the Netherlands, the United States, and some others, shows that the empirical evidence is rather limited, although whenever non-take-up of means-tested benefits is found, it is usually at a serious level. According to the author, 'only in a few rather specific cases are non-take-up rates less than 20 per cent.' The theoretical model used by van Oorschot reflects the idea that the causes of non-take-up are present not only at the client level, but also at the levels of scheme structure and administration. This implies that policy-makers and administrators, along with clients, have a clear and separate responsibility for the occurrence of non-take-up. The author's main conclusion from an empirical application of his model to means-tested benefits among elderly people and social assistance clients in two major Dutch cities is 'that realizing rights to benefits is not a matter of isolated individual beneficiaries deciding at a particular time to go out and claim or not. Instead it is a long process, which starts from the moment the structure of a scheme is defined, [... and it] ends when the benefit is actually received by those people who are entitled to it. In practice and on the macro-level, however, the process does not end, because at any one time there will always be eligible non-recipients left, usually marginal numbers in the case of non-means-tested benefits, but much higher proportions in the case of means-tested benefits.'

4.3 Methodological issues

Van den Bosch's analysis focuses on a methodological problem in the measurement of people's living standards. Since the pioneering work of Mack and Lansley (1985) it has become a routine task of survey research to collect information on the necessity and availability of a set of goods, services, and activities chosen as representative indicators of a minimum standard of living. From these data, various indices of (relative) deprivation can be computed, all of them assuming that there is a consensus in the population on what kind of goods, services, and activities constitute a minimum standard of living. Using data from the 1985 and 1988 waves of the Belgian Socio-Economic Panel, Van den Bosch tackles the question, 'to which extent people agree or disagree in their views about what goods, services, or activities are necessary for living in an affluent society such as Belgium.' The author convincingly shows that people, when asked the typical necessity question, take a 'publicly oriented view' and distinguish between what they want for themselves and what should be included in the society's minimum standard of living. However, when it comes to the items to be selected for this standard, respondents agree only on a few items. The reason for this lack of consensus 'is not so much that there are strong disagreements about this matter', says the author, 'but rather that individuals are apparently uncertain about the necessity of a range of items for modern living. Secondly, depending on a person's circumstances and characteristics, perceptions of necessities differ, indicating that the minimum standard of living is composed of different items for different groups in society.' Given this observation, the computation of a deprivation index can be improved in several directions. One of them is mentioned by the author: He argues that contrary to the method applied by Mack and Lansley (1985) all items should be included in the index (and not only the items termed as necessary by a majority of the respondents). Each item then should be weighted by the proportion of the population that regards it as a necessity (cf. Halleröd's deprivation index in this volume). According to Van den Bosch, 'this weight can be interpreted as the likelihood that the average person will regard the item in question as a necessity. Given the conclusion that differences in responses probably reflect uncertainty rather than disagreement, the weight can also be regarded as an indicator of how certain the average person is about the necessity of the item.' Another possible direction of research is the method proposed by Muffels, who controls for reference group behavior in his deprivation index (cf. the chapters by Muffels, Dirven, and Fouarge).

Kangas and *Ritakallio* compare five different methods to measure poverty with data from a Finnish mail survey that represents the total Finnish population between 18 and 70 in the beginning of 1995. Their measures include direct and indirect poverty indicators: low living standards (deprivation), low incomes, receiving social assistance benefits, scarce (economic) resources, and overindebtedness. Depending on the poverty indicator used, the overall poverty rate varies between 8.5% and 12.6% and the overlap between the five methods is surprisingly low (between 17.8% in the worst and 51% in the best case). Moreover, when looking at the socio-demographic characteristics of the populations classified as poor according to each indicator, the authors often observe conflicting results: One measure may classify some categories of the population as poor, while according to other indicators they may be rather well-off. Therefore, the main conclusion of their chapter is that different methods produce different pictures of poverty. This observation is not entirely new and has lead some scholars to give up poverty measurement completely, because the degree of poverty observed seems to be a question of definition. Kangas and Ritakallio, however, formulate it positively: 'Despite differences in results, each of these pictures may be correct and equally real. They only map a different slice of reality. Therefore, a simultaneous use of various measures may be advisable. By concentrating on one single "correct" measure, a great deal of valuable information may be lost.' A multidimensional approach to poverty measurement is especially necessary, if different poverty groups (according to the various criteria) need different policy responses, as the authors argue. Lack of economic resources can be alleviated by money transfers, but what should be done about deprived living conditions, especially if they occur together with income transfers from the state (e.g. social assistance payments)?

Similar results are observed by *Jeandidier* and *Kop* when reviewing the recent empirical literature on different measures of poverty in France. Firstly, they note two tendencies in French poverty research 'which are curiously contradictory' as they say: 'The quite systematic reference to a notion of poverty with a multi-dimensional approach, and the rarity of empirical attempts to construct composite scales.' But as with Kanga's and Ritakallio's analysis, the rare research in France that has been undertaken in this direction secondly concludes that the convergence between different measures of poverty is rather low. This is were Jeandidier and Kop's own empirical analysis starts: Using data from the Lorraine household panel, they study the interrelationship of three different poverty indicators over time: a) income poverty, b) (objective) living conditions (deprivation), and c) subjective evaluations of living conditions. They suspect that the low correlation between income poverty on the one hand and unfavorable living conditions (deprivation) on the other hand is due to the fact that time is not adequately taken into account. Temporary monetary problems, as measured by an income poverty indicator, do not necessarily change objective living conditions, nor do they result in feelings of poverty. Similarly to Kangas and Ritakallio, their cross-sectional analyses demonstrate that different poverty indicators classify different socio-demographic groups as poor. Besides that, the development of income poverty from 1986 to 1990 does not follow important macro-economic indicators, e.g. the regional unemployment rate. However, effects of the French social assistance program (Revenue Minimum d'Insertion, RMI), set up in January 1989, can be observed in higher exit rates out of and lower entry rates into income poverty in 1990. In order to test their hypothesis of low convergence because of temporal fluctuations in income, they study cross-lagged correlations and indicators averaged over the whole observation period. The results are mixed and the hypothesis is neither clearly rejected nor fully supported. While the correlations between the indicators rise when changing the length of the observation period, cross-lagged effects show that income poverty influences subjective feelings of poverty but not objective living conditions. Even if some of these divergent results can be ruled out by better methods, it could be, as the authors conclude, 'that even in a dynamic perspective the three poverties call upon three really different dimensions and that poverty cannot be understood without taking each of these dimensions into account.'

4.4 Using a multidimensional concept of poverty: Results from different countries

Muffels and *Dirven* examine the impact of increasing income inequality since 1980 on the evolution of poverty and deprivation in Germany and the Netherlands for three generations of the elderly. Both countries show a divergent pattern in their pension systems and social policies towards the elderly: While Germany uses a market-oriented pension system, the Dutch system consists of a mix of minimum pensions and supplementary private pensions. Given these systemic differences, the authors presume less poverty in the Dutch minimum pension system and higher income mobility in the market-oriented German system and, hence, lower poverty stability. Apart from these divergences, the authors expect lower real income growth or even a real income loss for both Dutch and German pensioners, because of the cuts in benefit levels and eligibility criteria in the 1980s in both countries. In connection with the aforementioned rise in income inequality, all (relative) income poverty indicators are supposed to show an upward trend for the elderly, because they measure the income position relative to the average of the total income distribution. Measures of actual living conditions on the other hand will show a different picture, because they, as the authors note, 'much more reflect the permanent consumption status and living standards of persons and households.' The empirical analysis uses data from the Dutch (1985-91) and the German (1985-89) Socio-Economic Panels and applies four different poverty indicators: less than half of median equivalized household income (European minimum income), the subjective income poverty line, a legal poverty line for the Netherlands (the Dutch Social Minimum Income), and

Muffel's subjective deprivation scale (only for the Netherlands). All analyses differentiate between three different generations of the elderly, because the authors assume that very old people with low or no occupational pensions are especially prone to increases in poverty. As expected, all poverty indicators do not show the same trend: Relative income poverty seems to be sensitive to the equivalence scale used to compare households of different size and structure, deprivation-based poverty is less dependent on temporary income fluctuations. Contrary to the authors' expectations, the results do not confirm the hypothesis that the market-oriented German system results in higher income inequality and poverty: It is the Dutch system that creates more inequality and poverty among the elderly. Income mobility is high in Germany as well as in the Netherlands, but more so in the latter than in the former country. Poverty persistence is much higher in Germany, particularly among the youngest and the oldest age group. 'A judgement on the German and Dutch pension system in terms of its performance to reduce (persistent) poverty among the elderly is hard to make', as the authors say, 'since it depends on what should be preferred: A highly mobile pension system with relatively many elderly people prone to transient poverty (the Netherlands) or a somewhat less mobile system with fewer aged persons in transient poverty, but more elderly running into persistent poverty (Germany).'

Dirven and *Fouarge* use different poverty indicators to study processes of impoverishment and social exclusion in Belgium and the Netherlands, which according to Esping-Andersen's (1990) characterization are similar, i.e. social-democratic, welfare regimes. More specifically, they use three measures of income poverty and two measures of living conditions (relative deprivation): less than half of median equivalized household income (European minimum income), the subjective income poverty line, a legal poverty line (according to the Dutch General Assistance Act and the Belgian guaranteed minimum income), Mack and Lansley's majority necessity index, and Muffel's subjective deprivation scale. Using log-linear models and panel data for the years 1985 and 1988, they test three main hypotheses: Firstly, relative deprivation is more stable than income poverty, secondly, relative deprivation and income poverty are mutually reinforcing, and thirdly, Belgium and the Netherlands are not statistically different. Only the second hypothesis is supported, while the two others are either rejected or only partially supported. It turns out that measures of relative deprivation are less stable because they are less reliable. This is especially true for Muffel's measure which includes subjective evaluations of one's own living standard. Both countries are statistically different, because income mobility is much higher in Belgium than in the Netherlands, which the authors explain both by different levels of income inequality and higher rates of labour market participation by married women in Belgium: 'Since two-earner households are more likely to experience labour market events [...], it can be expected that household incomes are less stable in Belgium.' Concerning Esping-Andersen's classification of both countries as social-democratic welfare regimes, the authors conclude 'that, even within the same world of welfare capitalism, people's living conditions may be more stable in some countries than in others.'

Halleröd compares the prevalence of deprivation and poverty in Great Britain and Sweden with data from the 1990 Breadline Britain Survey and the 1992 Swedish Standard of Living Survey. Both countries differ quite markedly in their welfare systems as well as in the state of their economy. Britain, as compared to Sweden, in the beginning of the 1990s is characterized by a more uneven income distribution, higher incidence of income poverty, higher unemployment rates, and correspondingly a higher proportion of long-term unemployed. Given these systemic differences and the strong connection between unemployment and poverty, it can be expected that actual living standards are much more endangered in Great Britain, yielding a much higher extent of deprivation than in Sweden. Like other researchers before, Halleröd uses Mack and Lansley's (1985) methodology to assess the number of items that are (involuntarily) missing in a given household although they are termed necessary by the majority of the population. To account for the relativity of deprivation, each item is weighted by the proportion of individuals regarding the given item a necessity. As expected, the amount of (relative) deprivation is much higher in Great Britain than in Sweden and increases disproportionally with decreasing equivalized household income. This disproportionality suggests a poverty threshold in Great Britain, but as Halleröd shows, this effect disappears when the unemployed are excluded from the analysis. 'Thus, it seems', as Halleröd says, 'as if deprivation is mainly a dilemma for people with an unemployment problem.' He then shifts the analysis from the aggregate to the individual level, and investigates how the amount of (relative) deprivation observed in each household correlates with the household's (equivalized) income, household structure, unemployment experiences, receipt of means tested benefits, age, and gender of the respondent. It turns out that the mechanisms that generate deprivation seem to be largely the same in both countries: 'Low income households, the unemployed, recipients of means tested benefits, and single parents suffer from an increased probability of being poor in both countries.' Because of this equivalence and because of the fact that the Swedish welfare state model currently faces similar economic problems,

Halleröd ends with the warning that in the near future Swedes will find themselves in a more 'British' society, unless new policies are found to adjust to an increasingly global economy.

4.5 Applying the dynamic approach

Buhr and *Weber* use duration data on the receipt of social assistance in the city of Bremen (Germany). The information comes from process-produced data files of the municipal authorities ('Sozialamt'). The authors compare two cohorts of new recipients of social assistance in 1983 and 1989 in order to assess the impact of social change on social assistance. Former research by the 'Bremen project' has shown that contrary to the expectations in the public - but in agreement with international research, especially from the United States - receipt of social assistance is a short-term experience for the majority. However, the risks of becoming a social assistance recipient are much more widespread than generally believed. With the new 1989 cohort, Buhr and Weber now ask the question, whether time on assistance has increased over time as often assumed because of increasing economic problems in Germany and what are the determinants of long-term receipt in the nineties as compared to the eighties. According to the authors, 'the empirical evidence does not point towards longer lasting social assistance careers in the nineties [...]. On the contrary, total time on assistance has decreased in the new cohort. This decline in duration is mainly due to the different composition of the two cohorts [...]: In the 1989 cohort there is a much higher proportion of immigrants and refugees. If such high numbers of immigrants had not appeared among the new recipients of 1989 - invited by politicians -, the number of new recipients would have been lower and total duration would have slightly increased.' Besides that, the structural determinants of spell duration have changed only slightly: While old age diminishes as a risk factor, it seems as if recipients with small children, single women, and young people have more problems leaving social assistance in the nineties.

Andreß and *Schulte* present a process-oriented model of coping with low income living situations. Ways into and out of income poverty are confronted with three very general hypotheses: the assumption of poverty persistence (the persistence hypothesis), the assumption of cyclically changing entry risks and exit chances (the life cycle hypothesis), and the assumption of individually varying poverty profiles with different developments that cannot be circumscribed with the classical socio-demographic variables (the individualization hypothesis). Labour-oriented coping strategies are modeled as the result of resources, restrictions, and subjective evaluations of living conditions of each household member. With data from the German Socio-Economic Panel the authors conduct case studies of a cohort of (income) poor households and study their ways into, through, and out of poverty over a period of nine years (1984-92). Summarizing the observed income profiles, changes in household composition, and labour force participation patterns in case studies for each household, they try to develop a typology of (income) poor households. With respect to poverty risks, this typology reveals several critical transitions within the life cycle of individuals and households, especially from less educated population groups. Individuals with less formal education have a much higher probability of entering poverty several times during their lives. This higher risk of recurrent poverty goes hand in hand with the traditional family cycle dominating in this group. This observation questions the validity of the individualization thesis, at least with respect to certain population groups.

4.6 Problems of poverty measurement: Lessons from Italy and Russia

The transition from centrally planned to market economies is associated with rising numbers of unemployed and poor people in virtually all East European countries. *Mikhalev* presents empirical results on poverty in the largest country, Russia, and discusses problems of poverty measurement in a country underlying rapid social change. Given the size of this country, the rapidly changing economic conditions, and the empirical knowledge available it is obvious that nearly all poverty standards become obsolete within a short period of time, that they do not capture the vast regional differences in living conditions, and that it is difficult to obtain the relevant data for answering all these important questions. Poverty measurement in Russia, therefore, relies mainly on income data, published by government agencies (e.g., the State Committee of Statistics, the Ministry of Labour, the Center for Economic Analysis and Forecasting) and by private and academic public opinion research institutes (e.g., the Russian Center for Public Opinion Research, the Moscow Institute of Socio-Economic Studies of the Population). Incomes are compared against a standard that in most cases consists of the money equivalent of a basket of minimum consumer goods and in a few cases of a representatively assessed minimum income, the so-called Leyden poverty line. Both approaches have their specific problems within a rapidly changing economy. The composition of the basket of minimum consumer goods will change, especially the relative prices of the goods and services included, making it difficult to maintain a constant standard of reference. Subjective evaluations of the minimum income necessary to make ends meet, on the other hand, 'are heavily influenced by the specific situation in Russia', as Mikhalev argues, 'where the average income has fallen sharply against a rapidly growing income disparity and the emergence of wealthy groups of the population. In their individual perceptions of a sufficient income, people naturally refer to standards typical of their previous rather than their current circumstances as well as to the living standards of the newly prosperous elites.' Besides these measurement problems it has been questioned whether money incomes alone are an adequate measure of the resources available to Russian households given the role of household assets, informal activities in the black market, and non-monetary forms of support. Further insights into the differences between household incomes and expenditures can be gained from the Russian Longitudinal Monitoring Survey initiated by the World Bank. All of these attempts to come up with better poverty measures have their merits, but as Mikhalev's results show, compared to the economic problems that large parts of the Russian population face today - i.e., far too low incomes whatever standard used, especially for those people dependent on the state sector, widespread wage arrears for those in gainful employment, etc. - this discussion of poverty measurement seems to be rather academic.

Kazepov's article deals with the problem of doing poverty research in a country, in which the socio-economic causes of poverty and the social policies against social exclusion vary dramatically at the local and regional level. In connection with the lack of sufficient empirical data, this situation makes it difficult to do any kind of analysis that captures all the different poverties that exist in the Italy of today. Kazepov, therefore, starts with a description of how the economic crisis affects the different regions of Italy, and then he continues by summarizing the available knowledge from different case studies on poverty. While the northern parts of Italy have suffered less from de-industrialization processes due to their diversified industrial system consisting of a dense network of many small and medium-sized firms, the southern areas with their more centralized industries and large state-run companies face severe economic problems accompanied by a concentration of long-term unemployment and precarious jobs. Accordingly, poverty rates are much higher in South than in North Italy, although the author's outlook for the North is rather pessimistic too. When looking at social policies, one has to bear in mind that the Italian welfare state has a strong bias towards the employed population (e.g., only Italians with a job are entitled to family allowances). Due to this subsidiary role of the state, the family is the traditional source of social security, especially in the South. Besides that, since 1977 all competencies for social assistance have been transferred to the regions and municipalities. This constitutes 'a differentiated system of social citizenship', as the author notes, 'within which citizens are entitled to different sets of rights, related not so much to their condition of need, but to the specific features these rights have in the place of residence and to the specific way in which social services are organized in that place.' The socio-demographic profile of the poor also reflects the North-South divide: Large families are affected in the South, while in the North singles and the elderly have the highest poverty risks. Because of the indexation of pensions, the situation of the elderly has greatly improved. There is a strong correlation between poverty and unemployment rates in the South, with young people and women mainly affected by unemployment, while in the North the picture is much more diverse since employment problems are less concentrated in certain population groups. These differences, as the author concludes, 'are consolidating on a national level an institutional system of regional inequality, which is not able to guarantee the right to similar minimum living conditions throughout the whole country.'

Some of the results presented in this book have been discussed on a conference on 'Empirical poverty research', which took place at the University of Bielefeld in November 1994. Since then a number of additional analyses from other European countries that were not represented at the conference have been added. Both the organization of the conference and the production of this book have been supported by grants from the Böckler-Stiftung, the foundation of the German labour unions, and the Ministry for Science and Research of Northrhine-Westfalia. The help of Dr. Mary Kenney with the proofreading of our English language is greatly acknowledged, as well as Doris Arriens' and Volker Verrel's expertise in typesetting the manuscript. The editor, of course, is responsible for all remaining errors. But he hopes that the wealth of empirical information and the different methodological approaches collected in this book prove useful for scientists doing empirical poverty research all over the world.

Note

[1] Given these social comparison processes the term preferences that was originally developed within the context of economic theory becomes compatible with sociological analysis. Within economic theory preferences are assumed as fixed, and the analysis of preferences is deferred to other disciplines (e.g. psychology). One exception is the theory of preference formation by the economist Kapteyn (Kapteyn 1977; Kapteyn et al. 1980), which - as the author notes himself - has an amazing similarity to Runciman's concept of relative deprivation.

References

Becker, G. (1975), *Human Capital*, 2nd ed., Chicago.

Berntsen, R., Rendtel, U. (1991), 'Zur Stabilität von Einkommensarmut im Längsschnitt', in Rendtel, U., Wagner, G. (eds.), *Lebenslagen im Wandel: Zur Einkommensdynamik in Westdeutschland seit 1984*, Campus: Frankfurt, pp. 457-487.

Bryant, W.K. (1990), *The Economic Organization of the Household*, Cambridge University Press: Cambridge.

Coleman, J.S. (1990), *Foundations of Social Theory*, The Belknap Press of Harvard University Press: Cambridge (MA).

Esping-Anderson, G. (1990), *The Three Worlds of Welfare Capitalism*, Polity Press: Cambridge.

Galler, H.P., Ott, N. (1993), *Empirische Haushaltsforschung: Erhebungskonzepte und Analyseansätze angesichts neuer Lebensformen*, Campus: Frankfurt am Main.

Garfinkel, I., Haveman, R.H., Betson, D. (1977), *Earnings Capacity, Poverty, and Inequality*, Academic Press: New York.

Glatzer, W. (1988), 'Die Wahrnehmung und Bewertung der Haushaltseinkommen', in Reich, U.P. (ed.), *Aufgaben und Probleme der Einkommensstatistik*, Vandenhoeck & Ruprecht: Göttingen, pp. 167-189.

Goedhart, T., Halberstadt, V., Kapteyn, A., Van Praag, B.M.S. (1977), 'The Poverty Line: Concept and Measurement', *The Journal of Human Ressources*, Vol. 12, pp. 503-520.

Hauser, R., Berntsen, R. (1992), 'Einkommensarmut - Determinanten von Aufstiegen und Abstiegen', in Schneider, H., Hujer, R., Zapf, W. (eds.), *Herausforderung an den Wohlfahrtsstaat im strukturellen Wandel*, Campus: Frankfurt.

Hauser, R., Neumann, U. (1992), 'Armut in der Bundesrepublik Deutschland', in Leibfried, St., Voges, W. (eds.), *Armut im modernen Wohlfahrtsstaat*, Kölner Zeitschrift für Soziologie und Sozialpsychologie, Sonderheft 32, pp. 237-271.

Haveman, R.H. (1987), *Poverty Policy and Poverty Research*, University of Wisconsin Press: Madison, WI.

Kapteyn, A., Wansbeek, T., Buyze, J. (1980), 'The Dynamics of Preference Formation', *Journal of Economic Behavior and Organization*, Vol. 1, pp. 123-157.

Kapteyn, A. (1977), *A Theory of Preference Formation*, Unpublished Ph.D. thesis, Leyden University: Leyden.

Mack, J., Lansley, S. (1985), *Poor Britain*, George Allen and Unwin: London.

McCubbin, H.I., Joy, C.B., Cauble, A.E., Comeau, J.K., Patterson, J.M., Needle, R.H. (1980), 'Family Stress and Coping: a Decade Review', *Journal of Marriage and the Family*, Vol. 42, pp. 855-871.

Muffels, R.J.A. (1993), *Welfare Economic Effects of Social Security. Essays on Poverty, Social Security and Labour Market: Evidence from Panel Data*, Tilburg University Press: Tilburg.

Piachaud, D. (1992), 'Wie mißt man Armut?', in Leibfried, S., Voges W. (eds.), *Armut im modernen Wohlfahrtsstaat*, Kölner Zeitschrift für Soziologie und Sozialpsychologie, Sonderheft 32, pp. 63-87.

Rainwater, L. (1974), *What money buys*, New York.

Ringen, S. (1988), 'Direct and Indirect Measures of Poverty', *Journal of Social Policy*, Vol. 17, pp. 351-365.

Runciman, W.G. (1966), *Relative Deprivation and Social Justice. A study of Attitudes to Social Inequality in Twentieth Century England*, University of California Press: Berkeley and Los Angeles.

Schäuble, G. (1984), *Theorien, Definitionen und Beurteilung der Armut*, Duncker & Humblot: Berlin.

Scheurle, U. (1991), *Statistische Erfassung von Armut*, Vandenhoeck & Ruprecht: Göttingen.

Simmel, G. (1968, first published in 1908), 'Der Arme', in Simmel, G. (ed.), *Soziologie. Untersuchung über die Formen der Vergesellschaftung*, Berlin.

Stouffer, S.A., Suchman, E.A., DeVinney, L.C., Star, S.A., Williams, R.M. jr. (1949), *The American Soldier. Adjustment During Army Life*, Princeton University Press: Princeton.

Townsend, P. (1979), *Poverty in the United Kingdom. A survey of Household Resources and Standards of Living*, University of California Press: Berkeley and Los Angeles.

Walper, S. (1988), *Familiäre Konsequenzen ökonomischer Deprivation*, München and Weinheim.

Wilson, W.J. (1987), *The Truly Disadvantaged. The Inner City, the Underclass, and Public Policy*, Chicago and London.

Zimmermann, G.E. (1993), 'Armut: Konzepte, Definitionen und Operationalisierungskonzepte in der BRD', *Soziale Probleme*, Vol. 2, pp. 193-228.

Part One
Conceptual issues

Rethinking poverty in a dynamic perspective

Robert Walker

This chapter begins with the sociologically familiar, moves on to consider the less familiar and concludes with the as yet unknown. In doing so, the aim is to contribute to the understanding of the nature of poverty, while simultaneously making links of both a theoretical and substantive nature with other chapters in this volume.

Throughout the paper judicious use is made of the statistics and experience of a number of different countries. Except in rare instances, direct comparisons are not intended nor should it be inferred that poverty is precisely the same everywhere irrespective of social context. On the other hand, there are some eternal verities which are the logical consequence of specified assumptions and others which relate to the shared experience of being poor.

1 Questioning old style poverty measurement

Commencing with the familiar, Figure 1 presents now quite old Eurostat data on the incidence of poverty in Europe in the first half of the 1980s. The measure of poverty used is based on income and, being set at 40 per cent of the *European Community* average, is severe. The diagram reveals that at that time poverty was much lower in the geographical and economic core of Europe and falling, and higher and rising in the peripheral areas. (The reasons for this pattern fall beyond the scope of this chapter but possibly reflect the restructuring inherent in the increasing economic integration of Europe (Cross 1993).)

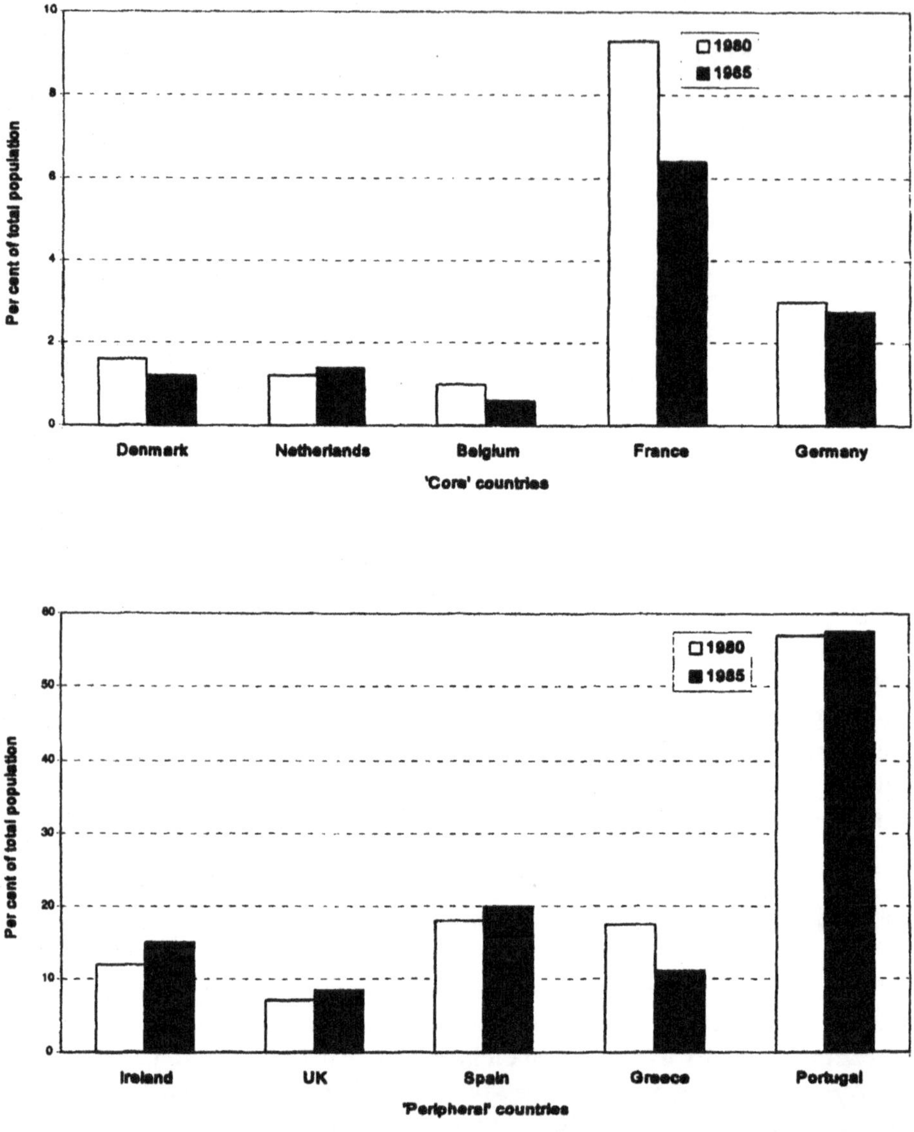

Figure 1 Individuals with income below 40 per cent of community average (1980-85)

Source: Commission of the European Countries 1991

Figure 2, which unfortunately excludes Germany takes an expenditure based measure for 1988 with poverty thresholds set at 50 per cent of *national* household expenditure. Despite the difference in definitions,[1] the statistics show broadly the same geographical pattern. Moreover, as can be seen from Figure 2, the incidence of poverty was noticeably higher among women than among men, especially in the European periphery.

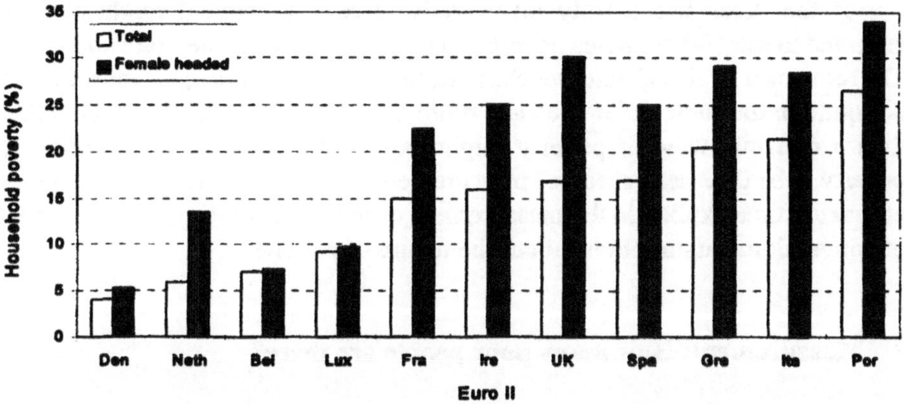

Figure 2 Poverty* in risk groups for Euro II (1988) - female headed
* Defined as 50 per cent of national average equivalent expenditure

Source: Eurostat 1991

These statistics are not without substantive significance and were very important politically: the furore that these and similar figures provoked in certain countries led to the erasure of the term 'poverty' from the European political lexicon (Room 1995). However, they reveal very little about either the nature or distribution of poverty. That this is so can be illustrated by the following thought experiment. Imagine an intelligent Alien visiting Earth with a mission to learn about poverty; and consider the questions that such a creature would ask. One could expect at least the following:

- What is the nature of poverty, what does it mean to the people who experience it?
- How many experience it?
- How long does it last?
- How severe is it?

The fact that Figures 1 and 2 contain insufficient information with which to answer this basic set of questions is not in itself surprising. More telling is the difficulty of identifying any study that contains answers to all of these questions and the small number of studies that ever address the issues of severity and duration. Moreover, as we shall show below, failure to answer a single one of these questions means that the answers given to at least two of the others will be partial and potentially misleading.

If the Alien had a truly investigative frame of mind it might also be expected to ask 'What causes poverty?' and even 'What can be done about it?'. The remainder of this chapter touches briefly on each of these questions, though not quite in the same order. Readers more accustomed to taking a static rather than a dynamic view of poverty might expect the definition or meaning of poverty to be discussed ahead of measurement. However, a direct consequence of making time explicit in the measurement of poverty is to trigger a reappraisal of conventional assumptions about the nature of poverty.

2 Measurement: How many poor people are there?

Poverty is usually defined in terms of a shortfall in resources relative to a legitimate set of needs. Clearly much has been written about the appropriate definitions of resources and needs although the debate about the rights and wrongs remains vigorous (Citro and Michael 1995; Poverty Summit 1992; Bradshaw 1993). Less has been said about the choice of the accounting period over which resources and needs are measured, although this can radically affect the recorded level of poverty.

2.1 The accounting period

Lengthening the accounting period has the effect of reducing the cross-sectional poverty rate. This happens because averaging over time evens out the temporary mismatches between income and needs, lessens the degree of dispersion in the population and, hence, reduces the proportion of individuals appearing in the tails of the income to needs distribution. The consequences of changing the accounting period can be considerable and depend on the stability of people's needs and the volatility of income flows. Measures of poverty will be more sensitive to the choice of accounting period in situations where circumstances are less stable. Given the recent development of a flexible labour market across Europe creating more precarious employment, one can presume that measures have become increasingly susceptible to the choice of accounting period.

As the accounting period is extended so the resultant estimates of poverty asymptotically approach the level of permanent poverty. This is because the shortfalls in income received by people who experience the shortest spells of poverty are the first to be offset by the higher income received during more prosperous periods. Also, the longer the accounting period, the more the characteristics of people counted as poor reflect those of persons who are in the midst of a very long spell.

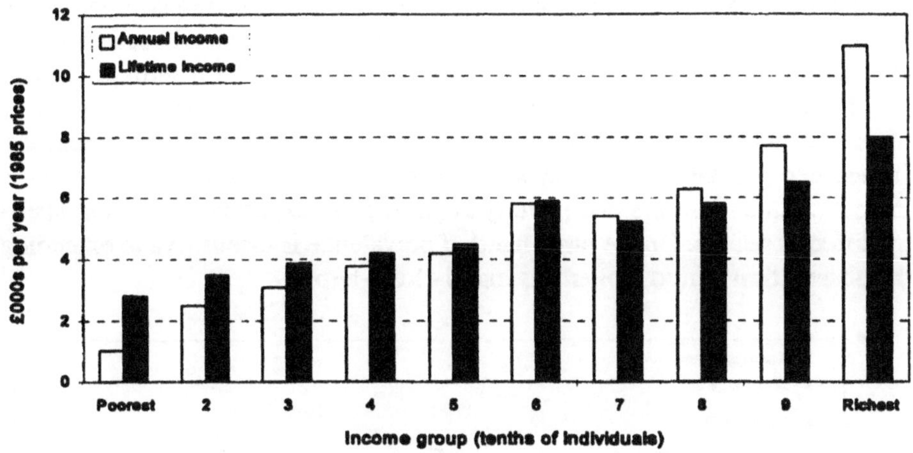

Figure 3 Annual and lifetime incomes in Great Britain
Source: Falkingham and Hills 1995

An example of this phenomenon comes from Britain and contrasts *annual* incomes with *life time* incomes based on a dynamic simulation model (Falkingham and Hills 1995). Consistent with theory, Figure 3 reveals that income measured over the life-time is much more egalitarian than annual income; indeed depending on the measure used, inequality is reduced by between a third and a half. Employing precisely the same data, and fixing an individual poverty line at 50 per cent of median income, causes the poverty rate to be approximately halved.

While there is probably no correct choice of accounting period, the choice makes a real difference. Various measures may need to be applied reflecting the purposes of the enquiry.

2.2 *Prevalence*

Thus far, we have focused on cross-sectional or static measures of poverty where assumptions about time are typically implicit. However, the assumptions need to be made explicit if a more dynamic view of poverty and social exclusion is to emerge. Moreover, with the advent of longitudinal data, additional decisions have to be taken concerning the period over which poverty is to be observed. A key concept, here, is 'prevalence': the proportion of a population that experiences a spell of poverty during a given period. This is the longitudinal equivalent of the cross-sectional poverty rate and suffers similar limitations. Prevalence is very sensitive to the length of the observation period; recorded values increase as the observation period is extended because of the enhanced opportunity to observe a greater proportion of short-term poverty.

However, this sensitivity offers a powerful tool for investigating the nature of poverty and for making comparisons between different countries or regions. If recorded prevalence rises linearly and rapidly as the observation period is increased, this indicates that poverty is principally experienced in short spells by different people. On the other hand, if prevalence is insensitive to extending the observation period, poverty is mainly long-term.

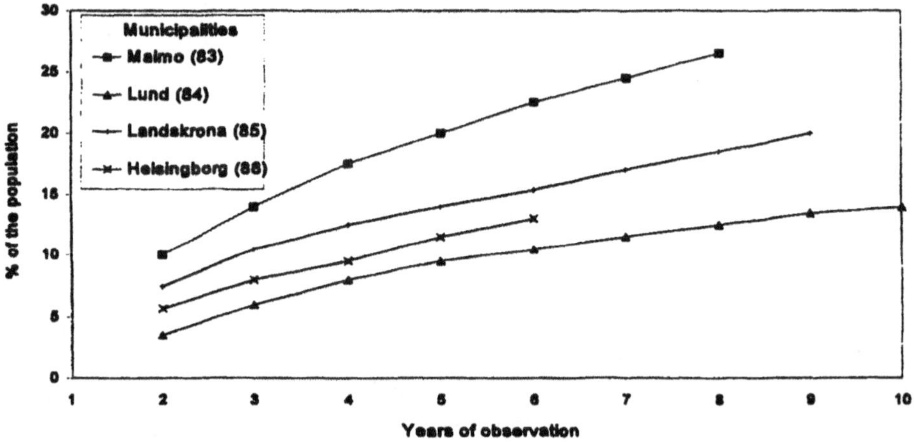

Figure 4 Percentage of population receiving social assistance in four municipalities in Sweden*

* The observation period for Malmo is 1983-89, for Lund 1984-92, for Landskrona 1985-92, and for Helsingborg 1988-92

Source: Salonen 1993

Prevalence, therefore, has value as an analytic concept as well as a descriptive one and this can be illustrated with Swedish data on social assistance receipt. Figure 4 arrays the numbers of people recorded as ever having received social assistance in four Swedish municipalities when the observation period is expanded from one to nine years. It shows that, depending on the locality, between four and ten per cent of people of working age make a claim for social assistance in any particular year, which is consistent with the widely accepted view that poverty in Sweden is comparatively rare and that social assistance fulfils a largely residual function. However, the fact that anywhere between 14 per cent and 28 per cent of the working age population will make a successful claim on social assistance in the longer term acts as an important corrective to the initial assumption. Moreover, it is evident that while the proportion claiming benefit is lower in Lund than in Malmo, people tend to receive benefit for a longer time (the slope of the curve is flatter).

The positive slope of the lines in Figure 4 reflects the fact that prevalence measures of poverty almost invariably exceed incidence; the number of households that ever suffer poverty often far exceeds the number in poverty at any particular time, a fact that politicians with a mission to dismantle welfare might do well to remember.

3 The meaning of poverty

Making time explicit, and focusing on the concept of prevalence rather than incidence, serves to remind us that the way in which poverty is distributed over time is related to the distribution of poverty within a population. This, in turn, helps to shape the experience of being poor and to mould its personal and social significance.

Given a fixed observation period, prevalence is determined by the total duration of poverty in the society, the length of spells and the degree to which the spells are recurrent. A lower boundary is set by the situation where the same group of people is continuously in poverty. The upper boundary describes the situation where poverty approaches a once in a life time event and where spells of poverty are as short as the global sum of poverty allows. Values in between imply that a variable proportion of the population is experiencing repeated spells of poverty of varying lengths.

Traditional discourse on poverty has implicitly assumed the kind of poverty associated with minimum, or at least minimal, prevalence. The poor have tended to be contrasted with the non-poor as if the two groups never changed places, that is as if the poor were permanently poor. Certainly, this concept underlies the rhetoric concerning the supposed growth in long-term dependency on benefits and is implicit in much of the discussion on social exclusion and the underclass (Deacon 1996). Indeed, other things being equal, the circumstances that foster the development of an underclass are most likely to arise when prevalence is low. Low prevalence suggests that that the poverty is experienced in long spells by a small number of people. As a consequence, poor people face low expectations of ever escaping poverty and come to have little in common with the wider society from which they are permanently excluded. Because the poor rarely change places with the non-poor, the lack of hope experienced by the former is matched by the latter's ignorance of any personal experience of poverty. Moreover, since low prevalence generally means that those who are not in poverty face little risk of ever becoming poor, they are likely to have little concern for poor people or policies to help them. (Self interest is arguably a powerful motivator of apparent altruism.)

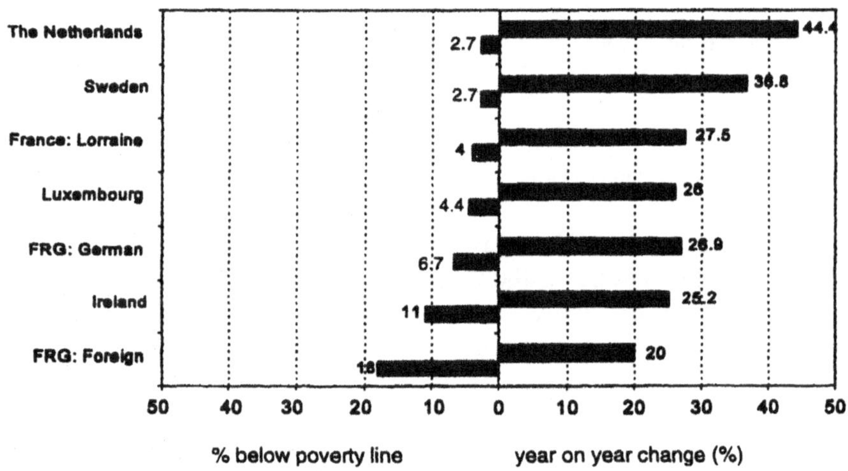

Figure 5 Static and dynamic poverty

* 50 per cent of the median equivalised income

Source: Duncan et al. 1995

However, the reality is often very different as is indicated by the graph presented in Figure 5. This compares poverty rates for selected European during the late 1980s and early 1990s, with the threshold set at 50 per cent of median national equivalised income. But, more important in the current context, the graph also records the proportion of poor people leaving poverty from one year to the next, a figure that ranges from 44 per cent in The Netherlands to 20 per cent among foreign nationals in Germany. While it is important not to underplay the extent of long-term poverty and the hardship and despair that undoubtedly accompanies it, significant numbers of people are escaping the clutches of poverty every year through their own efforts, or with the assistance of welfare services, or a combination of both. The suggestion, from Figure 5, is that the possibility of escape is highest where the overall incidence of poverty is lowest.[2]

Of course, not all of those who move out of poverty do so permanently; some return quickly and significant numbers repeatedly move in and out of poverty. In Europe, the best evidence of this phenomenon comes from studies of social assistance.[3] Salonen (1993), working in Helsingborg in Sweden, recognised four different patterns of usage over a five year period. Only eight per cent of recipients were permanent users whereas 82 per cent were variously categorised as occasional (42 per cent), sporadic (19 per cent) or recurrent (21 per cent) claimants.[4] Likewise, in Bremen, Germany, 40 per cent of people claiming social assistance over a six year period did so on at least two occasions (Brückner 1995).

At least some of the people who experience repeated spells of poverty or periods on benefit are moving in and out of employment. They are trying, albeit with limited success, to cling on to at least one of pivotal social structures that foster integration. It remains to be established what proportion of such people experience intermittent, or indeed permanent, exclusion from other aspects of social life on account of their repeated poverty.

Incidence measures of poverty are based on simple head counts of the number of people poor. Prevalence, as it has been defined to this point, additionally takes account of the duration of poverty although only indirectly. A more comprehensive measure, but the least that our inquiring Alien is likely to demand, would also need to take into account the severity of poverty, that is the shortage of resources as assessed against need. While the negative relationship between prevalence and average duration is logically unaffected by the added dimension of severity, it is an empirical question as to whether long spells of poverty are characterised by extreme severity, or whether severe poverty is experienced as short sharp shocks.

The empirical association between duration and severity is likely to be socially determined and, to date, readily available evidence is limited and based on experience in the United States (Table 1). There, according to analyses of the Panel Study of Income Dynamics, it would appear that the children who undergo the longest spells of poverty also suffer the greatest short-fall in family resources (Walker 1994; Ashworth, Hill and Walker 1994).

Table 1
Severity of poverty[a]

	Income to needs ratio during poverty spells[b] Mean (SD) ($)	Income to needs ratio during childhood[c] Mean (SD) ($)
Duration		
0	-	3.31 (1.60)
1 - 3	0.71 (0.23)	2.32 (1.13)
4 - 6	0.69 (0.15)	1.43 (0.37)
7 - 10	0.67 (0.14)	1.08 (0.18)
11 - 15	0.57 (0.13)	0.66 (1.60)
Experience[d]		
Transient	0.71 (0.26)	2.63 (1.60)
Occational	0.69 (0.21)	1.82 (0.49)
Recurrent	0.67 (0.15)	1.21 (0.45)
Persistent	0.70 (0.14)	1.66 (0.63)
Chronic	0.59 (0.09)	0.66 (0.08)
Permanent	0.46 (0.13)	0.46 (0.13)
Total	0.67 (0.20)	2.68 (1.63)

Notes:

a) Some of the distributions depart significantly from normal and the interpretation given in the text is informed by comparison of the full distributions
b) Average of ratios of income to needs for individual years in poverty
c) Ratio of income to needs for individual years averaged over the 15 years of childhood
d) *Transient poverty*, a single spell of poverty lasting a single year. *Occasional poverty*, more than one spell of poverty but none lasting more than one year, in practice, the duration of relative prosperity always exceeds the duration of poverty in this cohort. *Recurrent poverty*, repeated spells of poverty, some separated by more than a year and some exceeding a year in length. *Persistent poverty*, a single spell of poverty lasting between two and 13 years. *Chronic poverty*, repeated spells of poverty never separated by more than one year of relative prosperity. *Permanent poverty*, poverty lasting continuously for 15 years

American children growing up after 1968 who were poor throughout their childhood typically lived in households where resources were less than half of the PSID poverty line, whereas the resources available during shorter spells of poverty were generally above two-thirds of the poverty standard.

Such differentials are potentially explicable in terms of the carry-over of financial and social resources from previous periods of comparative prosperity, although the processes involved appear to be mediated by the exact patterning of spells (Table 1). The impact of a single year out of poverty has a dramatic effect on the level of resources available when poor, raising them from 46 per cent to 59 per cent of the PSID poverty standard. Children who experience recurrent, lengthy spells of poverty have marginally fewer resources while poor than children who encounter a single short lived spell but, whereas the former frequently experience a childhood spent on the margins of poverty, the latter are typically comparatively well-off throughout the rest of their childhood.

If long spells of poverty are generally the most severe, this points to poverty in its most pernicious form. Allied with low prevalence, this might exacerbate the segregation of the poor and non-poor in a society, creating a kind of economic Apartheid. However, in the American context, combining measures of duration and severity, and also taking account of the patterning of spells, does not suggest a dichotomy between the permanently, desperately poor and the never poor. Instead it reveals a distribution of different experiences. Plotting a measure of Dollar/years spent below the poverty line generates a Gini coefficient of 0.56; this suggests a degree of inequality *among* the people who experience poverty that is greater than that observed for annual incomes across the entire US population (Walker 1994).

In attempting to answer the Alien's three questions 'how many?', 'for how long?' and 'how severe?', it becomes apparent that poverty exists in different degrees and perhaps in different forms. While 'the poor', in the sense of being 'always poor', may still exist in advanced economic societies, together perhaps with an underclass, this is unlikely to be the typical experience of the very large minority of people who ever suffer poverty.

4 The experience of poverty

What is already apparent is that shifting attention from the cross-sectional poverty rate to a longitudinal measure of prevalence, forces a recognition of the different patterning of poverty over time. This, in turn, raises the question of whether these different patterns in fact index different kinds of poverty. If so, then our traditional cross-sectional measures have led us to combine the sociological equivalents of cabbages and kings with potentially disastrous consequences for policy development.

Our growing understanding of these different kinds of experience comes mainly from qualitative research and the accounts of poor people themselves. It emerges from British research that, far from time simply being the medium in which poverty occurs, it helps to forge the different experiences. Not only do people exchange places in the social order as spells of poverty start and finish, the fear of falling into poverty and the hope that it will one day end, a hope that sustains people but may fade over time, are all integral components of the experience of being poor.

Although poverties may differ, they impose a common discipline. Merely to make ends meet on a low income requires effective money management. Moreover, this management has a strong temporal component. Families facing an excess number of competing claims on limited resources respond by attempting to re-sequence the claims, deferring some until resources are available, and holding onto a little cash in order to meet both known and unpredictable future expenses. Ironically, 'when money is tight, managing the household spending [becomes] a full-time job' (Kempson et al. 1994).

In Britain it is typically the woman who carries the principal responsibility for budgeting, certainly when both partners are out of work. Management demands the setting of priorities: collective necessities, food, rent and fuel, are typically given higher priority than clothes, shoes or individual spending. The woman almost invariably tries to 'ring fence' the money to be spent on food, but this generally proves to be impractical since food is one of the few components of the budget which offers any degree of flexibility (Dobson et al. 1994; Walker et al. 1995).

In Britain welfare benefits are paid fortnightly.[5] But mothers typically shop for food weekly so that (1) they can save money in case of unexpected demands and (2) because food in the house is likely to be eaten. For the same reasons, women increase the frequency of their shopping when money is particularly short. Shopping is generally done alone in order to minimise expenditure.

Families have no choice but to adapt their expenditures, however preferences change much more slowly. Therefore, for example, families struggle to continue to eat a mainstream diet by adopting cheaper imitations of conventional eating patterns. Radically to rethink diet involves trial and error and there is no room for mistakes and waste on a low income.

The process of becoming poor is deeply distressing. Memories of better times are vivid. Having to pass the supermarket by in favour of the discount store is stigmatising. Moreover, the process may not become any easier over time, not least because the financial cushioning carried over from more affluent days is rapidly exhausted (Morgan 1994). Long term recipients of benefits may become habituated to the constraints inherent in their predicament such that their frustrations become less explicit. For people who incessantly move on and off benefit the experience must be one of repeatedly dashed hopes and frustrated aspirations when long-term planning is impossible or as likely as not to come to naught.

Children's preferences and needs are almost invariably placed first by parents both for altruistic and practical reasons (Middleton and Thomas 1994). They strongly believe that children should have access to a wide range of opportunities necessary for their social and intellectual development and, moreover, that they should not be singled out as a result of poverty but be able to participate in the activities of childhood.

Certainly British children appear to share a common culture of acquisition irrespective of parental incomes. Children from low income homes may make less demands in deference to family circumstances. They are also more likely to resort to tantrums and other forms of direct action when demanding things from parents. Low income parents feel themselves doubly disadvantaged in their financial dealings with children: (1) they both have to say 'no' more often and (2) they have to respond less consistently because of fluctuations in the family budget. Financial discipline over their children is exerted from necessity rather than from any decision about what is good or bad for their child to have or do.

Evidence of this kind is beginning to suggest, therefore, that the different patterning of poverty over time, and the varying trajectories that people follow, imbue poverty with different social meanings and impart differential risks. Within the very experience of poverty lie the seeds of social exclusion: increased social isolation, reduced morale, deviant behaviours and even the experience of ostracism that are all linked more or less directly to the limited choice and restricted opportunities imposed by inadequate resources. However, these seeds are likely to germinate more or less readily according to the type of poverty (Walker 1995).

5 Causes of poverty

Inadequate though our answers were to the Alien's first five questions, they appear erudite compared with attempts to explain the causes of poverty. The existing literature tends to reinforce a static view of poverty. At one end of the spectrum are those who view human frailty as the root cause of poverty. Individuals are believed to be poor as a consequence of their own capacities, attitudes and/or behaviour which must change if poverty is to be reduced. Few proponents of this view see change occurring quickly. Likewise, those who point to structural factors as the real cause of poverty offer a similarly pessimistic short-term scenario. Poverty reflects the prevalence of low paid jobs and processes in the labour market that push people into unemployment and economic inactivity. According to this view the incidence of poverty has much to do with the all embracing effects of class, mediated and largely compounded by gender and race, which exert their influence over income, wealth, education, career, family formation and inheritance. As a result, poverty is largely confined to the working class who 'walk along economic paths that are familiar to their parents' (George and Howards 1991, p.119).

Neither approach accords well with the enormous volatility in the financial and other circumstances of families in all sections of society which longitudinal research reveals. Large scale movements out of poverty have already been discussed above, while the findings of panel studies show that substantial variations in income to needs ratios from one year to the next are almost common place (Jarvis and Jenkins 1995; Duncan 1988; Walker 1994). Attempts to explain poverty need to focus on the triggers that precipitate poverty and the events associated with the end of spells. However, it is vitally important that the search for explanation moves on to consider the context in which such triggers occur, and the factors and circumstances which mediate the process by which an event becomes a trigger. Only in this way will it prove possible to unite the individualistic and structural explanations of poverty in a way that is likely both to convince our Alien visitor and to lay the foundations for sustainable policy solutions (Walker 1994).

Figure 6 provides a step towards this explanatory environment with a summary of the different triggers at work in five European countries. A reduction in employment within the household, often associated with life-course changes such as retirement or childbirth, is an important factor in all countries, but the degree of inter-country variation is striking and not instantly explicable. The initial presumption is either that these contingencies are relatively more common in Sweden and Luxembourg than elsewhere, or that their social welfare systems are less well developed to cope with them. However, an alternative proposition might be that these two societies have systems that are better adapted to protecting people against other social risks such as unemployment, which triggers a higher proportion of new spells of poverty in Germany and The Netherlands. The importance of institutional factors is further reinforced by the impact of social insurance rules in Luxembourg and among foreigners in Germany; in each case one in five new spells of poverty appears to be triggered by the exhaustion of insurance entitlement.

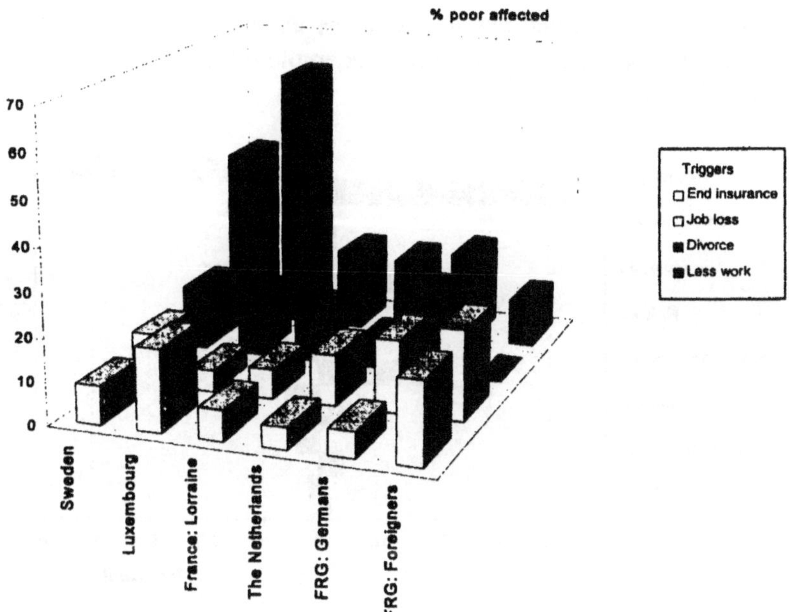

Figure 6 Events triggering poverty
Source: Duncan et al. 1995

There is, in fact, growing evidence that the events which trigger poverty are widespread but that poverty is a comparatively rare outcome. This means that any comprehensive explanation of poverty has to take account not only of the probability that any particular event occurs but also of the probability that the event triggers a spell of poverty. Both probabilities are likely to vary dramatically between (groups of) individuals for reasons that relate to personal characteristics and the plethora of structural factors associated with their prior social position and spatial location.

As yet we do not have comprehensive models of this kind but the first stages of elucidating these processes is underway in Britain, notably with respect to the receipt of Income Support. (Income Support is the main social assistance scheme in Britain and at any time will be supporting around five million households.) Figure 7 shows the routes that claimants and their adult dependants take on and off benefit. Most move onto Income Support directly from employment, with comparatively few arriving as a result of exhausted entitlement to social insurance schemes. This reflects the emphasis that Britain places on means-tested assistance at the expense of social insurance; indeed only 25 per cent of people becoming unemployed ever receive insurance-based Unemployment Benefit.[6]

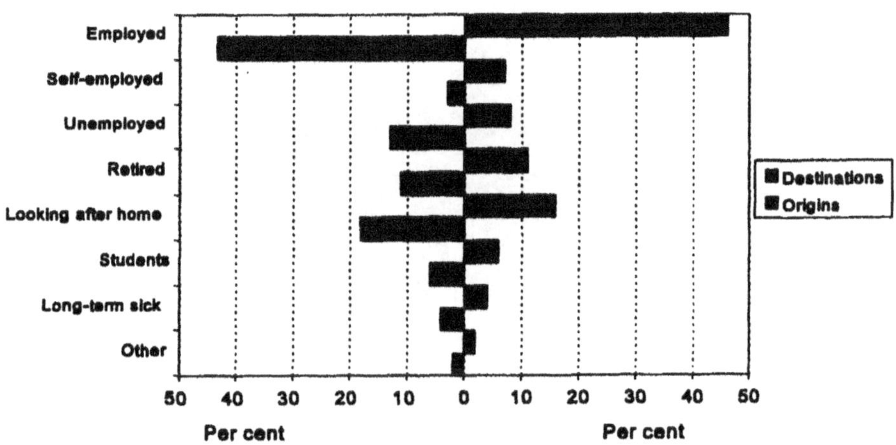

Figure 7 Routes on and off income support (1991/1 - 1992/3)
Source: Ashworth et al. 1995

It is also important to note that 28 per cent of people who become unemployed never receive cash benefits of any kind. Some of these unemployed will have resources of their own, such as savings and redundancy payments, that keep them above social assistance thresholds. Others will be protected financially by living with a more affluent partner. Either way, these people may find that unemployment triggers a change in social status but probably not a spell of poverty. Yet others, through ignorance, choice or force of other circumstance will fall beneath the state safety net for varying periods of time.

In thinking about the multiplicity of factors that can precipitate a spell of poverty or, in this instance, a period on social assistance, it is instructive to focus on the experience of women. In Britain significant numbers receive benefit as adult dependants rather than as claimants in their own right. In fact, only about two-fifths of women in partnerships receiving Income Support moved onto benefit following a change in their own employment status. Almost as many, a third, received benefit because their partner lost his job; from an economic perspective they arguably chose the wrong man.

An additional 25 per cent of women received social assistance benefit not because of any change in their employment status or that of their partner. Transitions of this kind clearly require attention to be paid to social trajectories other than those relating to employment and, although context is again important, relationship breakdown looms large as a factor precipitating claims for Income Support. About 17 per cent of people claim Income Support in the year following the dissolution of a family due to separation, divorce or death. However, this figure masks the precarious dependency of women who cease employment to look after the family home; 41 per cent[7] of these were forced to claim Income Support within a year of their relationship ending.

Interesting though these insights may be, they do not yet sum to the model of social causation demanded by the assiduous Alien. Admittedly we have begun to assign probabilities to the occurrence of selected events and to establish the likelihood that these will trigger spells of poverty, or periods on social assistance. However, this is a long way from understanding the processes that determine the probabilities, or building persuasive theories that account for the prevalence of the varying forms of poverty. Still less are we able with confidence to explain how individual experiences, the routines of daily living, relate to structural forces, or to specify the mediating role played by personal values, expectations and individual agency.

6 Conclusion

The Alien's questions have stimulated embarrassment, thought and a not inconsiderable reappraisal of the way that the study of poverty has traditionally been approached. In rethinking poverty, it is necessary to complement the question 'how many?' with others:

- How severe is the poverty?
- For how long does it last?
- Does it reoccur?

Answers to this battery of questions provide a basis for thinking about poverty in a dynamic way. This, in turn, drives home the truism that the nature of poverty is a function of its distribution, not only within a population, but also over time. Moreover, the patterning of poverty over time suggests that there may be more than one kind of poverty, each experienced in a different way, with a unique aetiology and, perhaps, demanding a different policy response.

Certainly the policy response (the Alien's final question) can no longer be to do nothing. Thinking dynamically destroys the excuse that, since the poor are always with us, anti-poverty strategies are proved worthless. Recognising that poverty occurs in spells, that mostly have beginnings and ends, predicates a new policy agenda that is proactive rather than reactive, which focuses on prevention rather than alleviation, and which aims explicitly to bring spells of poverty to an early end. A dynamic approach to poverty places us at the beginning of a new chapter of social enquiry. (Indeed, Gershuny (1997) sees it as the beginning of a new social science.) Perhaps, at least, we have begun to ask and answer the right questions.

Notes

[1] The definitions differ more than just the level at which the poverty threshold is pitched. They reflect radically different notions of poverty, the former based on a rights approach to poverty the latter based on a welfare perspective (Atkinson 1989).

[2] A low incidence of poverty may imply the availability of a large number of routes out of poverty. Empirically one might expect that a low incidence relative to other countries will be predictive of a low relative prevalence, although the relationship is of course mediated by the dynamic nature of the poverty in the countries concerned.

[3] Studies of the United States show that repeated spells of poverty are the norm rather than the exception; see Ashworth, Hill and Walker (1994) and Stevens (1994).

[4] *Occasional*: households with one period on social assistance or a maximum of three separate months. *Sporadic*: households with social assistance on several occasions but for brief periods. A maximum of nine months on social assistance in the five-year period. *Recurrent*: households with several periods, both long and short. The total time on social assistance is at least ten months. *Permanent*: households receiving social assistance continuously.

[5] The monthly pattern of social assistance payments in Gemany imposes a different budgeting cycle (Leisering and Walker 1996).

[6] Unemployment Benefit was replaced by Jobseeker's Allowance in October 1996 which is further evidence of the erosion of social insurance.

[7] This figure includes women who were retired at the time their relationship was dissolved.

References

Ashworth, K., Walker, R., Trinder, P., Jenkins, S. (1995), *British Benefit Dynamics*, Centre for Research in Social Policy: Loughborough.

Ashworth, K., Hill, M., Walker, R. (1994), 'Patterns of Childhood poverty: New Challenges for Policy', *Journal of Policy Analysis and Management*, Vol. 13, No. 4, pp. 658-680.

Atkinson, A. (1984), *The Economics of Inequality*, Oxford University Press: Oxford.

Atkinson, A. (1989), *Poverty and Social Security*, Harvester: Hemel Hempstead.

Bradshaw, J. (1993), *Technology, Employment and Income Distribution, mimeo*, School of Management, UMIST: Manchester.

Brückner, H. (1995), *Times of Poverty: Lessons from the Bremen Longitudinal Social Assistance Sample*, Universität München.

Buhr, P., et al. (1991), *Passages Through Welfare*, Centre for Social Policy Research, Discussion Paper 3: Bremen.

Burkhauser, R., Duncan, G. (1989), 'Economic Risks of Gender Roles: Income Loss and Life Events over Life Course', *Social Science Quarterly*, Vol. 70, No. 1, pp. 4-23.

Burkhauser, R., Holden, K., Feaster, D. (1988), 'Incidence, Timing and Events Associated with Poverty', *Journal of Gerontology*, Vol. 43, pp. 846-852.

Citro, C., Michael, R. (1995), *Measuring Poverty: A New Approach*, National Academy Press: Washington.

Commission of the European Countries (1991), *National Policies to Combat Social Exclusion, First Annual Report of the European Community Observatory*, Centre for Research in European Social and Employment Policy: Bath.

Cross, M. (1993), 'Generating the New Poverty: a European Comparison', in Simpson, R., Walker, R. (eds.), *Europe: For Richer or Poorer*, Child Poverty Action Group: London, pp. 5-24.

Daly, M. (1994), *The Syracuse University PSID and GSEP Equivalent Data File*, Paper presented at a conference on the Use of the PSID for International Comparative Research, Cologne, June.

Dawes, L. (1993), *Long-term Unemployment and Labour Market Flexibility*, University Centre for Labour Market Studies: Leicester.

Deacon, A. (1996), *Should we Worry about the Character of the Poor?*, The Beckly Lecture, June: Blackpool.

Dobson, B., Beardsworth, A., Keil, T. (1994), *Diet, Choice and Poverty: Social, Cultural and Nutritional Aspects of Food Consumption among Low Income Families*, Family Policy Studies Centre: London.

Duncan, G. (1988), 'The Volatility of Family Income over the Life Course', in Baltes, P., Featherman, D., Lerner, R. (eds.), *Life-Span Development and Behaviour*, Laurence Erlbaum Associates: Hillsdale, NJ, pp. 317-57.

Duncan, G. et al. (1993), 'Poverty Dynamics in Eight Countries', *Journal of Population Economics*, Vol. 6, pp. 214-234.

Elias, P., Steiner, V. (1993), *The Causes and Consequences of Recurrent Spells of Unemployment in Britain and Germany*, Anglo-German Foundation and European Commission Report: London.

Eurostat (1991), *Pattern of poverty in Europe*, Department of Economic Sociology and Psychology, Erasmus University: Rotterdam (unpublished paper prepared by A. Hagenaars, K. de Vos and A. Zaidi).

Falkingham, J., Hills, J. (1994) (eds.), *The Dynamic of Welfare*, Prentice Hall/Harvester Wheatsheaf: Hemel Hempstead.

George, V., Howard, I. (1991), *Poverty Amidst Affluence: Britain and the United States*, Edward Elgar: Aldershot.

Gershuny, J. (1997), 'Thinking Dynamically', in Leisering, L., Walker, R. (eds.), *The Dynamics of Welfare*, London.

Gregg, P., Wadsworth, J. (1994), *Opportunity Knocks? Job Separations, Engagements and Claimant Status*, National Institute of Economic and Social Research: London.

Headey, B., Habich, R., Krause, P. (1990), *The Duration and Extent of Poverty: Is Germany a Two-thirds Society?*, Wissenschaftszentrum, Working Paper P90/103: Berlin.

Jarvis, S. Jenkins, S. (1995), *Do the Poor Stay Poor*? Occasional Papers of the ESRC Research Centre on Micro-Social Change, 95, University of Essex: Colchester.

Jordan, B. et al. (1992), *Trapped in Poverty*?, Routledge: London.

Kempson, E. et al. (1994), *Hard Times*, Policy Studies Institute: London.

Leisering, L., Walker, R. (1996), *Social Assistance Dynamics: Anglo-German Similarities and Disparities*, mimeo: Loughborough.

Middleton, S. et al. (eds.) (1994), *Family Fortunes*, CPAG: London.

Middleton, S., Thomas, M. S. (1994), 'Budgeting for Survival: Strategies and Support', in Middleton, S. et al. (eds.), *Family Fortunes*, CPAG: London, pp. 119-132.

Morgan, C. (1994), *Family Resources Survey, Great Britain 1993/94*, Government Statistical Service: London.

Muffels, R., Berghman, J., Dirven, H.J. (1992), 'A Multivariate Approach to Monitor the Evolution of Poverty', *Journal of European Social Policy*, Vol. 2, No. 3, pp. 194-213.

Pissarides, C. (1986), 'Unemployment and Vacancies in Britain', *Economic Policy*, Vol. 3, pp. 500-559.

Poverty Summit (1992), *The Edinburgh Declaration*, University Department of Social Policy and Social Work: Edinburgh.

Room, G. (1995), 'Poverty in Europe: Competing Paradigms of Analysis', *Policy and Politics*, Vol. 23, No. 2, pp. 103-113.

Salonen, T. (1993), *Margins of Welfare*, Hällestad Press: Torna: Hällestad.

Sen, A. (1982), *Choice, Welfare and Measurement*, Blackwell: Oxford.

Stevens, A, (1994), 'The Dynamics of Poverty Spells: Updating Bane and Ellwood', *American Economic Review (Papers and Proceedings)*, Vol. 84, pp. 34-37.

Walker, R. (1995), 'The Dynamics of Poverty and Social Exclusion', in Room, G. (ed.), *Beyond the Threshold*, Policy Press: Bristol, pp. 102-28.

Walker, R. et al. (1995), 'Managing to Eat on a Low Income', *Nutrition & Food Science*, No. 3, May/June, pp. 5-10.

Walker, R., Shaw, A., Hull, L. (1995), 'Responding to the Risk of Unemployment', in *Risk, Insurance and Welfare*, Association of British Insurers: London, pp. 37-52.

Walker, R. (1994), *Poverty Dynamics: Issues and Examples*, Avebury: Aldershot.

Walker, R. et al. (1994), 'Pretty, Pretty Please - Just Like a Parrot', in Middleton, S. et al. (eds.), *Family Fortunes*, CPAG: London, pp. 88-104.

Walker, R. (1991), *Poverty and Poverty Dynamics*, Centre for Research in Social Policy Working Paper 135: Loughborough.

Webb, S. (1995), *Poverty Dynamics in Great Britain*, Institute of Fiscal Studies: London.

'Social exclusion' and 'underclass' - new concepts for the analysis of poverty

Martin Kronauer

1 The new social quality of poverty and unemployment, a challenge for research

Since the 1980s, persistingly high unemployment and growing poverty, combined with decreasing resources of the welfare states, are deeply transforming most Western societies. Youths in French 'banlieues' and English inner-city quarters demonstrate with sporadic eruptions of violence that they are set apart from the rest of society by a widening gap of despair. Even in the United States with its long history of Black ghettos, the isolation of poverty-stricken inner-city neighborhoods and the hopelessness of their inhabitants have increased. In Western Europe, less spectacularly but nevertheless present in the public mind, growing numbers of long-term unemployed are being forced out of the employment system. Everywhere the centrifugal tendencies of the highly developed capitalist 'work societies' become evident.

The present crisis of employment affects the selfperception and the institutions of those societies in particular ways: It has taken on a new historic quality. This holds true in three respects. Firstly, in the foreseeable future the employment effects of economic growth will not be strong enough to absorb the supply of labor. Even more, in manufacturing economic growth has itself become the driving force for the vanishing of jobs (see Dahrendorf 1988, p. 142; Europäische Kommission 1994, p. 11, p. 151). In Western Europe, therefore, for the first time after the Second World War unemployment on a high level threatens to become a permanent social reality.

Secondly, the historical context has changed for those who are most adversely affected by unemployment. While unemployment in the past had been embedded in a secular expansion of un- and semiskilled industrial work, this is no longer the case. For years the job opportunities for the unskilled in manufacturing have been sharply declining, and will decrease further in the future (for historical comparison see Pugliese 1987; Katz 1993, p. 446; Polanyi 1995, pp. 113; for the future composition of the workforce by qualification in Germany, see Tessaring 1994). At present it is more than questionable whether the gains in service-sector employment will make up for the losses in manufacturing (see Europäische Kommission 1994, p. 155). Qualifications, therefore, are of ever increasing importance as entry (or exclusion) criteria on the labor market. In Western Europe, this leads to a significant social division within unemployment itself: As a temporary experience, limited in time, unemployment affects ever larger segments of the skilled and even highly qualified workforce, causing a considerable amount of insecurity. As a long-term experience, however, it threatens the un- and semiskilled with permanent exclusion from regular employment. The price of the US-American 'alternative' to European mass unemployment, on the other hand, is an extreme income polarization within the workforce, with a growing number of 'working poor' (see Levitan et al. 1993).

Finally - and most importantly - , unemployment, poverty, and labor-market exclusion today represent historically new and distinct social realities because they are experienced in the light of an unprecedented period of collective upward mobility and accumulation of wealth. In addition, mainly in Western Europe but to a lesser degree even in the United States, the public responsibility for the welfare of the individual was politically recognized after the Second World War and institutionalized to an extent unknown before. For more than three decades, these factors together considerably increased the similarities in the living conditions of the population, despite persisting social inequality. Moreover, they shaped peoples' legitimate views on the standards of material and social well being which are necessary to fully participate in the life of society. In this respect, Western capitalist societies in the decades after the Second World War had become more socially integrated than ever before in their history.

It is only against this background of unprecedented material and social opportunities that the true historic dimension of the current employment crisis becomes visible. 'Underclass' and 'exclusion' are central categories with which the media and the social sciences discuss the social implications of these recent developments. The former was originally coined to cover developments in the United States (see Myrdal 1965, pp. 40) and was then exported to Europe. The latter concept originated in France but has meanwhile entered common

European language (see Paugam 1996; Commission of the European Communities 1993, pp. 7-17). Both notions not only refer to particular groups of people, the 'excluded', but also to a particularly critical state of society and its institutions. The very fact of 'exclusion' calls into question the future integrative capacities of most highly developed Western societies.

'Underclass' and 'exclusion' are new categories in that they introduce a new perspective into the traditional discourse on unemployment and poverty. If properly used, they shift the focus from living conditions to social relations, from characteristics of people to characteristics of society and what it does to people. Such a shift in perspective depends very much on historical context. The notion 'exclusion' would not have made much sense with reference to poverty and unemployment in a highly segmented nineteenth century European society. It presupposes its counterpart, a shared understanding of what it means to be socially 'included'. Both categories, therefore, are very 'modern' in the sense that they are based on the history of prosperity and the welfare state after the Second World War. As such they are even more controversial than other categories of poverty research. And as explicitely social, relational categories, they are also more difficult to handle empirically.

In the following I will discuss the specific contribution that the two concepts can make to unemployment and poverty research, but also important ambiguities which threaten their usefulness. My arguments will be based on studies from different European countries as well as the United States. First I will briefly consider the theoretical framework of the terms 'social exclusion' and 'underclass', and then discuss major questions which they address, and how they can guide empirical research.

2 Theoretical approach: 'Peripherization', 'social exclusion', 'underclass'

In the international discussion, the notions 'exclusion', 'social exclusion', and 'underclass' are theoretically and empirically highly controversial. At the present state of debate it seems to be most appropriate to use them as 'metaphors of social transformation' (Katz 1993, p. 440), i.e. as indicators of new social developments and new questions to be asked.

Theoretically they fit best into the categorial framework of 'center' and 'periphery'. The latter concepts were originally developed to characterize relations of dependence among economies and actors (nation states, corporations etc.) on the world market, and were later transferred to the analysis of social changes within the 'centers' themselves. Mainly researchers in the field of urban studies presently interpret 'exclusion' and 'underclass' as new forms of social inequality in the wider context of increasing 'marginalization' or 'peripherization' (see Mollenkopf and Castells 1991, pp. 16, pp. 399-418; Katz 1993, pp. 452-454; Dubet and Lapeyronnie 1994, p. 35; Wacquant 1995).

In Germany, Kreckel (1992) has in recent years most fruitfully adapted the notions 'center' and 'periphery' to the analysis of social inequality, speaking about these terms as 'metaphors' as well. They enlarge the vertical image of class and status stratification by adding further dimensions of social inequality which supplement and superimpose the positions within the structure of employment: inequality between the sexes, between those who are employed and those who are excluded from employment, between ascending and descending branches in the national economy, between national economies within the system of the world economy. The particular analytical vantage point of the center-periphery metaphor consists in its focus on unequal access to material and symbolic resources, i.e. on the problem of power: The 'center' is characterized by an accumulation of resources and a concentration of power, the 'periphery' by a lack of resources and a fragmentation of forces (see Kreckel 1992, pp. 41-44). Moreover, this analytical framework provides a means to address graduations in the power distribution, thereby to identify 'peripherization' as well as its result, the 'periphery'.

The notions 'exclusion' and 'underclass' stretch the idea of 'peripherization' even further. They point out that a social dividing line exists which does not fit into the traditional, employment centered scheme of class and status division. Already in the sixties Myrdal was convinced that a new term had to be invented in order to mark this particular social cleavage. He therefore introduced the Swedish 'underklassen' into the American language, changing in the process of translation its original meaning (see Myrdal 1965, p. 40). Ever more people are pushed to the margins, or even beyond, of the employment system. They thereby lose access to the relative prosperity of the majority of the population as well as to its ambitions for the future. In important dimensions of everyday social life they are - and perceive themselves as - excluded from the generally accepted and desired standards. They also no longer participate in the power of collective bargaining which the employed have - at least potentially - at their disposal. The only choices left for them are to develop survival strategies with the help of the welfare state and/or inside the informal economy, or to draw public attention to their plight with occasional riots.

Wilson summarizes the social situation of the 'underclass' or the 'excluded' in a short formula, emphasizing two characteristics: 'marginal economic position' and 'social isolation' (Wilson 1991, p. 475; cf. Wilson 1987, pp. 39-62). When both coincide, the 'periphery' splits away, so to speak, from the 'work society'.

While I have stressed so far the commonalities in the usage of the terms 'exclusion' and 'underclass', there are significant differences between them as well. 'Social exclusion' (or 'exclusion' in France) has the double meaning of the *state* of being exluded as well as the *process* of exclusion. It therefore directs our attention not only to characteristics of people but also to actors or institutions which are responsible for bringing exclusion about. 'Underclass', in contrast, denotes an already fixed social position and way of life. It is, therefore, much more prone to be misunderstood in a moralizing way. Mainly in the United States, but also in part in Great Britain, it has been taken up by the media and conservative social scientists in a discriminatory way, deprived of its originally critical, structural content, and turned into its opposite. In this conservative version, 'underclass' means deviant behavior for which the poor themselves are to blamed (for a critical discussion see Gans 1993a and 1995; Katz 1995; Pugliese 1995). Different are also the respective images of society to which both notions allude. 'Underclass' implies a hierarchically structured society, while 'exclusion' more strongly emphasizes an inside-outside dualism.

The conservative twist of the 'underclass' concept in the US has triggered sharp controversies. In the end, those social scientists who adhere to the original, critical intention of the term now distance themselves from its use. There are good reasons for this decision in the political and ideological context of the US. However, there is also a prize to be paid for it, which I would call the danger of a conceptual void. There is still great need to speak about the 'thing itself', i.e. the new social quality of persisting poverty and the fact of structural exclusion. The critics of the conservatively twisted 'underclass' category have demonstrated this again and again. But the problem of the appropriate language, of categories resistent to defamatory occupation, is so far by no means resolved - neither by resorting to quotation marks (see Katz 1993, pp. 440), nor by drawing upon new categories (such as 'undercaste', see Gans 1993b), nor by using, as far as possible, descriptive terms at the expense of analytical generalization (such as the term 'ghetto poor', see Wilson 1991, p. 463).

There are similar problems with the notion of 'social exclusion'. The dualism which it invokes between 'inside' and 'outside' can easily be interpreted as an apologetic affirmation of the 'inside'. What could be wrong with society when all that counts is to be 'included' in it? Here again the ambiguity of the notion leaves room for erasing its critical connotations, the reference to excluding institutions, processes, and actors, and to turn its original intentions upside down.

Maybe there is no convincing, unambiguous answer to this problem. It is not surprising after all that sociological categories which indicate social divisions become politically embattled and occupied. The more important it is, however, to be on guard by using these categories, to be precise and specific, and to explicate their meaning in empirical reality.

3 Empirical approach: Who is excluded, in which ways, and with which consequences for society?

In the following, the fruitfulness of the categories 'exclusion' and 'underclass' shall be judged by the questions which they allow us to ask vis-à-vis social reality, by their ability to guide empirical research, and by the knowledge which they thereby generate. When tested in this way, the unsolved problems also will show which need further theoretical consideration and empirical investigation. There are mainly four questions which the international research on 'exclusion' and 'underclass' addresses: Who is excluded (or threatend by exclusion) as a result of the current crisis of employment? What does 'social exclusion' mean for society at large? What does it mean for the individuals? How sharp is the division between the 'inside' and the 'outside'?

3.1 Who is threatened by exclusion?

The answers are manifold. At least five groups can be distinguished which draw particular attention in the international discussion.

- In the United States, the discussion about the 'underclass' concentrates on *the Black and Puerto Rican populations in the poor big-city neighborhoods*. The employment crisis comes into play in its direct as well as indirect consequences: Directly it shows in the retreat of many men in employable age from the labor market ('labor-market detachment'), indirectly in the growing poverty of single mothers (see the now classical study by Wilson 1987; for a critical discussion of its results see, among others, Fainstein 1987, Jencks and Peterson 1991). The farreaching social and ethnic/racial homogeneity of the urban neighborhoods is a historic peculiarity which has increased over the last decades (see Wilson 1987, pp. 46-62; Massey and

Denton 1993; Katz 1993, pp. 448). Only in England, if at all, the ghetto poverty of parts of the black population seems to have taken on similar features, though to a lesser extent. In this country the term 'underclass' is also sometimes used with reference to that particular group (see Dahrendorf 1988, p. 152; Morris 1994, pp. 95).

- The discussion about 'exclusion' and 'les exclus' in France refers mainly to *unemployed or marginally employed youths* (see Dubet and Lapeyronnie 1994; Wacquant 1995). In many cases they are second generation immigrants. Here again the spatial aspect, the social isolation in 'banlieues' of the big cities, plays a particularly influential role. Similar constellations of spatially concentrated youth unemployment can be found in other European countries as well, for instance in cities of Great Britain.
- A large part of the European literature on 'social exclusion', 'underclass', and 'soziale Ausgrenzung' concerns in addition the *long-term unemployed*, mainly those with fairly long work histories (see e.g. for Britain Smith 1992; Morris 1993; Morris 1994, pp. 93-110; for the Netherlands Engbersen et al. 1993, pp. 179-182; for Germany Kronauer et al. 1993, pp. 15, pp. 172-208, pp. 229-239; Kronauer 1995a; for France Paugam 1994).
- Sometimes the term 'underclass' is used as a catch-all category for different 'marginal groups' in the traditional sense, *the poor and the homeless*, who for various reasons ended up poor and without a home. However, there is a link to the current employment crisis in that unemployment since the 80s has become of ever increasing importance as a cause of poverty. Moreover, it is becoming increasingly difficult for populations which depend for their survival on casual work to find these kinds of jobs (see for the United States Wagner 1993, p. 2, p. 92; Jencks 1994, p. 53). In a similar way, Hess and Mechler in the 1970s already used the term 'Unterschicht' to characterize the living conditions of poor people in a big-city neighborhood of West Germany (see Hess and Mechler 1973).
- Finally, the literature on the 'underclass' sometimes includes the growing numbers of *illegal immigrants* (see Engbersen 1995).

It becomes obvious already by this selection how heterogeneous the groups are. Mainly two factors have a diversifying effect: On the one hand, the different historical and institutional contexts in the various countries determine who is especially affected by the processes of marginalization and exclusion on the labor markets, and in which particular ways. While in the United States, for instance, exclusionary practices are still based to a large extent on racial discrimination (see Kirschenman and Neckerman 1991), in Germany a long tradition of restrictive employment policy towards women and older workers clearly shows. On the other hand, there are considerable variations in the forms of exclusion even within each national context. In this respect, the differences in initial social position are of particular relevance. Exclusion can take place in the form of social decline (as in the case of long-term unemployed persons, kept out of employment after a long working life), or of barred first entry (as in the case of unemployed youths), or of a further deterioration in the employment chances and living conditions of people who have already been living at the margins of the 'work society' for a long time. Depending on those initial differences in social position, the consequences of exclusion and their perceptions will differ as well. In addition, each of these populations is characterized by specific internal social relations, which in turn can make their interaction with others even more difficult. And in the case of immigrants, differences in culture and legal status contribute to further divisions.

While comparative studies of 'social exclusion' in recent years have become more numerous on the international level, there is still a considerable lack of research dedicated to the comparison of different forms of exclusion within national contexts. In the United States, for example, there is meanwhile a wealth of studies on the 'urban underclass', but very little is known about unemployment in the declining industrial regions beyond the big cities, or the increasing 'white' poverty, not to speak of knowledge based on comparative studies. Only such a comparative approach, however, would allow us to weigh, and put in perspective, the farreaching conclusions in the literature on 'exclusion' and the 'underclass', which, as a rule, are based on quite limited empirical evidence relating to just one of those various populations.

3.2 What does exclusion mean for society?

Exclusion or marginalization on the labor market does not in every case also lead to social exclusion. There are ways in which some people can leave employment without being openly discriminated against by society, even when they are unemployed for a while and have no chance to find regular, gainful work again. Married women, forced out of employment, often resort to the role of the housewife. Older men can sometimes arrange the end of their working life as a transition to early retirement. However stressful the biographical break in these cases might be, the socially accepted status alternatives 'housewife' and 'pensioner' at least provide some protection from stigmatization. In countries such as Germany which until recently broadly applied early-retirement schemes, the distinction between labor-market exclusion and social exclusion, therefore, is particularly important. Wilson provides a clue for our understanding of this distinction by drawing upon two characteristics of the 'underclass' or the new poverty: marginal economic position and social isolation. Only when both coincide, I would argue, it is appropriate to speak of social exclusion.

The question, then, remains: What does 'social exclusion' in this strict sense, implying 'social isolation', mean? For a first approach, I suggest tackling the question on two levels, on the level of society at large, and on the level of the individuals confronted with exclusion. Obviously the two levels interrelate. For analytical purposes, however, it makes sense to distinguish them for a moment.

As Silver (1993, 1996) has shown in her comparative studies, the notions 'underclass' and 'exclusion' receive their particular meanings by implicitly referring to their opposite, the normative ideas of what it means to belong to and participate in society. After the Second World War, with the increasing importance of the welfare state and the spreading of mass consumption, those ideas have become more similar in the highly developed capitalist societies. However, particular national traditions are also still very much alive and supported by the actual working of institutions. They strongly influence peoples' sense of legitimate demands, of what they can rightly expect for themselves and from others, and of who (or what) is responsible for social hardships and for correcting them. In the following, I will call these particular traditions, combining normative orientations and their institutional support, 'modes of integration'.

Silver points out that the term 'underclass', as it is used in the United States, belongs to a much more individualistic tradition than the term 'exclusion' in France. The integrative counterpart to 'underclass' is the 'middle class', the members of which are striving for individual success and upward mobility, while 'inclusion' as the opposite to 'exclusion' in France implies the republican idea of universal rights, guaranteed by the state and public institutions. Accordingly, poverty is seen in the United States much more as individual failure, and therefore as a matter of private charity - if at all -, not of public responsibility (see also Wilson 1996, pp. 159). In the English tradition, on the other hand, 'underclass' has its opposite in the notion of 'social citizenship' (see Dahrendorf 1988, pp. 141; Morris 1994, pp. 44). The latter had been coined after the Second World War by Marshall to theoretically capture the historic enlargement of citizens' rights to include, besides civil and political rights, also 'social rights' as a result of the development of the welfare state (see Marshall 1992, pp. 65). In this tradition it is recognized that social security and material well- being are prerequisites for people's ability to fully participate in the political life of society. Everybody should, therefore, be entitled to a fair share of both. However strongly the present reality of English society contradicts the idea of 'social rights', the latter plays nevertheless the important role of a normative yardstick.

Any attempt to describe in similar ways the mode of integration in West Germany after the Second World War would have to take into account at least two aspects. Firstly, the notion of social integration is defined above all in negative terms, as avoidance of social conflict. As such it has been imbued with the significance of a collective ideal, institutionalized in rules of a class compromise between capital and labor (called 'social partnership'), and protected by extensive regulations of the welfare state. This ideal differs not only from the individualistic ideal which is predominant in the United States, but also from the republican ideal in France which is much more open to conflict. Secondly, in this particular mode of integration by means of intermediary institutions on the different levels of society, gainful employment plays the key role. Major provisions of the welfare state such as retirement and unemployment benefits accrue from mandatory social insurance and relate to the employment status; and the income distribution negotiated by the 'social partners' is, of course, also based on access to employment. Moreover, gainful employment is subjectively still pivotal for the male biography - this is most clearly shown in recent studies on the unemployed -, and it becomes ever more important in the biography of women as well. In Germany, therefore, the economic dimension of social participation - in the double sense of participation in regular employment and participation in the wealth of society - seems to be of particular relevance for 'inclusion'.

On the level of society at large, then, 'social exclusion' means that the employment crisis has rendered ineffective central elements of the national modes of integration for a growing number of people. In other words, it is a symptom of the crisis of basic social institutions. Myrdal already pointed this out in the early 1960s for the United States. He showed that the emergence of an 'underclass' results from the blocking of traditional ways of upward mobility which had been open for generations of immigrants (see Myrdal 1965, pp. 41-44). Others have taken up this idea in the present discussion with reference to parts of the black population in the inner cities (see Katz 1993, pp. 452). In France, on the other hand, the inside-outside division is discussed as indicator of a crisis, or even the end, of the 'mechanism of integration by conflict' (Dubet and Lapeyronnie 1994, p. 17), which had been a characteristic of the 'work society' within the republican consensus. Labor and capital were the main social agents on which this mechanism depended. By carrying out their social conflicts, they proved to be the two poles of industrial society which at the same time complemented and needed each other, thereby contributing to social integration. 'Les exclus' are no longer a part of this mutual relationship. Rather they are symptoms of the disintegration of working-class milieus and neighborhoods in the cities. Their mere existence demonstrates how far already the old contradictions, centered on work, have lost their integrative capacities. In Dahrendorf's view, finally, the crisis of 'social citizenship' caused by mass unemployment engenders the risk of anomy, the spreading of 'no-go areas' in the cites, and a growing number of people with 'no stake in society' (Dahrendorf 1988, p. 161, 163). If it is correct that employment - and mediated by employment the inclusion in collective regulations - plays a central role in the German mode of integration, then this integrative core is presently called into question by mass unemployment.

However, it is not integration for integration's sake that is up for debate in the question of 'social exclusion', but the social basis of democracy. In this respect, there is little reason to expect that a 'collapse of democratic society' (Dubet and Lapeyronnie) could be caused by a political, maybe anti-democratic, revolt of the 'excluded' themselves. More realistic seems to be a development which undermines democracy by destroying the material and social conditions for democratic participation. It is very possible - and in part it has already become a social and political reality in some countries - that a social segmentation emerges in which the majority largely excludes the economically 'superfluous' minority from participating in the wealth and political influence in society, without putting at risk its own ways of life. The larger the groups grow which depend on the financial support of the employed, the more the danger increases that the latter, themselves facing increasing financial insecurities, refuse to assume the financial responsibility for the welfare state (see Kronauer 1995a, pp. 209-212; Kronauer 1995b). This would historically represent a new fault line of conflict. A society divided in this way could well survive - keeping down the 'excluded' with repressive or other means of pacification. It would not be, however, a democratic society.

3.3 What does exclusion mean for the individuals?

The answers given in the literature vary, not only because the forms of exclusion differ, but also because the criteria delineating the 'inside' and the 'outside' change. However, there is one characteristic which is essential to every experience of social exclusion. To feel excluded presupposes a sense of inclusion, either as an experience in the past or as a simultaneous and utterly conflicting experience in the present. The latter is the case when 'inclusion' and 'exclusion' coexist and contradict each other on different levels in everyday life. Such a case is vividly described in French research on young, second-generation immigrants in the 'banlieues'. Assimilated to the values of consumption-oriented society through the educational system and the media, these youths are at the same time unable to live up to the standards prescribed by those values (see Dubet and Lapeyronnie 1994, pp. 135). The same contradiction has been pointed out by Nightingale in his study of kids in a poor Black inner-city neighborhood of the United States. The particular ways in which those children experience their alienation and exclusion, and in which they try to cope with them, are deeply informed by the fact that they are confronted and imbued to a historically unprecedented extent with the values of main-stream America concerning consumption, violence, and racism (see Nightingale 1993, p. 9, p. 12, p. 135). In these cases the paradox and the novelty of the current crisis become particularly apparent. Never before has 'inclusion' into the universal norms of the commodity-producing and consuming society been more advanced than today, with the consequence that the experience of exclusion also is more sharply pronounced than ever.

'Inclusion' extends into different dimensions of social life, it implies economic, cultural, social, and political participation. Despite the relative autonomy which characterizes each of these dimensions, they nevertheless closely correlate, as has been demonstrated in the discussion about the connection between civil, political, and social rights (see Marshall 1992, pp. 40). For the same reason, 'exclusion' on the other hand follows, as Luhmann points out, a logic of cumulative, negative reinforcement. Exclusion from one dimension of social life (or in Luhmann's terminology: in one 'functional system') leads to exclusion from others, in a steady process of 'marginalizations up to the point of total exclusion' (Luhmann 1995, p. 148). In the international literature there is a farreaching agreement on the central dimensions in which social exclusion manifests itself, regardless of the variations in conceptualization and realization of the studies:

- *Exclusion from the labor market*: This occurs when the return or entry to regular employment is permanently blocked. The criterion 'permanent', however, needs further clarification. In the strictest sense it is appropriate to speak about exclusion from the labor market when the individuals not only have very limited chances to find employment, but when they also react to this situation by finally retreating from the labor market. In this case, exclusion turns from an objectively high risk to a definite reality in a person's life (see Kronauer et al. 1993, p. 234; similarly Engbersen et al. 1993, pp. 170-174; see also the notion 'detachment from the labor force' in the American discussion, e.g. by Katz 1993, p. 448). People then are even no longer a part of the 'active reserve army of labor' (Marx) but belong to what Lenski called the 'superfluous' of the work society (see Lenski 1977, p. 509). However, whether exclusion from the labor market also leads to social exclusion depends - I repeat - on the social alternatives to which people can or must retreat: either to a socially accepted way of life beyond employment, or to the informal economy and/or permanent unemployment. Matters become even more complicated when, besides exclusion from the labor market, underemployment and other forms of marginal employment are considered as well (see Morris 1994, p. 108). Only in combination with exclusion from others of the following dimensions, will a precarious position on the labor market entail social exclusion.

- *Economic exclusion*: People are economically excluded when they have lost the ability to make a living for themselves or their household by regular employment. Important additional criteria are dependence on the welfare state or on socially disapproved forms of income (e.g. work in the informal economy). Economic exclusion, as a rule, means having to live in severely restricted circumstances - being 'poor'. In this dimension it becomes particularly obvious that exclusion is a social, relational category: Income poverty is measured against culturally defined standards of living and therefore changes with national contexts; dependence on the welfare state means institutional 'inclusion', but in this case only in a position which is negatively defined by society ('unemployed'; see Simmel 1983, pp. 372).

In the German discussion of the 1980s about the 'new' poverty caused by unemployment, receiving welfare benefits had been considered to be the decisive indicator of exclusion (see Balsen et al. 1984, pp. 69; Lompe 1987, pp. 157; Breckner et al. 1989, pp. 47). However important this indicator might be, it is not distinct enough. It is true that in Germany - as in other countries as well - unemployment considerably increases the risk of becoming dependent on welfare (see Ludwig-Mayerhofer 1992). Due to the German system of unemployment insurance, however, many older long-term unemployed - the group which bears the highest risk of labor-market exclusion in this country - have acquired long-time unemployment-insurance and unemployment-aid entitlements which keep them slightly above the official poverty line so that they do not receive welfare benefits ('Sozialhilfe'). Nevertheless, they often are economically excluded according to the criteria listed above: They depend for many years on other kinds of welfare-state support (first unemployment-insurance benefits and later unemployment aid), and suffer severe financial losses. In many cases this leads to a social decline if not into officially recognized poverty, but at least into relative income poverty (as measured by an income 50% or 60% of the average income level).

- *Cultural Exclusion*: This means to be cut off from the possibility of living according to the socially recognized and dominant patterns of behavior, life orientations, and values. But it also means facing social sanctions because it is not possible (or sometimes only with illegal or illegitimate means) to live up to the cultural expectations (with regard to unemployment see Kronauer et al. 1993, pp. 43). Sanctions are also in effect when people discard the socially prescribed goals and values because they are unable to realize them. For decades a sharp and controversial debate has been going on in the international literature on the forms and consequences of cultural exclusion caused by unemployment and poverty. Often the point of reference is Lewis' anthropological concept of a 'culture of poverty' from the late 1950s and early 1960s (see Lewis 1966, pp. xlii-lii). Essentially three positions can be distinguished. The first starts out from the assumption that a distinct culture of poverty actually exists. It views it as a kind of moral underworld of deviant behavior - deviant from the main-stream values - , which reproduces itself and represents the strongest obstacle against the overcoming of poverty. According to this line of thinking, the poor themselves are responsible for changing their situation by changing their attitudes, and the state should refrain from supporting the poor because this would only create welfare dependence (see Banfield 1968; Murray 1994). The second position already refutes the basic assumption of the first. It points out that even those who are excluded from the material well-being of main-stream society still adhere to its values (or, more specifically, to the values of the working classes), but in their daily lifes have to cope with the discrepancy between those values and their own possibilities. A 'shadow system' of alternative values (Liebow 1967, p. 213) might sometimes help to rationalize and endure this discrepancy, but it remains fragile and superficial (see also Glasgow 1980, p. 8; Gans 1995, pp. 2; Dubet and Lapeyronnie 1994, p. 108; Fryer 1995, p. 244; Tobias and Boettner 1992, pp. 88).

A third position has finally emerged in the American debate about the 'underclass' which takes up elements of the other two. It emphasizes more strongly than the second position the significance of particular behavioral patterns and orientations which develop under the conditions of spatially concentrated poverty and social isolation (see below). At the same time it distances itself from the 'culture of poverty' approach because the latter turns upside down the relationship of cause (unemployment and poverty) and effect (behavior and orientations; see Wilson 1987, pp. 13-19; Anderson 1990, pp. 2-4; Greenstone 1991; similarly with regard to unemployment Engbersen et al. 1993, pp. 158). There is empirical evidence for the second as well as for the third position. Both are, therefore, fruitful foundations for further research. A central analytical category which can stimulate inquiries on cultural exclusion is 'ambivalence'. It allows us to perceive and analyze the ambiguities in which the individuals experience attraction and repulsion by the dominant cultural patterns, and in which they try to deal with this experience (see e.g. the intriguing analysis by Liebow 1967, summarized p. 222).

In the cultural dimension of inquiry in particular it is indispensable to look at the populations which are in different ways confronted with the threat of exclusion, separately and in a comparative perspective. It is quite obvious, and also confirmed by pertinent studies, that young people when they are from the very beginning pushed to the margins of the employment system, experience their cultural exclusion very differently from older long-term unemployed. As French and US-American studies have pointed out, social alienation is for marginalized youths less a matter of barred access to gainful work than of exclusion from the material standards of middle-class life which have become the dominant norm of consumption (see Dubet and Lapeyronnie 1994, pp. 108-110; Anderson 1990, pp. 242). In contrast, older long-term unemployed at the end of their working life have to come to terms mentally mainly with the loss of employment, which most of all had provided a recognized status in society (see Kronauer et al. 1993). Cultural exclusion takes on even other forms when it coincides with ethnic differences.

- *Exclusion by social isolation*: This dimension refers to the scope as well as to the quality of social relations, therefore to social identity. In principal, social isolation can manifest itself in two ways, with different consequences. It can result in a farreaching reduction of social contacts (individual isolation), or in the concentration of contacts in a small circle of peers who are in the same disadvantaged position (group or milieu formation). In the first case it fosters dissociation and blockade of identity, in the second association and subcultural identification (for examples of dissociation and association among long-term unemployed see Kronauer et al. 1993, pp. 172-208). Both, the lack of material means to participate in social events with others, and the experience or expectation of stigmatization can lead into social isolation.

In the discussion about the 'underclass', social isolation has become topical mainly in two respects: on the one hand with regard to social networks which can be helpful as a resource for coping strategies to overcome unemployment and poverty, and on the other hand with regard to 'role models' for youths (see Wilson 1987, pp. 61, pp. 142-144; Anderson 1990, pp. 3, pp. 58-76). In these contexts social isolation means above all a lack of contacts with working and middle-class people who are positioned in the employment system, and therefore a shrinking of economic opportunities and social alternatives.

- *Spatial exclusion*: Spatial exclusion and social isolation are closely linked in the debate on exclusion and 'underclass'. The 'underclass' is as a rule not only urban but also concentrated in particular neighborhoods of the city. The same holds true for 'les exclus' in the French discussion. The limited scope of social contacts corresponds to the restricted space in which people move. Both combined make possible and at the same time force upon people similar ways of life.

  Spatial isolation from 'mainstream society', however, does not suffice to bring about an 'underclass', as has been pointed out in the US-American literature on the ghetto. Spatially limited and ethnically homogeneous, the ghetto nevertheless still might be characterized by a significant social stratification and possibilities of upward mobility. For the formation of an 'underclass' within the ghetto, therefore, social isolation is the decisive factor, i.e. the spatial concentration and segmentation of people who share the same or similar social characteristics and live under similar material and social conditions. Social isolation in this sense is nourished not only by the exodus of the Black middle classes from the ghetto but also by the linkage of a deepening crisis on the labor market with a deepening segmentation on the housing market. Besides the spatially concentrated forms of social isolation, but much less visible and acknowledged in research, there also exists the spatial dispersion of social isolation, mainly in the case of people who retreat to themselves or to the closest circle of relatives.

  Meanwhile urban sociologists in Germany also investigate whether in the big cities, facing the threefold pressure of employment crisis, immigration, and lack of financial means, the social and spatial preconditions for an 'underclass' emerge (see for Berlin Häußermann and Sackmann 1994; for Hamburg Dangschat 1995). There are already first insights in the consequences of the combination of spatial and social isolation in this country. In a comparison of several neighborhoods of the city of Hannover with a high share of welfare recipients, but different degrees of social isolation, Herlyn et al. (1991) were able to show that with a growing spatial distance to other social strata, the poor also loose important social networks as the basis for their coping strategies.

- *Institutional exclusion*: Unemployed and poor people can be confronted with institutional exclusion in different stages and different aspects of their life. Mainly three institutions are discussed in this context: Firstly, schools and other educational and training institutions. Their importance for the social positioning of people is constantly increasing. Moreover, they have a strong effect on people's perception of inequality. Since schools operate under the pretense of individual achievement and equal opportunities (without, however, rendering ineffective the actual social inequalities in starting positions), they also individualize the experience of failure which is so widespread among marginalized youths (see Dubet and Lapeyronnie 1994, pp. 19-22, pp. 29-32). Secondly, the institutions which administer unemployment and poverty very often act vis-à-vis their clientele in the paradoxical way of simultaneously including and excluding them from society. The less they are able to help people out of unemployment and poverty, the more they participate in reproducing the status quo. Thirdly, institutional exclusion is also evident in the withdrawal of public and private services from the poor (for the United States see Gans 1993b, pp. 330).

The forms which exclusion takes on in the different dimensions, and the relative importance of each dimension in the entire picture of social exclusion, vary from country to country. In the United States e.g. marginalization in the labor market plays a more important role than labor-market exclusion. On the other hand, this country shows a particularly high degree of social isolation and spatial concentration of the marginalized populations. In countries such as the Netherlands and Germany, in contrast, exclusion from the labor market is a particularly grave issue, while the social composition of the neighborhoods in which the poor and long-term unemployed live, is more heterogeneous than in American inner cities. Poverty also is less pronounced, due to the more extensive coverage and the better quality of social insurance and public benefits (see Engbersen et al. 1993, pp. 203; Kronauer 1995a, p. 209). In other words: What exclusion in the different countries means and where it begins, depends on the particular modes of social integration. On the other hand, only the individual and collective experiences with exclusion demonstrate where and in which ways the mode of integration is called into question.

3.4 How sharp is the division between 'inside' and 'outside'?

Especially in this question the positions differ widely. Mainly two points are controversial: Are the experiences of the excluded different enough from those of the precariously employed, so that it really makes sense to speak about an inside-outside division at the fringes of the employment system? And to which extent, if at all, is there persistence of unemployment and poverty in the individual biographies, so that exclusion in fact can have an enduring impact on people's lifes?

As to the first point, some social scientists question the assumption that longer lasting unemployment brings about a particular class position such as an 'underclass' (see e.g. Morris 1993; Fryer 1995). Instead, they argue, a social divison develops which separates those with steady employment, on the one hand, from the precariously employed and the long-term unemployed on the other, a dividing line which runs within the working class rather than between the working class and an 'underclass'. There are, however, in international research enough indications of significant differences in self and outside perception between those who are permanently excluded from regular employment, and the unemployed who manage time and again to reenter employment (see Morris 1993, p. 409; Morris 1994, pp. 108; Kronauer et al. 1993, pp. 172, Engbersen et al. 1993). How strongly these differences influence the daily interactions, needs further inquiry. The notion 'peripherization' can be helpful by guiding the research. It makes possible to consider gradations in social participation in the different dimensions, but also to detect and interpret qualitative differences.

As to the question of persisting unemployment and poverty, the controversies are even stronger. The empirical basis for the debate are sets of longitudinal data, produced for the first time in the 1980s, which allow us to trace life courses and work histories over extended periods of time. In Germany these are mainly the data of the Socio-economic Panel (see Hanesch et al. 1994, pp. 126), and regional data bases on welfare recipients (located at the university of Bielefeld, see Andreß 1994, and the university of Bremen, see Leibfried et al. 1995).

With the help of these data it is possible to demonstrate that considerable movements in and out of poverty occur. Looking at incidents of poverty over several years reveals that far more people become poor at certain points in their life than is shown in statistics based on cross-sectional data. On the other hand the longitudinal data also indicate that poverty in many (if not most) cases remains confined to a transitional, often quite short, period of life. The same holds true for unemployment. It is the great advantage of life-course research (or more specifically of so-called dynamic poverty research) that it provides more differentiated insights into the length of poverty spells and their biographical contexts, and thereby contributes to the analysis of the causes which lead to those differences (see the chapter by Walker).

Controversial, however, is the interpretation of the data and findings. Does the finding of fluctuation contradict the thesis of a structural hardening of poverty and unemployment, and if so, to what extent? In the United States where life-course research started, this was vehemently debated already in the 1980s (see Wilson 1987, pp. 9). Meanwhile it is possible to sum up the American discussion with a fairly secure result, based on many empirical studies: Both, a considerable fluctuation and a significant continuity are characteristic of poverty and welfare recipiency. In addition, there are a considerable number of people facing repeated poverty spells (see Rainwater 1992; Bane and Ellwood 1994, pp. 39-42). Bane and Ellwood, therefore, draw the conclusion that 'the only fair reading of welfare recognizes all three dimensions', i.e. all the three forms distinguished above (Bane and Ellwood 1994, p. 42).

In Germany the discussion is in danger of being deadlocked at this point. There is a strong tendency among some representatives of 'dynamic poverty research' to play off the fact of fluctuation against the fact of continuity. In their view, poverty today is characterized by 'Verzeitlichung' (limited time spells) and 'Entstrukturierung' (destructuration), and people who insist on the problem of exclusion are 'dramatizing' (see Leibfried and Leisering 1994; Zwick 1994; for critique see Gerstenberger 1994). The fact is, however, that also in Germany 'in considerable measure a reproduction of poverty takes place' (Hanesch 1995, p. 181; cf. Sopp 1994, pp. 65-67), and that the risks of becoming poor for an extended period of time are unequally distributed (see for the influence of education Schulte 1995 and the chapter by Andress and Schulte). And as to unemployment, it took on a new social quality in West Germany in the mid 80s when permanent unemployment (i.e. unemployment lasting two and more years, with sharply decreasing chances to ever find employment again) became a problem for the very first time. It has grown more serious ever since, and is grossly understated by official statistics (see Kronauer 1995a, pp. 203-205; for the misleadings of the German statistics on long-term unemployment in general see Wagner 1995).

The particular challenge to research as well as to social policy results exactly from the coincidence of the two phenomena, the spreading, on the one hand, of transitional unemployment and poverty into segments of the population which so far had rarely or never encountered them, and the persistence, on the other hand, of unemployment and poverty in the lives of people with the least resources on the labor market. The fact that poverty and unemployment in many cases represent transitional 'episodes' is no reason for comfort. Under the condition of an increasingly restrictive labor market, unemployment engenders considerable insecurity and fear of social decline, even for people who do not face the actual threat of exclusion. Those fears grow even stronger with the development of a population rendered 'superfluous' by the employment crisis (see Kronauer et al. 1993, pp. 126-172, pp. 223-229). How does a society in which inequality and insecurity grow, react to a minority in danger of exclusion and therefore more than ever in need of social solidarity? The United States present the disheartening example of a society in which large segments of the middle classes, worried about their own future after decades of income losses and social decline, dissociate themselves from the fate of the poor. The majority of voters have decided to withdraw even the small amount of support which the American state so far had granted to the disadvantaged (see Wacquant 1996). It is presently by no means clear whether Western Europe is going to adhere to its tradition of welfare state mediation, and if so to what extent. In this situation, if the social sciences want to get involved, based on their analytical competence, in the current struggles over the future of democracy, they will definitely have to pay attention to the dangers for social integration which arise from the interplay of the two sides of the employment crisis.

There is a question which still remains to be answered. When does exclusion become a feature of the social structure? There are two indicators which reflect the two aspects of the problem. Social exclusion becomes an enduring or even definite state in people's life when they see no longer any other chance for themselves but to adapt to their situation, thereby reproducing it by their own actions (see Kronauer et al. 1993, pp. 231-234; Kronauer 1995a, pp. 206-209). When society, on the other hand, perpetuates the processes of exclusion, either by pushing ever more people to the margins of the employment system or by passing exclusion on from one generation to the next, this social division establishes itself within the social structure.

Any attempt to name the new social formation - be it 'underclass', 'social stratum of the permanently unemployed' (Kronauer et al. 1993, p. 229) or 'no-class of non-workers' (Gorz as quoted by Offe 1983, p. 56) - ends in a paradox: There is no positive definition. The formation of the 'superfluous' of the work society differs from all other strata and classes in its essential characteristic of negativity. There is no economic, social, or cultural capital which could constitute a positive social identity. Identity is attributed either as stigma by the outside world, or, in its positive features, it is always threatened and broken by the experience of loss. Only in powerless, rebellious defiance, if at all, the young 'exclus' of the ghettos and banlieues identify with the stigma and play it back to society. At the same time, the 'superfluous' of the work society are a product and a part of society. Their exclusion is measured against society's ambitions, values, and material opportunities, their survival strategies relate to them. This is by no means a mere problem of definition. Being torn apart by belonging and not belonging at the same time is characteristic of the 'superfluous' condition itself. In this way the excluded represent the crisis - the dissolution of the developed capitalist work societies at the periphery.

References

Anderson, E. (1990), *Streetwise. Race, Class, and Change in an Urban Community,* The University of Chicago Press: Chicago, London.

Andreß, H.J. (1994), 'Steigende Sozialhilfezahlen. Wer bleibt, wer geht und wie sollte die Sozialverwaltung darauf reagieren?', in Zwick, M. (ed.), *Einmal arm, immer arm?,* Campus: Frankfurt am Main, New York, pp. 75-105.

Balsen, W., Nakielski, H., Rössel, K., Winkel, R. (1984), *Die neue Armut. Ausgrenzung von Arbeitslosen aus der Arbeitslosenunterstützung,* Bund Verlag: Köln.

Bane, M. J., Ellwood, D. T. (1994), *Welfare Realities. From Rhetoric to Reform,* Harvard University Press: Cambridge (MA).

Banfield, E. C. (1968), *The Unheavenly City: The Nature and Future of Our Urban Crisis.* Little, Brown: Boston.

Breckner, I., Heinelt, H., Krummacher, M., Oelschlägel, D., Rommelspacher, Th., Schmals K. M. (1989), *Armut im Reichtum. Erscheinungsformen, Ursachen und Handlungsstrategien in ausgewählten Großstädten der Bundesrepublik,* Germinal: Bochum.

Commission of the European Communities (1993), *Social Europe. Towards a Europe of Solidarity: Combating Social Exclusion, Supplement 4/93,* Brüssel, Luxemburg.

Dahrendorf, R. (1988), *The Modern Social Conflict. An Essay on the Politics of Liberty,* Weidenfeld and Nicolson: London.

Dangschat, J. (1995), '"Stadt" als Ort und als Ursache von Armut und sozialer Ausgrenzung', *Aus Politik und Zeitgeschichte, Beilage zur Wochenzeitung Das Parlament,* B 31-32/95, 28. Juli 1995, pp. 50-62.

Dubet, F., Lapeyronnie, D. (1994), *Im Aus der Vorstädte. Der Zerfall der demokratischen Gesellschaft,* Klett-Cotta: Stuttgart.

Engbersen, G. (1995), 'The Unknown City', *Berkeley Journal of Sociology: a Critical Review,* No. 40, pp. 87-112.

Engbersen, G., Schuyt, K., Timmer, J., van Waarden, F. (1993), *Cultures of Unemployment. A Comparative Look at Long-term Unemployment and Urban Poverty*, Westview Press: Boulder, San Francisco, Oxford.

Europäische Kommission (1994), *Wachstum, Wettbewerbsfähigkeit, Beschäftigung. Herausforderungen der Gegenwart und Wege ins 21. Jahrhundert, Weißbuch*, Luxemburg.

Fainstein, N. (1987), 'The Underclass/Mismatch Hypothesis as an Explanation for Black Economic Deprivation', *Politics and Society*, Vol. 15, No. 4.

Fryer, D. (1995), 'Beitrag zum Panel: Massenarbeitslosigkeit in Westeuropa: Die Entstehung einer neuen "Underclass"?', in Soziologisches Forschungsinstitut Göttingen (ed.), *Im Zeichen des Umbruchs. Beiträge zu einer anderen Standortdebatte*, Leske und Budrich: Opladen, pp. 240-254.

Gans, H. (1993a), 'The Danger of the Underclass: Its Harmfulness as a Planning Concept', in *People, Plans, and Policies. Essays on Poverty, Racism, and Other Urban Problems*, Columbia University Press, Russell Sage Foundation: New York, pp. 328-343.

Gans, H. (1993b), 'From "Underclass" to "Undercaste": Some Observations About the Future of the Postindustrial Economy and its Mayor Victims', *International Journal of Urban and Regional Research*, Vol. 17, No. 3, pp. 327-335.

Gans, H. (1995), *The War Against the Poor. The Underclass and Anti-Poverty-Policy*, Basic Books: New York.

Gerstenberger, H. (1994), 'Die dynamische Armutsforschung und das Elend der Welt', *Leviathan* 1/94, pp. 7-16.

Glasgow, D. G. (1980), *The Black Underclass. Poverty, Unemployment, and Entrapment of Ghetto Youth*, Jossey-Bass Publishers: San Francisco, Washington, London.

Greenstone, J. D. (1991), 'Culture, Rationality, and the Underclass', in Jencks, Ch., Peterson, P. (eds.), *The Urban Underclass*, The Brookings Institution: Washington, D.C., pp. 399-408.

Hanesch, W. (1995), 'Armut und Unterversorgung im vereinten Deutschland', in Andreß, H.J. (ed.), *Fünf Jahre danach. Zur Entwicklung von Arbeitsmarkt und Sozialstruktur im vereinten Deutschland*, Walter de Gruyter: Berlin, New York, pp. 165-195.

Hanesch, W., Adamy, W., Martens, R., Rentzsch, D., Schneider, U., Schubert, U., Wißkirchen, M. (1994), *Armut in Deutschland. Der Armutsbericht des DGB und des Paritätischen Wohlfahrtsverbands*, Rowohlt: Reinbek bei Hamburg.

Häußermann, H., Sackmann, R. (1994), 'Changes in Berlin: The Emergence of an Underclass?', *Built Environment*, Vol. 20, No.3, pp. 231-241.

Herlyn, U., Lakemann, U., Lettko, B. (1991), *Armut und Milieu*, Birkhäuser: Basel, Boston, Berlin.

Hess, H., Mechler, A. (1973), *Ghetto ohne Mauern. Ein Bericht aus der Unterschicht*, Suhrkamp: Frankfurt am Main.

Jencks, Ch. (1994), *The Homeless*, Harvard University Press: Cambridge (MA), London.

Jencks, Ch., Peterson, P. (eds.) (1991), *The Urban Underclass*, The Brookings Institution: Washington, D.C.

Katz, M. (ed.) (1993), *The 'Underclass' Debate. Views from History*, Princeton University Press: Princeton.

Katz, M. (1995), *Improving Poor People. The Welfare State, the 'Underclass', and Urban Schools as History*, Princeton University Press: Princeton.

Kirschenman, J., Neckerman, K. (1991), '"We'd Love to Hire Them, But...": The Meaning of Race for Employers', in Jencks, Ch., Peterson, P. (eds.), *The Urban Underclass*, The Brooking Institution: Washington, D.C., pp. 203-232.

Kreckel, R. (1992), *Politische Soziologie der sozialen Ungleichheit*, Campus: Frankfurt am Main.

Kronauer, M. (1993) (ed.), 'Unemployment in Western Europe. Individual and Social Consequences', *International Journal of Political Economy*, Vol. 23, No. 3.

Kronauer, M. (1995a), 'Massenarbeitslosigkeit in Westeuropa: Die Entstehung einer neuen "Underclass"?', in Soziologisches Forschungsinstitut Göttingen (ed.), *Im Zeichen des Umbruchs. Beiträge zu einer anderen Standortdebatte*, Leske und Budrich: Opladen, pp. 197-214.

Kronauer, M. (1995b), 'Die Entbehrlichen der Arbeitsgesellschaft. Zur sozialwissenschaftlichen Diskussion um eine neue "underclass"', *Frankfurter Rundschau, Forum Humanwissenschaften*, Vol. 28, No. 11, p. 10.

Kronauer, M., Vogel, B., Gerlach, F. (1993), *Im Schatten der Arbeitsgesellschaft. Arbeitslose und die Dynamik sozialer Ausgrenzung*, Campus: Frankfurt am Main, New York.

Kronawitter, G. (ed.) (1994), *Das Manifest der Oberbürgermeister: Rettet unsere Städte jetzt!*, Econ: Düsseldorf.

Leibfried, S., Voges, W. (eds.) (1992), *Armut im modernen Wohlfahrtsstaat*, Sonderheft 32 der Kölner Zeitschrift für Soziologie und Sozialpsychologie, Westdeutscher Verlag: Opladen.

Leibfried, S., Leisering, L. (1994), 'Das neue Bild der Armut', *Die Zeit*, 18. November 1994.

Leibfried, S., Leisering, L., Buhr, P., Ludwig, M., Mädje, E., Olk, Th., Voges, W., Zwick, M. (1995), *Zeit der Armut. Lebensläufe im Sozialstaat*, Suhrkamp: Frankfurt am Main.

Lenski, G. (1977), *Macht und Privileg. Eine Theorie der sozialen Schichtung*, Suhrkamp: Frankfurt am Main.

Levitan, S. A., Gallo, F., Shapiro, I. (1993), *Working but Poor. America's Contradiction*, The Johns Hopkins University Press: Baltimore, London.

Lewis, O. (1966), *La Vida. A Puerto Rican Family in the Culture of Poverty - San Juan and New York*, Random House: New York.

Liebow, E. (1967), *Tally's Corner. A Study of Negro Streetcorner Men*, Little, Brown: Boston, New York, Toronto, London.

Lompe, K. (ed.) (1987), *Die Realität der neuen Armut. Analysen der Beziehungen zwischen Arbeitslosigkeit und Armut in einer Problemregion*, Transfer: Regensburg.

Ludwig-Mayerhofer, W. (1992), 'Arbeitslosigkeit, Erwerbsarbeit und Armut. Längerfristige Armutsrisiken im Kontext von Haushalt und Sozialstruktur', in Leibfried, S., Voges, W. (eds.), *Armut im modernen Wohlfahrtsstaat*, Sonderheft 32 der Kölner

Zeitschrift für Soziologie und Sozialpsychologie, Westdeutscher Verlag: Opladen, pp. 380-402.

Luhmann, N. (1995), *Gesellschaftsstruktur und Semantik. Studien zur Wissenssoziologie der modernen Gesellschaft Band 4*, Suhrkamp: Frankfurt am Main.

Massey, D., Denton, N. (1993), *American Apartheid. Segregation and the Making of the Underclass*, Harvard University Press: Cambridge (MA), London.

Marshall, Th. H. (1992), *Bürgerrechte und soziale Klassen. Zur Soziologie des Wohlfahrtsstaats*, Campus: Frankfurt am Main.

Mollenkopf, J. H., Castells, M. (eds.) (1991), *Dual City. Restructuring New York*, Russell Sage Foundation: New York.

Morris, L. (1993), 'Is There a British Underclass?', *International Journal of Urban and Regional Research*, Vol. 17, No. 3, pp. 404-412.

Morris, L. (1994), *Dangerous Classes. The Underclass and Social Citizenship*, Routledge: London, New York.

Murray, Ch. (1994), *Loosing Ground. American Social Policy 1950-1980. Tenth-Anniversary Edition*, Basic Books: New York.

Myrdal, G. (1965), *Challenge to Affluence*, Vintage Books: New York.

Nightingale, C. H. (1993), *On the Edge. A History of Poor Black Children and Their American Dreams*, Basic Books: New York.

Offe, C. (1983), 'Arbeit als soziologische Schlüsselkategorie?', in Matthes, J. (ed.), *Krise der Arbeitsgesellschaft? Verhandlungen des 21. Deutschen Soziologentages in Bamberg 1982*, Campus: Frankfurt am Main, New York.

Paugam, S. (1994), *La disqualification sociale. Essai sur la nouvelle pauvreté. 3.edition*, Presses Universitaires de France: Paris.

Paugam, S. (1996), 'La constitution d'un paradigme', in Paugam, S. (ed.), *L'exclusion, l'état des savoirs*, Editions la decouverte: Paris, pp. 7-19.

Polanyi, K. (1995) (first published in 1944), *The Great Transformation. Politische und ökonomische Ursprünge von Gesellschaften und Wirtschaftssystemen*, Suhrkamp: Frankfurt am Main.

Pugliese, E. (1987), 'The Three Forms of Unemployment', *Social Research*, Vol. 54, No. 2, pp. 303-317.

Pugliese, E. (1995), 'Beitrag zum Panel: Massenarbeitslosigkeit in Westeuropa: Die Entstehung einer neuen "Underclass"?', in Soziologisches Forschungsinstitut Göttingen (ed.), *Im Zeichen des Umbruchs*, Leske und Budrich: Opladen, pp. 215-223.

Rainwater, L. (1992), 'Ökonomische versus soziale Armut in den USA (1950-1990)', in Leibfried, S., Voges, W. (eds.), *Armut im modernen Wohlfahrtsstaat*, Sonderheft 32 der Kölner Zeitschrift für Soziologie und Sozialpsychologie, Westdeutscher Verlag: Opladen, pp. 195-220.

Schulte, K. (1995), *Wege aus der Armut. Eine qualitative Analyse quantitativer Längsschnittdaten*, Diplomarbeit an der Universität Bielefeld, Fakultät für Soziologie: Bielefeld.

Silver, H. (1993), 'National Conceptions of the New Urban Poverty: Social Structural Change in Britain, France and the United States', *International Journal of Urban and Regional Research*, Vol. 17, No. 3., pp. 336-354.

Silver, H. (1996), 'Culture, Politics, and National Discourses of the New Urban Poverty', in Mingione, E. (ed.), *Urban Poverty and the Underclass*, Blackwell: Oxford, Cambridge (MA), pp. 105-138.

Simmel, G. (1983) (first published in 1908), *Soziologie. Untersuchungen über die Formen der Vergesellschaftung*, Dunker und Humblodt: Berlin.

Smith, D. (ed.) (1992), *Understanding the Underclass*, Policy Studies Institute: London.

Sopp, P. (1994), 'Das Ende der Zwei-Drittel-Gesellschaft? Zur Einkommensmobilität in Westdeutschland', in Zwick, M. (ed.), *Einmal arm, immer arm? Neue Befunde zur Armut in Deutschland*, Campus: Frankfurt am Main, New York, pp. 47-74.

Tessaring, M. (1994), 'Langfristige Tendenzen des Arbeitskräftebedarfs nach Tätigkeiten und Qualifikationen in den alten Bundesländern bis zum Jahre 2010', *Mitteilungen aus der Arbeitsmarkt- und Berufsforschung*, 1/94, pp. 5-19.

Tobias, G., Boettner, J. (eds.) (1992), *Von der Hand in den Mund. Armut und Armutsbewältigung in einer westdeutschen Großstadt*, Klartext: Essen.

Wacquant, L. (1995), 'The Rise of Advanced Marginality. Notes on its Nature and Implications', in van Kempen, R., Marcuse, P. (eds.), *The New Spatial Order of Cities*, New York.

Wacquant, L. (1996), 'Clinton reformiert Armut zu Elend', *Le Monde Diplomatique/ die tageszeitung*, 13. September 1996.

Wagner, A. (1995), 'Langzeitarbeitslosigkeit: Vielfalt der Formen und differenzierte soziale Lage', *WSI Mitteilungen*, 12/1995, pp. 749-760.

Wagner, D. (1993), *Checkerboard Square. Culture and Resistance in a Homeless Community*, Westview Press: Boulder, San Francisco, Oxford.

Wilson, W. J. (1987), *The Truly Disadvantaged. The Inner City, the Underclass, and Public Policy*, The University of Chicago Press: Chicago, London.

Wilson, W. J. (1991), 'Public Policy Research and The Truly Disadvantaged', in Jencks, Ch., Peterson, P. (eds.), *The Urban Underclass*, The Brookings Institution: Washington, D.C, pp. 460-481.

Wilson, W. J. (1996), *When Work Dissapears. The World of the New Urban Poor*, Alfred A. Knopf: New York.

Zwick, M. (1994b), 'Einmal arm, immer arm? Einleitung', in Zwick, M. (ed.), *Einmal arm, immer arm? Neue Befunde zur Armut in Deutschland*, Campus: Frankfurt am Main, New York, pp. 7-20.

Do poor neighborhoods make their residents poorer? Context effects of poverty neighborhoods on residents

Jürgen Friedrichs

Introduction

Research on city neighborhoods has a long tradition in urban sociology. It has addressed topics such as the description of life in a neighborhood, neighborhood stage models, problems of large new housing estates, and gentrification. With the deindustrialization of entire regions and urban economic decline, interest has turned to a further aspect of urban neighborhoods: poverty, social exclusion, and socio-spatial polarization.

The problem is not new, descriptions like Friedrich Engels' study of the working class in England (1845), the monumental publication by Charles Booth *Life and Labour of People in London* (1889) or subsequent studies by Rowntree (1901) and Townsend (1979) or the research on poverty in the U.S. by Harrington (1962, 1984) have given ample evidence of the concentration of poverty in urban areas.

The major reasons for a renewed interest in urban poverty areas since the 1980s seems to be that after decades of prosperity and liberal policies to increase social equality we find ourselves in a period of world-wide economic restructuring, economic recession, disappointment about the success of programs reducing social inequality, complemented by a severe cut-back of social welfare in favor of individual responsibility - all these changes adding up to a growing disparity of incomes and loss of the tenets of liberal policy.

The challenge this situation creates for social scientists is most vividly discussed by Wilson (1987). It was his work that has initiated a renewed interest in poverty. One of his central propositions is that living in a poor neighborhood leads to the social isolation of residents. This hypothesis has attracted additional interest due to the increase of poverty in all large European cities where a growing share of households lives under public assistance and the poor concentrate in a few urban areas. Hence, the question of neighborhood effects is not only a scholarly one but as well of interest for urban planners seeking adequate programs to fight poverty on the neighborhood level and to prevent a spiral of decline.

The most general assumption underlying all neighborhood research is that urban neighborhoods have an impact on the attitudes and the behavior of their residents. The specific effect of poverty can be framed into the following question: Do poor neighborhoods make their residents poorer? Although the question is simple, to answer it leads to both theoretical and methodological problems. Moreover, for reasons given below, this question has to be discussed in a more general framework: Under which conditions and by which mechanisms do neighborhoods, seen as contexts, influence attitudes and behavior of their residents?

To address the problem, I will first elaborate the assumptions underlying the effects of poor neighborhoods, Wilson's text serves as an example. In the following section, the propositions underlying the hypothesized neighborhood effects are discussed. Section three reviews the empirical evidence on neighborhood effects in general and more specifically on the impact of poverty. In the final section the findings are summarized and suggestions for further research designs are made.

1 Poverty effects: An explication of Wilson's theory

In the context of the underclass debate, William J. Wilson's publication *The Truly Disadvantaged* (1987) has attracted considerable attention to this topic. Since he makes clear statements on the impact of urban poverty neighborhoods on their residents, his book can serve as an excellent point of departure (although there is a growing body of literature on this topic from Europe, e.g., from France, Germany, the Netherlands, and the United Kingdom).

Wilson analyzes the extent of poverty in cities in the United States, but the majority of his analysis is devoted to poor and predominantly Black neighborhoods in Chicago. Based on a rich set of data, his empirical observations are that these neighborhoods exhibit higher rates of:

- school dropouts,
- teenage pregnancy,
- out-of-wedlock births,

- giving up searching for employment,
- deviance from norms of mainstream society,
- deviant behavior,
- physical deterioration of buildings.

He assumes that these high rates are a consequence of life in a high poverty area: High poverty rates in neighborhoods lead to greater social deviance among residents. Wilson argues further that the effects of these conditions are:

- deviant neighborhood norms become the dominant norms in the neighborhood,
- discrimination of the neighborhood's residents by the rest of urban residents, e.g. by giving a (negative) label to the area, discrimination of residents applying for jobs,
- resignation of residents.

The result is an increasing social isolation of the area and its residents from the urban fabric. In a more recent publication, Wilson (1991, pp. 10-11) posits that living in a poor neighborhood with high percentages of unemployed reduces the work discipline of the residents and leads to feelings of low self-efficacy. Wilson's mostly implicit hypotheses can be stated more formally:

H1: The neighborhood has an impact on the behavioral patterns in so far as the observed pattern serves as a model for social learning.

H2: Poverty neighborhoods have a larger segment of persons exhibiting behavior and norms deviating from the mainstream society.

H3: The deviance from the mainstream society is not perceived as deviant.

H4: Deviant norms and behavior spread among residents and become the dominant, i.e., majority norms and behavior.

H5: If a neighborhood exhibits above city average rates of deviance and this becomes known to other urban residents, residents from the neighborhood will be discriminated against. The attribution of a negative label to the area is an indicator of such discrimination.

H6: The more restricted the opportunities of the neighborhood's residents (including perceived discrimination), the more resigned and socially isolated from the rest of the city they become.

Finally, Wilson (1987, p. 57, chap.3) describes one mechanism through which this isolation is reinforced. Young female residents in these areas face a male partner market restricted to males with low education, high unemployment risk, or already making a living in the informal or illegal economy. This 'restricted male marriage pool' does not allow the majority of the women to find a partner who is (a) through his job able to alleviate the economic situation of the women or to help her out of the circle of poverty, and (b) willing to become a steady partner.

H7: Females' choice of a male partner is restricted to low-income or unemployed males.

H8: The choice of such a partner reinforces the women's poverty and restricts her behavioral options, eventually forcing her to adopt norms deviating from those of mainstream society.

H9: The male's responsibility for the mother and the child is reduced by a transfer of the costs of his actions to the welfary system.

H10: High rates of teenage pregnancy and out-of-wedlock births can partially be explained by young females receiving a constant transfer income in the form of welfare payments.

Wilson (1987, p. 10, chap. 3) also gives several clues about the probable sequence of events on the individual level. Although the dynamics on the micro level are not his main interest, some of his descriptive material and further evidence from French (Paugam 1991, 1993; Wacquant 1993) and German sources (Herlyn, Lakemann and Lettko 1991; Riede 1989) studies suggest the following sequence: Black, female -> school dropout -> low education -> not married -> child - > public assistance.

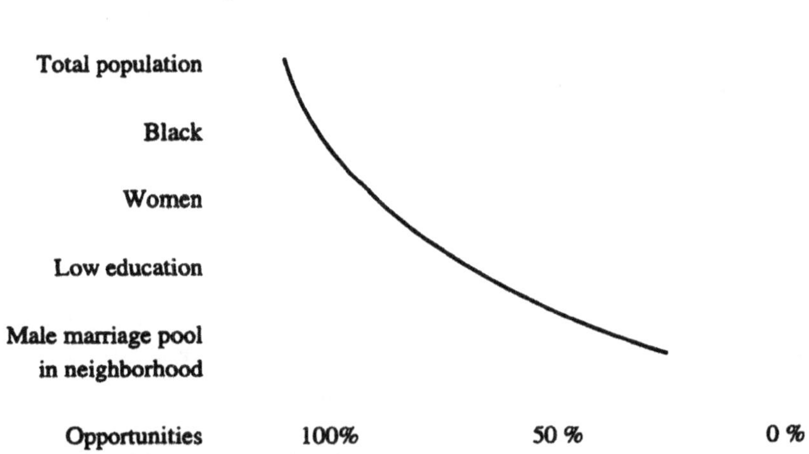

Figure 1 A diagrammatic presentation of successive reduction of opportunities

Certainly, this is a tentative ordering of events, which surely does not cover all cases. Event history analysis would reveal the modal sequence better, and multiple regression analyses would allow us to estimate the effects of the characteristics on poverty. Building upon this sequence, it can be extended theoretically by interpreting it as a series of successive steps of opportunity reduction or increasing constraints. In Figure 1, a hypothetical reduction curve is suggested.

The ten hypotheses represent a partial explication of Wilson's central arguments. If he is correct and in addition his propositions can be generalized to other poor urban neighborhoods in the United States and European cities, we have to assume that living in poverty areas has dramatic negative consequences for the residents of these areas. Wilson, however, does not systematically account for the mechanism that brings about the assumed context effects. These methodological problems are discussed in the following section.

A final note of caution. There are limitations to transferring the North American findings and propositions to the conditions in European cities. Afro-Americans in the United States are a minority that has suffered from prejudice and discrimination for a very long time. In contrast, no ethnic minority in an European country exhibits or has been subject to a comparable long-term situation of negative discrimination and restricted opportunities. Thus, we have to carefully evaluate the validity of generalizations drawn from the North American experience. The empirical results and conclusions Wacquant (1993) has offered, based on his comparative study of a Chicago and a peripheral Paris neighborhood, strongly support this view.

2 Neighborhood effects: Theoretical foundations

The basic question is, how social contexts can affect the attitudes and behavior of those living in or subjected to a given context. Three methodological problems are involved:

- the definition of the context,
- the delineation of the context,
- the specification of context and aggregation effects in a multilevel model.

Definition of the context In such a multilevel model, the macro level (neighborhood) is specified by a set of characteristics. In Wilson's study, like in all others studies reviewed below, the context variables are constructed from individual values, like mean income or percentage of households receiving public assistance. In the terminology of Lazarsfeld and Menzel (1962), these are analytical attributes, as opposed to global attributes, such as location in the metropolitan area or extent of pollution. A further solution would be to define contexts in terms of social networks. This fruitful approach would allow us to test the effects of networks vs. the effects of spatially defined contexts, namely neighborhoods.

In a more general sense, a context can be defined as a set of opportunities (and restrictions) available to the individual, or more precisely, the opportunities and restrictions perceived by individuals. In addition, in a neighborhood it is the probability to observe a given behavior *and* to interact with residents characterized by certain attitudes and behavior.

Delineation of the context If neighborhoods (and not networks) are chosen as contexts, the problem of delineating the neighborhood occurs. Almost all scholars have used census tracts or postal zip codes, assuming such official boundary marking to be a good approximation of the residents' mental maps of their neighborhood. This, however, is not necessarily the case. Rather, residents of the same area differ in their delineations of their neighborhood, as several studies have shown (Heuwinkel 1981, p. 92; Reuber 1993). This problem is also apparent in Crane's (1991, p. 1232) study.

Specifying the context effects This is evidently the crucial problem in the analysis. In line with the general definition of contexts given above, the context effect is the impact a set of options (and restrictions) has on the behavior and attitudes of the individuals. But how can this impact be specified? Which are the mechanisms linking the context to the individuals? These questions bring us back to Wilson's analysis.

The mechanisms that account for these context effects are far from clear (cf. Tienda 1991). In their careful discussion of the problem, Erbring and Young (1979) have suggested four possible mechanisms: social telepathy (contagion), common fate, group norms, and endogenous feedback. Only the latter mechanism, interaction, appears to them as a fruitful assumption to account for the diffusion of attitudes and behavior in a neighborhood. However, as I shall discuss below, the epidemic or contagion hypothesis has been refined and deserves attention (e.g., Brooks-Gunn et al. 1993; Crane 1991; Jencks and Mayer 1990).

Other authors (e.g., Skogan 1990, pp. 65-84; Taub, Taylor and Dunham 1984, pp. 119-141) have argued that not only interaction, but also the visibility of certain neighborhood characteristics has an impact on the attitudes and the behavior of residents. These include litter, physical decay, visible acts of aggression and crime, or drug use. The basic assumption is, that such behavior will be perceived as normal and shift the norms of the residents (further) away from those of the mainstream society towards the deviant norms. Empirical support for this assumption comes from the work of Skogan (1990).

The main mechanisms specifying the context effects are interaction and social learning. Interaction, in turn, is a function of spatial propinquity. The propinquity-contact hypothesis has been suggested by many other authors, e.g. by Gans' articles on the 'balanced community' (Gans 1961a, 1961b), in the research on spatial proximity and social contacts by Festinger, Schachter, and Back (1968), or more recently in the study of interracial friendship by Jackman and Crane (1986). It has been reframed in network research (Blau 1977, 1994; Verbrugge 1977, 1983). Verbrugge (1977, p. 577) argues, that meeting is a function of status homogeneity and spatial proximity. Mating, in contrast, does not only require these opportunities, but attraction as well. Attraction, in turn, is highest among status-similar persons, and this holds for all socio-demographic groups. Unfortunately, Verbrugge does not test spatial proximity effects on friendships. He only imputes friends as having similar 'daily routines' (ibid., p. 592).

From this body of literature, several propositions emerge to account for neighborhood effects:

Proposition 1: The neighborhood as an opportunity structure determines - at least in part - the contacts of residents.

Proposition 2: Spatial proximity fosters social contacts.

Proposition 3: Behavioral and attitudinal models available in the neighborhood determine or influence the range and type of behavior and attitudes of the neighborhood's residents. Thus, the options and restrictions available to the resident enrich or restrict his or her behavior.

Proposition 4: The mechanism of diffusion of norms and behavior are interaction and visible behavior.

None of these propositions is empirically valid without further specification. To give just one example: Most of us interact with some people in the neighborhood, but there is a great variation in the number of such local contacts, as several network studies have shown (see below). There is no automatic mechanism leading from spatial proximity to contacts, and even if such contacts exist, they may make up only a small share of our total contacts - as network analyses have proven as well.

Hence, to test these propositions requires elaborate research designs. We would first have to define contexts. We would further need to survey the type and range of behavior and attitudes towards a given set of objects and issues in the neighborhood in order to construct from these context variables. Furthermore, we would have to analyze changes over time, *since we assume a socialization process reproducing the dominant norms of the neighborhood.* This clearly can only be assessed by panel studies. None of the studies I read has attempted to do this. Hence, there is no test of propositions P3 and P4 due to the high cost of the empirical research required.

Aside from these more technical limitations, there are theoretical objections, too. Proposition (3) implies, that the assumed effect is not counterbalanced by contacts to persons outside the neighborhood. In the framework of Feld's theory (Feld 1981), the neighborhood is not the only focus of interaction available to the residents. In addition, we exclude mass media effects. It is hard to believe, that residents are restricted to the neighborhood focus, with all other foci, such as kinship, associations and place of work being either irrelevant or located as well in the neighborhood.

Further, proposition (4) holds that interaction is the crucial mechanism of social learning. Again, this excludes mass media effects. More importantly, it raises the question of why we do not study the networks of neighborhood residents and contrast their impact to those effects attributed to the neighborhood? These qualifications are captured in an additional proposition:

Proposition 5: The assumed neighborhood effects are more significant when both the social network and the action spaces of a resident are restricted to the neighborhood.

To sum up: The explicit and implicit hypotheses of a strongly negative effect of poor neighborhoods on their residents presumably are valid only under a further set of propositions. The basic assumptions are a) poverty is concentrated in few urban areas and b) the very fact of living in such an urban area has negative impacts on the life chances of its residents. To extend the argument, we may even assume a vicious circle to occur: Living in a poor neighborhood decreases the probability of escaping from poverty and reinforces social inequality. Blau (1977, p. 62) has argued in a similar way when referring to segregation: 'the segregation of social strata reinforces the negative effect of inequality'.

The most important proposition, P5, is that the hypothesized effects will be observed only if both the social networks and the action spaces of the residents are restricted to the neighborhood. It is only under these conditions that a disorganized neighborhood will further restrict the options of individuals and eventually lead to social isolation, as Wilson posits. More precisely, we have to assume that:

Proposition 6: Social networks of poor people are smaller than networks of other individuals and their networks have recently become even smaller; social networks of poor persons are spatially less extended and more restricted to their neighborhood.

We therefore posit that proximity increases the probability of interaction, and interaction, in turn, results in some forms of adaptations, diffusion of attitudes, and behavior patterns. Two further mechanisms can be proposed: Social learning and normative adjustment. The first can be based on the theory of Bandura and Walters (1963). From their social learning theory we can derive the proposition that residents of an urban district imitate or adopt patterns they observe in their neighborhood.

Part of this social learning is a mechanism that can be designated 'normative adjustment'. The basic assumption here is that, in urban areas with a high concentration of poverty, participation in public assistance programs is less stigmatized and more acceptable (Wilson 1987, p. 56), especially when the relatively better-off move out of such areas. Thus, the number of 'positive' behavioral models are reduced.

Hirschl and Rank (1991, p. 226, p. 233) found a positive correlation between the population density in a community and the welfare participation rate, even when controlling for other variables. They suggest two explanations: better access to social welfare programs in more densely settled communities, and the formation of subcultures. The latter argument is drawn from Fischer's theory of urban subcultures (Fischer 1975), where he suggests that the diversity of urban subcultures with specific norms will increase with the size of the city. Hence, a 'culture of poverty' (Lewis 1968) will be facilitated with increasing size of the city. The observation of poverty and deviant types of behavior in an urban area will gradually 'lower' the normative level of all residents. Poverty and deviant behavior will eventually become a regular and legitimate behavior.

Social learning can be viewed as the most general explanation to account for the imputed effect of contextual traits of the neighborhood on the behavior of its residents. It comprises both the interaction and the normative adjustment hypotheses. Three conclusions can be drawn from this approach:

1. There must be some individuals or households serving more than others as behavioral models. Can we empirically identify such models? Are they necessarily 'negative' or deviant models or do positive ones exist as well? A positive model might be a person who has been striving successfully to escape from the conditions of poverty and/or exclusion.
2. Selective moves into and out of an urban neighborhood play a crucial role. While mixed neighborhoods will exhibit less negative consequences of poverty (as a contextual effect), selective outmigration will decrease the number of positive models and thereby increase the negative effects of poverty (cf. Wilson 1987, p. 56). Evidence for the hypothesis of selective outmigration from a distressed neighborhood by the relatively better-off comes from several studies, e.g. for poor neighborhoods in the United States (Weicher 1990) and from large new housing estates in Germany (Friedrichs 1988, 1991), leading to a spiral of decline. The same processes of selective moves out of and into a neighborhood have been said to occur in deprived areas, the net result being an increase of poor households in urban districts already exhibiting an above average percentage of poverty. We therefore wish to analyze the dynamics of migration and population composition in deprived neighborhoods.
3. If it holds true that specific behavior is diffusing in a neighborhood regarded as deviant by the society at large, e.g. teenage pregnancy, *and* this becomes an accepted behavior, we have to study in greater detail how this process occurs. To approach this problem, we can build upon theoretical models and empirical research pertaining to thresholds and the diffusion of behavior (Granovetter 1978; Granovetter and Soong 1988; Oliver and Marwell 1988; Oliver, Marwell and Teixeira 1985; Schelling 1971, 1978). The basic idea is that individuals have thresholds for participating in a given activity, be it participating in a demonstration, joining a group, collecting money for a common good, or migrating into or out of a neighborhood. A simple way to define individual thresholds is to ask how many people from this group must participate until the specific individual in question will also participate. The threshold value can be expressed either in absolute numbers (10, 30, 100 persons) or in percentages (5, 20 or 50 per cent) of the group. The application of these models to our research agenda is straightforward: How many people or households must exhibit a given deviant behavior, until person x will accept this behavior and perform it in a given situation? We can further ask about the distribution of these thresholds over the total number of residents in a given neighborhood: Is it a normal or a very skewed distribution? Depending on the distribution we can then model

diverse behavioral processes by different production curves as Marwell and associates have used to describe the production of a common sentiment or behavior.

3 Empirical evidence

The analysis so far has shown that the neighborhood-impact assumption rests upon several implicit premises (and additional methodological problems). In this section, I will review some of the available empirical evidence for the assumption in general and the above stated propositions in particular. Before turning to accounts of poor neighborhoods let me first discuss the results of several empirical studies on neighborhood effects on different variables.

3.1 General studies

Evidence contrary to the basic neighborhood-impact proposition comes from a study of Yugoslav and Turkish guestworkers of the first and second generation in several German cities (Alpheis 1988; Alpheis and Friedrichs 1991; Esser and Friedrichs 1990). In a multivariate analysis separating context effects of the neighborhood from effects of individual traits on various measures of assimilation we found the neighborhood to have an impact of beta = 0.10, whereas individual factors resulted in much higher betas. The coefficients were only slightly different when the level of an urban district, a block or even the building were used as measures of the spatial context. Individual traits had a much greater effect in minority member's assimilation than the composition of the neighborhood.[1]

These findings may hold only for such phenomena as assimilation of members of a minority. We do not know whether this can be generalized to the poverty and exclusion problem. However, other studies corroborate the result.

Context effects by neighborhoods are only one source of variation in the behavior of individuals. As Jencks and Mayer (1990, pp. 113-115) have argued, we have to account as well for family and institutional effects, such as schools. Many studies confound neighborhood and school effects. Typically, children go to elementary schools located in their neighborhood. If it is correct that interaction is the crucial element in the process of integration, further, that interaction is more frequent in schools, then the impact of schools and classmates would be stronger than the effect of the neighborhood. Thus, if school effects are not controlled, neighborhood effects are overestimated and may eventually be close to zero. A good example is Hogan and Kitagawa's study on teenage pregnancy among unmarried female Afro-Americans aged 13-19 in Chicago. In their carefully designed study, they matched census tract and survey data for the same neighborhoods. They found significant bivariate correlations beween sexual activity and social class, parental control of dating, number of siblings, and neighborhood quality. However, when controlling for the other variables, neighborhood quality had an insignificant effect (Hogan and Kitagawa 1985, pp. 844-845).

A similar result was obtained by Brewster (1994). She analyzed neighborhood effects, such as SES, racial composition, female full-time employment rate, and individual characteristics on nonmarital first intercourse among 2,210 women aged 15 to 44. As the analysis, a multivariate hazard model, revealed, when controlling for individual characteristics, of all seven neighborhood covariates only full-time female employment has a significant effect on adolescent sexual activity; this finding holds for Whites and all minority groups (Brewster 1994, p. 417).

Several studies have addressed the proximity-contact hypothesis. From earlier studies (e.g., Deutsch and Collins 1951) we know that proximity per se does not lead to contacts, but that the probability increases, if actors have equal status. Further, the type of contact has to be taken into account. This was done in a recent survey by Sigelman et al. (1996). They studied casual contacts and friendships among 1,124 White and Black residents in the Detroit area in 1992. Further, they compared their data with the results of the Detroit Area Study conducted in 1968/69. Their major findings with respect to changes over time were an increase in mixed school attendance, in interracial contact on the job and in the neighborhood, but almost no change in the percentage visiting the homes of neighbors. Contacts occur predominantly during shopping (Blacks: 83%, Whites: 84%), on the job (72% vs. 64%), and at sports events (59% vs. 56%), less at children's events (40% vs. 28%) and church attendance (36% vs. 20%).

Turning to the determinants of casual contact, several socio-demographic variables, such as age, sex, education, and SES were introduced, in addition place of work, per cent of Blacks in the neighborhood, early life neighborhood composition, and early life school composition. This model explains 25% of the variance, with place of work, church attendance, early life school composition, and age having the strongest effects. Of the neighborhood variables, only early life neighborhood composition had an effect, but only on Blacks ($b = 0.37$ and $b = 0.06$ for Whites). The same variables were entered into a probit model to estimate the effects on friendships. This model performed worse for Blacks than for Whites (Pseudo R^2 = 0.11 and 0.23), with only early life school composition having a significant effect of 0.07 for Blacks and 0.08 for Whites. Thus, casual contacts seldomly turn into friendships.

The study as well sheds further light on the relationship of racial mix and contacts. Sigelman et al. (1996, p. 1321) found a significant nonlinear relationship between racial mix and casual contacts. Casual contacts raise from 0 to 20% Blacks, slows down from 20 to 50%, then steadily decreases. This holds only for casual contacts, the friendship relation is linear. Summarizing their findings, the authors conclude: 'Where white people live strongly affects their contact with blacks, but where black people live has little effect on their contact with whites' (ibid., p. 1322, cf. p. 1326); but early life school composition had an effect for both Blacks and Whites, while early life neighborhood composition has an effect for Blacks only. But we may even interpret the latter result not as a neighborhood effect: If ethnic mix is more important for Blacks than for Whites, and elementary schools are located in the neighborhood, then the early neighborhood effect is simply due to the correlation of school and neighborhoods.

Racial mix proved to be a strong predictor in a study of the epidemic hypothesis by Crane (1991). He estimated the effect of per cent professional and managerial workers of all workers in a neighborhood on high school drop-out rates and childbearing of teenagers aged 16-19. He obtained extreme effects on low drop-out rates when there were only 0 to 5 per cent managerial or professional workers in the neighborhood. Thereafter, as their share grows, drop-out rates decline only slightly. Functions for Whites and Black were nonlinear, linear for Hispanics. Neighborhood effects were stronger in central cities of large urban conglomerations. Effects for Black males were stronger than for Black females, the effect for males being 'almost 38 times greater below the key point than above it' (Crane 1991, p. 1239). Crane obtained similar results, a strong effect of very low percentages of managerial and professional workers, for teenage childbearing. Functions for both White and Black were non-linear.

These studies strongly correspond to the type of neighborhoods Wilson refers to in Chicago. Two conclusions emerge with respect to the above listed propositions (and some of Wilson's hypotheses): First, neighborhood effects are very small if individual variables and the effects of institutions are controlled. Second, effects are nonlinear and presumably higher if certain thresholds are crossed.

3.2 Poverty area studies

A consistent finding of many studies is the spatial distribution of poverty neighborhoods in urban space. Research from the early Chicago school has shown the spatial concentration of crime, poverty, and psychoses. Further evidence comes from studies on inner-city poverty, e.g., in London and Paris (Madge and Willmott 1981).

The studies further indicate that there are two types of poverty areas in European cities: older neighborhoods close to the city center and large new housing estates at the urban periphery, like in Britain (Jones 1996; Shepherd, Westaway and Lee 1974), France (Dubet and Lapeyronnie 1994; Jazouli 1992; Paugam 1993; Rhein 1994, 1996), or Germany (Herlyn et al. 1991; Hess and Mächler 1973; Podzuweit, Schütte and Swiertka 1992; Stadt Essen 1993; Landeshauptstadt München 1991).

Studies pertaining to changes in poverty areas consistently conclude that the great majority of these areas have exhibited increasing poverty since 1970 (e.g., Massey and Denton 1993; Paugam 1993; Weicher 1990; Wilson 1987). This finding is supported by data on German cities as well. The two main reasons for such a spiral of decline are selective moves out and into such areas and increasing poverty among the residents in the areas.[2]

Finally, the studies find very similar characteristics of the residents in poverty areas: the households designated 'problem families' or 'multiple distressed families'. Although conceptually vague, these terms are attributed to households exhibiting two or more of the following characteristics: low income, living from transfer payments (unemployment aid, public assistance), living in bad or substandard housing conditions (e.g., high internal density, substandard equipment of the dwelling), membership in an ethnic minority, low level of schooling, often incomplete schooling, single-headed (mother) households with child or children, out-of-wedlock birth of child/children, teenage pregnancy, abuse of alcohol or drugs, violence as an everyday pattern of intra-family conflict resolution, deviant behavior (crime). Evidently, these characteristics closely correspond to North American findings (e.g., Jargowski and Bane 1990). What we now observe and discuss is not new, but a numerical growth of this segment of the population due to a world-wide economic restructuring.[3]

Much less consistent and conclusive is the evidence on the impact of poor neighborhoods on their residents. Most of the studies are predominantly descriptive and based on small samples. More important, they are highly selective, since only neighborhoods with high poverty rates have been sampled. In the above outlined theoretical frame they represent areas where the conditions of small and predominantly locally restricted networks and restricted action spaces of individuals prevail. *It is under this premise that the empirical evidence, although unsystematic, can be viewed as a preliminary test of some of the propositions stated in Section 2.*

1. Residents of poor neighborhoods are not a homogeneous group, instead there is internal differentiation. There are at least two different groups: First, those who have succeeded in managing their lives according to mainstream norms - these are the 'consolidated' (Tobias and Boettner 1992) or 'organized' (Paugam 1991). Second, those who became marginalized - the 'Trinkhallen-Gruppe (pub group)' (Tobias and Boettner 1991) or the 'banned' (Paugam 1991). These groups may be interpreted as the extremes of a continuum of marginalization, social exclusion, or social isolation.
2. Irrespective of the exact typology of subgroups, their members hardly communicate with others. In addition, members of the relatively better-off group avoid contact at least with those at the other end of the continuum. For example, they inhibit contacts of their children with children of marginalized families in order to prevent them from adopting behavior patterns of the marginalized (Tobias and Boettner 1992, pp. 68-69).

   Groups also differ by their opinions about the possible causes of poverty. In his empirical study of two neighborhoods in Cologne, Düppe (1995) found that in the lower poverty area poverty was significantly more often attributed to individual causes, whereas in the high poverty area it was attributed to external causes, such as economic conditions.

   This differentiation among groups and their different attitudes falsifies the straightforward propositions of diffusion of deviant behavior and deviant norms to become the dominant norms in a poverty neighborhood.
3. A crucial element in the neighborhood impact theory are the social networks of the residents. We expect networks of such households to be small and spatially more constrained to their vicinity than the networks of other individuals, irrespective of their social class. The empirical evidence, however, contradicts this expectation.

   Several studies of urban networks, such as Böltken (1987), Fisher (1982), Pappi and Melbek (1988), or Wellmann (Wellmann 1979; Wellmann, Carrington and Hall 1988) indicate a very low percentage of the total network members to be living in close proximity. Although neighbors play a role, it is in the majority of the cases limited to basic help.

   These findings seem to conflict with the assumption of the significant influence of other persons living in the same neighborhood on the attitudes and behavior of the residents of poor areas. But these research results may nonetheless not contradict the hypothesis, since the surveys include only a small fraction of households living in poverty, or characterized as being socially excluded, and thus, for the same reason, only a small number of deprived neighborhoods.

In poor neighborhoods, the action spaces and social networks of most residents indeed seem to be restricted to the local area. Further, the restrictions increase with duration of poverty (somewhat confounded with duration length of living in the poverty area). As Tobias and Boettner (1992, p. 70) conclude: 'Consolidation of household and family is linked to minimal everyday mobility, and an almost complete loss of social contacts, leisure activities and other forms of participation beyond the area. [...] The horizon of everyday life shrinks to the neighborhood and the positive social status individuals attribute to themselves depends almost exclusively upon comparisons with people in the area.' Similar observations can be found in the work by Herlyn, Lakemann and Lettko (1991), the poverty reports from Hamburg (BAGS 1993) and Munich (Landeshauptstadt München 1991, p. 14), and the French studies by Dubet and Lapeyronnie (1994).

4. All network studies agree that lower class persons have smaller networks and a larger percentage of relatives in their networks. Neighbors are often not chosen for social support, since individuals are afraid of letting their neighbors obtain intimate knowledge of their life style. The reduction of social contacts thus increases the dependency on institutions and the family. But the alleviating function of the family is limited, 'the longer people utilize this network, the more tense it becomes until it finally breaks down' (Landeshauptstadt München 1991, p. 17).
5. Given this spatial restriction, the local social infrastructure, e.g. leisure facilities, becomes an important element of the neighborhood's overall opportunity structure. Most of the poverty areas have a low number and diversity of social facilities. This deficit reduces the options of the residents, and is aggravated by their disability to compensate for the deficit by trips to such facilities outside their neighborhood (Herlyn, Lakemann and Lettko 1991; Pincon-Charlot et al. 1986). In the framework of focus theory, the residents lack opportunities to meet people from mainstream urban society and eventually engage in status-heterogeneous relations.
6. The reduction of action spaces and social contacts is not only due to such external restrictions and negative labels attributed to the poor neighborhood. It is accompanied by a cognitive process of dissonance reduction: Meeting persons from outside the neighborhood implies a confrontation of own

prospects and opportunities with mainstream society - resulting in demotivation and hopelessness. Hence, such contacts are avoided.

In sum, the empirical studies reviewed support the propositions P3 to P6. They suggest poverty neighborhoods as impacting negatively on the lives of a significant share of the residents. They also do not contradict the assumptions on social learning via social contacts, neither do they let us refute the notion of visible forms of deviant behavior. But, contrary to Wilson's hypothesis, they indicate that deviant forms of behavior, albeit visible, are negatively judged by a section of the residents and thus do not become dominant. Dominance of deviant norms and behavior presumably occurs only via selective population exchange.

4 Conclusions: Do poor neighborhoods make their residents poorer?

The general evidence presented on neighborhood effects indicates low or negligible effects; most context effects can be explained by either individual or institutional effects or both. With respect to poor neighborhoods exerting an influence on its residents, the tentative result is: Poor neighborhoods do indeed aggravate the poverty of their residents. But this conclusion only holds under specific conditions.

Firstly, residents have to have their action spaces limited to the neighborhood and their social networks have to be restricted to the neighborhood. The more restricted both are, the higher the probability for the neighborhood to impact on the attitudes and the behavior of its residents. Secondly, although the relationship seems to be linear, is it is highly probable that it is exponential, the assumption being that effects occur only if both action spaces and social networks are strongly restricted to the neighborhood. (Although we are not yet in the position to give an empirical threshold value.)

Thirdly, the impact of the neighborhood may differ among social groups, such as children, housewives, or the unemployed. In the absence of such information we may apply the above reasoning by scaling residents according to the time they spent in the neighborhood, and thus measuring the degree of exposition to neighborhood influences.

However, more precise statements are required; we lack systematic research based on a theoretical framework and larger samples. The existing research on poverty areas - and neighborhood effects in general - has several methodological fallacies and therefore cannot be conclusive. Let me point to some of these methodological problems.

The studies on neighborhoods characterized by poverty are selective since they pertain to neighborhoods with a high percentage of poor individuals or households. Hence, further research should be devoted to a broader sample of neighborhoods ranging from very low to high percentages of the poor.

Furthermore, we need more elaborated studies including both social networks and action spaces (and foci) of the residents. We also have to consider other definitions of contexts, such as networks. Presently, in almost all studies context variables are constructed from individual variables. In the studies reviewed, the neighborhood (context) effect is measured by the concentration or high share of low-income households in a neighborhood. Hence, only analytical attributes are used. Truely global attributes (as defined by Lazarsfeld and Menzel), in contrast would be 'modernization area', 'new housing high-rise estate' or 'area with far below average social infrastructure'. The latter definition of a context could be linked to the concept of opportunity structure, this being a context effect. We may, for instance, assume low status or poor neighborhoods to have a low diversity in social infrastructure, whereas neighborhoods characterized by mixed social status households have a greater variety of social infrastructure and shops - a diversity from which poor households could profit (Sarkissian 1976).

Hence, and most important, studies should be more sophisticated allowing us to separate the neighborhood effects from institutional and individual effects - under varying values of the contextual variable.

Notes

[1] The example allows us as well to draw an important conclusion concerning policy formulations. If the neighborhood does not have an impact on ethnic integration, why then should we implement programs promoting neighborhood diversity and reducing ethnic homogenous neighborhoods? Our policy recommendations for assimilation would be entirely different and no longer be directed towards spatial units.

[2] A further factor contributing to the increases are housing conditions, which have worsened in almost all European countries. This holds especially true for public sector housing. Here we observe a deficit since the mid 1980s due to the rising demand wich in turn was spurred by the increase of low-income households.

[3] There are good reasons to assume that the distribution of poverty over the urban neighborhoods and the concentration of poverty in few of them is a function of the economic conditions of a city. A city experiencing decline, due to a shrinking

economic base, has higher rates of unemployment and of persons on public assistance than a growing or regenerating city. As Massey, Gross and Eggers (1991) have shown for the fifty largest North American SMSA's (comprising a total of 54,442 urban tracts), a group's poverty rate at the metropolitan level has a positive effect upon the extent and the disproportionate distribution of poverty among urban tracts.

References

Alpheis, H. (1988), *Kontextanalyse*, Deutscher Universitätverlag: Opladen.

Alpheis, H. (1990), 'Erschwert die ethnische Konzentration die Eingliederung?', in Esser, H., Friedrichs, J. (eds.), *Generation und Identität*, Westdeutscher Verlag: Opladen, pp. 147-184.

Alpheis, H., Friedrichs, J. (1991), 'Housing Segregation of Immigrants in West- Germany', in Huttman, E.D., Blauw, W., Saltman, J. (eds.), *Urban Housing Segregation of Minorities in Western Europe and the United States*, Duke University Press: Durham, London, pp. 116-144.

BAGS (Behörde für Arbeit, Gesundheit und Soziales der Freien und Hansestadt Hamburg) (1993), *Armut in Hamburg*, BAGS: Hamburg.

Bandura, A., Walters, R. H. (1963), *Social Learning and Personality Development*, Holt, Rinehart and Winston: New York.

Blau, P. M. (1977), *Heterogeneity and Inequality: A Primitive Theory of Social Structure*, Free Press: New York.

Blau, P. M. (1994), *Structural Contexts of Opportunities*, University of Chicago Press: Chicago, London.

Böltken, F. (1987), 'Soziale Disparitäten und soziale Netzwerke im regionalen Vergleich', *Informationen zur Raumentwicklung*, Heft 9/10, pp. 543-549.

Booth, C. (1989), *Life and Labour of People in London*, Williams and Margate: London.

Braddock, J. H., Dawkins, M. P., Trent, W. (1994), 'Why Desegregate? The Effect of School Desegregation on Adult Occupational Desegregation of African Americans, Whites and Hispanics', *International Journal of Contemporary Sociology* , Vol. 31, pp. 273-283.

Brewster, K. L. (1994), 'Race Differences in Sexual Activity Among Adolescent Women', *American Sociological Review*, Vol. 59, pp. 408-424.

Brooks-Gunn, J., Duncan, G. J., Klebanov, P. K., Sealand, N. (1993), 'Do Neighborhoods Influence Child and Adolescent Development?', *American Journal of Sociology*, Vol. 99, pp. 353-395.

Crane, J. (1991), 'The Epidemic Theory of Ghettos and Neighborhood Effects on Dropping Out and Teenage Childbearing', *American Journal of Sociology*, Vol. 96, pp. 1226-1259.

Deutsch, N., Collins, N.E. (1951), *Interracial Housing*, Minneapolis.

Dubet, F., Lapeyronnie, D. (1994), *Im Aus der Vorstädte. Der Zerfall der demokratischen Gesellschaft*, Klett: Stuttgart.

Düppe, W. (1995), *Wahrnehmung von Armut und die Einstellung gegenüber armen Menschen unter Berücksichtigung des Umfeldes*, University of Cologne, unpublished Masters Thesis: Köln.

Engels, F. (1845), *Die Lage der arbeitenden Klasse in England*, Otto Wigand: Leipzig (Engl.: The Condition of the Working Class in England, Panther Books: London 1969.).

Erbring, L., Young, A. A. (1979), 'Individuals and Social Structure', *Sociological Methods and Research*, Vol. 7, pp. 396-430.

Esser, H., Friedrichs, J. (eds.) (1990), *Generation und Identität*, Westdeutscher Verlag: Opladen.

Farley, R., Steeh, C., Krysan, M., Jackson, T., Reeves, K. (1994), 'Stereotypes and Segregation: Neighborhoods in the Detroit Area', *American Journal of Sociology*, Vol. 100, pp. 750-780.

Feigelman, W., Bernard, S. (1990), 'Blacks Who Live Near Whites: 1982 and 1987', *Sociology and Social Research*, Vol. 74, pp. 202-207.

Feld, S. L. (1981), 'The Focused Organization of Social Ties', *American Journal of Sociology*, Vol. 86, pp. 1015-1035.

Festinger, L., Schachter, S., Back, K.(1968), 'The Spatial Ecology of Group Formation', in Barnlund, D. C. (ed.), *Interpersonal Communication: Survey and Studies*, Houghton Mifflin: Boston, pp. 91-107.

Fischer, C. S. (1975), 'Toward a Subcultural Theory of Urbanism', American Journal of Sociology, Vol. 80, pp. 1319-1341.

Fischer, C. S. (1982), *To Dwell Among Friends. Personal Networks in Town and City*, University of Chicago Press: Chicago, London.

Friedrichs, J. (1988), 'Large New Housing Estates: The Crisis of Affordable Housing', in Friedrichs, J. (ed.), *Affordable Housing and the Homeless*, de Gruyter: Berlin, New York, pp. 89-102.

Friedrichs, J. (1991), 'Middle-Class Leakage in Large New Housing Estates: Empirical Findings and Policy Implications', *Journal of Architectural and Planning Research*, Vol. 8, pp. 287-295.

Gans, H. J. (1961a), 'Planning and Social Life. Friendship and Neighbor Relations in Suburban Communities', *Journal of the American Institute of Planners*, Vol. 27, pp. 134-140.

Gans, H. J. (1961b), 'The Balanced Community: Homogeneity or Heterogeneity in Residential Areas?', *Journal of the American Institute of Planners*, Vol. 27, pp. 176-184.

Granovetter, M. S. (1978), 'Threshold Models of Collective Behavior', *American Journal of Sociology*, Vol. 83, pp. 1421-1443.

Granovetter, M., Soong, R. (1988), 'Threshold Models of Diversity: Chinese Restaurants, Residential Segregation, and the Spiral of Silence', *Sociological Methodology*, Vol. 18, pp. 69-104.

Halligan, M. T. (1978), 'The Process of Friendship Formation', *Social Networks*, Vol. 1, pp. 193-210.

Harrington, M. (1962), *The Other America: Poverty in the United States*, Macmillan: New York.

Harrington, M. (1984), *The New American Poverty*, Holt, Rinehart and Winston: New York.

Herlyn, U., Lakemann, U., Lettko, B. (1991), *Armut und Milieu*, Birkhäuser: Basel.

Hess, H., Mächler, A. (1973), *Ghetto ohne Mauern. Ein Bericht aus der Unterschicht*, Suhrkamp: Frankfurt/Main.

Heuwinkel, D. (1981), *Aktionsräumliche Analysen und Bewertung von Wohngebieten*, Christians: Hamburg.

Hirschl, T. A., Rank, M. R. (1991), 'The Effect of Population Density on Welfare Participation', *Social Forces*, Vol. 70, pp. 225-235.

Hogan, D. P., Kitagawa, E. M. (1985), 'The Impact of Social Status, Family Structure, and Neighborhood on the Fertility of Black Adolescents', *American Journal of Sociology*, Vol. 90, pp. 825-855.

Jackman, M. S., Crane, N. (1986), 'Some of Our Best Friends Are Black: Interracial Friendship and Whites' Racial Attitudes', *Public Opinion Quarterly*, Vol. 50, pp. 459-486.

Jargowski, P. A., Bane, M. J. (1990), 'Ghetto Poverty: Basic Questions', in Lynn, L. E.M., McGeary, G.H. (eds.), *Inner-City Poverty in the United States*, National Academy Press: Washington, D.C., pp. 16-67.

Jazouli, A. (1992), *Les années banlieue*, Seuil: Paris.

Jencks, C., Mayer, S. E. (1990), 'The Social Consequences of Growing up in a Poor Neighborhood', in Lynn, L. E., McGeary, M. G. H. (eds.), *Inner-City-Poverty in the United States*, National Academy Press: Washington, D.C., pp. 111-186.

Jones, E. (1996), 'Social Polarization in Post-Industrial London', in O'Loughlin, J., Friedrichs, J. (eds.), *Social Polarization in Post-Industrial Societies*, de Gruyter: Berlin, New York, pp. 19-44.

Landeshauptstadt München (1991), *Münchner Armutsbericht '90*, Landeshauptstadt, Sozialreferat: München.

Lapeyronnie, D. (1993), *L'individu et les minorités. La France et la Grande Bretagne face leurs immigrés*, PUF: Paris.

Laumann, E. O., Pappi, F. U. (1979), *Networks of Collective Action: A Perspective on Community Influence Systems*, Academic Press: New York.

Lazarsfeld, P. F., Menzel, H. (1962), 'On the Relation Between Individual and Collective Properties', in Etzioni, A. (ed.), *Complex Organizations*, Holt, Rinehart and Winston: New York, pp. 422-440.

Lewis, O. (1968), 'The Culture of Poverty', in Moynihan, D. P. (ed.), *On Understanding Poverty: Perspectives from the Social Sciences*, Basic Books: New York.

Madge, C., Willmott, P. (1981), *Inner City Poverty in Paris and London*, Routledge and Kegan Paul: London.

Massey, D. S., Denton, N. A. (1985), 'Spatial Assimilation as a Socioeconomic Outcome', *American Sociological Review*, Vol. 50, pp. 94-106.

Massey, D. S., Denton, N. A. (1993), *American Apartheid. Segregation and the Making of the Underclass*, Harvard University Press: Cambridge, MA, London.

Massey, D. S., Gross, A. B., Eggers, M. L. (1991), 'Segregation, the Concentration of Poverty, and the Life Chances of Individuals', *Social Science Research*, Vol. 20, pp. 397-420.

Massey, D. S., Condran, G. A., Denton, N. A. (1987), 'The Effect of Residential Segregation on Black Social and Economic Well-Being', *Social Forces*, Vol. 66, pp. 29-56.

Oliver, P., Marwell, G. (1988), 'The Paradox of Group Size in Collective Action', *American Sociological Review*, Vol. 53, pp. 1-8.

Oliver, P., Marwell, G., Teixeira, R. (1985), 'A Theory of Critical Mass', *American Journal of Sociology*, Vol. 91, pp. 522-556.

Pappi, F. U., Melbeck, C. (1988), 'Die sozialen Beziehungen städtischer Bevölkerungen', in Friedrichs, J. (ed.), *Soziologische Stadtforschung*, Sonderheft 29 der Kölner Zeitschrift für Soziologie und Sozialpsychologie, Westdeutscher Verlag: Opladen, pp. 223-250.

Paugam, S. (1991), *La disqualification sociale. Essai nouvelle sur la pauvreté*, PUF: Paris.

Paugam, S. (1993), *La société francaise et ses pauvres*, PUF: Paris.

Pincon-Charlot, M. et al. (1986), *Ségrégation urbaine et classes sociales en région parisienne*, Anthropos: Paris.

Podzuweit, U., Schütte, W., Swiertka, N. (1992), *Datenhandbuch Hamburg*, Fachhochschule Hamburg: Hamburg.

Reuber, P. (1993), *Heimat in der Großstadt*, University of Cologne, Institute for Geography (Kölner Geographische Arbeiten, Heft 58): Köln.

Rhein, C. (1994), 'La division sociale de l'espace parisien et son évolution (1954-1975)', in Brun, J., Rhein, C. (eds.), *La ségrégation dans la ville*, L'Harmattan: Paris, pp. 229-258.

Rhein, C. (1996), 'Social Segmentation and Spatial Polarization in Greater Paris', in O'Loughlin, J., Friedrichs, J. (eds.), *Social Polarization in Post-Industrial Societies*, de Gruyter: Berlin, New York, pp. 45-70.

Riede, T. (1989), 'Problemgruppen', in Statistisches Bundesamt (ed.), *Datenreport 1989*, Bundeszentrale für politische Bildung: Bonn, pp. 514-523.

Rowntree, B. S. (1901), *Poverty: A Study of Town Life*, Macmillan: London.

Sarkissian, W. (1976), 'The Idea of Social Mix in Town Planning: an Historical Review', *Urban Studies*, Vol. 13, pp. 231-246.

Schelling, T. C. (1971), 'Dynamic Models of Segregation', *Journal of Mathematical Sociology*, Vol. 1, pp. 143-186.

Schelling, T. C. (1978), *Micromotives and Macrobehavior*, Norton: New York.

Shepherd, J., Westaway, J., Lee, T.(1974), *A Social Atlas of London*, Clarendon Press: Oxford.

Sigelman, L., Bledsoe, T., Welch, S., Combs, M. W. (1996), 'Making Contact? Black-White Social Interaction in an Urban Setting', *American Journal of Sociology*, Vol. 101, pp. 1306-1332.

Skogan, W. G. (1990), *Disorder and Decline. Crime and the Spiral of Decay in American Neighborhoods*, University of California Press: Berkely, Los Angeles.

Stadt Essen (1993), *Soziale Ungleichheit im Stadtgebiet*, Amt für Stadtentwicklungsplanung, Statistik, Stadtforschung und Wahlen: Essen.

Taub, R. P., Taylor, D. G., Dunham, J. D. (1984), *Paths of Neighborhood Change. Race and Crime in Urban America*, Chicago University Press: Chicago, London.

Tienda, M. (1991), 'Poor People, Poor Places: Deciphering the Neighborhood Effects on Poverty Outcomes', in Huber, J. (ed.), *Micro-macro Linkages in Sociology*, Sage: Newbury Park, CA, pp. 244-262.

Tobias, G., Boettner, J. (eds.) 1992, *Von der Hand in den Mund. Armut und Armutsbewältigung in einer westdeutschen Großstadt*, Klartext: Essen.

Townsend, P. (1979), *Poverty in the United Kingdom*, Penguin: Harmondsworth.

Verbrugge, L. M. (1977), 'The Structure of Adult Friendship Choices', *Social Forces*, Vol. 56, pp. 576-597.

Verbrugge, L. M. (1983), 'A Research Note on Adult Friendship Contact: A Dyadic Perspective', *Social Forces*, Vol. 62, pp. 78-83.

Wacquant, L. J. D. (1993), 'Urban Outcasts: Stigma and Divison in the Black American Ghetto and the French Urban Periphery', *International Journal of Urban and Regional Research*, Vol. 17, pp. 366-383.

Weicher, J. C. (1990), 'How Poverty Neighborhoods are Changing', in Lynn, L. E., McGeary, M. G. H. (eds.), *Inner-City Poverty in the United States*, National Academy Press: Washington, DC, pp. 68-110.

Wellmann, B. (1979), 'The Community Question: The Intimate Networks of East Yorkers', *American Journal of Sociology*, Vol. 84, pp. 1201-1231.

Wellmann, B., Carrington, P. J., Hall, A. (1988), 'Networks as Personal Communities', in Wellmann, B., Berkowitz, S.D. (eds.), *Social Structures. A Network Approach*, Cambridge University Press: Cambridge, pp. 130-184.

Wilson, W. J. (1987), *The Truly Disadvantaged*, Chicago University Press: Chicago.

Wilson, W. J. (1991), 'Studying Inner-City Social Dislocations: The Challenge of Public Agenda Research', *American Sociological Review*, Vol. 56, pp. 1-14.

Failing selectivity: On the extent and causes of non-take-up of social security benefits

Wim van Oorschot

To alleviate the financial problems of the poor, welfare states provide them with financial benefits which are specifically targeted at those in greatest need. By way of means-testing need is assessed followed by payment of benefits for those satisfying the means-test and meeting other supplemental criteria. In the ideal situation a benefit scheme is implemented effectively: all those entitled receive the benefit and there is no abuse of rights. However, in practice ineffectiveness occurs in the implementation of many means-tested schemes. Often there is either underconsumption of rights (non-take-up), overconsumption (misuse), or both. From the viewpoint of the poor at least, the first form of ineffectiveness is more serious than the latter. And, as we shall see, there are good reasons for policy-makers and academics to be concerned about underconsumption of rights too. However, looking over the literature on the functioning of welfare states in general, or the literature on how people cope with poverty or react to the supply of welfare state benefits, it quickly becomes clear that overconsumption - the misuse of benefits - usually receives much more attention than non-take-up (Van Oorschot and Kolkhuis Tanke 1989). Somehow it seems that the importance of non-take-up, which is the phenomenon whereby people or households do not receive the amount of benefit to which they are legally entitled, is not self-evident.

There may be several reasons for this bias but we believe that one of the most important factors is the widespread idea that the modern, Western citizen is a rational, calculating individual seeking personal profit from any relationship with the state. From this perspective the proper functioning of social policy is seen as being endangered more by overconsumption than by underconsumption of social rights. As a consequence the existence of underconsumption may easily be underrated.

In fact, a common set of interrelated ideas exists with regard to the problem of non-take-up, holding that this problem is not, nor can be, very serious. The central idea in this set is that only very few people in a population eligible for a benefit do not receive it, because people will seek profit and will not deliberately renounce a financial gain. In the few cases of non-take-up that may exist it is believed that people do not *want* the benefit, either as a result of calculation (they do not think the benefit is worth the effort), or on principle (they do not want to depend on what they believe is 'charity'). In both such situations, according to the common view, the non-claimants do not really *need* the benefit to which they are entitled. Coupled with the assumed low frequency of the non-take-up this leads to the judgement that there is not generally a serious problem; at least not for the non-claimants themselves, and, usually therefore, neither for the administration nor for policy-makers.

Although there will be cases of non-take-up which accord with this common view, results from studies on the topic show that such cases are rare. Such studies show that in the case of means-tested benefits (and sometimes also for non-means-tested benefits) it is a normal situation for large proportions of eligible populations not to receive the benefits in question. They show also that many people who are eligible for social security benefits do not behave as rational, calculating individuals, and that only in a minority of cases do non-claimants explicitly not want the benefit to which they are entitled.

All this implies that non-take-up, contrary to common belief, may be a serious problem in social policy. Some authors take a strong standpoint by evaluating the existence of non-take-up as evidence of the failure of the means-test as an instrument for social security (Hartmann 1985), or even as indicating the failure of the very principle of selectivity, which principle is central to any means-tested scheme (Lynes 1972, p. 505). Lister (1974, p. 21) concludes in this respect from her review of early British (non) take-up studies that '*The selectivist solution to poverty has been tried, and it has failed*'. Others take a more moderate standpoint by stating that non-take-up generally should be regarded as an important problem in social policy, but not, or to a lesser extent, if only small amounts are forgone (Bendick 1985), if people genuinely do not want to claim (Beltram 1984), if non-take-up is only frictional (Adler 1977), or if people are entitled but non-claiming only for a short period of time (SBC 1978; Richardson and Naidoo 1978). Atkinson (1984) would assert that in all such cases non-take-up nevertheless indicates the existence of non-trivial costs associated with claiming. These costs, which claimants will also experience, may justify attention to the problem apart from the amount of unclaimed money or the non-claimants' motivations.

Although we believe that there is not a single standard answer to the question of how to judge the importance or seriousness of a given case of non-take-up of benefits, we do believe that non-take-up in general is a phenomenon in social policy worth studying by academics in the field and being taken seriously by policy-makers as well as by administrators.

First, the existence of non-take-up can tell us about a dis-functioning policy, in the sense that it indicates ineffectiveness in a scheme's implementation, as well as being a cause of poverty and other problems related to low incomes. Secondly, non-take-up in itself implies a fundamental injustice, because of the inequality that exists between claiming and non-claiming citizens in realising their rights. Especially in the field of social security, injustice in a scheme's implementation should be a matter of concern, not only because social security is the institution par excellence which can promote a just distribution of resources in modern society, but also because many people who are entitled to a benefit are in a situation of real need. And thirdly, the role of the selectivity principle, i.e. means-testing, to which non-take-up is inherent, has expanded in the social security systems of nearly all Western European countries since the economic crisis of the early eighties. This has led to *a shift from insurance to assistance* (see Van Oorschot and Schell 1991, but also more recently e.g. Gough 1994). As a result the importance of studying non-take-up has increased.

Given that the phenomenon of non-take-up deserves more attention than it usually is given up till now in poverty studies and debates, and wishing to offer those interested a quick and broad view on the body of knowledge which already exists, this article has three specific aims: (1) to give an international review of non-take-up figures from a number of western countries: (2) to present recently developed theoretical models for understanding the underlying causes of non-take-up, and: (3) to present some results of an empirical application of the models.

1 The extent of non-take-up

To offer an idea of what is generally known about non-take-up, and at what levels it usually is present, we shall briefly present an international overview of figures. Although different types of non-take-up can be distinguished the figures presented here will relate only to the main type of non-take-up, i.e.

people not receiving their full benefit entitlement. This is because few reports refer to partial non-take-up (people only receive part of their entitlement). Reports usually do not distinguish either between primary non-take-up (people do not claim) and secondary non-take-up (people claim but withdraw or are rejected), or between permanent and temporary non-take-up.

Furthermore, the figures presented express the extent of non-take-up by way of a caseload-based rate (in stead of an expenditure-based rate). Exact definitions of such rates may differ, however. The problem is that many of the documents from which figures presented are taken do not clarify the definitions used. For this reason the different rates between schemes and countries and over time should be interpreted and compared with care.[1]

Britain

Britain occupies a unique position among European countries with regard to research on non take-up. From the 1960s on many studies were carried out, nationally as well as locally, and almost all of the existing means-tested benefits have been subjected to research (for reviews of this research see Lister 1974; Corden 1983; Falkingham 1985; Van Oorschot and Kolkhuis Tanke 1989; Craig 1991).

The non take-up of non means-tested benefits is generally believed to be very low, take-up of these benefits is estimated at close to 100% (DHSS 1983). There are, however, important exceptions mainly in respect of the non means-tested benefits for handicapped and disabled people.[2]

However, most British research on non-take-up has been directed mainly to means-tested benefits. The most important schemes are *Supplementary Benefit* (*SB*) which was replaced by *Income Support* (*IS*) in 1988 (*SB/IS* is the national 'safety-net' social assistance scheme), *Housing Benefit* (*HB*), and *Family Income Supplement* (*FIS*) which was replaced by *Family Credit* (*FC*) in 1988 (*FIS/FC* supplements the income of working parents with low earnings and acts as a passport benefit e.g. to some health benefits). Since the 1970s the Department of Social Security (DSS) has published regularly estimates of the take-up of these benefits. It uses administrative data for assessing the number of benefit receipts, and the *Family Expenditure Survey* (*FES*) to estimate the number of entitled non-recipients. Throughout the years the non-take-up of these three benefits has been fairly stable (see also Fry and Stark 1993, p. 39), and rather high, despite the permanent attention paid to the take-up problem in the British social policy debate. For instance, non-take-up of *SB/IS* was estimated at 30% in 1979 and at 26% in 1990. Non-take-up of *FIS/FC* is generally higher: 49% in 1979 and 36% in 1991. For *HB* the figures vary between 25% (rent rebates) and 45% (rent allowances) in 1979 and 37% (standard housing benefit) in 1990. In local studies usually higher, though variable, rates of non-take-up for these benefits are usually found (Lister 1974; Corden 1981; Deacon and Bradshaw 1983; Falkingham 1985). It is not entirely clear why this happens, but a factor of importance here may be that low income families are underrepresented in the *FES*. In addition, the official *FES*-based estimates of the Department of Social Security (DSS) make use of the number of officially registered recipients, which are not corrected for unentitled recipients, and therefore tend to underestimate non-take-up. One would expect correction for unentitled recipients to increase the estimated rates of non-take-up, and this is actually shown to be the case for *HB* and *FIS* by Fry and Stark (1993).

Belgium

Interest in the problem of non-take-up has emerged only recently in Belgium. Although there are hardly any figures available it is believed that non-take-up does occur in several schemes. A general indication of non-take-up is the fact that 2.7% of all Belgian households have incomes which are below the national subsistence minimum (Cantillon 1992). Nicaise and Cassey (1987) found a discrepancy between the numbers of students theoretically entitled to education allowances and the actual number of students claiming. From this he estimated that non-take-up of this allowance was about 25% among eligible students in lower and higher secondary education. Dhooghe et al. (1988, cited in Cantillon 1992) found strong evidence for the non-take-up of medical and social provisions for elderly people. A survey by the 4th World Movement among households on low incomes in Brussels showed that 39% were entitled to the Belgian social assistance (*Bestaansminimum*), while only 10% received it (Cantillon 1992). This would suggest a non-take-up rate of about 80%.

Recently it appeared that among the households in Brussels and Antwerp which were cut off from public utilities (gas and electricity) 24% had an income below the national subsistence minimum, giving them a right to social assistance. Only 6% had actually claimed (and still were below the minimum) (Cantillon 1992). Baert et al. (1991) report that administrators from municipal social services (*OCMW's*) express the opinion that non-take-up of social assistance occurs. And finally, Driessens (1989) presents an overview of Belgian social security schemes together with comments about possible 'bottlenecks' which could give rise to non-take-up problems of varying severity.

The former West Germany

In the former West Germany the first evidence of non take-up was found in a study on poor families with children (Knechtel 1960). Blume (1970) found that non take-up was one of the factors contributing to poverty among elderly people. Dick (1986, p. 159) reports a non-take-up rate of more than 50% of German housing allowances in the early 1970s. Albrecht and Reidegeld (1977) present evidence that not every household entitled to housing allowance (*Wohngeld)* receives it. When discussions on poverty revived in the mid-1970s, non take-up became a subject of concern. Since then estimates about the non take-up of social assistance (*Sozialhilfe*: a means-tested 'safety-net' benefit) have been made on a regular basis (Geissler 1976; Bujard and Lange 1978; Klanberg 1979; Hauser et al. 1981;, Hauser et al. 1993). Estimates ranged from 36 to 79%, depending on the method of calculation. These estimates were mainly based on analyses of data from the national, socio-economic survey (*Einkommens- und Verbrauchsstichprobe)*. Because of certain inadequacies in this survey Hartmann (1981) carried out a large scale, national survey (N= 25.000 households) to estimate the rate of non take-up rate of *Sozialhilfe*, and the reasons underlying this non take-up. His conclusion was that at the end of the 1970s 48% of all entitled households did not receive the benefit. In the 1980s the non-take-up rate of German *Sozialhilfe* did not change. Hauser et al. (1993, p. 54) conclude from calculations, using income data and the number of *Sozialhilfe* recipients, that in the first half of the 1980s non-take-up of the benefit was between 33 and 50%.

The Netherlands

In the Netherlands the non-take-up of housing benefit (*Individuele Huursubsidie, IHS*) has attracted attention over the longest period of time, mostly as part of broader research on housing needs and problems (see for details Van Oorschot and Konings 1990). There is quite a large variation in estimated non-take-up rates of the *IHS*. There are variations among samples of the general population of tenants: among sub-groups of tenants; over time (year of sampling) and according to method of calculation. We can not say definitely that any of the rates found is the correct one, but some general observations can be made.

Over the years the estimates based on the large *Woning Behoefte Onderzoek* (*WBO*) samples (N=70,000 persons) vary between 35 and 48% non-take-up. Given the fact that receipt of the housing benefit tends to be under-reported in surveys the true rate will be probably somewhere between 30 and 40%. We think that this range indicates the general extent of *IHS* non-take-up, which was, over the 1980s, quite stable. A second observation is, that it is likely that there is lower non-take-up among tenants of low incomes (see In 't Groen et al. 1989). Reasons for this might be their greater need for the subsidy due to their low income, the fact that most of them rent their dwelling from (municipal) housing corporations, and the information that the social assistance beneficiaries among this group receive from the municipal social service.

With regard to other Dutch benefits some occasional figures and evidence exist. For instance, 43% of eligible self-employed people did not take up the 1984 lump sum supplement for low income families (*Wet Eenmalige Uitkering, WEU*) (CBS 1985). There is evidence that non-take-up of this benefit was not confined to the self-employed. In 1981 people had to take the initiative to claim the benefit themselves. In that year 44% of the unemployed among the social assistance beneficiaries claimed the benefit, and 78% of the non-unemployed (who are mostly single parents). In 1982, however, social assistance beneficiaries did not have to take the initiative, but were invited to claim in a letter from the municipal social service. In that year the proportion of claimants among the two groups increased to 73 and 88% respectively (CBS 1985), suggesting that in the previous year many of these (especially the unemployed) had not claimed.

General Social Assistance *(Algemene Bijstandswet, ABW)* is the main Dutch means-tested benefit. No overall non-take-up figure for this benefit is known, but there is some evidence of non-take-up, found by Van Bijsterveldt (1975) and Filet (1974). In our own research project (Van Oorschot 1995) we found non-take-up of the *ABW* among elderly people in Rotterdam who were entitled because of the shortfall in their state pensions.

Special Assistance (*Bijzondere Bijstand*) is part of the General Social Assistance Act and provides people on low incomes with a grant or a loan in case they are confronted with 'special costs' (i.e. costs which are exceptional but necessary). From several studies it is known that non-take-up of this benefit is at a serious level, i.e. between 50 to as much as 82% (see Konsumenten Kontakt 1989; Mullenders 1993; Smolenaars 1991; Van Oorschot 1995).

United States of America

In the USA a range of means-tested federal, state and local social welfare programs exists, in which non-take-up, or nonparticipation as it is usually called in American literature, is common. Bendick (1980) presents a table in which participation-rates (recipients relative to eligible people) of several of these benefits are taken together. The figures are from different sources and date from 1967 to 1977. They vary from 4 to 90% depending on type of benefit, year and region. If we take from the table the most important federal programs for the year 1975 then the nationwide non-participation-rates (100% minus participation-rate) are: 13% for *Aid to Families with Dependent Children* (*AFDC*), 84% for *AFDC for Unemployed Fathers*, 40% for *Supplemental Security Income* (*SSI*) among disabled people, and 40% for *SSI* among elderly people (see also Bendick 1986).

The non-take-up of *SSI* seems to have been fairly stable over the years since its introduction in 1974. Menefee et al. (1981) used variables identified in the 1973 *Survey on Low Income Aged and Disabled* (*SLIAD*) to identify nonparticipation in 1974 *SLIAD* follow up responses. The overall nonparticipation rates they found were 45% among eligible elderly people and 46% among eligible disabled people. A major pilot study of *SSI*-participation among elderly people found a nonparticipation rate of 30 to 40% in 1980 (Urban Systems 1981). This rate was confirmed in analyses by Drazga et al. (1982) of the same data set using, however, the Social Security Administration calculation method. Nine years after its introduction nonparticipation in *SSI* was still approximately 45%. This was the rate found by Zedlewski and Meyer (1987) using the *Current Population Survey* data of 1983.

Regrettably we could not obtain a sequence of figures on *AFDC* nonparticipation.

Other countries

As far as we were able to collect relevant data we found that in European countries like Ireland, France, Denmark, Luxembourg, Italy, Sweden, Switzerland and Finland little, if any, systematic information is available on non-take-up. A little evidence has emerged, in some of these countries, that suggests there is non-take-up of benefits.

In France, for instance, it is known that poor families in comparable situations receive supplements to their incomes from a variety of sources and to varying levels (Dumont 1987). Furthermore, 22% of *minimum-veillesse*-claimants waited more than five years after becoming eligible before they claimed, and the use of allowances for families with handicapped children is far less than would be expected on the basis of the number of handicapped children (according to information we received from prof. J.C. Ray, University of Nancy II). The *Centre d'Etudes des Revenus et des Coûts* estimates, on the basis of a special enquiry, a non-take-up rate of 16% for the French widows' pension (Duclos 1992, p. 6). And, in a comprehensive evaluation of the new *RMI*-scheme non-take-up of this benefit is estimated at 10% maximally, on the basis of evidence from a number of different studies (Vanlerenberghe 1992).

In Sweden a survey suggested that the non take-up of the *socialbidrag* (a means-tested 'safety-net' benefit) could be as much as 80% (Gustafsson 1987).

And lastly, in the Republic of Ireland Cousins and Charleton (1991) report on the first major survey on benefit take-up. The survey showed a high level of possible non-take-up of different benefits, i.e. 85% of the responding households were not claiming at least one benefit to which they were entitled. The main Irish benefits with possible non-take-up were *Supplementary Welfare Allowance*, *Exceptional Needs Payments*, school-books entitlements, *Treatment Benefit* and *Medical Cards*.

Conclusions

In most of the countries discussed very little, if anything, is known about the non-take-up of benefits, except in Britain and, to a lesser degree, the USA, the Netherlands and (the former West) Germany. It appeared that only in a few rather specific cases non-take-up rates are less than 20%. This implies that whenever non-take-up of means-tested benefits is found, it is usually at a serious level. Purnell (1973, p. 17) suggests from a multi-benefit study, which included 'small' schemes like welfare milk, free prescriptions, and remission of dental and optical charges, that '*...there will always be a substantial minority of means-tested benefits (20 %) which will go unclaimed...*'. Purnell appears to have been judging the general situation better than the former British Supplementary Benefits Commission, which suggested that a minimum rate of 10% non-take-up was likely to occur in all means-tested schemes (SBC 1978, p. 6).

2 The underlying causes of non-take-up

Reviews of non-take-up research show that traditionally the causes of non-take-up of social security benefits are studied at the client-level only (Corden 1981; Falkingham 1985; Van Oorschot and Kolkhuis Tanke 1989; Craig 1991). That is, in trying to explain why people do not receive the benefits to which they are entitled the focus has been on eligible people's knowledge, perceptions, attitudes, motivations, experiences and circumstances. Influencing factors possibly operating at the levels of scheme structure and administration have largely been ignored thus far (see also Whyley and Huby 1993; Corden 1995). Furthermore, the leading theoretical model of claiming decisions taken at the client level, the Kerr-model, which has been applied in nearly all of the latest (non-econometrical) take-up studies, has shown to contain some apparent deficiencies (see e.g. Ritchie 1988; Buckland and Dawson 1989; Craig 1991; Van Oorschot 1991; Vincent et al. 1991).

In this section we shall introduce new approaches to the causes of non-take-up, tackling both the confinement to the client level, as well as the need for a more consistent and valid client-level model. With regard to each of both issues a new theoretical model will be presented.

Different levels: clients, administration, scheme

The idea that factors influencing non-take-up are situated at different levels, and not only at the client level, has been referred to earlier in the literature, but only implicitly (SBC 1978; Adler 1977; Bendick 1980). Nevertheless, the literature on non-take-up contains much empirical evidence on the importance of influential factors at the levels of scheme and administration, although there is little direct proof. It is commonly acknowledged that the *administration* of services and benefits can have a great influence, generally, on what citizens actually receive compared to what is originally intended by policy-makers (see, among others, Blau 1955; Handler and Hollingsworth 1971; Kramer Gordon 1975; Catrice-Lorey 1976; Leibfried 1976; Ringeling 1981; Lipsky 1980; Mashaw 1983; Walker 1985). About administrative influences on the non-take-up of means-tested benefits in particular, however, little is yet known exactly. This is especially so in the case of *direct* influences, which occur when administrators decide wrongly to reject a claim, or when they award a smaller amount than a claimant is actually due. Examples of such wrong decisions can be found in Berthoud (1983, 1984) and Vos (1991). Other studies have shown that administrators of means-tested social security schemes tend to make decisions on the basis of biased and/or insufficient information (Howe 1985; Vos 1991; Beltram 1984; Knegt 1986), leading most probably to false rejections in at least some cases. In comparison with the direct influences, there is more documentation about *indirect* influences of the administration on a scheme's non-take-up. Such indirect influences arise from practical administrative arrangements and administrators' behaviour which can set constraints on clients or lay stumbling blocks in their paths. Clear examples can be found in Briggs and Rees (1980), Corden (1983 and 1987), Graham (1984), Richardson and Naidoo (1978), Davies and Ritchie (1988). From these studies the main factors at the level of administration which enhance the probability of non take-up can be summarized as follows:

- a way of handling claims and claimants that is experienced by claimants as humiliating or degrading
- combining a 'service'- and a 'fraud control'-function
- poor quality of communication with clients, giving insufficient information and advice
- using complex application forms
- poor quality of decision-making, e.g. taking decisions on the basis of insufficient information or on the basis of client stereotyping
- poor quality of technical administrative procedures
- wrong interpretation of scheme rules by administrators.

Recently, Corden (1995) elaborated this list of main factors on the basis of British findings and improved it by offering and applying an alternative, sequential classification of administrative aspects that are influential: aspects of information supply, of service provision, and of application procedure and outcome. Corden presents a wide variety of evidence on the influence of these administrative aspects on non-take-up, and concludes that '... *every aspect of administration can potentially affect take-up*.' (p. 58).

Factors at the level of *benefit structure* will not lead directly to non-take-up, but indirectly, because they constitute to a large extent the context in which the behaviour of administrators and clients takes place, thereby offering opportunities for and constraints on the behaviour of both sets of actors. From the rather scattered information available we concluded elsewhere (Van Oorschot and Kolkhuis Tanke 1989) that the probability of the occurrence of non take-up is larger in schemes that:

- have a 'density' (a large number) of rules and guidelines
- contain complicated rules
- contain vague, i.e. imprecise, indistinct and/or discretionary entitlement criteria
- contain a means-test
- supplement other sources of income
- are aimed at groups in society which are the subject of negative valuation
- provide only small amounts of benefit
- leave the initiative to start the claiming process fully to the applicant
- provide for a variety of expenses (comprehensive schemes)
- provide for incidental instead of regular expenses
- offer an unstable entitlement.

Corden (1995) also applied this list to the British social security system, and claimed to have found considerable supporting evidence of its validity, at the same time offering a few additional features which certainly are of relevance. She suggests that not only may a test of means have a deterrent effect on take-up, but also, mainly because of feelings of shame involved, a test of disability (proof of which can be found in e.g. Bradshaw and Lawton 1982; Blunn and Small 1984; Corden 1987). Furthermore, she suggests effects from overlap and interaction between different benefits in respect to the criteria for entitlement, from structural aspects of benefits which challenge cultural norms, and she rightly points to the fact that structural aspects of time influence (non) take-up. Of course, of the structural aspects the presence of a means-test is most widely recognised as a factor inherently associated with non-take-up.[3]

The three different levels - scheme structure, administration and client - can be distinguished analytically quite easily, but the research literature and reviews of it show that in practice the factors influencing non take-up form a complex whole. We propose to see non-take-up as the result of a mix of interrelated factors from different interacting levels. These factors may be directly or indirectly influential and the actual mix of factors may and usually will differ between particular situations, i.e. between different schemes, administrative arrangements, client groups, times and places. Looking at the causes of non-take-up in this way for one thing helps us understand how different studies focusing on the reasons for non-take-up at the client level have come to quite different, indeed sometimes opposite conclusions about the relative influence of separate factors, as e.g. 'knowledge', 'stigma', 'perception of eligibility', and 'need' (see Craig 1991 for examples). Namely, these studies were about different schemes and different client groups (pensioners, lone parents, working poor, or social assistance beneficiaries); they were carried out at different times; in different places, and in the context of different administrative arrangements. The view on the causes of non-take-up as a mix of multi-level factors furthermore leads to recognizing that it is not only citizens who are responsible for the problem of non take-up. Policy-makers and administrators also play their role and can be held responsible. Denying this would be a clear case of 'blaming the victim' (Townsend 1979). As for the question of primary responsibility one must realise that often the answer is just a matter of which viewpoint is taken. For instance, who is responsible for the non-take-up resulting from lack of sufficient knowledge by eligible people? Is it the clients, as is commonly assumed, or the administration, for not being active enough in distributing information and giving advice, or the policy-makers, for designing a large number of complex, vague and therefore incomprehensible rules and guidelines?

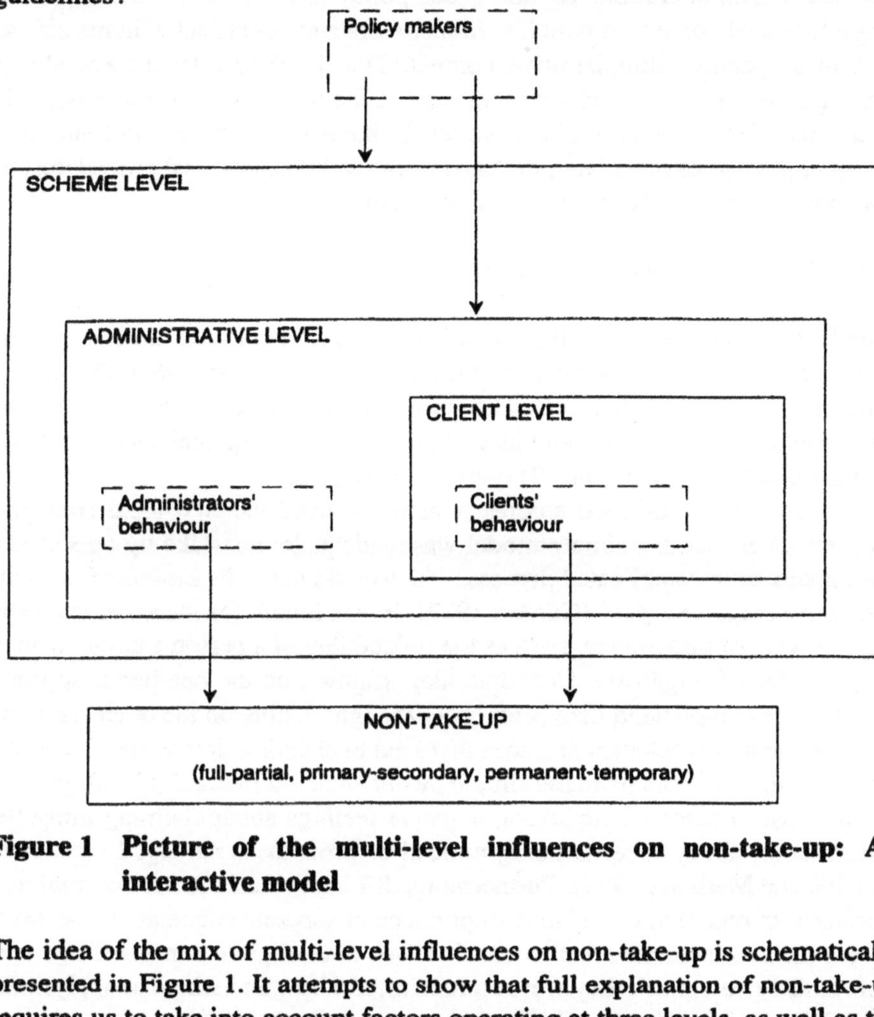

Figure 1 Picture of the multi-level influences on non-take-up: An interactive model

The idea of the mix of multi-level influences on non-take-up is schematically presented in Figure 1. It attempts to show that full explanation of non-take-up requires us to take into account factors operating at three levels, as well as the behaviour of three distinct groups of actors. The levels are scheme, administration and client; the actors are policy-makers, administrators and clients. Non-take-up is represented as the direct result of the specific behaviour of two groups of actors: administrators (who may make false decisions regarding applications of clients) and clients (who may omit putting in a claim or withdraw a claim). The third main group of actors, policy-makers, is of importance because of their role in setting the scheme's rules, in deciding on the budget and personnel available and outlining the main factors of the scheme's administration. In doing so, policy-makers define the legal and organizational context in which administrators and clients act. Clients also act within a specific administrative context. That is, their relevant knowledge, perceptions, attitudes, experiences and behaviour are all influenced by characteristics of the administrative level, like e.g. the amount and quality of information and advice given, the barriers raised in the practical procedures, the location of offices, and their treatment by administrators.

Modelling non-take-up at the client level

The first generalizations on the client level causes of non-take-up came from a number of small-scale British studies carried out in the 1960s.The overall picture emerging was that non-take-up was generally caused by three distinct main factors: (1) ignorance and lack of information, (2) (perceived) complexity of the claiming process, and (3) (perceived) stigma.

From better designed studies, which followed the first local studies, it became clear that this simple model was inadequate: non-take-up appeared to be a much more complicated process, which could not '*...be explained in simple all-embracing concepts.*' (Corden 1987). It was found, for instance, that other factors were of importance, such as the (in)stability of a person's circumstances which affected eligibility. Concepts like 'stigma', on the one hand, appeared much more complicated than previously thought, while, on the other hand, did not capture all the relevant attitudes involved in claiming. It was also found that the three main factors from the simple model were interrelated (like stigma and knowledge in cases where strong negative feelings about claiming prevented information about benefits being noticed or processed; see e.g. Lewis 1975; Ritchie and Mathews 1982). Furthermore, different studies led to contradictory results with regard to the relative importance of separate concepts. What struck researchers as most remarkable was that even after eligible non-claimants were told exactly how much they were entitled to, and how and where to apply, some still did not claim (as was e.g. found by Taylor-Gooby 1974).

The many factors found, their indistinct relationships, the sometimes obscure meaning of central concepts, and the contradicting empirical findings led the Supplementary Benefit Commission in 1978 to remark that '*...reluctance to claim appears to come from some mixture of pride, ignorance, a sense of stigma, reluctance to make the efforts which a claim calls for, a desire for self-sufficiency on the part of an individual or family, an unwillingness to become involved with a government agency and a feeling that* *the whole business is not worthwhile.*' (SBC 1978, p. 7). In the report the Commission doubted whether a complete and coherent picture of the many factors involved would ever be reached.

An important breakthrough towards such a picture has been the model on the decision whether or not to claim developed by Kerr in the early 1980s (Kerr 1983). In this model the most important factors previously found to influence non-take-up are interrelated by placing them in a sequential order. Each main factor represents a barrier, or *threshold* as Kerr calls it, which has to be passed before the next one can be crossed. Eligible people passing all thresholds will decide to claim; failing to cross one of the thresholds will result in not claiming. Kerr distinguishes six thresholds. First, people have to perceive difficulties in making ends meet and therefore a need for a benefit; if that threshold is crossed they have to become aware of a benefit's existence; next they must perceive themselves as eligible; they have to perceive some utility of the benefit to meet their need; the total of their attitudes to benefit support must be positive; and finally, they must be in a stable situation (Kerr 1983). The solution to the problem of assessing the relative importance of factors is rather simple: because of the postulated sequentiality, the first uncrossed threshold is taken to explain non-claiming. Consequently, the most important factor is the threshold which functions as a sufficient obstacle for the greatest number of non-claimants.

Kerr's model was applied heuristically, i.e. as a guiding framework for design and analysis, in most of the studies on non-take-up which were carried out in the years after its introduction.[4] The results of all these studies did not leave Kerr's model uncriticized. From reviews of these studies (notably Craig 1991; Van Oorschot 1991, 1995) the main critiques can be summarized.

A first point is that the model is not valid in respect to the fundamental mechanisms at work. That is, the logic of sequentially ordered thresholds does not seem to be adequate, because several studies found that many claimants had experienced high thresholds and had claimed anyway (e.g. Davies and Ritchie 1988); that extreme scores on a separate construct can overrule negative scores on other constructs (e.g. Graham 1984); and that covariation among constructs of the model exist. The alternative of a trade-off, as the fundamental logic underlying the decision whether or not to claim, is therefore proposed by several authors, offering not only a critique of the threshold character of constructs, but also on their order of appearance in Kerr's model (see e.g. Ritchie 1988). Secondly, the model seems to miss some fundamental factors, like: (1) triggers, which are sudden disruptive events with the power of inducing claims quickly (Van Oorschot 1991); (2) strong negative attitudes towards social security benefits and being dependent on society in general, which have the power to block any considerations and behaviour in respect of claiming at an early stage of the decision process (Graham 1984); (3) information: although basic knowledge, i.e. being aware of a benefit's existence, is found to be a prerequisite for claiming, the general role played by different aspects of information in the decision process is neglected (Van Oorschot 1991); (4) time: Kerr's model is static in the sense that it seems to conceive of non-take-up as a steady state, reached once and for all after meeting a serious threshold. Many studies, however, found relatively large numbers of delayed claiming. In addition, Kerr's model neither takes into account the duration of the different stages in the decision process (Vincent et al. 1991). Finally, the model is limited in scope, even as a client level model, because it is confined to the decision whether or not to apply. It therefore excludes all the relevant factors in the total claiming process which are found to play a role before and after this decision. It notably lacks the application stage which follows after the decision (Buckland and Dawson 1989; Corden 1983).

Given these criticisms there is a need for an alternative model in which the missing factors are incorporated, as well as the processes before and after the decision, and in which the threshold mechanism is accorded less significance in favour of greater attention paid to trade-off and trigger mechanisms. In Van Oorschot (1995) we have developed such a new, more elaborate model. This dynamic model of benefit receipt is presented in Figure 2.

Briefly explained the Figure 2 expresses the following. The process of claiming is conceived of as taking place between two populations, namely those who do not receive the benefit involved, and those who do.[5] It makes no diference in this respect whether recipients or non-recipients are eligible or not. The core of the model, the process of claiming, consists of three stages. We conceive of the whole of the first stage as a *threshold*, which has to be crossed before the second stage can be reached in which with more or fewer considerations the decision is made. In the first stage the issue of claiming has to become salient which basically demands awareness of the scheme in question. Having achieved such basic knowledge, however, people still will be prevented from considering claiming if they perceive themselves to be ineligible (PE), if they have a really strong attitudinal barrier against claiming (AB), if they do not perceive any need (N), or if they are in a very unstable situation (US). People who have crossed the first threshold stage enter the *trade-off* stage. That is, when people come as far as considering claiming, they will trade off claim inhibiting and claim stimulating factors.

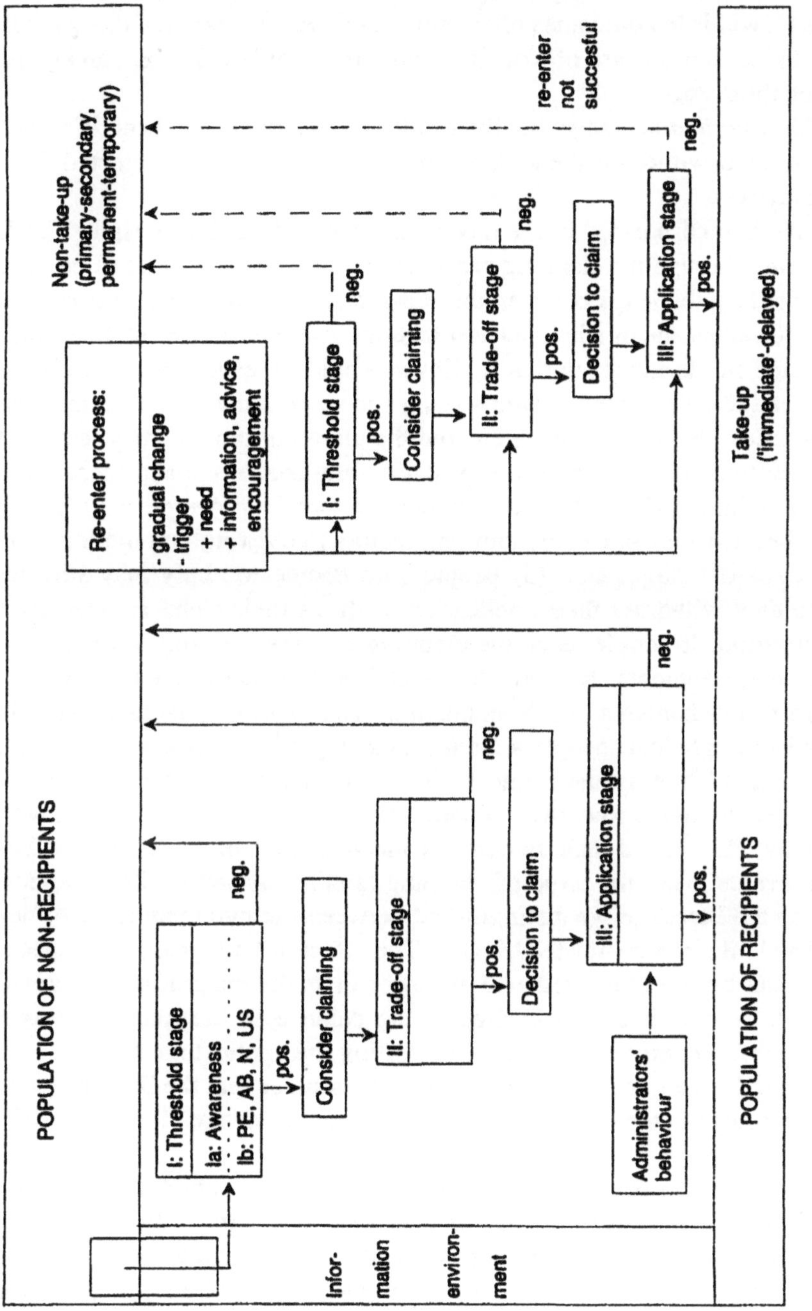

Figure 2 The dynamic model of benefit receipt

Factors involved here are perceptions of need, of eligibility and of utility, attitudes towards the outcomes of claiming, and the perception of the instability of one's situation. In case of a positive outcome people will claim and thereby enter the third stage.

This *application* stage finally results in receiving the benefit at issue, unless people withdraw their claim, or unless the claim is rejected by the administration.

Time is incorporated in the model and passes from left to right. The fact that moving through the claiming process will always take at least some time is represented by the leaps between the separate stage-boxes. These leaps, then, point to the existence of frictional non-take-up. Another important time element is reflected in the model in that it allows people to leave the initial claiming process and re-enter later on. This leaving and re-entering may even take place several times. People who have entered the claiming process may leave it for certain reasons: (1) they may not pass the threshold stage and therefore not consider claiming; (2) without experiencing a threshold, people may leave the process because they perceive inhibiting factors to outweigh promoting factors in the trade-off stage; and, (3) people who decide to apply may still leave because they withdraw their application, or have their claim rejected by the administration. If people leave the claiming process they regain the status of inactive non-recipients. Re-entry to the claiming process may be induced by two main mechanisms, each containing two specific factors. The first mechanism is gradual: people's circumstances gradually change and they are aware of this bringing them into entitlement, or there is gradually growing need, as people move towards a situation in which they can no longer manage financially. The second main re-entrance mechanism is through triggers. These sudden events make the issue of claiming (again) instantly salient to people. Based on the literature we distinguished between the two main types of need-related and information-related triggers. The effect of both gradual changes and triggers can be threefold: either they lower or make insignificant a previous threshold; or they induce a change in the balance in the trade-off between opposing influences; or they induce re-starting the application stage.

As for the start of the process, the model assumes that the first entry to the claiming process takes place when people become aware (first hear) of the benefit's existence.

The single box representing the information environment includes conceptually all relevant informational factors. We agree with Vincent et al. (1991) that aspects of information such as content, character, sources and channels, the time and place it is received and processed and the persistence with which it is sought, are all factors which may play an important role during the different stages of the claiming process. Elsewhere we argued for higher priority to be given to refining the information factor (Van Oorschot 1991). But, there are too many aspects to it, about which too little is known yet, to make it feasible to incorporate the information factor into our model at this stage. As such, then, the box representing the information environment on the one hand reflects the complexity of the information factor, and on the other hand it reminds us that the factor is important.

The dynamic model in Figure 2 can directly be placed into the client level box of the interactive model in Figure 1. Such a placement would show clients' behaviour as the outcome of going through the processes pictured in the dynamic model of benefit receipt, and the model would be directly linked to the administrators' behaviour, because administrators may reject claims wrongly. Such a placement would also express the ideas discussed earlier: that clients' behaviour, and thus all the stages in the dynamic model, take place in a specific administrative and structural context, implying that they are influenced directly or indirectly by features of administration and scheme structure.

An important feature of the model is that it pictures both non-take-up and take-up as states which may be reached through different 'paths' or 'routes'.

The most direct path to *take-up* would be: when people are already aware of the benefit's existence at the moment of becoming eligible; when they do not experience thresholds at that point; when they go on almost immediately to make a positive trade-off, thereby quickly deciding to claim, and actually put in the claim; when they do not withdraw the claim afterwards; and when finally an award is made and the benefit is paid by the administration without much delay. In our model such a process could be pictured as an arrow running nearly vertically from the population of non-recipients to the population of recipients. In practice, routine claiming by eligible people who have previously already received the benefit involved probably comes close to this most direct path. At the other extreme the most direct path to *non-take-up* might be represented by an horizontal arrow. This would show such a situation, when people becoming eligible and not being aware of the benefit's existence remained ignorant right up to the point at which they went out of eligibility. Between these two extremes there are many other possible routes to take-up as well as to non-take-up. This possibility of following distinct paths is connected not only with the existence of different types of (non) take-up, but also with the fact that cases of (non) take-up, although all of the same type, may still have quite different causal backgrounds.

3 Some empirical results

The theoretical ideas expressed in Figures 1 and 2 were applied in a cross-sectional study of non-take-up of means-tested benefits among elderly people (N= 1370) and social assistance clients (N=520) in two major Dutch cities. In 1990/1991 surveys were carried out measuring receipt of, and entitlement to, a number of national and local means-tested benefits. The surveys furthermore tried to measure extensively the possible reasons and underlying causes of non-take-up. The main national schemes included in the study were housing benefit (IHS) and special assistance (SA). The main local schemes were exemption from paying property tax (EPT) and garbage tax (EGT), and the Nijmegen Declaration fund (Df).[6] The results of the surveys are reported in full in Van Oorschot (1995). Here we can only present briefly some of the central outcomes related to the above presented models.

Stages and triggers: Analyses at the client level

Let us first address the causes of non-take-up found in our empirical study from the client level and focus on two main questions, which were derived from the characteristics of the dynamic model of benefit receipt: (1) What is the relative significance of different stages in the claiming process? (2) What is the role played by delayed claiming and by trigger events?

Question 1: Stages in the claiming process In contrast to earlier theoretical models the dynamic model of benefit receipt contains three successive stages. Although much evidence exists to justify distinguishing the three stages, there was nothing in existing reports about the extent to which non-take-up can be explained either by eligible people experiencing thresholds, by negative outcomes of trade-offs or by unsuccessful progress through the application stage. Here we can show the relative importance of the stages, for the non-take-up found in our study. Analyses were carried out on 14 cases (that is, 14 combinations of benefits and sub-groups).[7] It was found that in the *general case* (that is, in most of the combinations analyzed) most of the non-take-up can be explained by the fact that non-recipients have not succeeded in crossing existing thresholds: this counts for 60% to 70% of all eligible non-recipients (in one case this was even 90%). In all cases these thresholds are either lack of basic knowledge (i.e. not being aware of a scheme's existence), or a perception of ineligibility as opposed to perceiving oneself (possibly) eligible. Generally, the knowledge threshold has a greater role than the eligibility threshold: about

50 to 60% of the non-recipients experience the first, and 10 to 20% the second. Furthermore, in the general case the trade-off stage has only a minor role, because only about 20 to 35% of the cases of non-take-up are due to negative outcomes of a process in which promoting and inhibiting factors are weighed up against each other. The application stage, measured as the proportion of unsuccessful claimants, is least important. Only up to 15% of all cases of non-take-up are due to withdrawal of initial applications, or subsequent rejection.

There were two clear exceptions to this general picture. Among the schemes, housing benefit was the exception, because here very small proportions of non-recipients, ranging from only 2 to 12%, are unaware of the scheme's existence. Here, the most important reason for non-take-up is non-recipients' perception of ineligibility (30 to 60%). Compared to the general case, the overall importance of the threshold stage remained about the same. Among the sub-groups, the social assistance clients from Nijmegen are the exception, again because of the relatively low proportion of non-recipients lacking basic knowledge (20 to 30%). Compared to the general case, the threshold of perception of ineligibility as well as the trade-off stage are more important here.

Furthermore, we found that the other three thresholds suggested by the dynamic model of benefit receipt - strong negative attitudes, very low perceived need and a very unstable situation - were not found in our analyses: we did not find non-recipients with basic knowledge who perceived themselves to be in a very unstable situation, and, although some non-recipients had strong negative attitudes or very low need, the recipients were the same in this respect, implying that these characteristics do not ultimately block claiming, as they would if the characteristics functioned as thresholds.

Thus, far more than being the result of rational decisions, or of practical difficulties in applying, the non-take-up found in our study generally is the result of people simply not being aware of, or misinterpreting, their entitlement. The threshold stage plays the most important role.

Question 2: Delayed claiming and triggers There was delayed take-up of all schemes, varying from 5% to as much as 45% among the recipients of the different sub-groups. Within groups, delayed take-up was generally more common in respect to special assistance, exemption schemes and the Nijmegen Declarationfund, while it was least common in the case of housing benefit. Because this is a similar order to that found for the rates of non-take-up we suggest that the extent of non-take-up and the extent of delayed take-up (or of temporary non-take-up) are positively related: higher non-take-up generally goes with a higher degree of delayed take-up. This in turn would indicate that temporary and permanent non-take-up are subject to the same underlying factors and processes, which in fact is implied by the dynamic model of benefit receipt presented in Figure 2.

With regard to the role of triggers, our analyses aimed at answering questions which have never been properly addressed in previous research, like: to what extent are claimants induced to claim by specific events in their lives; what kinds of events usually play the most important roles; and, do role and type of claim inducing events vary according to different stages of the claiming process? A first conclusion from the analyses was that triggers have a universal importance in the take-up process, because 70 to 80% of all recipients said they were induced to claim by a specific event. These events may vary considerably in nature, but most of the events mentioned are either need-related or information-related. New findings are the apparent trends we discovered. Need-related triggers were mentioned more in the case of benefits which are directed at substantial costs (housing benefit and special assistance), while information-related events were mentioned more in the case of benefits which are directed at relatively low costs (exemption from paying garbage tax and Declaration-fund). Furthermore, compared to the non-delayed recipients, a greater proportion of delayed recipients reported having been triggered, and they tended to be induced more by information-related events (advice) than need-related events.

Mixes of multi-level influences

Next to analyzing the causes of non-take-up occurring at the client level, we also explored influencing factors operating at the other two relevant levels of scheme structure and administration (see Figure 1). We will present the results of one of a number of questions posed in this respect: (1) why do non-take-up rates differ according to types of benefit and sub-groups?

Differences among rates of non-take-up We found considerable variation in the non-take-up percentages of the schemes included in our study (ranging from 8% to as much as 72%). One of the patterns was that within all sub-groups non-take-up of housing benefit is relatively (very) low compared to that of the other schemes. This pattern cannot be understood fully from client level factors alone, because there is a large overlap of 80% to 90% between the scheme's population of eligible people and the populations of the other schemes. That is, to a large degree the people involved in the high take-up of housing benefit are the very same people involved in the low take-up of the other schemes. Therefore, the answer mainly has to come from comparisons of characteristics of structures of schemes and of administrative practices.

At the *structural* level housing benefit is no different from the other schemes in terms of being means-tested and supplemental to other sources of income. The scheme is not much less complicated, nor does it contain much clearer entitlement conditions, and as with the other schemes it leaves to the applicant the initiative to start the claiming process. Nevertheless, housing benefit does have some distinctive structural features which create a strongly claim promoting context. These features are related to the types of household and the types of cost at which housing benefit is directed, as well as to features of the benefit itself. The following mix of favourable characteristics is typical for Dutch housing benefit: it offers a relatively large amount of benefit which is awarded for a whole year; the scheme is directed at a single type of expense which recurs regularly (monthly rent); it offers a stable entitlement over a period of some years (entitlement criteria do not change much, and most people do not move frequently); it has a fixed application date (making possible well-targeted campaigns); the eligibility criterion is last year's taxable income (which for clients is a rather easy definition of the means-test); and finally, it is not directed only at the poorest households, i.e. it is less selective (depending on their rent, families with incomes up to about 150% of the minimum wage may be entitled).

We also compared housing benefit's position at the *administrative* level with that of the other schemes. The relevant features apparent to us were that the atmosphere surrounding the housing benefit application process is less dominated by the administration's function of fraud control, and most importantly that each year during June, the month preceding the application deadline of July 1, housing corporations undertake intensive and well-targeted information campaigns directed at stimulating housing benefit take-up. Both these claim promoting administrative features are directly linked to certain structural features of the scheme. The first is linked to the fact that for housing benefit what counts as means is last year's taxable income (which is easy to check in most cases), and the second is linked to the fixed application date (campaigns of the quality and intensity of those organised by the housing corporations in June could not be sustained throughout the year).

To complete the exploration of multi-level influences we compared at the *client* level the people eligible for housing benefit with those eligible for the other benefits on two sets of factors: (1) benefit specific informational factors, including: awareness of a benefit; the type of source of the first information about the benefit; the degree of knowledge of the entitlement criteria, and whether people have searched intensively for information about the benefit, and; (2) image factors, including the expected amount of a specific benefit; the perceived character of the benefit (i.e. whether one sees it mainly as a right or as a matter of charity); the expected degree of disapproval from acquaintances with regard to claiming the benefit, and the expected difficulty of applying for that benefit. The analyses showed that the high take-up of housing benefit can be understood at the client level from the facts that it is a much better known scheme, and also a more acceptable scheme. That is, among the population of eligible people the level of awareness is much higher compared to other schemes (nearly 100% against on average 75%) and, in contrast to the other schemes, it is thought to offer large amounts of benefit, be easy to apply for and being less stigmatizing (more seen as a matter of right and less disapproval of acquaintances is expected).

So, the lower level of non-take-up of housing benefit can be understood from a mix of multi-level factors: structural and administrative features form the context in which the claiming behaviour of the eligible people takes place, and some of these features are directly linked to factors found to play a role at the client level. That is, the higher level of basic knowledge is directly linked to the intensive claim promoting activities undertaken at the administrative level, which are specific for housing benefit. And the image factors are linked to administrative as well as to structural features: the justified expectation of substantial amounts of benefit, of being easier to get (linked to simpler means-test, more information and help), and of being less stigmatized (linked to less fraud control and less selectivity).

4 Concluding remarks

The implications of the phenomenon of non take-up of social security benefits with regard to the functioning of social policy, i.e. to the effectiviness of the implementation of social security schemes, and the incidence of poverty, make it a relevant subject to be studied by academics in the field of social policy. The fact that non take-up is strongly related to means-testing, combined with the growing significance of means-testing in the social security systems of European countries, supports our opinion that non-take-up is a phenomenon worthy to be put on the agenda of academic research. This would give the subject the place that it deserves in the debate on the functioning of social policy and on the design of social security systems, i.e. for instance in the choice between universal or selective benefits.

Till now in Europe non take-up has extensively been studied in Great-Britain only, although some studies were also carried out in West-Germany and in the Netherlands. Nearly all studies show high to very high rates of non take-up of means-tested benefits.

From an academic point of view, but also from the viewpoint of any policy-maker trying to take measures which could solve the problem, the reasons for non take-up are of utmost importance. We have seen that research on the factors affecting take-up has mainly been confined to the client-level, and within that level to factors affecting the decision to put in a claim. In contrast we have emphasized here the role played by factors on the levels of policy making and administration, and we also tried to improve the modelling of factors and stages which are of importance at the client level.

Regrettably space did not allow us to present more than just some main results of initial empirical applications of the models proposed on data from a number of surveys carried out in the Netherlands. For the full results we refer to Van Oorschot (1995). Our main conclusion is that realizing rights to benefits is not a matter of isolated individual beneficiaries deciding, at a particular time, to go out and claim or not. Instead it is a long process, which starts from the moment the structure of a scheme is defined, i.e. when the concrete eligibility criteria are determined by policy-makers. These criteria establish, to a considerable extent, the degree to which administrators and clients will experience serious obstacles later in the process. Analytically, on the micro-level, the process ends when the benefit is actually received by those people who are entitled to it. In practice and on the macro-level, however, the process does not end, because at any one time there will always be eligible non-recipients left, usually, marginal numbers in the case of non-means-tested benefits, but much higher proportions in the case of means-tested benefits. Between the establishment of a scheme's structure and benefit receipt, administrative bodies and administrators play an important role. They have to implement the scheme, with a primary aim to ensure that the benefit reaches its eligible population. Whether they fulfil this task completely depends not only on contextual constraints over which they usually have no control (elements of scheme structure, budget, time and/or prescribed procedures), but also on their own efforts and activities within such constraints. Delivery of entitlements within each scheme can meet higher or lower standards, in a technical administrative or procedural sense, along with variable degrees of conviction and commitment to clients' needs. The clients of the administration, the people who are or might be entitled to the benefit, are not discharged from any responsibility within the administrative process. On the contrary, they are justifiably expected to try as hard as possible to find solutions to problems experienced, e.g. by seeking (further) information about possible benefits and by claiming those available. However, this is different from expecting them to be self-confident, rational, active and bureaucratically competent. Only if all clients were like this would it be justifiable to allot the main responsibility for the actual realization of their rights to the clients themselves.

Notes

[1] See Appendix 1 of Van Oorschot (1995) for an elaborate discussion of definitions of rates.

[2] See Bradshaw and Lawton (1982) on non-take-up and delayed take-up of the non-means-tested Family Fund, Blunn and Small (1984) on families with handicapped children who had not applied to the Family Fund, Cohen (1983) on cases of non-take-up of Attendance Allowance and Mobility Allowance for disabled people, and Corden (1987).

[3] In most British empirical studies on non-take-up the relationship is taken for granted. Elsewhere no opposing views or research results are present. See e.g. Bendick (1980) for the American case, Leibfried (1976) and Hartmann (1985) for the situation in (the former West) Germany, and Van Oorschot (1995) for the Netherlands.

[4] See e.g. Corden 1983 and 1987; Corden and Craig 1991; Graham 1984; Ritchie and England 1984; Millar and Cooke 1984; Davies and Ritchie 1988; Van Oorschot 1992.

[5] The model assumes that moving from the population of non-recipients to the population of recipients is only possible by moving through this process as it is pictured. In the case of benefits in which the initiative to apply is more or less taken over from the individual eligible person by another actor (e.g. the administration of a scheme or a welfare institution) this may not be a valid assumption. Here we are concerned, however, with means-tested benefits, which generally leave the initiative to apply entirely to the individual eligible person.

[6] Dutch housing benefit (IHS) is a national scheme administered by housing corporations and the Department of the Environment. It offers a monthly rent subsidy to households who's rent is too high in relation to the income. Special assistance (Bijzondere Bijstand) is assistance for households which face exceptional but necessary costs. Dutch municipalities levy property tax and garbage tax. Households on (very) low incomes can be exempted from paying these taxes. The Nijmegen Declaration fund is an example of a municipal fund which offers small amounts of benefit to low income families with the aim of stimulating them to participate in socio-cultural activities.

[7] There are four sub-groups: elderly people in Rotterdam and in Nijmegen, and social assistance clients in both cities. Schemes included in the analyses here are: housing benefit, special assistance, exemption from paying garbage tax, and the Nijmegen Declaration fund.

References

Adler, M. (1977), *Research Priorities for Improving the Take-up of Benefits*, Social Security Research Policy Committee: Edinburgh.

Albrecht, R., Reidegeld, E. (1977), 'Öffentliche Verwaltung, Verständlichkeit und Wohngeld', *Soziale Sicherheit*, pp. 323-335.

Atkinson, A. B. (1984), *Take-up of Social Security Benefits*, Discussion Paper 65, International Centre for Economics and Related Disciplines: London.

Baert, H., Cras, A., Deelen, B. (1991), *Bereikt het OCMW de armen? Gebruik en niet-gebruik van financiële en materiële hulpverlening*, Referaat 3e beleidsdag 'OCMW: wij nemen uw rechten ter harte': Brussel.

Beltram, G. (1984), *Testing the Safety Net, an Enquiry into the Reformed Supplementary Benefit Scheme*, Bedford Square Press: London.

Bendick, M. (1980), 'Failure to Enroll in Public Assistance Programs', *Social Work*, Vol. 25, No. 4.

Bendick, M. (1985), *Improved Program Administration can Benefit Both Public Assistance Recipients and Oregon Taxpayers*, The Urban Institute: Washington.

Bendick, M. (1986), 'Targeting Benefit Payments in the British Welfare State', in McKinney, Jerome B., Johnston, Michael (eds.), *Fraud, Waste and Abuse in Government. Causes, Consequences and Cures*, Institute for the Study of Human Issues: Philadelphia.

Berthoud, R. (1983), *Study of the Reformed Supplementary Benefit Scheme: Working Paper D; Welfare Rights Advice Experiment*, Policy Studies Institute: London.

Berthoud, R. (1984), *The Reform of Supplementary Benefit: Working Paper E; Analysis of DHSS Records of Single Payment Decisions*, Policy Studies Institute: London.

Blau, P.M. (1955), *The Dynamics of Bureaucracy*, Chicago.

Blume, O. (1970), 'Die Position älterer Menschen in der Leistungsgesellschaft', in Deutscher Verein für öffentliche und private Fürsorge, *Die Fürsorge im sozialen Rechtsstaat*, Frankfurt, pp. 537-546.

Blunn, C., Small, M. (1984), 'The Anomalies of Attendance Allowance', *Community Care*, Vol. 16, pp. 18-20.

Bradshaw, J., Lawton, D. (1982), 'Utilisation of the Family Fund', *Child: care, health and development*, Vol. 8, pp. 227-237.

Briggs, E., Rees, A. M. (1980), *Supplementary Benefits and the Consumer*, Bedford Square Press: London.

Buckland, S., Dawson, P. (1989), 'Household Claiming Behaviour', *Social Policy and Administration*, Vol. 23, No. 1, pp. 60-71.

Bujard, O., Lange, U. (1978), *Theorie und Praxis der Sozialhilfe. Zur Situation der Einkommensschwachen alten Menschen,* Eine Untersuchung des Instituts für Sozialforschung und Gesellschaftspolitik: Stuttgart.

Bijsterveldt, Q.M., van (1975), *Een sociale voorziening en haar cliënten: een onderzoek naar de bijstandsverlening aan vrouwelijke gezinshoofden,* Proefschrift, Katholieke Hogeschool Tilburg: Tilburg.

Cantillon, B. (1992), *De verzadigde social zekerheid,* Centrum voor Sociaal Beleid, Universiteit Antwerpen UFSIA: Antwerpen.

Catrice-Lorey, A. (1976), 'Inegualités d'accès aux systèmes de protection sociale et pauvreté culturelle', *Revue Française des Affaires Sociales,* Vol. 4.

CBS (1985), 'Grote verschillen tussen bevolkingscategorieen in het beroep op de eenmalige uitkering 1982', *Sociaal- economische Maandstatistiek,* No. 7, pp. 6-9.

Cohen, R. (1983), *Able to Claim? A Report of Work with Occupational Therapists and Physiotherapists to Improve Take-up of Disability Benefits,* Islington Peoples Rights: London.

Corden, A. (1981), *The Process of Claiming FIS: Background Paper II- Review of Previous Studies on the Take-up of Means-tested Benefits and their Relevance to a Study of FIS-take-up,* SPRU, University of York: York.

Corden, A. (1983), *Taking up a Means-tested Benefit: the Process of Claiming Family Income Supplement,* Department of Health and Social Security, HMSO: London.

Corden, A. (1987), *Disappointed Applicants. A study of Unsuccessful Claims for Family Income Supplement,* Avebury: Aldershot.

Corden, A. (1995), *New Perspectives on Take-up: a Literature Review,* HMSO: London

Corden, A., Craig, P. (1991), *Perceptions of Family Credit,* HMSO: London.

Cousins, M., Charleton, B. (1991), *Benefit Take-up: a Report of a Benefit Take-up Project in Dublin,* Free Legal Advice Centres: Dublin.

Craig, P. (1991), 'Costs and Benefits: a Review of Research on Take-up of Income-related Benefits', *The Journal of Social Policy,* Vol. 20, No. 4, pp. 537-565.

Davies, C., Ritchie, J. (1988), *Tipping the Balance: a Study of Non-take-up of Benefits in an Inner City Area,* DHSS Research Report No. 16, HMSO: London.

Deacon, A., Bradshaw, J. (1983), *Reserved for the Poor: the Mean-test in British Social Policy,* Robertson: Oxford.

DHSS (1983), *The Take-up of Supplementary Benefits: Characteristics of Nonclaimants,* Department of Health and Social Security: London.

Dick, E. (1986), 'Use of Simulation Techniques in Developing a Housing Allowance Allocation System', in Orcutt, G., Merz, J., Quinke, H. (eds.), *Microanalytic Simulation Models to Support Social and Financial Policy,* Elsevier: Amsterdam, pp. 155-167.

Drazga, L., Upp, M., Reno, V. (1982), 'Low-Income Aged: Eligibility and Participation in SSI', *Social Security Bulletin,* Vol. 45, No. 5, pp. 28-3.

Driessens, K. (1989), *Het niet-gebruik van uitkeringen van de sociale zekerheid en van de bijstand: op zoek naar wat niet is,* Departement Politieke en Sociale Wetenschappen, Universitaire Instelling Antwerpen: Antwerpen.

Duclos, J.Y. (1992), *The Take-up of State Benefits: an Application to Supplementary Benefits in Britain Using the FES*, Discussion Paper WSP/71, WSP/STICERD/LSE, London School of Economics: London.

Dumont, J.-P. (1987), *La Coordination des Aides Multiples et la Lutte contre la Pauvreté*, Centre National d'Etudes Supérieures de Sécurité Sociale: Paris.

Falkingham, F. (1985), *Take-up of Benefits: a Literature Review*, Benefits Research Unit Review Paper 1:85, Department of Social Administration, University of Nottingham: Nottingham.

Filet, B.C. (1974), *Kortsluiting met de bureaucratie*, Samson: Alphen a.d. Rijn

Fry and Stark (1993), *The Take-up of Means-tested Benefits, 1984-90*, Institute for Fiscal Studies: London.

Geissler, H. (1976), *Die neue Soziale Frage*, Herder Verlag: Freiburg i. Breisgau

Gough, I. (1994), *Means-tested Benefits in a Comparative Perspective*, The Richard Titmuss Memorial Lecture, Hebrew University of Jerusalem, May 31, 1994.

Graham, J. (1984), *Take-up of FIS: Knowledge, Attitudes and Experience, Claimants and Nonclaimants*, Social Research Division, PPRU, Department of Finance and Personnel: Stormont.

Gustafsson, B. (1987), 'Som et isberg? Om underutnyttjande av socialbidrag', *Nordisk Sosialt Arbeid*, No. 3, pp. 43-51.

Handler, J., Hollingsworth, E. J. (1971), *The Deserving Poor: a Study of Welfare Administration*, Markham Publ. Company: Chicago.

Hartmann, H. (1981), *Sozialhilfebedürftigkeit und 'Dunkelziffer der Armut'*, Kohlhammer: Stuttgart.

Hartmann, H. (1985), 'Armut trotz Sozialhilfe. Zur Nichtinanspruchnahme von Sozialhilfe in der Bundesrepublik', in Leibfried, Stephan, Tennstedt, Florian (eds.), *Politik der Armut und die Spaltung des Sozialstaats*, Suhrkamp: Frankfurt am Main, pp. 169-189.

Hauser, R., Cremer-Schafer, H., Nouvertné, U. (1981), *Armut, Niedrigeinkommen und Unterversorgung in der Bundesrepublik Deutschland*, Campus Verlag: Frankfurt, New York.

Hauser, R., Hübinger, W. (1993), *Arme unter uns; Teil 1: Ergebnisse und Konsequenzen der Caritas-Armutuntersuchung*, Deutscher Caritasverband, Lambertus Verlag: Freiburg im Breisgau.

Howe, L.E.A. (1985), 'The "Deserving" and the "Undeserving": Practice in an Urban Local Security Office', *Journal of Social Policy*, Vol. 14, No. 1, pp. 49-72.

In 't Groen, J., Konings, M. (1989), *Niet-gebruik van sociale zekerheid onder Tilburgse bijstandscliënten*, Scriptie, Vakgroep Sociale Zekerheidswetenschap, KUB: Tilburg.

Kerr, S. (1983), *Making Ends Meet: an Investigation into the Non-claming of Supplementary Pensions*, Bedford Square Press: London.

Klanberg, F. (1979), 'Einkommensarmut 1969 und 1973 bei Anlegung verschiedener Standards', *Sozialer Fortschritt*, Vol. 6, pp. 127-131.

Knechtel, E. (1960), 'Die Zahl der einkommensschwachen kinderreichen Familien in der Bundesrepublik', *Soziale Welt*, pp. 330-339.

Knegt, R. (1986), *Regels en redelijkheid in de bijstandsverlening: participerende observatie bij een Sociale Dienst.* Proefschrift, Universiteit van Amsterdam: Amsterdam.

Konsumenten Kontakt (1989), *Hoe bijzonder is de bijzondere bijstand?*, Den Haag.

Konsumenten Kontakt (1990), *Profijt van het gemeentelijk minima-beleid?*, Den Haag.

Kramer Gordon, L. (1975), 'Bureaucratic Competence and Success in Dealing with Public Bureaucracies', *Social Problems*, Vol. 23, pp. 197-208.

Leibfried, S. (1976), 'Armutspotential und Sozialhilfe in der Bundesrepublik: zum Prozess des Filterns von Anspruchen auf Sozialhilfe', *Kritische Justiz*, pp. 376-393.

Lewis, T. (1975), *Haringey Rent Allowance Project; Second Interim Report*, Sociological Research Branch, Department of Environment: London.

Lister, R. (1974), *Take-up of Means-tested Benefits*, Poverty Research Series 18, Child Poverty Action Group: London.

Lipsky, M. (1980), *Street Level Bureaucracy: Dilemmas of the Individual in Public Services*, Russell Sage Foundation: New York.

Lynes, T. (1972), 'Welfare Men', *New Society*, September issue.

Mashaw, J.L. (1983), *Bureaucratic Justice: Managing Social Security Disability Claims*, Yale University Press: New Haven.

Menefee, J. A., Edwards, B., Schieber, S. J. (1981), 'Analysis of Nonparticipation in the SSI Program', *Social Security Bulletin*, Vol. 44, No. 6, pp. 3-21.

Millar, J., Cooke, K. (1984), *A Study of the Take-up of One-parent Benefit in Hackney*, Department of Health and Social Security: London.

Minkman, M., Slot, J. (1991), *Inkomens- en budgetonderzoek.* O+S, het Amsterdamse Bureau voor Onderzoek en Statistiek: Amsterdam.

Mullenders P. (1993), *Minimaal gebruik I: omvang van het niet-gebruik*, Gemeente Utrecht: Utrecht.

Nicaise, I., Cossey, H. (eds.) (1987), *Methoden van studiefinanciering (3 volumes).* Katholieke Universiteit Leuven: Leuven.

Oorschot, W. van, Kolkhuis Tanke, P. (1989), *Niet-gebruik van sociale zekerheid; feiten, theorieën, onderzoeksmethoden*, COSZ-series, 16: The Hague.

Oorschot, W. van, Konings, M. (1990), *Het niet-gebruik van de Individuele Huursubsidie: de omvang*, Working Paper, KUB: Tilburg.

Oorschot, W. van (1991), 'Non Take-up of Social Security Benefits in Europe', *The Journal of European Social Policy*, Vol. 1, No. 1, pp. 15-30.

Oorschot, W. van, Schell, J. (1991), 'Means-testing in Europe: a Growing Concern', in Adler, M., Bell, C., Clasen, J., Sinfield, A. (eds.), *The Sociology of Social Security*, Edinburg University Press: Edinburgh.

Oorschot, W. van (1992), *Onbenutte Rechten I: het niet-gebruik van sociale zekerheid onder Rotterdamse bijstandsontvangers*, Dienst Sociale Zaken en Werkgelegenheid: Rotterdam.

Oorschot, W. van (1995), *Realizing Rights: a Multi-level Approach to Non-take-up of Means-tested Benefits*, Avebury: London.

Purnell, C. (1973), *The Prospect for Rent Allowances*, Wandsworth Peoples Rights.

Richardson, A., Naidoo, J. (1978), *The Take-up of Supplementary Benefits: a Report on a Survey of Claimants*, Chelsea College, University of London: London.

Ringeling, A. (1981), 'The Passivity of the Administration', *Policy and Politics*, Vol. 9, No. 3, pp. 295-309.

Ritchie, J., England, J. (1984), *Unclaimed Benefits in Hackney*, Paper ESRC Workshop, ESRC.

Ritchie, J., Matthews, A. (1982), *Take-up of Rent Allowance; an in Depth Study*, Social and Community Planning Research: London.

Ritchie, J. (1988), *Income Related Benefits: the Causes of Non take-up; a Review of Recent Research Evidence*, Social and Community Planning Research: London.

SBC (1978), *Take-up of Supplementary Benefits*, Supplementary Benefits Administration Papers No. 7, HMSO: London.

Smolenaars, E. (1991), *Niet-gebruiks aanwijzingen: een explorerend onderzoek naar de oorzaken van het niet-gebruik van sociale zekerheid*, Gemeentelijke Sociale Dienst: Rotterdam.

Taylor-Gooby, P. (1974), *Means-Tests and Social Policy*, M.Phil. Thesis, University of York: York.

Townsend, P. (1979), *Poverty in the United Kingdom: a Survey of Household Resources and Standards of Living*, Penguin Books: Middlesex.

Urban Systems (1981), *SSI Aged: a Pilot Study of Eligibility and Participation in the Supplemental Security Income Program*, Urban Systems Research and Engineering: Cambridge, Massachusetts.

Vanlerenberghe, P. (1992), *RMI: le pari de l'insertion*, TOME 1, Commission Nationale d'Evaluation du Revenu Minimum d'Insertion, La Documentation Francaise: Paris.

Vincent, J., Ashworth, K., Walker, R. (1991), *Taking Account of Time in the Targeting and Administration of Benefits*, Centre for Research in Social Policy (CRSP), Loughborough University of Technology.

Visser, P. M. (1992), *Duurloop voor doven; onderzoek naar de doventolkvoorziening in Nederland*, Rapport 92/2, Sociale Verzekeringsraad: Zoetermeer.

Vos, J.G. (1990), *Ongekende rechten: potentieel gebruik van bijzondere bijstandsverstrekkingen en minimafondsen*, Gemeentelijke Sociale Dienst: Den Haag.

Vos, J.G. (1991), *Recht hebben en recht krijgen: een studie over beleidsvrijheid, niet-gebruik van rechten en verantwoord ambtelijk handelen*, Vermande: Lelystad.

Walker, R. (with A. Hedges) (1985), *Housing Benefit: the Experience of Implementation*, Housing Centre Trust: London.

Whyley, C., Huby, M. (1993), *Take-up and the Social Fund: Applying the Concept of Take-up to a Discretionary Benefit*, SPRU, University of York: York.

Zedlewski, S., Meyer, J. (1987), *The Supplemental Security Income Program: its Role in Alleviating Poverty*, The Urban Institute: Washington, D.C.

Acknowledgement

This article is based on research funded by the Dutch Ministry of Social Affairs and Employment, the Science Shop, and the city councils of Rotterdam and Nijmegen.

Part Two
Methodological issues

Perceptions of the minimum standard of living in Belgium: Is there a consensus?

Karel Van den Bosch

1 Introduction

In this chapter, I will study answers to the following survey question: 'Here you have a list with 20 goods, services, and activities. Which of these do you think are necessary, in the sense that every family (or person) should be able to afford them, and that nobody should have to live without them?' It is assumed that the answers to this question provide indicators of people's perception of the minimum standard of living. This contribution will focus on the issue of whether there is a consensus on this matter, or, in other words, to which extent people agree or disagree in their views about what goods, services, or activities are necessary for living in an affluent society such as Belgium.

The chapter is organised as follows. In the next section, the notion of a consensual minimum standard of living is elucidated in the context of the measurement of poverty. In the third section, the basic results are presented about how many respondents perceive which items as necessities. Section four looks at the relation between individual possessions and perceptions of necessity. In sections five and six the question is considered whether different groups and categories have different views about necessities. In section seven we look at the relationships between perceptions of necessity of different items. Section eight is about the total number of items classed as necessities. In section nine the changes over time in individual perceptions of necessity are studied. Section ten concludes, reconsidering the question: is there a consensus among the Belgian population about the minimum standard of living.

Data are from the 1985 and 1988 waves of the Belgian Socio-Economic Panel, a household panel survey conducted by the Centre for Social Policy at the University of Antwerp. The sample is representative for the population of private households in Belgium. Total sample size was 6471 in 1985 and 3779 in 1988. For more information see Van den Bosch et al. (1993).

2 A consensual minimum standard of living

An important, if not the main problem in the measurement of poverty is how to identify the poor. Whether poverty is measured in the income space, in the space of actual goods and services consumed, or on any other dimension, one always needs a minimum standard of some kind below which persons, families, or households are regarded as poor. A number of methods have been proposed in the literature (see Callan and Nolan 1991, Van den Bosch 1993, or Gustafsson 1995 for overviews). None of these methods is completely satisfactory or has gained full acceptance.

One possible way to identify minimum standards is the so-called consensual approach, where a sample of individuals from the general population is asked about their views on this point. The consensual method that has been used most often is to ask respondents in sample surveys how much income a family of a given type needs in order to reach a particular level of living. Probably the most well known question of this kind is the so-called 'get-along' or Gallup question: 'What is the smallest amount of money a family of four needs each week to get along in this community?' (Rainwater 1974, 1990). A problem with this kind of question is that people may have difficulties in translating a certain standard of living into an income level. For this reason, Mack and Lansley (1985) have devised a method to identify a minimum standard of living in a direct way, by asking a sample of people to indicate which items of a list of goods and activities were 'necessities' for living in Britain in the 1980s.

Following in Mack and Lansley's footsteps, the 'necessities' question with a similar list of items was used in a later survey in Britain in 1990 (Gordon et al. 1994) and also in surveys carried out in Denmark (Mack and Lansley 1985), Finland (see the chapter by Kangas and Ritakallio), Germany (Andreß and Lipsmeier 1995), Ireland (Callan et al. 1989), Sweden (Halleröd 1994a, 1994b, see also the chapter by Halleröd) and Belgium (Deleeck et al. 1991). In this chapter, I will look only at results for Belgium.

Consensual methods are to be distinguished from what could be called *subjective* methods, where people are asked questions about their *own* income or standard of living. The latter are sometimes referred to as 'consensual' as well, but in my view this is misleading. While the consensual methods, at least according to the most straightforward interpretation, presuppose that a social consensus on a minimum income or standard of living exists, this is not true for subjective methods. The distinction between consensual and subjective methods corresponds to the one Barry (1990, pp. 12-13) makes between publicly-oriented and privately-oriented evaluations. The latter have oneself or one's family as their object, while the former have everyone or a large group such as a country as their object. It seems to me that one can properly talk about a consensus only in the context of publicly-oriented evaluations, simply because privately-oriented judgments by different persons are about different things. You and I can agree or disagree about what income is needed to, say, make ends meet in our community. If we agree, there is consensus. However, if I state how much income I think I need, while you say how much income you need, then there is neither agreement nor disagreement, because we are talking about different matters. Consequently, in the latter case, it is beside the point to ask whether there is consensus.

An important issue is, of course, whether the distinction between publicly-oriented evaluations and privately-oriented evaluations is actually recognised by respondents when answering consensual or subjective survey questions. While this cannot be ascertained directly, the recorded answers can provide indications. In particular, because publicly-oriented evaluations are to be made with a larger reference group in mind than privately-oriented ones, and thus from a more general point of view, one would expect them to be less influenced by the personal circumstances of respondents.

In this contribution, I will therefore look at two conditions that must be met before we can speak about a consensus on a minimum standard of living. In the first place, respondents should take a publicly-oriented point of view when answering the 'necessities' question, i.e. they should take a more general point of view than when they are answering questions about their wishes and needs. Secondly, people should actually agree (more or less) in their judgments about the necessities of living in an affluent modern society such as Belgium.

3 Basic results

Table 1 gives the main results, showing the percentages of respondens who classed an item as a necessity, as well as the percentage of people that actually had the item. The most important result is that a wide range of items are regarded as necessities by a large majority of respondents in Belgium.

Table 1
Percentage of all respondents regarding item as necessity and percentage actually possessing it, Belgium, 1985 and 1988

Item	1985 Necessity	1985 Possession	1988 Necessity	1988 Possession
Heating to warm living areas of the home if it's cold	95	95	97	97
Indoor toilet (not shared with another household)	97	97	97	95
Damp-free home	97	94	98	92
Bath or shower (not shared with another household)	93	90	94	90
A warm water-proof coat	97	97	98	96
Two pairs of all-weather shoes	92	94	90	91
A meal with meat, chicken or fish every second day	94	97	94	95
Three meals a day for children*	98	99	97	97
To be able to save	83	58	85	60
Own bedroom for every child over 10 of different sex	94	93	91	86
Refrigerator	93	98	96	97
Washing machine	86	88	92	89
Vacuum cleaner	-	-	80	90
A holiday away from home for one week a year, not with relatives	56	50	57	50
Leisure equipment for children, e.g. sports equipment, or bicycle*	91	95	84	91
A colour television	39	83	55	87
Central heating in the house	40	62	45	64
A telephone	51	74	64	83
A daily newspaper	34	51	31	46
A car	46	72	58	76
A video-recorder	-	-	8	24

* Items for families with children only

Source: Belgian Socio-Economic Panel, waves 1985 (N=6471) and 1988 (N=3779)

There is virtual unanimity about the necessity of heating, an indoor toilet, a damp-free home, and a bath. But also, a large majority regard labour-saving household goods (such as a washing machine and a refrigerator) as 'necessities'. As Mack and Lansley (1985, p. 55-56) remark, this partly reflects 'shifting standards and expectations; but it also reflects the fact that, in a practical sense, items that become customary also become necessary because other aspects of life are planned and built on the very fact that these items are customary.'

We also observe that for the items regarded by the majority as necessities, possession is widespread. Conversely, in general, the fewer people have an item, the less often it is seen as a necessity. This, as Mack and Lansley remark, comes as no surprise; most poverty studies are based on the assumption 'that those styles of living that are widespread are equivalent to those that are socially approved, encouraged or expected' (1985, p. 67). But there are some interesting exceptions, which show that other factors come into play. A holiday is classed as a necessity by relatively many respondents, given the proportion who say they actually go on holiday. The discrepancy is even more glaring for the item 'being able to save': while more than 80% of all respondents indicate that saving is a necessity, the number of respondents that actually do save is much smaller. Conversely, a (colour) television is present in a large majority of households, but only slightly more than half, or even fewer, of all respondents regard it as a necessity. To a certain extent, these exceptions may be explained by price differences. A holiday is rather expensive, while a television is fairly cheap (when the purchasing cost is properly discounted; cf. Gordon et al. 1994, pp. 19-21). For a poor family, it makes sense to buy a cheap 'luxury', if the price of a necessity is so prohibitively high, that it would not be able to afford the latter, even if it would forego the luxury. (Indeed, 'holiday' is one of the few items which large proportions of the respondents say they do not have, because they cannot afford it; Deleeck et.al. 1991, p. 720.) But, especially regarding the items 'saving' and 'a television', it seems that moral considerations are also of importance. In any case, it is clear that people's judgements about necessities are not just a reflection of what is customary.

The replication of the survey in 1988 allows us to observe how perceptions of necessity evolve over time. Respondents show a clear tendency to consider more, rather than less items as necessary. There are five items which were regarded as a necessity by fewer respondents in 1988 compared to 1985, but the changes are small (less than five percentage points) except for the item 'leisure equipment for children' (minus seven percentage points). For a few items large increases are recorded in the proportions of people regarding them as necessities: 'a colour television', 'a telephone' and 'a car'.

These changes are difficult to interpret. A general increase in the number of respondents considering any item to be necessary was to be expected, as average real income of households increased during the period of time passed between the two surveys. As Gordon et al. (1994, p. 67) state: 'The relative theory of poverty predicts that, if a society gets richer, the number of people who perceive common possessions and activities as necessary will increase.' But this theory cannot explain why there is so much variation in the changes in perceptions of necessity. Where the average perception of the necessity of an item has considerably changed, there has in most cases been no comparable change in the number of people actually having the item. In some cases, perceptions of necessity may have been in the process of catching up with increases in possession rates that occurred before the year of the first survey. This may be true for the items 'refrigerator', 'colour television', 'telephone' and 'a car'. Some of the findings may be data quirks with no real significance. Nevertheless, the results show that perceptions of necessity can change considerably in a fairly short span of time.

4 Individual possessions and perceptions of necessity

Which factors influence people's perceptions of necessities? This can be an interesting question in itself, but it becomes also important for the validity of a minimum standard derived from these perceptions. If disaggregated results were to show that great differences of opinion exist across different social groups and categories in society classing items as necessities, it would be difficult to maintain that such a minimum standard reflects a social consensus. We have seen that at the aggregate level the extent of ownership is fairly closely related to the number of people classing an item as a necessity. It seems reasonable to expect, therefore, that a similar relation applies to the individual level.

I look not only at differences between those who have an item, and those who do not, but also subdivide the 'have nots' into those that did not want the item, and those that could not afford it (cf. Table 2). It turns out that people who have an item are the most likely to class it as a necessity. The next group most likely to classify an item as a necessity are those who don't have it, because they can't afford it. Those who do not have an item and do not want it are the least likely to regard it as a necessity. For all items except one ('colour television' in 1985; 'video recorder' in 1988), the majority of those who have it class it as a necessity.

Table 2
Percentage regarding item as necessity by personal possession of item

Item	1985 Have	1985 Don't have can't afford	1985 Don't have don't want	1988 Have	1988 Don't have can't afford	1988 Don't have don't want
Waterproof coat	99	(89)	[45]	99	[69]	(54)
Damp-free home	99	94	[80]	99	85	89
Indoor toilet	99	75	(58)	99	[51]	(69)
Heating in living room	97	(70)	46	98	[69]	(65)
Refrigerator	95	[60]	(38)	98	[57]	(44)
Meal with meat etc.	97	(72)	(23)	97	[58]	(20)
Bath or shower	97	79	51	98	(71)	58
Washing machine	92	60	40	98	(67)	44
Waterproof shoes	96	69	29	95	54	31
Regular saving	93	78	48	93	75	64
Telephone	63	31	13	72	29	22
Car	59	21	9	71	25	15
Holiday	78	43	24	78	43	28
Colour TV	45	16	8	60	21	11
Central heating	55	30	10	62	21	14
Newspaper	58	23	7	58	12	5
Vacuum cleaner	-	-	-	85	34	15
Video-recorder	-	-	-	21	5	3
Three meals a day*	98	-	-	99	-	[60]
Separate bedrooms*	96	(77)	(42)	95	(74)	81
Leisure goods*	93	(66)	[37]	90	(51)	(33)

Notes:

* Items for families with children only
() Figures based on less than 100 cases
[] Figures based on less than 50 cases
- Less than 20 cases in cell

Source: Belgian Socio-Economic Panel, waves 1985 (N=6471) and 1988 (N=3779)

Among respondents who do not have an item because they cannot afford it, there are majorities classing items as necessities for 12 out of 19 items in 1985 and 12 out of 21 items in 1988. Within the group who did not have an item and did not want it, 3 items in 1985, and 6 items in 1988 were regarded by the majority as a necessity. It should be noted that for each item these groups are composed of different persons. In spite of these differences, there is roughly the same ranking in all groups: all items classed as a necessity by at least 50% of the 'don't haves' were on the top of the 'necessities' list, and were regarded by at least 93% of the 'haves' as a necessity. These results are similar to those reported by Mack and Lansley (1985) for Britain.

Two important conclusions can be drawn from these results. In the first place, a person's own situation, and her own personal desires are important for her judgments about the necessities of modern living. Nevertheless, they do not determine these judgments. This works in two directions. On the one hand, many of those who 'could not do without' a car or a telephone, do not regard these items as necessities, in the sense that no one should have to do without them. On the other hand, for a range of items, a majority, or at least a large minority, of those who do not have it and do not want it for themselves, still class it as a necessity. This, as Mack and Lansley (1985, p. 72) remark, may indicate a degree of selfishness on the part of the first group, but it is not inconsistent. It shows that people distinguish between what they want for themselves, and what they think are needs from a general, public, perspective. As argued above, only if respondents make such a distinction, and answer the 'necessities' question from the public perspective, is it appropriate to say that a minimum standard derived from these answers reflects a social consensus on these matters.

A second conclusion is that a person's subjective attitude towards an item (i.e. how much he or she wants it for him- or herself) is important for his judgment about its necessity, independently of the objective circumstance whether he or she possesses it or not. This is important because it follows that it is less likely that what people perceive as necessity is directly related to their actual living standard. If persons with a high standard of living regarded many more items as necessities than those with a low living standard, it would be more difficult to speak of a consensus about the needs of present-day living.

5 Background characteristics and perceptions of necessity: Bivariate results

An obviously important question is whether different social groups and categories have different views about necessities. I have looked at family composition, age, education, socio-professional status, household income, and region. The results are shown in Table 3. For the items 'waterproof coat', 'damp-free home', 'indoor-toilet', 'heating in living quarters', 'refrigerator', 'meal with meat etc.', 'waterproof shoes', and 'video-recorder', and for those items specific for families with children, the differences were so small that it did not seem worthwhile to report them (almost everyone in every social group regards these items as necessities, except for the video-recorder, which almost no one classes as a necessity).

Overall, *family composition* and *age* seem to have the greatest impact on judgments about necessities. Single elderly people regard a bath or shower, a car, and a holiday as necessities relatively less often. Single people - elderly or not - attach less importance to a washing machine. Conversely, elderly persons - either couples or single - more often than younger persons say that a telephone, a colour TV, and a newspaper are necessities. On the other hand a car is classed as a necessity by couples with children more often than by persons in other family types.

Judgments about necessity vary according to *education* for only three items: the higher a person's education, the more inclined he or she is to class a holiday and a car as necessities, and the less often a colour TV is regarded as a necessity. It seems that there is no direct bivariate relationship between education and the perception of a newspaper as a necessity.

The higher a respondent's *socio-professional status* (occupation or former occupation of head of household) the more often he or she regards a holiday, a telephone, a car, and central heating as necessities. The opinions of the (small) self-employed and the white-collar or senior white-collar levels tend to be alike, though the former appear to attach more importance to a telephone. People in the employer / liberal category are relatively more prone to regard a newspaper as a necessity. These findings contrast with those for Britain in 1990, where persons with more education and from higher social classes are considerably *less* likely to consider some items as necessities (Gordon et al. 1994, pp. 184-193).

Table 3
Differences in perceptions of neccessities*

	Bath or shower		Washing machine		Regular saving		Holiday		Telephone	
	'85	'88	'85	'88	'85	'88	'85	'88	'85	'88
Household type										
Single elderly	-15	-17	-18	-20	-8	-9	-18	-18	+8	+19
non-elderly	-3	-7	-28	-23	-7	-5	+5	-3	-	-
Couple elderly	-6	-6	-6	-5	-	-	-7	-8	+15	+20
non-elderly	-	-	-6	-6	-	-	-	-	-	-
with children	*97*	*97*	*92*	*97*	*87*	*86*	*59*	*60*	*49*	*59*
One-parent	-	-	-	-	-9	-9	-	-	+1	+6
Other	-	-	-	-	-	-	-8	-3	+4	+11
Age (head)										
16 - 29	-	-	-10	-9	-5	-1	-2	-11	-11	-14
30 - 49	*97*	*97*	*90*	*94*	*87*	*85*	*61*	*62*	*49*	*59*
50 - 64	-	-	-	-	-	-	-	-	+6	+10
65 - 74	-6	-5	-5	-2	-	-	-9	-7	+9	+18
75 +	-15	-18	-14	-18	-7	-8	-22	-25	+12	+19
Education (head)										
only primary	*90*	*88*	*89*	*89*	*86*	*82*	*47*	*44*	*51*	*70*
lower secondary	+5	+7	-1	+5	-	-	+6	+13	-4	-10
higher secondary	+7	+9	-	-	0	+5	+15	+18	+1	-9
higher	+7	+10	-6	+1	-	-	+22	+22	+8	-4
Status (head)										
Blue collar	*92*	*92*	*89*	*93*	*87*	*86*	*49*	*50*	*44*	*58*
White collar	+4	+5	-	-	-	-	+12	+12	+7	0
Senior white c.	+5	+6	-	-	-5	0	+18	+17	+13	+8
Self-employed	-	-	-	-	-4	-5	+10	+10	+20	+18
Employer	+5	+7	-	-	-6	-3	+22	+17	+23	+18
Income										
25,000 BF or less	-13	-19	-16	-15	-10	-9	-13	-17	+5	+4
25,000-40,000	-	-	-5	-5	-	-	-3	-9	-	-
40,000-60,000	*97*	*96*	*90*	*94*	*87*	*85*	*55*	*58*	*48*	*62*
60,000-80,000	-	-	-	-	-	-	+6	+3	+6	-1
80,000 or more	-	-	-	-	-	-	+12	+5	+11	+5
Region										
Flanders	*96*	*94*	*87*	*91*	*90*	*87*	*57*	*58*	*51*	*64*
Wallonia	-	-	+6	+3	-9	-6	-9	-9	-	-
Brussels	-	-	-22	-11	-16	-10	+21	+21	+10	+6

* Figures in italics refer to reference category of respective variable. They indicate the percentage in that category perceiving the item as necessary. Other figures show the deviation (in % points) in the particular category, relative to the reference category. Deviation is not shown, when it is smaller than 5% both in 1985 and 1988. The reference category is always the modal category (i.e. the one with the largest number of cases).

Car		Colour TV		Central heating		Newspaper		Vacuum cleaner	Number of cases in category**	
'85	'88	'85	'88	'85	'88	'85	'88	'88	'85	'88
-42	-45	+8	+16	-14	-2	0	+8	-6	605	322
-18	-16	-	-	-5	-8	-	-	-7	453	164
-23	-18	+16	+26	-	-	+18	+27	+7	604	431
-6	-5	-	-	-	-	+5	+9	-	1207	655
57	*68*	*36*	*48*	*43*	*46*	*32*	*24*	*79*	2696	1631
-22	-8	-	-	0	-8	-8	-1	-6	204	102
-8	-6	+10	+13	-5	+4	+8	+14	-	512	344
-	-	-9	-8	-4	-8	-3	-7	-9	811	304
56	*67*	*36*	*46*	*42*	*44*	*31*	*24*	*79*	2497	1494
-7	-9	+10	+15	+1	+5	+7	+14	-	1680	1003
-24	-19	+12	+25	-5	+5	+11	+21	+6	793	522
-37	-39	+11	+17	-8	-2	+8	+17	-7	484	326
39	*50*	*49*	*66*	*34*	*43*	*35*	*36*	*75*	2059	1069
+8	+8	-6	-8	+6	0	-1	-7	+6	1517	947
+15	+15	-10	-18	+12	+6	0	-7	+9	1491	778
+17	+15	-17	-31	+9	+4	+3	-6	+3	1116	663
43	*57*	*42*	*59*	*34*	*39*	*32*	*29*	*77*	2580	1260
+6	+5	-5	-12	+10	+8	-	-	-	1896	858
+10	+4	-8	-15	+13	+9	+6	+3	-	512	411
+9	+6	-	-	+11	+9	+7	+6	-	960	457
+15	+13	-6	-10	+18	+23	+15	+13	+8	155	115
-29	-38	-	-	-11	-7	-	-	-12	784	352
-15	-17	+2	+9	-	-	-	-	-	1492	701
52	*65*	*39*	*55*	*39*	*43*	*34*	*32*	*80*	1750	966
+5	+3	0	-5	+7	+5	-	-	-	1251	825
+7	0	-1	-8	+8	+12	-	-	-	1004	805
49	*59*	*43*	*57*	*41*	*48*	*37*	*34*	*85*	3632	2290
-6	-2	-10	-4	-8	-10	-6	-4	-18	2068	1199
-	-	-4	-11	+15	+1	-2	-12	-	581	160

** Number of cases for item with largest number of missings, i.e., the number reported equals the minimum number of cases. Figures for 1988 are unweighted.

Source: Belgian Socio-Economic Panel, waves 1985 and 1988

Variations in perceptions of necessity by *household income* seem to fall into two distinct patterns. Where an item is classed as a necessity by a large majority - bath, washing machine, saving, vacuum cleaner - it is only the lowest income group which differs from the rest. For other items - holiday, car, and central heating - the proportion of respondents judging it to be a necessity increases with household income up until a much higher level of income, or there is no clear pattern whatsoever (viz. telephone, colour TV, and a newspaper).

People in the *region* of Wallonia are less likely than those living in Flanders to consider a range of items as necessities; the only exception is a washing machine. This finding is partly but not wholly explained by lower possession rates in Wallonia for most items (see also next section).

The patterns of differences in judgments about necessities described in the preceding paragraphs remain more or less the same from 1985 to 1988 for most items. The interesting exceptions are a telephone and a colour TV. For both items, the overall proportion of respondents classing these items as necessities has increased considerably. But what is remarkable is that this increase is much stronger among the elderly than among the middle-aged, even though the elderly in 1985 were already more inclined to perceive a telephone and a colour TV as necessities. It contrasts with the increasing number of people who say that a car is a necessity, where the similarly strong increase seems to have been fairly uniform across social categories.

6 Background characteristics and perceptions of necessity: Multivariate results

Of course, the bivariate relationships shown in Table 3 may be misleading, in the sense that an apparent relationship between perceptions of necessity and, e.g., education may in fact be due to a relationship between these perceptions and age and the fact that people in older age brackets tend to have had less formal education. For this reason multivariate analyses have been carried out. Given the binary nature of the dependent variable, logistic regression is an appropriate technique (cf. Aldrich and Nelson 1984). A multivariate model also enables us to examine whether differences in views about necessities across social categories only reflect differences in patterns of personal possession and personal wants (which, as we saw above, have an important effect on perceptions of necessity), or are independent from the latter.

All background variables shown in Table 3 were used in the logistic regression models. Because of their strong interrelatedness, household type and age of head were combined into one variable.[1] Household income was entered as a continuous variable in logarithmic form. Possession status was coded a follows: 1) has; 2) has not, can't afford; 3) has not, doesn't want; 4) has not, no answer on can't afford / doesn't want question (about 15-20% of the respondents who did not have an item did not answer the latter question). Logistic regressions were run for all items in Table 3, except for 'regular saving' and 'central heating', since the differences in views about the necessity of these items did not seem particularly interesting.

The chi-square statistics for the variables in the model are given in Table 4. Chi-square statistics are mainly used as test-statistics in order to evaluate the hypothesis that a given variable has a significant effect on the dependent variable, as against the null hypothesis that there are no differences (i.e. effects of all categories are zero).[2] It is therefore equivalent to the F-statistic in multivariate regression (Aldrich and Nelson 1984, pp. 59-61). Since the chi-square statistic is directly proportional to the size of the coefficient estimates, and inversely proportional to their standard errors (which are themselves functions of the number of cases in the respective categories), it can, very roughly, be interpreted as the gain in the predictive ability of the model, due to the inclusion of the particular variable. However, they are certainly not comparable across different equations.

In the discussion below I will only consider effects that are found to be statistically significant both in 1985 and 1988. Since there is generally no reason why an effect should change across these years, differences in chi-square statistics between 1985 and 1988 are probably due to either the larger sample size in 1985, or to peculiar data anomalies.

If we look first at the models without possession status, we can see that in the multivariate models household type (incorporating age) has a significant effect on perceptions as a necessity of all the items that are analysed, except for 'bath or shower'. Education is found to have an independent effect on views about the necessity of a holiday, a colour TV, and a washing machine. The direction of the effect is the same as in the bivariate table: the higher the educational level, the more likely a person is, ceteris paribus, to regard a holiday as a necessity, and the less prone he or she is to perceive a colour TV and a washing machine as necessities. Socio-professional category exerts an independent effect only on the perception of the necessity of a telephone. Self-employed persons are, ceteris paribus, more likely than others to say that a telephone is a necessity. Income has an influence on judgments about the necessity of a bath or shower, a holiday, a telephone, and a car; all effects are in the expected direction.

Table 4
Results of logistic regression of perceptions of necessity of various items: Chi-square statistics for various variables*

Item	Year	Household type		Education head		Soc.-prof. status head**	
		(1)	(2)	(1)	(2)	(1)	(2)
Bath or shower	'85	29.0	[15.5]	[9.9]	[1.3]	[6.6]	[1.1]
	'88	[13.6]	[7.7]	[7.7]	[1.1]	[3.4]	[2.0]
Washing machine	'85	142.4	39.6	27.6	31.2	[7.9]	[6.0]
	'88	90.0	[14.0]	11.4	[8.7]	[1.0]	[1.2]
Holiday	'85	63.3	33.3	15.9	[0.8]	[8.6]	[6.3]
	'88	22.0	[20.1]	30.0	[6.5]	[4.2]	[1.9]
Telephone	'85	172.4	104.6	16.1	[11.3]	85.9	26.0
	'88	126.2	83.7	[4.8]	13.3	53.1	32.1
Car	'85	139.6	[13.7]	[5.1]	[3.3]	13.9	[8.4]
	'88	73.2	29.9	[2.1]	16.8	[7.9]	[3.6]
Colour TV	'85	100.3	89.4	42.8	34.2	[3.5]	[6.6]
	'88	79.8	65.9	44.2	38.8	[3.7]	[3.5]
Newspaper	'85	125.0	29.5	[3.3]	[2.0]	16.7	[8.7]
	'88	154.7	45.8	[1.4]	[7.7]	[11.3]	[4.5]
Degrees of freedom***		9	9	3	3	4	4/5

Notes:

* Chi-square statistics in brackets if not significant at the 1%-level
Column (1): Chi square without 'possession status' in model
Column (2): Chi square with 'possession status' in model

** In 1988 the category 'unknown' was added to the variable 'socio-professional status', which therefore has then 5 degrees of freedom

*** Base: model with intercept only
(a) change for model without 'possession status'
(b) additional change after adding 'possession status' to model

HH Income (log)		Region		Possession status	-2 Log Likelihood***			N
(1)	(2)	(1)	(2)	(2)	Base	(a)	(b)	
32.7	10.3	9.3	17.5	325.5	2489	253	323	6019
19.9	8.9	[2.8]	[3.0]	198.8	1382	176	205	3431
16.3	[3.1]	187.0	109.5	405.2	4620	588	418	6092
[1.0]	[0.2]	27.9	16.6	294.6	1634	228	346	3431
61.2	12.4	119.9	65.6	903.0	8289	426	1035	6052
10.8	[0.2]	41.6	23.1	508.7	4609	199	581	3362
45.7	8.5	22.4	28.6	600.8	8419	360	778	6076
22.7	[3.3]	[5.9]	[2.2]	332.2	4408	260	411	3389
47.0	6.8	[8.8]	[9.0]	458.3	8402	527	581	6072
21.7	[1.5]	[5.8]	[8.2]	344.1	4546	255	443	3372
28.5	8.0	63.5	57.2	323.9	8142	279	476	6071
[1.0]	[0.4]	14.4	[7.4]	207.9	4636	258	304	3362
19.0	[0.1]	20.4	22.5	1077.4	7749	191	1548	5992
[5.5]	[0.8]	[8.1]	[0.2]	658.5	4200	216	1034	3344
1	1	2	2	3		19/20	3	

Source: Belgian Socio-Economic Panel, waves 1985 and 1988

In the multivariate analysis, region continues to have a significant effect where this was already apparent from the bivariate table: it affects views about the necessity of a washing machine, a holiday, and a colour TV.

Possession status (i.e. whether or not the household possesses the given item, and if not, whether it desires it or not) has evidently a very large effect on perceptions of necessity, which generally surpasses that of all other variables combined. After the inclusion of possession status, the effects of the other variables are generally much smaller, and in many cases they are no longer significant. This suggests that possession status works as an intervening variable: views about necessities are much influenced by the personal possessions and personal desires of respondents, which in turn are affected by the social conditions of the latter. But there are a few instances where background variables exert an effect which is independent from possession status. Household type has an independent effect on views about a telephone, a colour TV, and a newspaper, education on those about a colour TV, socio-professional category on those about a telephone, and region on those about a washing machine and a holiday.

Since coefficients in logistic regression models are somewhat difficult to interpret, they are not shown here. (They are available on request.) Moreover, for most items the coefficient patterns seem to confirm the bivariate percentage-point differences shown in Table 3. An interesting exception are the coefficients for holiday: in contrast to the bivariate results, older persons apparently are in general not less likely than younger persons to perceive a holiday as a necessity; the bivariate finding was presumably a result of their lower education and / or income. Instead, two particular groups stand out: young single persons and also older middle aged couples are most prone to claim that a holiday is a necessity. Inclusion of possession status into the models does not change the patterns of coefficients very much (where they remain significant), though the size of the estimates is more or less attenuated.

As regards the effects of possession status, the interested reader is referred back to Table 2. Because other variables had only very limited effects, the simple percentages shown there reflect well the impact of possession status as estimated in the multivariate model. As noted above, respondents who do not have an item are much less likely to perceive it as a necessity, compared with those who have it. Furthermore, among the former, whether the item is desired or not by the respondent for him- or herself also exerts a considerable influence. Comparing across items, the percentages for the various groups appear to move in tandem, i.e., the size of the effects of the categories of possession status is roughly similar for the various items.

7 Relationships between perceptions of necessity of different items

Until this point the perceptions of necessity have been examined item by item. The question can be asked whether and how these perceptions are related across items. Such relationships could be interesting for what they reveal both about respondents and items. Some people might be systematically more ready than other people to regard any item as a necessity. Conversely, a subset of items could be related in the sense that people who perceive one item as a necessity are more likely to regard the other items in the subset as necessities as well.

Among the items about which Table 1 showed that there is almost total consensus about their necessity, the answers appear hardly or not related. This is most easily checked by counting the number of these items each respondent regards as necessities and comparing the resulting distribution with the binomial distribution. The binomial distribution is the distribution which would result when the answers to the various items would be independent of each other. This has been done for those respondents who answered all these items (Table 5a). The binomial distribution shown is the expected distribution when each respondent would answer each item with a propability of 0.943 of a positive answer (i.e., the item is a necessity), and the answers were completely independent of each other. 0.943 is the average overall probability of a positive answer on these items, both in 1985 and 1988.

Table 5a
Number of items regarded as necessity of those highest on the list of necessities* (compared with a binomial distribution with number of trials = 10 and probability = 0.943)

Number of items regarded as necessity	1985 (% of sample)	1988 (% of sample)	Binomial distribution (N=10, p=0.943)
10	63.6	64.2	55.6
9	23.5	22.8	33.6
8	8.1	8.8	9.1
7	2.9	2.7	1.5
6 or less	1.9	1.5	0.2
Number of cases	6112	3557	100

* These items are: damp-free home, coat, indoor toilet, heating in living rooms, meal with meat or fish, bath or shower, all weather shoes, refrigerator, washing machine, and regular saving. Only records of respondents who answered all of these items (94% of total) were used in the analysis

Source: Belgian Socio-Economic Panel, waves 1985 and 1988

The number of respondents regarding all ten items as necessities, as well as the size of the small minority perceiving only seven or less of these items as necessities, is slightly larger than expected under the hypothesis that all answers would be independent of each other. But the distributions in both years are quite close to the binomial one, indicating that the answers are generally almost independent of each other. More detailed cross-tabulations show that two pairs of items are consistently somewhat related to each other: 'coat' and 'all weather shoes' on the one hand, and 'indoor toilet' and 'bath or shower' on the other; both relationships seem to make sense. In any case, Table 5a shows that there is hardly any respondent who does not regard the majority of these items as necessities. Most judgments of non-necessity come from respondents who perceive only one or two of these items as non-necessities.

The situation is quite different for the six items which are regarded as necessities by between one third and two thirds of all respondents (holiday, telephone, car, colour TV, central heating, and newspaper, cf. Table 1). Here we find that a sizable minority regards all of these items as necessities, and also that there is another one which says that none of them are (Table 5b). The comparison with the corresponding binomial distributions shows that these proportions are much larger than would be expected when the answers to different items would be independent of one another. The answers thus seem related, though not very strongly.

Table 5b
Number of items regarded as necessity among the items where there is no consensus about their necessity* (compared with a binomial distribution with number of trials = 6 and probability = 0.446 for 1985 and 0.516 for 1988)

Number of items regarded as necessity	1985 (% of sample)	1988 (% of sample)	Binomial distribution (N=6) p=0.446	p=0.516
6	9.5	10.0	0.8	1.9
5	10.3	14.3	5.9	10.6
4	14.1	17.2	18.2	24.9
3	16.3	20.0	30.2	31.2
2	18.4	18.0	28.1	21.9
1	16.9	13.4	14.0	8.2
0	14.5	7.1	2.9	1.3
Number of cases	N=6162	N=3467	100	100

* These items are: holiday, telephone, car, colour TV, central heating, and newspaper. Only records of respondents who answered all six items were used in the analysis (95% of all in 1985; 92% of all in 1988)

Source: Belgian Socio-Economic Panel, waves 1985 and 1988

Further analysis shows that there are correlations of about 0.3 between almost any pair of these six items. The fact that those correlations do not vary much across different pairs of items suggests that these correlations are the result of a general tendency of respondents either to perceive many things as necessities, or few things. The alternative would be that some items are especially related, in the sense that a person who finds central heating important is also likely to regard good heat insulation as a necessity, but may be indifferent with respect to other items. To test this hypothesis a factor analysis has been carried out, trying to extract common factors. A common factor is a latent unobservable variable that is assumed to explain the *correlations* among a set of variables.[3] Factor analysis is not really suited to binary data, such as the one at hand, and therefore the results can only be regarded as indicative. But, as far as they go, they are quite clear: in both years there is only one common factor for these six items, with which all items are more or less correlated.[4] (When the ten other items are included this is no longer true; since these are essentially uncorrelated with the other items and with each other, with the exception of the two pairs of correlated items noted above, they do not load on any common factor.)

8 Background characteristics and the total number of necessities

A further question in this context concerns the total number of items people class as necessities. We have seen above that, in most cases, social characteristics of respondents have only limited effects on perceptions of necessity of individual items. However, the item-by-item analysis might fail to reveal a substantial effect on the aggregate level. Since perceptions of necessity are to some extent correlated across items, small effects on individual items that are all in the same direction, might add up to a substantial effect when we look at the total number of items that respondents class as necessities. To investigate this issue, the total number of items which each respondent has classed as necessities (only the sixteen items which are applicable to all respondents) was calculated, and this sum was regressed on the same variables as were used in the logistic regressions for individual items.[5] The results (not shown here, but available on request) indicate that the influence of the background variables on the number of items classed as necessities is rather small. In all social categories about 12 out of a total of 16 items (that are applicable for all households in 1985) are regarded as necessities. Of all background variables (apart from the number of possessions) household income has the strongest influence on the number of items classed as necessities. Nevertheless, the results imply that a trebling of income corresponds to only one additional item being classed as a necessity. In any case, the effect of income wholly disappears after controlling for the number of possessions.

The number of items that a respondent actually possesses exerts a substantial effect on the number of items classed as necessities. On average, if the number of items possessed increases by 2.5, the number of items regarded as necessities grows by 1. The interpretation of this result is not straightforward, however. At first sight, it may seem to suggest that the higher a person's standard of living, the more extended the range of goods and services she or he will regard as necessities. But this interpretation may be slightly misleading. Above we saw that the circumstance of whether or not the respondent has an item to a great extent determines her perception of its necessity. Presumably people who are used to having a certain good or service come to regard it as indispensable, while, conversely, persons who find a certain amenity important will tend to buy or obtain it. More detailed analyses have shown that the correlation between the number of possessions and the number of items classed as necessities is indeed largely the result of this item-on-item effect. That is, people with a higher standard of living are not much more likely to regard any item as a necessity, but only those they themselves actually possess.

This finding is of some importance, since it indicates that the views on necessities of the better-off and the worse-off are less different than at first sight might appear to be the case, or at least that the difference is not situated at a very fundamental level. People with a high standard of living are not, because of that circumstance alone, more inclined than persons with a lower standard of living to regard any good or service as a necessity. Rather, it is the case that persons who have a particular good or service tend to regard it as a necessity. And, of course, well-off persons are more likely to possess any item than less well-off persons.

9 Stability of perceptions of necessity in Belgium across time

We have seen above that the proportions of people perceiving the various items as necessities remain generally rather stable over time. The panel data of the Belgian Socio-Economic Panel make it possible to investigate whether perceptions of necessity are also stable at the individual level. What do we hope to find? At first sight, it might seem that it would enhance the validity and credibility of the approach if people would stick to the same opinions about necessities three years later.

After all, one might say, if people change their minds very much about what they regard as necessities, these opinions are apparently not deeply held, and there is less reason to take them seriously. But there is another side to this matter, which has to do with the consensual nature of the approach. As we have seen above, in Belgium, as in other countries, there is a range of items about which opinions whether they are necessities or not are divided fairly evenly. This does not look much like a consensus, even if the differences in views do not follow political party lines, or class, or other social divisions. After all, we would not speak of a 'consensus' if, say, 50% of the population in a country would favor joining the E.C., while the other half is against it, even if the controversy would cross-cut social and political boundaries. But the interpretation would be different if it could be shown that the apparent difference of opinion at the aggregate level corresponds to uncertainty at the individual level. In other words, if it would be the case that those who class, say, a car as a necessity are much less sure of this than about the necessity of an indoor toilet, while those who do *not* class a car as a necessity are also less confident about this than about the same judgment as regards a video-recorder, then the difference of opinion is much smaller than it appears to be. An indicator of such uncertainty is that respondents give different answers to the same question after some time has elapsed. (It is unfortunate, in this context, that respondents have only two possible answers to the necessities question to choose from, and thus cannot indicate the degree of their conviction.)

Taking the two considerations mentioned into account, what we hope to find, therefore, is that there is stability at the individual level for the items at both ends of the necessities scale - those which almost everybody regards as necessities and those which almost nobody regards as necessities, and, at the same time, more change for the items in the middle of the scale, where opinions are more evenly balanced.[6] In fact, the results reported in Table 6 confirm these expectations almost perfectly. The items have been ordered according to the proportions classing them as a necessity in 1985, from high to low. For the first ten items, up to regular saving, which at least 85% of the sample regards as necessities, we observe that a very large majority of those who did so in 1985 stick to their judgment in 1985. On the other hand, an almost equally large majority of those who did not class these items as necessities in 1985, have changed their minds in 1988. In fact, for several of the items the difference between the two groups is so small that it is not statistically significant.

Table 6
Stability of perceptions of necessities across time at the individual level, Belgium, 1985-1988

Item	Nec. '85	Nec. '88			
			Nec. '85		
	All	All	Yes	No	Diff.
	(1)	(2)	(3)	(4)	(5)
Damp-free home	99	98	98	100	
Coat	98	98	98	97	
Indoor toilet	98	97	98	88	10
Heating in living rooms	97	97	97	97	
Meal with meat or fish	95	95	95	85	11
Bath or shower	95	94	95	73	22
All-weather shoes	95	90	90	88	
Refrigerator	94	96	97	89	8
Washing machine	90	93	95	77	18
Regular saving	87	85	87	75	12
Holiday	56	57	67	44	23
Telephone	51	65	77	53	24
Car	49	59	72	47	26
Colour TV	39	56	68	48	19
Central heating	38	46	58	38	20
Newspaper	35	33	48	25	24
Three meals a day*	99	98	98	96	
Separate bedrooms*	93	92	93	83	10
Leisure equipment*	91	86	87	76	11

Notes:

(1) Percentage saying item is a necessity in 1985, of those answering the question both in 1985 and 1988
(2) Percentage saying item is a necessity in 1988, of those answering the question both in 1985 and 1988
(3) Percentage saying item is a necessity in 1988, of those saying item is necessity in 1985
(4) Percentage saying item is a necessity in 1988, of those saying item is not a necessity in 1985
(5) Difference between(3) and (4); only reported if significantly at the 1% level
* Items for families with children only

Log-linear estimates of correlation (6)				N (9)	N (10)
Simple (7)		Possession factored out (8)			
Est.	S. e.	Est.	S. e.		
-0.072	0.358	0.330	0.213	3553	3397
0.127	0.164	0.057	0.190	3569	3405
0.441	0.096	0.068	0.154	3580	3434
0.028	0.138	0.040	0.168	3534	3331
0.327	0.057	0.167	0.105	3553	3393
0.497	0.047	0.236	0.071	3567	3424
0.071	0.056	0.038	0.080	3542	3369
0.342	0.057	0.113	0.108	3578	3458
0.444	0.038	0.205	0.064	3564	3430
0.194	0.030	0.142	0.038	3513	3337
0.235	0.017	0.140	0.024	3508	3331
0.269	0.018	0.195	0.043	3524	3377
0.272	0.018	0.153	0.041	3498	3350
0.202	0.018	0.223	0.048	3488	3347
0.204	0.018	0.126	0.034	3479	3330
0.265	0.019	0.151	0.034	3490	3339
0.254	0.214	0.210	0.252	1828	1659
0.245	0.065	0.228	0.094	1773	1510
0.180	0.050	0.040	0.126	1767	1588

(6) Estimates of the correlation of perceptions of necessity obtained with log-linear analysis; Est. = estimate, S. e. = standard error; underlined estimates are statistically significant at the 5%-level

(7) Estimates from 2x2 table necessity '85 - necessity '88; estimate is equal to 1/4 log (odds ratio)

(8) Estimates of second level effect necessity '85 - necessity '88 in 2x2x2x2 table necessity '85 - necessity '88 - possession '85 - possession '88 (saturated model)

(9) Number of cases for columns (1) to (7)

(10) Number of cases for column (8)

Source: Belgian Socio-Economic Panel, waves 1985 and 1988

Also in view of the nature of these items, one may wonder whether most of the recorded answers classing these items as non-necessities are not in fact due to mistakes, either by the respondent or by the interviewer, or at the data-entry stage. (For the item 'two pairs of all weather shoes' the clause 'two pairs' may be a source of confusion, some people thinking that one pair is sufficient, others overlooking it.) It seems, therefore, that as far as these ten items are concerned, people classing them as necessities are rather sure of their opinion, while people who do not are very uncertain about it.[7]

As regards the other six items, both those who in 1985 had classed it as a necessity, and those who did not, are fairly likely to change their opinion. In fact, across items, the proportions in both groups saying that an item is a necessity move in tandem, the difference being between 19 and 26 percentage points. The more often an item is regarded as a necessity overall, the less often people classing it as a necessity in 1985 changed their mind, and the more often people who had the opposite opinion did. The results show that, as far as these items are concerned, there is only a fair degree of correlation over time in the perceptions of necessity. Looking at the percentage differences, it seems, though, that there is more correlation across time for the items which are less often classed as a necessity than for the items which almost everyone regards as a necessity. But if one uses log-linear estimates of correlation, the situation is less clear: for some items high up on the list of necessities, the correlation is stronger than for items further down the list.[8]

The log-linear model has the advantage, in any case, that it enables us to investigate to what extent the correlations across time in perceptions of necessity are mediated by the possession of these items. That is, a correlation across time might be solely or mainly the result of the fact that at both points in time people who possess the item are more likely to regard it as a necessity (assuming, of course, that possession is strongly correlated across time). The results in Table 6 show, however, that after the effects of possession status (i.e., whether the item is possessed or not, in 1985 and in 1988) have been factored out, the correlation generally drops, but in most cases by less than half (except for washing machine). The correlation for a colour TV does not drop at all, which again suggests that normative considerations are important when respondents make judgments about the necessity of this item. These results show that the judgments about necessities have some stability independent of that induced by the inertia of possession patterns.

Until now we have looked at the results across time for individual items. I have suggested that the instability of the judgments about the necessity of some of these items reflects uncertainty in respondents' minds about these judgments.

This interpretation would be difficult to maintain if it could be shown that in fact some people change their judgments a great deal, while others do not alter them at all. But this does not seem to be the case. Looking only at the people who at both points in time answered at least 14 of the 16 items that are applicable to everyone (95% of all those whose records could be linked), it turns out that less than 6% of these respondents do not change their judgment about any item, while 90% make between 1 and 6 changes. If attention is restricted to the items lower down on the list of necessities, holiday to newspaper, where the bulk of the changes occur, it is found that 13% make no changes in their judgments and 68% make 1, 2 or 3 changes. These figures indicate that the changes in judgments for different items are not completely independent of each other,[9] but it is certainly not the case that there is a large number of people who do not change their mind at all.

10 Summary and conclusions

In this section I will first summarize the empirical findings, and then try to answer the main question posed in the introduction: is there a consensus about a minimum standard of living?

When a random sample of people in Belgium are asked which items, out of a list of activities and amenities, they think are necessary, a range of items is classed as necessities by a very large majority (more than 80%). These items do not only include amenities that are needed to maintain health and decency (such as a damp-free home), but also household goods that save time and effort (such as a washing machine). There is also a wide range of items about which opinions are divided, in the sense that the proportion of respondents regarding them as necessities lies between 30% and 70%. Similar results are obtained in other Western European countries.

In general, we find that items for which possession rates are high, are also very often classed as necessities, and vice versa. This seems natural: people will tend to regard things as necessities which are customary in society, and, conversely, they will tend to acquire the items that are socially approved, encouraged, or expected. But there are some exceptions to this rule, a colour TV being the most notable example, where normative considerations apparently predominate.

The correlation between possession and perceptions of necessity is also found at the individual level. Whether or not the respondent possesses the item is by far the most important determinant of his or her perception of its necessity. Furthermore, among those who do not possess an item, there are large differences between those who say they do not have it because they cannot afford it, and those who say they do not want it. This finding shows that not only objective circumstances, but also subjective wants strongly influence perceptions of necessity.

Correlations of perceptions of necessity with other characteristics of respondents are generally not large. For the items which are on the top of the list of necessities there are virtually no differences between various social categories, and for the other items they are mostly fairly limited. The largest differences occur between different age groups, in particular between the elderly and the non-elderly. Whether the respondent lives as a single or as a couple, and whether he or she has children also exerts an influence. Persons with more education and from higher social classes are more likely to consider some items as a necessity, but the differences are not large. (This is in contrast to findings for Britain in 1990.) Most of these differences between social categories are related to differing item possession rates.

Perceptions of necessity of different items are not strongly correlated, i.e. people who class one item as a necessity are not much more likely than the average person to class any other item as a necessity. Partly as a consequence of this, differences in the total number of items regarded as necessities across social categories are quite small. The only variable with an important effect is the total number of items possessed. However, this reflects a tendency of people who have a particular item to consider it a necessity, rather than a correlation between the standard of living in general and perceptions of necessity.

The Belgian panel data also allow us to look at changes in perceptions of necessity across time at the individual level. There is a range of items which virtually everyone regarded as a necessity at both points in time. For the other items lower down on the list of necessities, however, it is found that although there is a fair amount of correlation across time, many respondents have changed their perceptions of necessity after a few years.

Conclusion: Is there a consensus about the minimum standard of living?

Having reviewed the empirical findings, we must now address the question: is there a social consensus about the minimum standard of living? In section 2 I have argued that two conditions must be met before we can say that such a social consensus exists. In the first place, respondents should be able to take a 'publicly-oriented' point of view when considering this matter, and to distinguish between what they want for themselves, and what should be included in a community minimum standard of living. Secondly, the views on this matter in society should not be too divergent.

It seems to me that the first condition is reasonably well met. As reported above, many people who do not have an item and do not want it for themselves, still say that it is a necessity in the sense that everyone should be able to afford it. Conversely, it also happens quite often that respondents who say they themselves could not do without a particular item, still do *not* class it as a necessity. This shows that respondents do make the distinction between their own private wishes and a more public point of view. Of course, their publicly-oriented judgments are coloured, if not largely shaped, by their personal circumstances and experiences, but that is an unavoidable fact of life, and does not detract from the validity of the distinction.

The second condition is perhaps more of a problem. We have seen that there is near unanimity about the necessity of a number of items. But there is also a range of items where opinions are more or less evenly divided. We have also seen that, in general, these divisions of opinion do not coincide very much with social boundaries. Mack and Lansley (1985, p. 86) conclude on the basis of the latter finding that: 'The survey found widespread agreement between all groups in society about the items that are classified as necessities. The homogeneity of views is striking. People from all walks of life [...] share the same view of the kind of society Britain should be in terms of the minimum standards of living to which all citizens should be entitled. Their views are based, it seems, on a general cultural ethos of what is decent and proper.' But this interpretation is not wholly convincing. If, for instance, about half of all respondents class a holiday as a necessity, while the other half does not, it seems somewhat forced to talk about a consensus, even if the same balance of opinion is found to exist across all social and political groups. To use an analogy with a different domain: a country where half of all inhabitants want to join the European Community, while the other half does not, would not be described by most observers as showing a great deal of consensus, even if the controversy would cross-cut all social and political divisions.

One might try to circumvent this problem or objection by saying that there is at least virtual consensus about the items which at least 80% of respondents class as necessities. But if a minimum standard of living were to be defined using only these items, it would be difficult to maintain that it reflects a social consensus, as it would not include items that a large majority regards as necessities. Mack and Lansley (1985) use a cut-off point of 50% to select the items which go into the minimum standard of living. The 50% cut-off point could be defended by analogy with a voting procedure (although Mack and Lansley do not do this). If a vote were to be taken on each item whether or not it should be included in the minimum standard of living, then presumably those items would be included which a majority class as necessities (assuming voting outcomes for one item would not influence those for another). However, as Halleröd et al. (1994, p. 4) remark, 'majority is not the same as consensus'.

Thus the results do not warrant the conclusion that there is consensus about a minimum standard of living in Belgium. But there seems to be no dissensus either. There are a number of items where the answers to the question whether it is a necessity are about equally divided. But the available empirical evidence suggests that in general respondents do *not* have strong feelings about these items. Above I compared differences in perceptions of necessity with a hypothetical controversy in a country about joining the European Community. This comparison was somewhat misleading, since there is likely to be a real social and political controversy about joining the EC, which there is not about the necessity of, say, an annual holiday. In fact, where opinions are evenly balanced at the aggregate level, this seems to correspond to uncertainty at the individual level. Few people appear to have settled views on these issues. Walker (1987, p. 219) may well be justified in his suspicion that many people might modify their perceptions of necessity after receiving additional information or discussing the matter with other people. There is a range of goods and services which almost everyone classes as necessities. There is also another range of items which everyone agrees are not necessities. But in between there is a large grey area, where there is not so much disagreement as uncertainty about the necessity of goods, amenities, and activities.

In this context, the finding that differences between 'vertical' strata, i.e. between people with varying levels of education, from different social classes, and with different incomes are generally small, is very important. Some critics of the consensual method have argued that 'the opinions of the poor, of the rich, of the middle income bands, of the tax payers will almost certainly clash and differ' (Stitt, 1994, p. 73). These critics seem to expect that people in more favourable social positions will have a more stringent view on the minimum standard of living. In that case, it would be clearly inappropriate to talk about a consensus. However, the results show clearly that this is simply not the case in Belgium (it may apply somewhat better to Britain). Views on necessities do not differ much between different social strata, whether these are distinguished according to income, education, or professional class. We have seen that in Belgium people who are richer or better educated or who have more prestigious jobs are, if anything, more, not less generous than the average person.

As shown above, the largest differences in perceptions of necessity are often found between different social or demographic groups, such as age groups and household types. In contrast to the 'vertical' stratifications according to education, income, or social class, we might call these kinds of classifications 'horizontal'. These 'horizontal' differences do not seem to be the result of divergent views about how stringent or generous the minimum standard of living should be, but, rather, reflect the fact that some items are more important for some kinds of people than for others. Older people, for instance, have more need for a telephone and a television, and less need for a car, while the reverse is true for younger people. Mack and Lansley (1985) implicitly recognized that what counts as a necessity may vary according to the circumstances of individuals when they introduced special items for families with children. But otherwise their method implies that an item is either a necessity for everyone or for no one. The results show that this is not a realistic assumption (cf. Halleröd et al. 1994, p. 5, who reach a similar conclusion for Britain). People in different circumstances need different things to reach a minimum standard of living.

This conclusion raises a somewhat theoretical problem: in what sense is it possible to maintain that the minimum standard represents the same standard of living for different people, when it is composed of different goods and services? There is no straightforward answer to this question, but to deny that the needs for goods and services differ across persons would be evidence of a rather strong form of commodity fetishism. A typical 85 year old person with a car but without a telephone does not have the same standard of living as a 25 year old person in the same circumstances. Account must be taken of 'horizontal' differences in perceptions of necessity.

The main conclusions of this chapter can now be stated as follows. First, there is not a well-defined public consensus on the minimum standard of living. The reason is not so much that there are strong disagreements about this matter, but rather that individuals are apparently uncertain about the necessity of a range of items for modern living. Secondly, depending on a person's circumstances and characteristics, perceptions of necessities differ, indicating that the minimum standard of living is composed of different items for different groups in society.

In view of the conclusions reached, it seems inappropriate to follow Mack and Lansley's method, which divided all items sharply into necessities and non-necessities. It is much more defensible to follow the method proposed by Halleröd et al. (1994, p. 9; see also the chapter by Halleröd), who give each item a weight based on the proportion of the population that regards it as a necessity. This weight can be interpreted as the likelihood that the average person will regard the item in question as a necessity. Given the conclusion that differences in responses probably reflect uncertainty rather than disagreement, the weight can also be regarded as an indicator of how certain the average person is about the necessity of the item. An advantage of this method is that we do not need a more or less arbitrary cut-off point to classify items into necessities and non-necessities. Furthermore, the method provides a simple way to take account of differences in perceptions of necessity between different demographic groups. Instead of having the same set of weights for all persons, the weights for each item could be allowed to vary from one group to another. A disadvantage of the weighting method, compared with Mack and Lansley's index of deprivation, is that the former may have less appeal for a lay audience. Mack and Lansley were able to present a list of necessities, and consequently, when they identified a household as living in deprivation, it was very clear what this meant. With the weighting method, some of this clarity is lost.

Notes

[1] This variable had the following categories: 1) single person aged 65+; 2) single person aged 40-64; 3) single person aged less than 40; 4) couple, head aged 65+; 5) couple, head aged 40-64; 6) couple, head aged less than 40; 7) couple with children, head aged 40 or more, 8) couple with children, head aged less than 40; 9) one-parent families; 10) other household types.

[2] More precisely, this statistic, which is also called the Wald statistic, is asymptotically distributed as a Chi-square distribution (Menard 1995, p. 39). It is calculated as follows: $c = b'S^{-1}b$, where c is the chi-square statistic, b the vector of coefficient estimates for the categories of the variable, and S the variance-covariance matrix of these estimates (Aldrich and Nelson 1984, p. 60).

[3] The difference with the, perhaps better known, type of analysis called principal components is that the aim of the latter technique is to catch as much as possible of the total variance among a set of variables in a limited number of new variables (cf. Tacq 1991, pp. 251, 274).

[4] More technically: the first factor had an eigenvalue of 1.61 in 1985 and 1.25 in 1988; subsequent factors had eigenvalues smaller than 0.03 in both years; no residual correlation after extracting the first factor was higher than 0.07. Estimated correlations of items with this factor (factor-loadings) ranged from 0.39 to 0.57 in 1985 and from 0.33 to 0.52 in 1988.

[5] Some readers might question whether adding up respondents' scores on individual items into a sum-score is appropriate, given that in the previous section I have reported that the answers to the various items do not correlate very much with each other. I think that this is not inappropriate, as long as it is recognized that the sum-score has no meaning beyond the the total number of items that respondents class as necessi-

ties, and does not, for instance, measure an underlying tendency on the part of the respondent to be more or less generous in her perceptions of necessities. Another methodological issue is that the number of items regarded as necessities is not really a continuous variable, since it can only take on a limited number of discrete values. Therefore, the regression errors might not be distributed normally, but rather as a Poisson distribution. However, since the variable of interest has in fact a fairly wide range (from 1 to 16), and the aim of the analysis was not to get very precise estimates, ordinary least-squares regression was considered appropriate.

[6] In a sense, this statement amounts to the hypothesis that answers to the former kind of items are more reliable than those to the latter. However, rephrasing the issue in terms or reliability is more likely to confuse than to enlighten matters.

[7] One might object to the first part of this statement by pointing out that it could hardly be otherwise, given that in both years there is virtual unanimity about the necessity of these items. That is, if both in 1985 and 1988 95% of the respondents regard an item as a necessity, then, even at the maximum rate of change, at least 90% of those who did so in 1985 must continue to do so in 1988. Mathematically this argument is of course quite correct, but in the real world it was, equally obviously, not a preordained fact that the overall proportion classing the item as a necessity remained unchanged. Rather, the 1988 situation is a result of the changes that occurred between 1985 and 1988.

[8] The choice between a percentage difference as an estimate of correlation and a log-linear estimate is in fact a choice between an additive model and a multiplicative one, and no clear criteria for making this choice seem to exist.

[9] For each of the six items from holiday to newspaper about 61% of respondents gave the same answer in both years. Thus, if these changes were statistically independent of each other, 0.61**6 = 5% would give the same answer to all six items, instead of 13%.

References

Aldrich, J., Nelson, F. (1984), *Linear Probability, Logit, and Probit Models*, Sage University Paper Series on Quantitative Applications in the Social Sciences, 07-045, Sage: Beverly Hills, London.

Andreß, H.J., Lipsmeier, G. (1995), 'Was gehört zum notwendigen Lebensstandard und wer kann ihn sich leisten? Ein neues Konzept zur Armutsmessung', *Aus Politik und Zeitgeschichte, Beilage zur Wochenzeitung Das Parlament*, B 31-32/95 (28. Juli 1995).

Barry, B. (1990), *Political Argument. A reissue with a new introduction*, Harvester Wheatsheaf (first edition in 1965): New York, London.

Callan, T., Nolan, B. (1991), 'Concepts of Poverty and the Poverty Line', *Journal of Economic Surveys*, Vol. 5, No. 3, pp. 243-261.

Callan, T., Nolan, B. et al. (1989), *Poverty, Income and Welfare in Ireland*, General Research Series Paper No. 146, The Economic and Social Research Institute: Dublin.

Deleeck, H., Cantillon B., Meulemans, B., Van den Bosch, K. (1991), 'Indicateurs sociaux de la securité sociale, 1985-1988', *Revue Belge de Securité Sociale*, Vol. 33, No. 10-12, pp. 689-756.

Goedhart, Th., Halberstadt, V., Kapteyn, A., Van Praag, B. (1977), 'The Poverty Line, Concept and Measurement', *The Journal of Human Resources*, Vol. 12, No. 4, pp. 503-520.

Gordon, D., Pantazis, C., Townsend, P., Bramley, G., Bradshaw, J. (1994), *Breadline Britain in the 1990's.* A Draft Report to the Joseph Rowntree Foundation.

Gustafsson, B. (1995), 'Assessing Poverty. Some Reflections on the Literature', *Journal of Population Economics*, Vol. 8, No. 4, pp. 361-381.

Hagenaars, A. (1985), *The Perception of Poverty*, Academic Thesis, University of Leyden, published 1986, North-Holland: Amsterdam.

Halleröd, B. (1994a), *A New Approach to the Direct Consensual Measurement of Poverty*, Social Policy Research Centre Discussion Paper No. 50, The University of New South Wales: Sydney.

Halleröd, B. (1994b), *Poverty in Sweden: a New Approach to the Direct Measurement of Consensual Poverty*, Umea Studies in Sociology No. 106, Sociologiska Institutionen, Umea Universitet: Umea.

Halleröd, B., Bradshaw, J., Holmes, H. (1994), 'Adapting the Consensual Definition of Poverty' in Gordon et al. (1994), *Breadline Britain in the 1990's.* A Draft Report to the Joseph Rowntree Foundation.

Mack, J., Lansley, S. (1985), *Poor Britain*, George Allen and Unwin: London.

Menard, S. (1995), *Applied Logistic Regression Analysis*, Sage University Paper Series on Quantitative Applications in the Social Sciences, 07-106, Sage: Thousand Oaks, CA.

Rainwater, L. (1974), *What Money Buys. Inequality and the Social Meanings of Income*, Basic Books: New York.

Rainwater, L. (1990), *Poverty and Equivalence as Social Constructions*, LIS Working paper No. 55, The Luxembourg Income Study: Walferdange.

Stitt, S. (1994), *Poverty and Poor Relief: Concepts and Reality*, Avebury: Aldershot.

Tacq, J. (1991), *Van probleem naar analyse: de keuze van een gepaste multivariate analyse-techniek bij een sociaal-wetenschappelijke probleemstelling*, Academisch Boeken Centrum: De Lier.

Van den Bosch, K. (1993), 'Poverty Measures in Comparative Research', in Berghman, J., Cantillon, B. (eds.), *The European Face of Social Security, Essays in honour of Herman Deleeck*, Avebury: Aldershot, pp. 3-23.

Van den Bosch, K., Callan, T., Estivill, J., Hausman, P., Jeandidier, B., Muffels, R., Yfantopoulos, J. (1993), 'A Comparison of Poverty in Seven European Countries and Regions, using Subjective and Relative Measures', *Journal of Population Economics*, Vol. 6, No. 3, pp. 235-259.

Walker, R. (1987), 'Consensual Approaches to the Definition of Poverty: Towards an Alternative Methodology', *Journal of Social Policy*, Vol. 16, No. 2, pp. 213-226.

Different methods - different results? Approaches to multidimensional poverty

Olli Kangas and Veli-Matti Ritakallio

1 Introduction

Intuitively, everyone knows what poverty is. Poverty is deprivation and misery. Poverty also involves moral obligations: we must try to eliminate it. But as soon as we address the practical question of what the poor are actually deprived of, our definition of poverty becomes much less unanimous. What kind of misery can be defined as poverty? What should be done to decrease poverty?

Following Peter Townsend's (1979) famous proposition, the majority of researchers more or less agree that poverty in the industrialised world means that a person's ability to function in society is restricted because of insufficient economic resources, i.e., that he or she is unable to live in a way that is customary in his or her environment (e.g. Townsend 1979). Absence of poverty thus means not only secure physical conditions (appropriate housing, nutrition, clothing, and health) but also the ability to live, consume and participate in a way that allows for the satisfaction of needs according to certain socially prevalent quality requirements. Even as researchers continue to define poverty along Townsend's lines as exclusion from 'normal' social life, there is much debate on research methods. The main dividing issue has been whether to use methods based on resources or way of life, i.e., whether to study lack of economic wellbeing indirectly through incomes and/or other resources, or directly through living conditions or consumption (Ringen 1988, 1995). Within both schools, there are further disputes: What data to use? What concepts of income and living conditions to adopt? How to draw the line between poor and non-poor? How to make different kinds of living situations commensurable? What weight to give to objective factors and what to subjective ones based on individual experience? How to distinguish between those who have chosen a 'poor' way of life and those who live in involuntary poverty? How these issues are resolved affects not only research methods but probably results as well. The extent of poverty appears different depending on the measures and poverty lines used. Similarly, the methods applied may classify different population groups as poor.

Indeed, previous research (e.g. Halleröd 1991; Callan, Nolan and Whelan 1993) has shown that different groups are identified as impoverished depending on whether research is based on resources or way of life. There is not much overlap between pictures of poverty produced by different methods. This finding has generally been interpreted as a weakness of the resource-based approach (McGregor and Borooah 1992), and many researchers have attempted to develop alternative measures for revealing 'true' poverty (Mack and Lansley 1985). The proponents of each of these alternative strategies have declared their own approach superior to the other ones. But is aiming for the one and only 'correct' indicator too ambitious? Does it do reality justice to reduce what in principle is a multidimensional societal phenomenon to one dimension only? Does not poverty have so many facets that its proper description requires the use of several complementary approaches? The aim of this study is to investigate to what degree the picture of the distribution of poverty depends on the measure used. We want to find out which sectors of the population are identified as poor when applying different income-based resource measures, indices of social deprivation and indicators based on subjective experience. How much overlap is there? Or do the different measures create completely different pictures of poverty?

The comparison of different measures is justified both on research-related and practical sociopolitical grounds. Because of limitations of data, international studies have often been restricted to comparing only one or two measures at a time. An analysis of several different measures even with cross-sectional data from only one country, as in this study - may produce potentially useful information for comparative research on which measures accentuate the various aspects of poverty. From the point of view of social policy, the comparison of different approaches is important because it yields a wider picture of which sectors of the population are more vulnerable to different forms of poverty. Thus, our approach hopefully offers some guidelines how to reform the present welfare state to better meet demands of multidimensional poverty.

The structure of this paper is as follows: We will first present an overview of the basic approaches to poverty research and the applied methods, and examine the strengths and weaknesses of each approach. Our empirical research questions and poverty measures are anchored in this theoretical overview. Next, we introduce our data and the measures to be analysed. In the empirical analysis, we first examine the extension of poverty and then portray the pictures created by the different measures, i.e., we look at where poverty falls according to each measure. The final section of the paper summarizes the results and examines the implications of our findings for social policy.

2 Earlier studies and approaches

2.1 Poverty criteria

'There is no one correct, scientific, agreed definition because poverty is inevitably a political concept, and thus inherently a contested one,' claims Pete Alcock (1993, p. 3). Indeed, there is an abundance of studies attempting to operationalize and measure poverty (for a summary see e.g., Saunders 1994b). Each study has been justified by its contribution of new perspectives to the phenomenon of poverty. Moreover, each new approach has been claimed to be better than the previous ones.

Table 1 displays a summary of the main approaches adopted in earlier studies. In the Table, empirical poverty research is divided into three different types depending on whether the focus is on economic resources, deprivation in need satisfaction, or both simultaneously. Each type of approach is further divided into subsections depending on how the poverty line is defined. With the exception of subjective measurements of poverty, all these methods are still commonly used. Our purpose is not to give a comprehensive critical analysis of the various methods but a general justification of our multidimensional approach.

2.2 Indirect approaches

When measuring poverty indirectly, one must first establish an adequate concept of economic resources that would best measure subsistence. Second, one must decide how to make different kinds of households comparable. Third, a decision has to be made on where and how to draw the poverty line. The fourth issue, important but largely ignored so far, is the duration of poverty.

Table 1
Approaches to poverty

Method	Who defines the poverty line	Poverty line (example of studies)
Indirect		
Political-administrative income line	Political decision	Minimum pension/social assistance (Gustafsson & Uusitalo 1990)
Relative income line	Expert	50 % of the median or mean income (poverty lines used by OECD and EU)
Minimum subsistence budget	Expert	The cost of a basket of minimum needs (official poverty line in the U.S.)
Deprivation standard	Expert	Income-poverty line derived from the deprivation index (Townsend 1979)
Consensual poverty line	Public opinion	Derived from the public opinion (Hagenaars 1986)
Direct		
Subjective	Individuals themselves	Agrees completely with the statement 'Considering the present income level, my family has problems with managing'
Relative expenditure line	Expert	50 % of the median expenditures (Ritakallio 1994a)
Political-administrative expenditure line	Political decision	Expenditure is below the level of minimum pension/social assistance (McGregor & Borooah 1992)
Accumulation of deprivation	Expert	Cumulative deprivation (Heikkilä 1990)
Dual criterion		
Recipiency of social assistance	Political decision and application for assistance	Recipiency of assistance (Most poverty studies in the Nordic countries)
Dual condition	Expert	Low income and deprivation of needs satisfaction simultaneously (Ringen 1987)
Consensual deprivation	Public opinion and expert	Enforced lack of socially perceived necessities (Mack & Lansley 1985)

(1) Disposable income is the concept generally used to measure economic resources. It is the part of gross income (including social income transfers) that remains after the deduction of taxes and taxlike payments. Critics of this income measure have stressed that in reality, many other factors besides income provide resources. It is possible to maintain a livelihood by such stopgap measures as borrowing money or selling assets (see Ringen 1987, pp. 141-165, Ringen 1988). Participation in the informal economy, for example barter between households, may also be a significant economic resource. The problem is that many of these kind of additional sources of livelihood do not appear in official statistics. When information of unofficial net income is not included in studies, a weak correlation between the income measure and the actual economic resources can be anticipated.

(2) Another basic deficiency of research based on income only is that people are lumped together as if their household needs were identical. However, similar households with equal net incomes and comparable housing may have big differences in such necessary expenses as housing, health care, child care, commuting, etc. Thus, the one with the higher net income may have a lower amount of freely disposable income. In principle, similar situations may exist at the poverty line: those above the income poverty line may remain below it in terms of freely disposable income, and vice versa. Despite sophisticated speculations and scientific debates on what income should be included and what excluded, complete agreement is unlikely, and scholars are obliged to make some ad hoc decisions in doing practical research. More information is therefore needed on the differences in results produced by the different methods.

(3) Resource-based studies differ visibly from each other in their determination of the poverty line. The so-called *political-administrative (policy) method* defines poverty according to the fundamental standards of the welfare state itself, for example, by using as determinants minimum pensions and social assistance. The welfare state 'provides income for various categories of people who are not working. The level of disposable income for them can be used as a poverty line.' (Gustafsson and Lindblom 1993). This definition of the poverty line provides means for estimating how well the welfare state has succeeded in guaranteeing its citizens the minimum level of subsistence it has set as a goal. Thus, the measure is most useful for evaluating the deficiencies of the social security system since the criteria of the shortcomings are defined through the system itself. This method is most problematic when used in comparative

research, where it may produce odd results: welfare states with the lowest social benefits may display the lowest poverty rates. Furthermore, changes in the minimum level of social security are reflected as reduced or increased poverty. Therefore, the method is vulnerable to political manipulation: the most effective way to reduce poverty would be to lower the level of social benefits (Ringen 1987).

In recent years, the most commonly used way to determine the poverty line has been the *relative income method* (e.g., Mitchell 1991; Ritakallio 1994). This method is purely relative. Poverty is defined as a fraction of the median (or mean) income, generally 50%. As the median income changes, so does the criterion of poverty. By this definition, the proportion of the poor in the population is tied to the shape of the income distribution rather than to their real income levels, which has its own problems. 'Measured poverty will change only if, and whenever, the distribution of income changes, and measured poverty will be the same in two countries with the same distributions of income even if the level of income is twice as high in one country as in the other' (Ringen 1987, 1988). Another problem caused by the use of the relative income method is the arbitrariness of the poverty line. There never has been, nor will be, information that would provide for a scientifically 'correct' determination of the relative poverty line. Here again, the limit has to be set somewhere, and one half of the median income is only one possibility. The problem is that increases or decreases in poverty as well as comparisons of poverty between countries have been shown to be sensitive to poverty line changes (e.g., Mitchell 1991). In comparative studies and in studies pertaining to intracountry changes, the effects of the poverty line level on research findings can be controlled by sensitivity analyses. This analysis compares on a ranked scale whether different levels of poverty lines (for example 40, 50, and 60% of the median income) produce a congruent picture of the direction of change in poverty within a country, or of the ranking of countries in comparative analyses. Findings are indisputable only in situations where all poverty lines produce a congruent result (see Atkinson 1989).

(4) A look at previous research reveals certain, rather consistent, differences in the way how the duration of poverty is handled. Some cross-sectional data reflect mainly short-term poverty, as if in a snapshot view. When research is based on this kind of data, there is no information on the duration of poverty. A poverty category will include both the permanently and temporarily impoverished, but it is hard to differentiate between them. Other data-bases measure annual income and therefore more enduring poverty, but here,

information on different forms of short-term poverty may be lost. In the current sociopolitical discussion, more emphasis has been laid on analyses of lifetime income, but because of the lack of sufficient data bases, persistent poverty that may last a lifetime has hardly been investigated at all. Probably mostly because of the dearth of the necessary long panel data-sets, no poverty studies have gauged the dimension of depth by comparing temporary, cyclical, phase-of-life and life-long manifestations of poverty.

The idea of the *minimum subsistence budget method* is to create lists of minimum needs for households of different sizes. The poverty lines are determined by calculating the cost of the minimum needs. This method was the first one to be used by poverty researchers (e.g., Rowntree 1901), and is still in use in the United States (see Poverty in the United States 1991). The setting of the poverty line is no less arbitrary with this method than with others (see Saunders 1994a, 1994b, pp. 247-256). Not only what items are to be included in the basket of minimum subsistence but also who defines what these items are, is an issue of endless disputes (see Piachaud 1987).

Peter Townsend introduced in his mammoth study (1979) the widely debated *deprivation standard*. According to Townsend, a comparison of the distribution of income and the index that measures participation in various lifestyles will show a point in the income distribution - a poverty threshold - below which withdrawal from ordinary lifestyles is disproportionately faster than the decrease of income. What was problematic in Townsend's method was that he used directly the index that measured the realized satisfaction of needs and took it as a means of determining an income poverty line. One consequence was that some of those deprived according to the deprivation index were not included in the poverty category, and vice versa.

In the recent past, the demands of political relevance have been a major motivation for the increased pursuit of establishing poverty criteria on the basis of public opinion (Veit-Wilson 1987). The *social consensus method* was originally developed by Goedhart et al. (1977), and it has been used, on the one hand, for determining the indirect income poverty line and, on the other hand, for picking items for the deprivation index (originally developed by Mack and Lansley 1985). In order to determine the consensual poverty line, a sample of persons is first asked the following minimum income question (MIQ): 'What in your opinion is the lowest sum of money to cover the expenses of your household?' The responses to the MIQ are then used to estimate a consensual poverty line for different types of households. After the poverty line has been determined, the analysis in the consensual income method proceeds similarly as in other income methods. Those whose incomes fall under the poverty line are poor, others are not. This approach has its own deficiencies. The wording of the MIQ is problematic. For example, people's idea of the minimum living standard to be guaranteed in society does not necessarily agree with their idea of their own minimum needs. In sum, the consensual poverty line method is not immune to the problems that plague all indirect income measures.

2.3 Direct approaches

When studying poverty directly from the vantage point of social deprivation, decisions have to be made on how to operationalize deprivation and on where to draw the deprivation line. Information on the duration of poverty is based on survey-type panel data since no statistical information is available. In principle, direct approaches are divided into two groups according to whether they operate on the basis of expenditure data or with data that approach material living conditions from a wider perspective.

One relevant perspective on poverty is *subjective perception*. It is essential to know where poverty and economic hardships are being experienced in society and how these feelings relate to indications achieved through the more objective approaches. Naturally, at least on an individual level, personally perceived poverty cannot function as the only criterion for decision-making, say, in deciding who gets social benefits; and, of course, serious scholars would hardly suggest using a subjective poverty measure alone to uncover the poverty existing in society.

It has been emphasized in many conceptual analyses that poverty means, above all, deficient consumption (e.g., Mack and Lansley 1985). Comparing consumption is thus a logical approach. Many countries conduct household consumption expenditure surveys based on precise book-keeping by selected households. These data sets can be used in the same way as income data. Analogically, the poverty line can be politically determined (the political-administrative expenditure line) or it can be set at 40, 50, 60, etc. per cent of median consumption expenses (the relative expenditure line).

In principle, the *political-administrative expenditure* method and the *relative consumption expenditure method* have the same problems as the income based methods in defining the poor. There are also some additional problems. For practical reasons, it is not possible to follow consumption over a longer period of time. For example, in the Finnish Household Budget Surveys, the book-keeping period is two weeks. In comparing households with low consumption with low income households, it must be taken into account that the length of the observation period may change the picture of poverty and affect the overlap of both measures. If the book-keeping period is short temporary spells of income poverty do not necessarily coincide with temporary poverty in consumption. Another problem is that in some cases those who are classified as poorest on the basis of consumption expenditure (in Finland, for example, pensioners) may have more money than other groups to put into savings (Ritakallio 1994). For these reasons, the correlation between income and consumption measures may be rather weak.

According to Ringen (1987, p. 162) poverty is the result of an *accumulation of deprivation* in both resources and the way of life. In practice, however, the decision of what to include in the concept of deprivation or in indices of deprivation has proved to be even more problematic than the operationalisation of the concept of economic resources. What should be the basis for selecting the items for the deprivation index? Conceptually, deprivation items must be expected to have a fairly direct connection to the lack of resources. Poverty is the flip side not just of welfare, but of economic welfare in particular (cf. Heikkilä 1990; Halleröd 1991, pp. 91-93).

The selection of items for the deprivation index becomes even more complex when poverty is being studied from a comparative perspective. According to the relative concept of poverty, the criteria will change when the conditions in society change. When investigating trends within one society or doing cross-national comparative research, how do we establish deprivation indicators that would be relevant to each point in time or to each country? In the end, arbitrariness is unavoidable even with this method. In addition, unless special conditions are set, the deprivation index also identifies as poor those people who have 'consciously chosen an unassuming way of life', which tends to diminish the credibility of the purely objective deprivation index.

2.4 *Combination approaches (dual criteria)*

Many researchers define poverty as restricted social functioning caused by insufficient economic resources, thus establishing dual conditions. Both conditions must apply at the same time, and there must be a causal relationship between them (see Callan, Nolan and Whelan 1993). Poverty is not just any limited social functioning, but specifically isolation that stems from the lack of economic resources. Thus, the choice of deprivation indicators must exclude those aspects of living standards which are not clearly money-related. Poverty in money-based societies generally means life in the shadow of monetary shortages that make it difficult to provide for such everyday needs as food, sufficient housing, clothes, mobility, and leisure. That is, poverty in modern societies means restricted consumption possibilities and these restrictions in a very fundamental way limit everyday life.

The dual-conditions definition has a practical application in *social assistance recipiency*. Some empirical studies on social assistance indicate that the problems encountered in recipients' daily activities are the very problems included in the two-condition definition of poverty: restricted consumption possibilities because lack of money continuously shadows everyday life activities of assistance recipients (Fridberg 1993; Ritakallio 1991). There are pros and cons to using the social assistance recipiency method. The strength of this method is that it reveals repeated periods of temporary poverty that could not have been identified by studies using data on annual income (Ritakallio 1991). The weakness of the measure is connected to the way in which the eligibility for social assistance is determined. Firstly, the political-administrative (policy) process sets an income norm below which a person's income has to fall in order for him or her to receive assistance. Then the individual need assessment is used to determine the person's right to assistance. Most importantly, social assistance is only given on application and every case is evaluated separately. These steps also form the basic shortcomings of this measure of social assistance. Since the rules for social assistance may change considerably over time, the validity of this measure is limited for analyzing trends within one country. In cross-national comparisons, the method is beset with all the shortcomings of the political-administrative method as described above. In addition, many of those under the income norm do not claim benefits for one reason or another and thus remain in 'hidden poverty' (Gustafsson 1987).

Some of the more sophisticated approaches (e.g., Ringen 1987; Mack and Lansley 1985; Halleröd 1995) are stricter in demanding that economic problems and accumulated deprivation must appear simultaneously. There are many differences in the ways these approaches have been put into practice in research (dual condition and consensual deprivation standard in Table 1).

Mack and Lansley (1985) define poverty as an 'enforced lack of socially perceived necessities'. Their method involves identifying necessities on the basis of people's opinions. A sample of persons is given a list of items that are closely related to economic welfare. The purpose is to find out which of the items the majority of people consider necessities. The questionnaire also includes another battery of questions where the same list of items is given to indicate ownership or lack of ownership. The responses are then dichotomised so that the deprived become a separate group. An index is compiled of the items considered necessities by the majority of the population. The index is aptly called the majority necessity index (MNI). A lack of ownership of an index item is a necessary, though not sufficient condition for being classified as deprived. The additional condition is that a person expresses the subjective opinion that the lack of ownership is due to insufficient financial resources, i.e., the lack of necessities is involuntary. A crucial question in this approach is where on the deprivation index the poverty line should be drawn. Mack and Lansley (1985) used as a cut-off point an unwanted absence of at least three necessities. This is just as arbitrary as any other cut-off point (Piachaud 1987). The question remains how to deal with those respondents who appear to be cumulatively deprived, yet own items, such as a car, that require large outlays of money? These questions have so far remained unanswered in the applications of the social consensus method.

Some studies (e.g., Halleröd 1995) set out to identify the 'truly poor' by using a *consensual dual condition*. In practice, this means that the criteria for true poverty is an income below the consensual poverty line and a designation as poor in the consensual deprivation index. Double measurement doubles the amount of problems. Generally speaking, all the problems of the various measures remain when the dual condition is understood as a technical combination of the indirect and direct methods (e.g., Heikkilä 1990; Halleröd 1991).

2.5 Earlier research on interrelationships between poverty measures

The few comparative studies on approaches to poverty measurement have in essence yielded the result that different approaches will only partly categorize the same groups of the population as poor. Overlap has been quite weak. The extent of poverty has also been found to be dependent on what measure is used. A number of studies have shown how singular methodological solutions affect the results produced by different income methods.[1] In the studies investigating the interrelations of poverty measures, two or three measures have generally been investigated at a time.

Ringen (1987) compared the pictures of changes in poverty in Sweden between 1968 and 1981 produced by the relative income method and the cumulative deprivation method. Low income poverty was set at 40% of the median income for all families. The condition for cumulative deprivation was simultaneous presence of low personal capability (the respondent does not judge himself/herself to have the ability to make a written complaint against an authority) and inferior housing (crowded and/or low standard). During the observation period low income poverty fell from 3.6 to 3.1%. In 1968, 21% of the low-income poor satisfied the cumulative poverty condition, and only 5% in 1981. The rapid decrease in the overlap of these two measures is partly explained by the methodology used: Ringen applied a fixed measure for deprivation (the criterion for inferior housing was the same in 1981 as in 1968) but not for low-income.

In their nearly identically arranged studies of Finland and Sweden, Heikkilä (1990) and Halleröd (1991) analyzed the political-administrative (policy) income method, a cumulative deprivation measure, and the social assistance recipiency method. They defined as political-administratively poor those whose income was below the social assistance norm. The measure of cumulative deprivation in both studies was an index that gauged lack of wellbeing multidimensionally. Heikkilä's index had six items, and his criterion for cumulative deprivation was deprivation indicated simultaneously by at least two items. Halleröd utilized nine items, and cumulative deprivation required a lack of wellbeing on at least three dimensions. As poverty measures, both of these cumulative deprivation indicators are inadequate, because many of their items measure in large part something other than restricted consumption capacity. Poor health, problems in social relationships, or political passivity do not necessarily, on a personal level, have anything to do with poverty. Used in this way, the cumulative deprivation indices can classify a lonely, politically passive and ailing millionaire as poor. This helps to explain why these studies found only a weak connection between poverty and cumulative deprivation (Heikkilä 1990, p. 91; Halleröd 1991, pp. 108-11 and pp. 134-6). Low income and social assistance recipiency were also only slightly overlapping. On the other hand, in both Heikkilä's Finnish data and Halleröd's Swedish data, the correlation between social assistance recipiency and cumulative deprivation was significantly higher.

McGregor and Borooah (1992) operated on the political-administrative income and consumption expenditure methods. Measured with consumption expenses, the poverty rate was higher (12.2 vs. 15.0%), whereas the poverty gap was not dependent on whether the measurement was based on income or expenditure. In McGregor and Borooah's study, expenditure-based and income-based poverty measures classified different groups as vulnerable to poverty. Using income measures, the proportion of the unemployed is accentuated; using expenditure-based measures, the poverty risk of large families and the elderly is prominent.

In his study of poverty in Finland, Ritakallio (1994b) applied the relative income and expenditure method (the poverty line was 50% of the median) and the social assistance recipiency method. He also concluded that different poverty measures identified mostly differing groups. In 1990, the poverty rate measured by the relative income method (2.5%) and social assistance recipiency (6.3%) covered a total of 8.3% of the population when the criterion was belonging to either or both categories. Yet only 0.5% were poor in both categories at the same time. In comparing the relative income method and the relative expenditure method (5.0%), the result was that 6.9% of the population was poor according to at least one measure, while poverty by both measures was 0.6%. An even weaker correlation existed between social assistence and expenditure methods, with 10.6% of the population being poor by one measure or both, and only 0.6% identified as poor by both measures. The simultaneous use of all three measures rendered 0.1% of the population being poor.

In sum, results from earlier research indicate that it may be questionable to consider the different approaches to poverty measurement interchangeable. The aim of the next sections is to try to answer how and to what extent the picture of poverty will change when measurement methods are changed.

3 Data and poverty measures

Data used in this study was collected by a mail survey by the Department of Social Policy at the University of Turku in the early part of 1995. The survey broadly mapped the level of welfare and subsistence of Finns, and their views on social policies. The sample was collected from the data of the Population Register Center using random sampling and it represents the total Finnish population between ages 18 and 70. The effective response rate was 65% (n = 1859). A non-response analysis did not reveal systematic bias associated with such traditional background variables as age, education, gender, and socioeconomic position. As a rule, such unprivileged groups as the recipients of social assistance and the unemployed are underrepresented in survey data. Although the former group is also somewhat underrepresented in our data, our figures match approximately with register data. As much as 9.0% of the respondents reported that they had received social assistance in the preceding year. This figure corresponds quite closely to official data according to which 10.7% of Finns between 18 and 70 years of age received social assistance in 1993 (Living Allowance and Draftees' Dependents Allowance 1993; Statistical Yearbook of Finland 1994). Contrary to the recipients of social assistance, the unemployed are somewhat overrepresented in our sample: 21.4% compared to

19.1% in official statistics. Thus, our data rather satisfactorily represent the actual (January 1995) unemployment level.

The survey had two objectives. Firstly, we wanted to get concrete information on wellbeing of Finns at a time when the country had spiraled into the deepest depression of its history.[2] Our second objective was methodological. The questionnaire included several different poverty measures that represent alternative theoretical approaches to poverty. The methodological objective was to investigate the degree to which these different approaches lead to the same conclusions concerning the extent and location of poverty. The five measures used in the survey are: relative income, consensual deprivation, subjective feeling of scarcity in the form of subsistence problems, overindebtedness, and recipiency of social assistance. In the following sections, we briefly investigate each measure to see how severe the poverty problem is according to each of them.

3.1 Relative income measure (RELINC50)

In market economies, money is the basic medium of exchange: it is considered one of the most essential resources for living a good life. Money makes people either rich or poor. Therefore, income based measures are the most commonly used indicators of poverty. It has become general practice to define as poor those whose disposable incomes fall below a line drawn at a certain fraction of median income. In order to test the sensitivity of our findings, we first applied three alternative poverty lines: 40, 50, and 60% of the median income per OECD consumption unit (median = 4 350 FIM per month). The poverty rates produced by these lines were 4.5, 8.5, and 13.3%, respectively. Because of space considerations, in the subsequent comparisons only results produced by the half-of-the-median line are reported.

The income data used in the analysis is based on questionnaire responses, and measures monthly net income. At this point it is not possible to compare the questionnaire responses on income with the current information in register data, but since depression has kept wage levels in Finland fairly constant during the 1990s, the latest available register data on income - from 1993 - is usable for purposes of comparison. The median income of the respondents is about 80% of the register-based median income. Unfortunately, the response data does not make it possible to clarify how this 'hidden income' is distributed between different population groups, and we must therefore assume that the distribution is unbiased. This appears to be a reasonable assumption, since income-based poverty risks in survey data seem to be distributed rather similarly to those in register-based data (cf. Ritakallio 1994b).

However, there seem to be certain problems with the income measures of the survey. For example, the survey income data reveal quite a different picture of the extension of poverty than register-based data display. In the survey, the poverty rate is 8.5%, whereas the preliminary figure based on the 1993 income register is only 2.9%. Halleröd (1995) discovered a similar, though smaller, difference in Sweden: his survey gave a poverty rate of 13.2%, whereas register information suggested not more than 7.7%.

The differences between register and survey data can be interpreted in various ways. First, the difference may be due to the fact that the register information usually pertains to annual income, whereas our data measure monthly income. The longer time span in the registers may eliminate fortuitous income-lowering factors, such as sickness, unemployment, uncompensated days waiting for social benefits etc. The strength of cross-sectional, survey based income data is that it also picks up shorter periods of poverty, while annual data may conceal shorter and temporary spells of low income. Second, the overall reliability of survey data may also be questioned: for one reason or another, respondents may not report their incomes accurately. If we choose to rely on income registers and accept the picture served by them we can conclude that, at least for the time being, the Finnish welfare state is functioning excellently: despite the drastic and unprecedented changes in unemployment, the poverty rate has not gone up much from the 2.5% in 1990 (Ritakallio 1994b). Unfortunately, we do not have survey data from the 1980s or from the early 1990s with which to compare our results.

3.2 Consensual deprivation (CON50)

The consensual deprivation index was constructed on the basis of two different batteries of questions (cf. Table 1). To start with, respondents were given a list of 37 items related to consumption and way of life (Table 2), and asked to indicate which items they considered necessary for everyone. The list was compiled largely utilizing earlier studies (Mack and Lansley 1985; Breadline Britain 1990; Halleröd 1994).

Table 2
The public's perception of necessities and the extent of possession of the items (percentages)

Consumption item	a)	b)	c)	d)	e)
Medical teatment and medicine if necessary	96.4	85.3	9.7	0.2	4.8
A hot meal every day	95.0	87.4	10.4	0.2	2.0
Washing machine	88.4	82.2	9.1	2.7	6.0
Dental examination once a year	82.3	61.6	19.3	4.0	15.2
Vacuum cleaner	80.0	80.0	17.0	0.9	2.1
Modern dwelling (bath/ shower WC, central heating, stove, refrigerator)	77.9	83.3	13.2	0.4	3.1
Public transportation according to one's needs	76.5	34.8	50.7	9.5	5.0
Householders' comprehensive insurance	66.2	57.6	25.1	7.7	9.6
Telephone	66.0	73.9	20.5	1.6	4.0
Not more than two persons in each bedroom	59.3	58.2	30.1	3.5	8.3
A hair cut every third month	58.8	56.7	29.3	3.9	10.1
Daily paper	53.2	53.7	29.4	7.1	9.7
Freezer	51.6	60.1	28.7	4.9	6.3
Possibility for regular free-time activity	46.2	32.9	45.1	7.7	14.3
TV	45.8	55.3	40.2	2.8	1.7
Possibility to buy new clothes regularly	32.8	9.7	46.1	12.4	31.8
Balcony or garden	29.5	54.0	29.4	7.1	9.7
Large enough dwelling	27.5	41.0	32.9	4.8	21.3
Celebrations on special occasions	26.2	12.0	57.2	13.3	17.5
Save at least 500 FIM each month	26.0	14.2	27.2	7.4	51.1
Car	22.1	53.2	22.9	11.9	12.0
A 'best outfit' for special occasions	21.0	27.5	40.6	14.0	17.9

Consumption item	a)	b)	c)	d)	e)
Presents for family or friends at least once a year (except Christmas and special days)	20.7	15.3	48.7	13.1	23.0
A holiday away from home for one week a year	16.2	10.1	37.7	12.8	39.3
Invite friends for a meal once a month	10.2	6.9	52.3	21.9	18.9
Private pension insurance	10.1	4.9	8.0	57.2	29.9
Microwave oven	9.2	19.2	60.3	13.5	7.2
Clothes that to some degree correspond with fashion	9.0	10.8	49.6	17.1	22.5
Go to cinema, theatre, or concert at least once a month	8.8	5.9	52.6	21.6	19.9
A special meal once a week	7.1	4.8	38.8	36.9	19.5
Stereo equipment	6.8	15.3	51.9	23.9	8.9
A night out once a fortnight	6.1	4.3	46.6	24.6	24.5
Dish-washer	6.0	12.6	40.7	34.3	12.4
VCR	5.2	11.6	58.4	22.2	7.8
Access to summer cottage	4.3	14.8	32.6	22.7	30.0
Mobile telephone	1.6	6.0	13.0	63.5	17.5
Personal computer	1.5	5.3	16.6	57.3	20.8

Notes:

a) It is necessary, everyone should be able to afford it

b) I have it, and could not do without it

c) I have it, but could do without it

d) I don't have it and don't want it

e) I want it, but cannot afford it

The services and commodities that the majority of respondents felt everyone should be able to afford were: health services (96% of the respondents), warm meal at least once a day (95%), a washing machine (88%), dental services once a year (82%), a vacuum cleaner (80%), satisfactory level of modern conveniences (78%), availability of public transport (77%), home insurance (66%), telephone (66%), enough living space in housing (59%), quarterly hair care (59%), newspaper (53%), and a refrigerator (52%). In a nearly identical Swedish study (Halleröd 1994), in addition a television set and a two-week minimum yearly vacation trip were considered necessities by the majority of the Swedish respondents. It is interesting to note that all along, Swedes were more likely than Finns to see list items as necessities, reflecting that necessity, too, is a relative concept closely bound to time and place.

The second battery of questions was a replica of the first, but the respondents were now asked whether they owned the items listed. The response alternatives were: '1) I have it, and could not do without it. 2) I have it, but could do without it. 3) I don't have it and don't want it. 4) I want it, but cannot afford it.' The responses were dichotomized so that the 'I want it, but cannot afford it' responses became their own class of deprivation. We were particularly interested in involuntary lack of those thirteen items that had been classified as necessities by the majority of respondents. Contrary to Townsend's deprivation index, for example, we categorized only involuntary lack of necessities as deprivation. Deprivation was involuntary nearly without exception regarding the thirteen necessary items. The only exception was that of those respondents who indicated no access to public transport: two thirds responded that they did not want it (Table 2).

As in some earlier studies (Mack and Lansley 1985; Breadline Britain 1990; Halleröd 1994), the criterion for poverty was set at involuntary lack of three or more necessities in the household of the respondent. With this method, the consensual poverty turned out to be 12.6%, which is somewhat higher than poverty indicated by the income measurement. Like the relative income measure, the definition of the poverty line is a bit arbitrary. The picture of the severity of poverty will change if the number of necessities is changed. If we use the lack of two items as the criterion, the poverty rate will rise to 20.4%. Correspondingly, if we increase the number of items to four instead of three, 7.3% of the respondents will be classified as poor.

3.3 Scarcity

Feeling poor is different from being poor. Poverty measurement through subjective experience indeed has its problems. First, it may be that someone who is characterized by a relatively high level of need satisfaction in terms of objective measures might feel him- or herself to be poor. On the other hand, as Runciman (1966) has pointed out, individuals who have become isolated from mainstream society may only compare themselves with others in similar circumstances. Wishes and goals are adjusted to fit whatever meager opportunities seem available at a time. Consequently, many of those who can be identified as poor on objective grounds do not subjectively feel themselves to be poor. Yet, the subjective aspect of poverty is of interest (see for example Alcock 1993, p. 91), and it is worthwhile to investigate to what degree subjective experience and other measures identify the same groups as poor.

According to Steinar Stjernö (1985), a distinctive feature of modern poverty is economic scarcity that casts a shadow on everyday life. Stjernö calls this the tyranny of scarcity. We measured this tyranny of scarcity by using two statements: 1) 'I have in the past year had difficulties in making necessary payments (for food, rent etc.)' and 2) 'It is very difficult for my family to manage on the present level of income'. The correlation between these two items was relatively strong (gamma correlation = 0.86). Of those who indicated that their family has trouble managing with its current income, 91% also reported that they have experienced difficulties in making necessary payments. (Only 28% of the other respondents reported such difficulties.) Those who totally agreed with both statements were characterized as experiencing scarcity. Measured in this way, 8.8% of the respondents were classified as poor, which is close to the figure attained through the income measure.

3.4 Subjective overdebt (OVDEBT)

The impact of overindebtedness has not been widely addressed in international poverty research. Overindebtedness may be a justifiable indicator of poverty in circumstances where freely disposable income is highly curbed by obligatory expenditures. For example, in countries that heavily rely on house ownership, housing costs may be that kind of factor. In such circumstances, people - young families in particular - who have invested in high-priced homes often have financial difficulties even when their nominal incomes are relatively high. This is precisely the situation in Finland where the current recession accentuates problems in housing policy. Toward the end of the 1980s, house prices went up exponentially and those who bought homes at that time had to finance them with considerably high mortgages. With the 1990s recession, prices suddenly collapsed, and many Finns are now in an unfortunate situation where their loans clearly exceed the present sales value of their homes. Furthermore, decreased earnings and unemployment have pushed many families into economic straits, and many find that it is no longer possible to cope with housing loans or other debts. This category of people, in common usage called the 'new poor', are in financial troubles despite their nominally high income.

In this study, we had one question about subjective overindebtness: 'Considering my income and debt management expenses, I feel I am overindebted.' All those were classified as overindebted who in a five step scale completely agreed with the statement. The overindebted constituted 10.9% of all respondents.

3.5 *Recipiency of social assistance* (SOC.ASS)

Researchers in Nordic countries have often used the recipiency of social assistance as a measure of poverty (see Halleröd et al. 1996). This has been motivated by the fact that, in advanced welfare states, social assistance services are the last resort for securing a satisfactory livelihood when other sources of income have failed. In theory, those who receive social assistance are at any given point in time the most indigent members of society and remain so even after receiving assistance. This theoretical statement is also fortified by some recent Scandinavian opinion surveys indicating that in popular opinion social welfare recipients are regarded as excluded from the rest of society. In Sweden, 60% of the population agreed with the statement: 'Social assistance recipients are excluded' (Halleröd et al. 1993, p. 114). In our data, the corresponding figure is 63%.

Despite its many shortcomings and the criticism heaped upon it (see above), social assistance recipiency deserves its place among poverty measures; it works better than other measures to pinpoint those unstable circumstances of life marked by repeated periods of temporary poverty (see Ritakallio 1991). The use of this kind of poverty measure, that is sensitive to continuous fluctuations in citizens' welfare, is warranted especially now that the labour market in most industrial countries has become highly unstable resulting in lower standards of living. In this context, some scholars speak of an urban or new underclass (Jencks and Peterson 1991).

As shown above, the picture of the severity of poverty changes somewhat depending on the measure used. What is common to all the measures is that they display higher poverty rates than official income statistics. The low income measure produces the lowest poverty rate in the survey (9%), whereas the consensual poverty indicator gives the highest figure (13%). Besides that, the poverty rates are relatively close to each other. But how well do the figures correlate, and how good is the overlap?

4 Measures, correlations, and poverty risks

4.1 Correlations of the poverty measures

Table 3 confirms the findings from earlier studies (e.g., McGregor and Borooah 1992; Callan, Nolan and Whelan 1993): the connection between low-income poverty and poverty indicated by other measures is relatively weak. As can be seen in Table 3, less than one third (31.9%) are poor also on the consensual scale. The correlation between other poverty measures and income is weaker still: only about one fifth of low income earners has been classified as poor on the basis of scarcity, overdebt and recipiency of social assistance.

Table 3

The overlap between different poverty measures (percentages)

	RELINC50	CON50	SCARCITY	OVDEBT	SOC.ASS
RELINC50	100.0	31.9	20.7	18.9	17.8
CON50	18.9	100.0	34.9	25.8	30.7
SCARCITY	19.5	50.3	100.0	51.0	35.1
OVDEBT	14.0	29.6	39.9	100.0	22.2
SOC.ASS	16.7	45.2	35.3	27.5	100.0

Note:

Rows indicate the overlap. For example, the first row tells how many per cent of the 'income poor' are poor according to the other measures

Consensual poverty correlates somewhat better with the other measures than the income approach does. Over one third of those who were found poor on the consensual scale appear poor also in the dimensions of scarcity. One fourth of the consensual poor are overindebted, and less than one third receive social assistance. When it comes to subjective feelings of scarcity, they are linked to some degree to overdebt and lack of necessities. About one half of those who had experienced economic difficulties felt that they were overindebted, and about one half were poor on the consensual scale as well.

Overindebtedness is not particularly dependent on income level. Only 14% of those who had been classified as overindebted were poor on the relative income scale. The explanation might be that housing and other loans have been stretched to the upper limits of income and loan servicing capabilities: the higher the income, the bigger the debts. Overindebtedness does have a clearer relationship to subjective feelings of poverty and to financial difficulties. The result is logical in the sense that the overindebted are bound to have trouble managing their households, and are likely to perceive themselves as poor.

Social assistance recipiency correlates most strongly with non-ownership of necessities (45%) and with scarcity. It appears that the dimension created by the combination of these measures highlights the sector of the population that is traditionally perceived as deprived, that typically receives social assistance, and is seen as excluded from mainstream society. Interestingly enough, only 17% of social assistance recipients are poor on the income scale.

In criticizing earlier poverty measures as insufficient, Ringen (1987, 1988) set up two conditions to define poverty: an individual has to be classified as poor by both the income and deprivation measures. In the present study, 28% of the respondents were classified as poor through one measure and 72% were not poor by any measure. Of those 28% classified as poor through one measure, about one half were found poor also by some other method. Thus, roughly speaking about 15% of the population fullfill the dual condition. The proportion of the poor goes rapidly down with each additional condition, e.g., only 2% were poor according to four measures, and none of the nearly 2000 respondents is poor on all five scales. Different measures obviously classify different individuals as poor. But in which particular groups do the different measures locate the highest risks of poverty?

4.2 Poverty risks

Knowing which groups face the greatest risk of becoming poor has important sociopolitical significance. Table 4 (below) gives a picture of what each of the above mentioned five measures tells us about the incidence of poverty in different population categories. The background factors chosen (labour market position, socioeconomic status, socioeconomic status and social assistance recipiency of one's parents, education, type of household, number of children, marital status, age, gender, and area of residence) have been found in earlier studies to have the strongest association with poverty.

Much of life in Western societies is structured around work and the *labor market position*. Classic studies on the effects of the 1930s depression in Marienthal (Jahoda, Lazarsfeld and Zeisel 1971) showed that lack of employment not only deprived people of income, but in many instances also meant exclusion from social relations that normally serve as a foundation for everyday life. In a workorientated society, having no work means exclusion from socially prevalent practices. Therefore, it is hardly surprising that unemployment is one of the most important background factors associated with poverty (Callan et al. 1989, 1993; McGregor and Borooah 1992; Muffels, Berghman and Dirven 1992; Halleröd 1994). Our study is in this respect in line with earlier studies. All of our five measures indicate clearly that the risk of poverty is radically higher for the unemployed than for any other group. In addition, our results show that at least in Finland, the change from full-time to part-time work will increase the risk of poverty. In the Finnish case, the shift from a full-timer to a part-timer status seems to be a gradual shift towards the margins of society and not a gate to the inner circles of society. The incidence of unemployment also indicates this: as much as 56% of part-timers had experienced unemployment during the last five years compared to 26% among the full-timers.

Traditionally, retirement increased individuals' economic risks, largely because of insufficient pension security. However, welfare states in many countries have essentially changed this situation, and pensioners are no longer necessarily the economically weakest group in society (see e.g., Hedström and Ringen 1990; Jäntti, Kangas and Ritakallio 1996). Table 4 shows that the differences between pensioners and the fully employed are minor. In fact, pensioners experience scarcity less and are less often overindebted than any other group. All in all, in terms of labour market position, full-time workers and pensioners seem to have more secure circumstances than all others, whereas the unemployed are the most vulnerable category. In this respect, most measures give a congruent picture.

The majority of our scales indicate that students are highly exposed to poverty but since their low income position may be regarded as a temporary phenomenon and as a result of deliberate choice, student poverty is a disputable issue. In order to get a better picture of poverty, it is necessary to look at its development by collecting data for longer periods of time. Panel set-ups where the same individuals are followed through many years would give a clearer picture of the dynamics of poverty than cross-sectional data. In an ideal research situation, income-related poverty measures would be based on decades-long series of data, or perhaps even cover entire life spans.

In developed societies, *education* has been seen as a means of rising in the social hierarchy (see e.g., Erikson and Goldthorpe 1992). Conversely, in an education-oriented society, those who for one reason or another fail to gain an education may be faced with particular difficulties. Where education opens doors, a lack of education closes them. The stronger the educational orientation in a society, the bigger the risk of exclusion for the uneducated.

Table 4
Extension of poverty (percentages) according to different measures (p-values in parentheses)

	RELINC50	CON50	SCARCITY	OVDEBT	SOC.ASS
Total population	8.5	12.6	9.7	10.9	9.0
Labor market status	(0.000)	(0.000)	(0.000)	(0.003)	(0.000)
Full-time work	1.9	7.4	5.2	9.8	2.5
Part-time work	11.0	14.9	13.3	12.0	15.6
Unemployed	15.8	27.7	24.4	18.5	29.1
Student	25.5	23.9	12.2	10.0	19.1
Retired	9.5	8.1	4.4	8.1	4.3
Education	(0.002)	(0.003)	(0.018)	(0.047)	(0.043)
Basic level	11.3	14.7	11.2	13.4	8.9
Vocational/college	7.6	12.7	7.7	10.0	10.2
University	3.4	4.7	6.1	7.9	4.1
Socioeconomic status	(0.000)	(0.000)	(0.001)	(0.271)	(0.000)
Farmer	21.5	5.8	4.9	12.9	1.5
Self employed	7.1	6.7	6.3	13.6	10.0
Worker	7.6	17.3	12.3	12.8	10.4
Lower white-collar	4.8	10.9	7.6	9.9	7.9
Upper white-collar	0.8	4.6	4.0	7.5	2.8
Parents	(0.095)	(0.000)	(0.000)	(0.030)	(0.001)
Farmer	10.3	6.8	5.7	8.6	4.8
Self employed	1.3	17.5	15.3	14.6	13.4
Worker	7.8	17.7	11.6	13.5	10.5
Lower white-collar	7.7	12.5	10.9	13.3	14.5
Upper white-collar	5.9	9.0	4.5	6.5	7.9
Parents' recipiency of social assistance	(0.579)	(0.000)	(0.000)	(0.000)	(0.000)
No	8.5	12.4	7.9	9.6	8.5
Yes	6.7	23.0	19.9	21.7	18.6
Type of household	(0.002)	(0.000)	(0.000)	(0.051)	(0.000)
Single	9.9	28.8	12.3	12.9	17.8
Couple, no children	6.7	8.3	5.8	9.0	5.8
Couple with children	7.5	7.6	10.1	12.5	5.7
Single mother/father	4.3	32.6	19.1	15.8	36.4
Number of children	(0.005)	(0.009)	(0.114)	(0.058)	(0.155)
No children	9.2	14.9	7.6	9.7	9.8
One	4.9	9.4	10.1	10.4	6.6
Two	6.3	9.1	11.9	15.6	6.9
Three or more	14.4	9.2	9.8	12.3	11.7

	RELINC50	CON50	SCARCITY	OVDEBT	SOC.ASS
Age	(0.000)	(0.000)	(0.000)	(0.002)	(0.000)
- 24	21.9	29.6	9.3	5.8	24.7
25 - 34	6.7	15.1	7.9	11.7	11.1
35 - 44	5.3	10.3	13.8	15.5	7.3
45 - 54	7.3	10.3	11.1	11.4	6.3
55 - 64	4.4	6.2	3.8	8.1	3.7
65 - 70	17.3	5.6	1.7	7.0	0.9
Family status	(0.000)	(0.000)	(0.000)	(0.000)	(0.000)
Bachelor	17.2	26.7	8.1	6.7	18.6
Married	6.4	7.0	7.9	11.1	5.1
Divorced	7.0	31.4	21.0	23.5	21.1
Widow	4.9	7.1	3.8	4.9	2.3
Gender	(0.231)	(0.986)	(0.824)	(0.201)	(0.909)
Male	9.3	12.7	9.0	11.9	9.1
Female	7.6	12.5	8.6	9.9	8.8
Place of residence	(0.000)	(0.534)	(0.642)	(0.040)	(0.006)
Village	13.5	11.4	9.6	13.5	6.2
Town	7.5	12.1	8.4	8.9	8.5
Larger city	4.7	13.6	8.2	10.2	11.7

Table 4 supports these assertions to some degree. The different measures give a rather similar picture with minor exceptions. Those with only basic education have the highest risk of poverty in the sense of ownership of necessities and by the subjective experience measure. For those with middle-level schooling, the lack of necessities is also a problem, and they often receive social assistance. People with university degrees suffer mostly overindebtness and scarcity, indicating that their problem is not low income, but rather an imbalance between income and spending. The problem of these 'new poor' is emphasized by the recent economic recession. With the 1980s trust in economic growth, many acquired housing by stretching their paying power to the extreme. Therefore, even slight cuts in household income - not to speak of major losses due to unemployment - can now cause insurmountable economic hardships. All in all, the story told by looking at education is that education still gives a protection against poverty.

An individual's *socioeconomic position* is one of the most important background variables in matters ranging from opinions and choice of leisure activities to income levels and poverty risk. In Table 4, respondents have been divided into five groups: farmers, other entrepreneurs, labourers, and upper and lower white-collar workers.

For wage earners and salaried staff, different approaches give very similar results: the problem of poverty is most severe among labourers, and least severe on all scales among managerial personnel. The situation is fundamentally different for farmers and entrepreneurs, with different measures giving different pictures of the incidence of poverty. On the income scale, for example, farmers are the poorest of all: as much as 22% of them are below the poverty line but on the other dimensions farmers are pretty well-off. This result is largely due to the applied income concept, which does not take into account all income components. For self-employed, above all for farmers, monetary income is only a portion of all available resources. A large part of their subsistence comes from various in-kind sources connected with their occupation, and it is difficult to estimate this either in surveys or in official statistics. Therefore, the traditional income concept measuring individual's economic resources functions least well with self-employed, something which indicates that cash income does not always satisfactorily assess one's poverty status and, furthermore, this assessment may be biased in favor of certain categories of the population.

Of all poverty measures overindebtness correlates least with socioeconomic status, which again is due to the Finnish peculiarity mentioned above of overextending mortgage and other debts to the extremes of one's ability to pay.

Family background has proven to be a major determinant of whether individuals seek further education and it consequently determines what kind of social status is later acquired (e.g., Eriksson and Goldthrope 1992; Eriksson and Jonsson 1993). We can therefore assume that family background will also have an effect on poverty risk. Another aspect of the connection of family background to poverty - the so-called *culture of poverty* - has become an issue of public debate especially in the United States. It has been argued that families receiving social assistance develop a distinctive culture of dependency that is transmitted from one generation to the next (e.g., Lewis 1968; Murray 1984; see also Dean and Taylor-Gooby 1992; Leibfried et al. 1995) and family members are conditioned to receiving social assistance and other welfare benefits to a large degree. Because of this passivity or helplessness learned at home, their income level is directly dependent on various welfare provisions. Indeed, some empirical studies confirm the positive link between social assistance recipiency for parents and their children (Gottschalk 1992; Stenberg 1995).

Table 4 shows that family background does have an influence on poverty risk, but both the direction and strength of this influence are sensitive to the measure used. Like farmers, farmers' children have the highest risk of income-poverty. The obvious reason is that nearly without exception, farmers are offspring of farmers. What is interesting here is that those children of farmers who are employed outside agriculture still display a high level of risk of income-poverty. However, with other measures it appears that a farming background and the family background of white-collar workers clearly diminish the poverty risk. Interestingly enough, especially farmer background reduces the risk of social assistance recipiency. 10% of all entrepreneurs receive social assistance, whereas only 2.8% of those enterpreneurs who are from farmer homes rely on assistance. Corresponding figures for workers are 10.4 vs. 6.8%, for lower white-collar workers 7.9 vs. 2.9%, and for upper white-collar workers 2.8 vs. 2.0%. Thus, the Finnish farmers and their offspring seem to share some kind of selfsuffiency ethos that is hostile to recipiency of social assistance.

An entrepreneurial background has inverse implications to those of a farming background. The poverty risk for the income measure is the lowest, but as far as scarcity, social assistance recipiency, and overindebtness are concerned, children of entrepreneurs are in an even worse position than those who hail from working-class homes. Table 4 also reveals the interesting information that social welfare recipiency seems to correlate somewhat more strongly with a lower white-collar than with a laborer background.

It also appears that a history of social welfare recipiency, the 'culture of poverty' of the childhood home has some effect (cf. Stenberg 1995). By all measures but one, the poverty risk for children of social assistance recipients is distinctly higher than for those whose childhood households did not receive social assistance. Interestingly enough, low-income poverty seems to be lowest among those coming from 'social assistance homes' but despite this, all other indicators display higher poverty risks for them. The result thus seems to support the culture of poverty hypothesis. However, it must be emphasized that the second generation recipients of social assistance is a rather limited phenomenon. Not more than 2.5% of the respondents belong to this category.

Many earlier studies have shown that poverty risk widely varies among different *household types*. According to some studies, the most severe poverty risk is in households headed by single parents (Mitchell 1991; Smeeding and Torrey 1988). However, these results obviously depend on the social policies of each country. Ritakallio (1994a), for example, showed that low income poverty risk varied more between countries than between different sectors of the population within countries. In the Scandinavian countries, the situation of single parents in relation to the other family types is better than in Australia, the United States, or Germany.

Finnish research has shown that those who live alone - especially single men - constitute the 'the hard core' of social deprivation (Heikkilä 1990). The measures used in this study give a somewhat conflicting picture of poverty in different types of household. According to the income measure, the situation of single parents is not particularly bad. However, as far as ownership of necessities, experiencing economic hardships, overdebt, and social assistance recipiency are concerned, single parents are a clear at risk group. Social assistance recipiency is especially high among single parents. Table 4 indicates that people living alone are also in the danger zone. For them, ownership of necessities, subjectively felt poverty, and social assistance recipiency measures clearly display higher poverty figures compared to the average. A partial explanation is that singles are younger, and the poverty measures in question do point out the young as especially vulnerable to poverty, as will be discussed later.

According to a Finnish proverb, when a child is born, the bread will follow. But if there are very many children, a lot of bread will be needed. In most cases it is impossible to raise the household incomes to meet the new needs, and social redistribution measures compensate only in part for the additional consumption needs. Many empirical studies using the income measure have shown a direct link between poverty and the *number of children* (Smeeding and Torrey 1988; Ritakallio 1994a). Our data give a somewhat unambiguous picture of the relationships between the number of children and poverty. The income-based poverty measure confirms the earlier results: the risk of poverty increases in tandem with the number of children. Social assistance recipiency is also more common in families with many children. By the other measures, large families are not significantly worse off than other types of families.

Seebohm Rowntree's classic 1901 study showed that poverty is closely tied with *age* or stages of life. It is worse for the groups with dependent children. After the children leave home, the family's poverty rate goes down, but goes up again in old age with ebbing work capacity. Many later studies have tried to substantiate Rowntree's poverty cycle more precisely, often with conflicting results. Some of the studies have confirmed the cycle; in others, this feature has either not been found or has turned out to be different from what it was in York a century ago. Of course it is clear that the development of welfare societies has made a big difference in which age groups are vulnerable to poverty in today's world (e.g., Hedström and Ringen 1990; Jäntti, Kangas and Ritakallio 1995). And it is equally clear that different types of poverty profiles for different countries produce different types of poverty profiles for different age groups. Old-age poverty, for example, is nearly unknown in Sweden because the country has such a good pension security system (Hedström and Ringen 1990). Also in many other countries, there is a clear trend towards decreased old-age poverty (Room et al. 1987).

Table 4 does not show a clear correlation between poverty and age. The pictures produced by the subjective and objective measures conflict greatly. The traditional income measure pinpoints the youngest group as poorest, but according to the subjective measures, young people's poverty is below average. Like the youngsters, the oldest age group (65 to 70 years), the 'grey panthers', also have relatively low incomes but appear to be well off in all other dimensions. Only 2% of the oldest age group felt economic hardship. The corresponding figure for the rest of population was 10%.

Most of the measures are sensitive to the respondent's age. Ownership of necessities and recipiency of social assistance display a linear relationship. In the former case, deprivation decreases in tandem with age. In the latter case similarly, recipiency of social assistance is most common among the young age brackets. Subjective feelings - whether in terms of scarcity, overindebtness or feelings of being poor - are curvilinearly related with age: gloomy feelings are most common among the middle-aged groups.

Family may be both a burden and a resource. Some Finnish studies (Heikkilä 1990) speak in favor of the latter: single persons, particularly men who for one reason or another have never managed to marry, have the highest risk of poverty and social exclusion. Also widowhood has traditionally increased the poverty risk. Therefore, we also look at the distribution of poverty according to the respondent's *marital status*.

The income measure used in Table 4 confirms the connection between single status and poverty. For the unmarried, income-based poverty, the lack of necessities, and the recipiency of social assistance are significantly more common than for the other groups. However, being widowed is not associated with financial hardships at all. In fact, widows appear to be one of the most privileged groups in today's Finland, where survivors' and widows' pension systems are quite well-developed. The dissolution of families, however, makes a big difference on all scales except the income scale. In comparison to the other groups, divorced people own fewer necessities, they feel themselves to be poor, experience more financial difficulties, are overindebted and receive social assistance more often than others. All in all, our data portray the lives of the divorced in rather gloomy colours. Marriage appears to give a protection against poverty. Only overindebtness is above the average among the married.

The feminisation of poverty has become an important part of the international debate on poverty (see e.g., Gimenez 1989; Zopf 1989; Roche 1992). Many researchers have shown that poverty is *gender* sensitive and characteristically hits women harder. On the basis of our data, none of the five measures gives support to the hypothesis of poverty being more common among women. In fact, poverty is not associated with gender. This result has been verified also by household surveys and by income-based data (Heikkilä 1990; Ritakallio 1994b). Marklund (1990) came to the same conclusion in his analysis of Sweden. Apparently, the combination of Nordic women's high labor force participation with the universal social security programs has created a situation where poverty is not gender-related in the same way as in certain other countries where feminisation of poverty has been clearly detected.

The last of the Table 4 background variables, *area of residence*, has emerged as a poverty determinant in earlier studies (e.g., Ritakallio 1994b, p. 66) with social welfare recipiency being more conspicuous in towns, and low income poverty in the countryside. Table 4 shows a similar outcome: welfare recipiency is most common in larger cities, low incomes on the other hand is a poverty feature in small localities. Overdebt and subjective feelings of poverty are also problems prevalent in smaller localities.

All in all, our results show that different measures tend to identify poverty with different groups.[3] Moreover, the stories told by our measures are often ambiguous: some categories of the population are poor according to some measures while in terms of other indicators they may be rather well-off. In addition to these conflicting findings, there are some findings that are less affected by the measure adopted. First of all, the lack of employment is the most important factor causing poverty, be it measured as a lack of economic resources or as different forms of social deprivation. Also higher education and upper white-collar position, gender and the recipiency of social assistance by one's parents behave consistently across the poverty measures: the two former reduce the probability of being poor, while the latter clearly increases the incidence of poverty. According to our data, there is no correlation between gender and poverty.

5 Summary

Poverty is a very demanding concept. It also suggests a moral imperative to eliminate poverty, or at least to alleviate its most extreme forms (Piachaud 1987, p. 161; Saunders 1994a,b). The problem is that researchers tend to use different definitions and measures, thereby producing different pictures of poverty. But, if we take the moral imperative as our social policy goal we may be confused: Who are the poor? Who should be helped? What should be done? Therefore, comparing concepts and measures is not just semantic or scientific acrobatics. Comparative analysis also has important sociopolitical implications. In order to reduce poverty, it is highly essential to know what kind of a societal problem poverty is and in which population groups different poverty measures locate social hardships. The purpose of this study was not to try to uncover the 'true' nature of poverty but just to investigate to what extent, if any, different methods commonly used in poverty research yield the same results on the incidence of poverty.

The main finding is that the poverty rates picked up by our five measures are rather similar but the overlap of those indicators is rather weak. The poverty rate varied from 9% (low income) to 13% (the consensual deprivation measure). Methodologically it is worthwhile to note that all of our cross-sectional measures yield remarkably higher poverty rates than register-based income measures. Differencies can be explained by variation in the reference period to which income data pertain. Register data usually refer to annual income, whereas our data refer to monthly income. The longer reference period in registers may eliminate or smooth temporary income-losses, thus concealing short term spells of poverty. For these reasons, annual incomes tend to diminish the incidence of poverty, whereas cross-sectional snap-shots may magnify the extension of poverty.

Not only the magnitude of the problem but also the identification of risk categories is sensitive to the methods used. The overlap of our measures is poor. At best, the overlap between two measures is about 50%, usually considerably lower revolving between 20 and 30%. Especially the connection between income and the other poverty measures used is surprisingly low. All these results indicate that different methods tend to classify different population categories as poor. Despite this, there are also some important similarities. First of all, there is a strong causal connection between unemployment and poverty. According to all indicators examined, the unemployed have the highest poverty risk. Examples from other OECD countries with high unemployment clearly indicate that the growth of unemployment, long-term unemployment in particular, will generate persistent poverty problems that will be obvious in all poverty measures - something which may be helpful for poverty research but not for the unemployed.

One of the most important underlying ideals in welfare state ideology has been the accomplishment of equal opportunity by abolishing at least the most striking economic barriers which retard individual fulfilment. As a rule, the main tool to achieve these goals has been income transfers. Or to put it in more general terms, equality of opportunity is obtained by equality of monetary resources. However, the fact that direct and indirect measures produce such a different picture of poverty is somewhat problematic for the adequacy of the welfare state relying on transfers. Why are the monetary resources provided by the welfare state not better transformed into well-being in other arenas of life? This question is highly relevant when looking at the problems of those respondents whose parents received social assistance. According to our data, the children of assistance recipients are not suffering from lack of economic resources (relative income poverty) but their poverty rates according to the other measures are significantly higher than those of the rest of the population. If money is not enough, what kind of new approaches and policies should be adopted in order to combat those manifestations of poverty that are revealed by direct poverty measures? How can the individual's capabilities to fully utilize those opportunities that are available to them be improved? The following Table tries to answer these questions (for a closer description, see Ritakallio 1991).

Table 5
Individual's possession of resources and the control over resources

		Control over resources	
Has resources		No	yes
	No	*excluded*	*can be helped by transfers*
	Yes	*will be excluded*	*no problems*

Those respondends who are not classified as poor by any of our five indicators can be placed into the 'yes-yes box': they have resources (money etc.) and command over them, and in principle, they live on their own without major interventions of the welfare state. People in the 'no-yes box' do not have resources but they would have the capacity to control their resources if they had any. For example, those who are overindebted because of unemployment could be placed in this box. Money would relieve their misery. To some extent, this goes for scarcity experiences and income poor as well. Also some of the consensual poor would be helped by transfers.

Money alone is not a remedy for those belonging to the two remaining boxes. Those in the 'no-no box' neither have resources nor a capacity to control their lives. The traditional core of social assistance recipients and consensual poor are in such a situation: they lack knowledge and skills to manage in a society that values social and cultural capital. In the long run, also those who lack the capacity to control their resources (the 'yes-no box') will be in the same position. Because of deficiencies in control over their life they will gradually lose all they have. The problem picture of these persons indicates that standard measures of social policy, undertaken in accordance with the ideology of the welfare state, do not help to solve the problems having to do with control of one's life. Along with the standard income transfer measures there is obviously a need for selective strategies for individual cases.

The main conclusion of our paper is that different methods produce different pictures of poverty. Despite differences in results, each of these pictures may be equally correct and realistic. They only map a different slice of reality. Therefore, a simultaneous use of various measures may be advisable. One measure gives one result, another reveals something else. By concentrating on one single 'correct' measure, a great deal of valuable information may be lost. A full analysis requires a multidimensional method of measurement. In that way we can reveal the many faces of poverty and social exclusion that, in turn, can be combatted by different remedies.

Notes

[1] The studies in question have investigated, among other things, the effects of equivalence scales (Buhmann, Rainwater, Schmaus and Smeeding 1988), differences produced by different concepts of income (Whiteford 1993; Jansson 1992), and effects of the unit of analysis (Ritakallio 1994b, p. 41).

[2] The Finnish national income fell by about 15% between 1991 and 1993 with a direct effect on rising unemployment. In 1990 the out-of-work population was less than four per cent of the labour force - one of the lowest unemployment rates among the OECD countries - unemployment then exploded and by 1994, nearly 20% of the labour force was without work (OECD 1994, p. 6). As a consequence, social expenditure skyrocketed (from 25% of GDP in 1990 to 35% in 1994) putting the state budget out of balance. The growth of public debt forced the government to cut expenditure, causing deterioration in social security and decline in living conditions for those living on social assistance and public income transfers.

[3] Table 4 only shows the bivariate relationships. However, a logistic regression model basically shows the same results. Since logistic regression coefficients are somewhat hard to interpret, they are not reported here, but can be obtained from the editor on request.

References

Alcock, P. (1993), *Understanding Poverty*, MacMillan: London.

Atkinson, A. (1989), *Poverty and Social Security*, Harvester Wheatsheaf: New York.

Breadline Britain 1990s (1991), *The Findings of the Television Series*, Weekend Television (Booklet): London.

Buhmann, B., Rainwater, L., Schmaus, G. and Smeeding, T. (1988), 'Equivalence Scales, Well-Being, Inequality and Poverty: Sensitivity Estimates across Ten Countries Using Luxembourg Income Study (LIS) Data-Base', *Review of Income and Wealth*, Vol. 34, No. 2, pp. 115-142.

Callan, T., Nolan, B., Whelan, B. and Hannan, D. (1989), 'Poverty, Income and Welfare in Ireland', *The Economic and Social Research Institute, General Research Series*, paper no. 146: Dublin.

Callan, T., Nolan, B. and Whelan, C. (1993), 'Resources, Deprivation and the Measurement of Poverty', *Journal of Social Policy*, Vol. 22, No. 2, pp. 141-172.

Dean, H. and Taylor-Gooby, P. (1992), *Dependency Culture. The Explosion of a Myth*, Harvester and Wheatsheaf: London.

Erikson, R. and Goldthorpe, J. (1992), *The Constant Flux. A Study of Class Mobility in Industrial Societies*, Clarendon Press: Oxford.

Erikson, R. and Jonsson, J. (1993), *Ursprung och Utbildning - Social snedrekrytering till högre studier (Origin and Education)*, Statens offentliga utredningar 1993:85, Utbildnings-departementet: Stockholm.

Fridberg, T. (ed.). (1993), *On Social Assistance in the Nordic Capitals*, Nordic Council of Ministers: Copenhagen.

Gimenez, M. (1989), 'Feminization of Poverty: Myth or reality?', *International Journal of Health Services*, Vol. 19, No. 1, pp. 45-61.

Goedhart, T., Halberstaad, V., Kapteyn, A. and van Praag, B. (1977), 'The Poverty Line: Concept and Measurement', *Journal of Human Resources*, Vol. 12, No. 4, pp. 503-520.

Gottschalk, P. (1992), 'The Intergenerational Transmission of Welfare Participation: Facts and Possible Causes', *Journal of Policy Analysis and Management*, Vol. 11, No. 2, pp. 254-272.

Gustafsson, B. (1987), 'Som ett isberg?– Om underutnyttjande av socialbidrag (Like Iceberg? - About the non-take-up of Social Assistance)', *Nordisk Socialt Arbeid*, Vol.7, No. 3, pp. 43–51.

Gustafsson, B. and Lindblom, M. (1993), 'Poverty Lines and Poverty in Seven European Countries, Australia, Canada and the USA', *Journal of European Social Policy*, Vol. 3, No. 1, pp. 21–38.

Gustafsson, B. and Uusitalo, H. (1990), 'The Welfare State and Poverty in Finland and Sweden from the Mid-1960s to the Mid-1980s', *Review of Income and Wealth*, Vol. 36, No. 3, pp. 249–266.

Hagenaars, J. (1986), *The Perception of Poverty*, Elsevier Science Publishers: Amsterdam.

Halleröd, B. (1991), *Den svenska fattigdomen. En studie av fattigdom och socialbidragstagande* (The Swedish Poverty), Arkiv avhandlingsserie 36: Lund.

Halleröd, B. (1994), 'Poverty in Sweden: a New Approach to the Direct Measurement of Consensual Poverty', *Umeå Studies in Sociology*, No. 106.

Halleröd, B. (1995), 'The Truly Poor. Direct and Indirect Consensual Measurement of Poverty in Sweden', *Journal of European Social Policy*, Vol. 5, No. 2, pp. 111-129.

Halleröd, B., Heikkilä, M., Mäntysaari, M., Ritakallio, V-M. and Nyman C. (1996), 'The Nordic Countries: Poverty in a Welfare State', in Öyen, E., Miller, S. and Samad, S. (eds.), *Poverty. A Global Review. Handbook in International Poverty Research*, Scandinavian University Press: Oslo, pp. 325-353.

Halleröd, B., Marklund, S., Nordlund, A. and Stattin, M. (1993), 'Konsensuell fattigdom – en studie av konsumtion och attityder till konsumtion (Consensual Poverty)', *Umeå Studies in Sociology*, No. 104.

Hedström, P. and Ringen, S. (1990), 'Age and Income in Contemporary Society', in Smeeding, T., O'Higgins, M. and Rainwater, L. (eds.), *Poverty, Inequality and Income Distribution in Comparative Perspective*, Harvester Wheatsheaf: London, pp. 77–103.

Heikkilä, M. (1990), 'Köyhyys ja huono-osaisuus hyvinvointivaltiossa. Tutkimus köyhyydestä ja hyvinvoinnin puutteiden kasautumisesta Suomessa (Poverty and Deprivation in a Welfare State; with English Summary)', *National Board of Social Welfare*, Publications 8.

Jahoda, M., Lazarsfeld, P. and Zeisel, H. (1971), *Marienthal; The Sociography of an Unemployed Community*,. Aldinen-Atherton: Chicago 1971 (Die Arbeitslosen von Marienthal 1933).

Jansson, K. (1992), *Low Income is not Enough to Measure Poverty. A Study of Distribution of Poverty in Sweden including Data about Assets and Debts*, Paper presented at the multidisciplinary research conference on poverty and distribution, 16-17 November 1992, Oslo.

Jencks, C. and Peterson, P. (eds.) (1991), *The Urban Underclass*, The Brookings Institution: Washington, D.C.

Jäntti, M., Kangas, O. and Ritakallio, V-M. (1996), 'From Marginalism to Institutionalism: Distributional Consequences of the Transformation of the Finnish Pension Regime', *Review of Income and Wealth*, Vol. 42, No. 4, pp. 473–491.

Leibfried, S., Leisering, L., Buhr, P., Ludwig, M., Mädje, E., Olk, T., Voges, W. and Zwick, M. (1995), *Zeit der Armut. Lebensläufe im Sozialstaat*, Suhrkamp Verlag: Frankfurt am Main.

Lewis, O. (1968), *La Vida, a Puerto Rican Family in the Culture of Poverty: San Juan and New York*, Panther Books: London.

Living Allowance and Draftees' Dependents Allowance 1993. National Research and Development Centre for Welfare and Health. Social Security 1995 1: Helsinki.

Mack, J. and Lansley, S. (1985), *Poor Britain*, George Allen and Unwin: London.

Marklund, S. (1990) 'Structures of Modern Poverty', *Acta Sociologica*, Vol. 33, No. 2, pp. 125-140.

McCregor, P. and Borooah, V. (1992), 'Is Low Spending or Low Income a Better Indicator of Whether or Not a Household is Poor: Some Results From the 1985 Family Expenditure Survey', *Journal of Social Policy*, Vol. 21, No. 1, pp. 53–69.

Mitchell, D. (1991), *Income Transfers in Ten Welfare States,* Avebury: Aldershot.

Muffels, R., Berghman, J. and Dirven H-J. (1992), 'A Multi-Method Approach to Monitor the Evolution of Poverty', *Journal of European Social Policy,* Vol. 2, No.3, pp. 193-213.

Murray, C. (1984), *Losing Ground: American Social Policy 1950-80,* Basic Books

OECD (1994), *Employment Outlook,* Paris.

Piachaud, D. (1987), 'Problems in Definition and Measurement of Poverty', *Journal of Social Policy,* Vol. 16, No. 2, pp. 147-164.

Poverty in the United States (1991), *Current Population Reports, Consumer Income,* Series P-60, No. 181.

Ringen, S. (1987), *The Possibility of Politics. A Study in the Political Economy of the Welfare State,* Clarendon Press: Oxford.

Ringen, S. (1988), 'Direct and Indirect Measures of Poverty. Discussion', *Journal of Social Policy,* Vol. 17, No. 3, pp. 351–365.

Ringen, S. (1995), 'Well-being, Measurement, and Preferences', *Acta Sociologica,* Vol. 38, No. 1, pp. 3-15.

Ritakallio, V-M. (1991), 'Köyhyys ei tule yksin. Tutkimus hyvinvointipuutteiden kasautumisesta toimeentulotukiasiakkailla (Poverty Does not Come Alone. A Study of Accumulated Welfare Deprivation among Social Assistance Recipients; with English Summary)', *National Agency for Welfare and Health,* Research Report 11. Helsinki.

Ritakallio, V-M. (1994a), 'Finnish Poverty: A Cross-National Comparison', *Luxembourg Income Study, Working Paper* 119.

Ritakallio, V-M. (1994b), 'Köyhyys Suomessa 1981-1990. Tutkimus tulonsiirtojen vaikutuksista. (Poverty in Finland 1981-1990. A Study of Effects of Income Transfers; with English Summary)', *National Research and Development Centre,* Research Report 39.

Roche, M. (1992), *Rethinking Citizenship,* Polity Press: Cambridge.

Room, G., Lawson, R. and Laczko, F. (1987), 'New poverty in the European Community', *Policy and Politics,* Vol. 17, No. 2, pp. 165-176.

Rowntree, S. (1901), *Poverty. The Study of Town Life,* Macmillan: London.

Runciman, W. (1966), *Relative Deprivation and Social Justice,* Routledge and Kegan Paul: London.

Saunders, P. (1994a), 'The Role, Value and Limitations of Poverty Research', *SPRC, Discussion Papers* 53, The University of New South Wales.

Saunders, P. (1994b), *Welfare and Inequality. National and International Perspectives on the Australian Welfare State,* Cambridge University Press: Cambridge.

Smeeding, T. and Torrey, B. (1988), 'Poor Children in Rich Countries', *Science* 242 (November 11), pp. 873-877.

Statistical Yearbook of Finland 1993. Statistics Finland 1994, Helsinki.

Stenberg, S-O. (1995), 'The Inheritance of Welfare Dependency: An Intergenerational Study in Postwar Sweden', *Swedish Institute for Social Research,* Stockholm University (stencil).

Stjernö, S. (1985), *Den moderne fattigdommen (The Modern Poverty)*, Universitetsforlaget AS: Oslo.

Townsend, P. (1979), *Poverty in the United Kingdom. A Survey of Household Resources and Standards of Living*, Penguin Books, Harmondsworth: London.

Veit-Wilson, J. (1987), 'Consensual Approaches to Poverty Lines and Social Security', *Journal of Social Policy*, Vol. 16, No. 2, pp. 183–211.

Whiteford, P. (1993), *The concept of income in international comparative research*, Paper presented at ISA RC 19 Conference On Comparative Research of Welfare State in Transition, Oxford, September 1993.

Zopf, P. (1989), *American women in poverty*, Greenwood Press: Westport.

The convergence between different measures of poverty in a static versus dynamic perspective: An empirical illustration in France

Bruno Jeandidier and Jean-Luc Kop

Introduction

The *theoretical* literature relating to individual processes which lead to poverty or relating to the characterisation of poor populations shows a broad consensus regarding the multidimensional character of poverty (income, employment, health, housing, social relations, etc.). This plurality justifies the thesis which emphasises that poverty is a cumulative phenomenon of either concurrent handicaps at a given moment or of a series of difficulties in various areas leading to exclusion. On the other hand, in the literature relating to the *measurement* of poverty, methodologists generally stick to *only one* of the three classic types of measures: monetary measures, subjective measures, or measures of objective living conditions, even if they do not reject the idea of the multidimensionality of poverty. The result is either internal debates within each of these approaches, or a simple statement of divergence regarding the measures resulting from these three approaches.

The hypothesis we are testing in this article is: *one of the reasons for divergence in these different measures lies in the fact that time is not taken into account.* As a matter of fact, one can understand intuitively that, for example, a temporary monetary difficulty may not involve any alteration of objective living conditions, nor result in a subjective feeling of poverty. Also, a personally stigmatising event (e.g. the recent death of a husband or wife) may lead the individual to express at the time a very negative opinion about his situation, whereas objectively, from the viewpoint of his living conditions and/or his monetary standard of living, his situation has not significantly worsened. On the contrary, one can imagine easily that a critical financial situation over a long period may be correlated with a degradation of living conditions and with negative feelings (despair, complaints, etc). In other words, our hypothesis is that, if time is taken into account, the various measures of poverty may be reconciled, even if the diagnoses (poor / non-poor) made on the same individuals may differ when being measured staticly.

As a first step, we will show briefly that, even if we can find some attention given to the monetary and non-monetary forms of poverty in French literature, few studies directly tackle the question of concordance between the different measures. As a second step, we will discuss our own results, elaborated from French data, which compare the extent of concordance between the three methods using the static or the longitudinal approach.

1 The partial absence of a methodological debate regarding the (non) convergence between monetary and non-monetary measures

Our - non-exhaustive - reading of the French literature on the statistical analysis of poverty seems to indicate two tendencies which are curiously contradictory: the quite systematic reference to a notion of poverty with a multidimensional approach, and the rarity of empirical attempts to construct composite scales. As far as we know, the question of methodological confrontation between monetary and non-monetary measures has been the subject of very few studies whose main conclusions we will evoke here.

1.1 A desire to combine income criteria with non-monetary characteristics without getting to the point of constructing composite scales of poverty

The French works we have recorded may be classified into three categories. A first set of studies are those which refer very little to non-monetary poverty indicators, i.e. those for which the construction of such indexes is not the object nor the main methodology. These studies develop a non-monetary problematic of poverty but, from the methodological viewpoint, they do not propose the construction of synthetic indicators; items of living conditions are analysed separately. However, the link between income and objective living conditions is quite present in these studies as the authors emphasize the specificity of the living conditions of the low income population compared to those of the whole population (Debonneuil 1978; Willmott et al. 1978; Tran Ap 1992).

The second category brings together studies which are meant to emphasise the hypothesis of an accumulation of disadvantages, by using exploratory statistical methods enabling the classification of multiple qualitative criteria, but which are not designed to compute measurement scales (Tabard 1980; Tallard and Valetas 1981; Dupré et al. 1986; Fénelon et al. 1988; Croutte et al. 1991; Euvrad et al. 1991; Paugam, 1991). In all these studies, the multidimensional character of poverty is the central hypothesis and it is interesting to see that the methodological approach is systematically the same: descriptive analysis of living conditions for each field, then a synthetic approach using correspondance analysis and, finally, a typology of disadvantaged groups of individuals or families. Even if the relation between income and living conditions is generally not a central question for the authors, it nevertheless exists in the analyses: income is either used (explicitely or implicitely) as a selection variable, or it is introduced as an additional variable in the correspondance analysis.

In this second category of works, we must also evoke those of the French National Institute of Statistics (INSEE) using the survey 'Etudes des Conditions de Vie 1986-87' (Borkowski et al. 1991; Villeneuve 1991) whose methodology is slightly different. As a matter of fact, the target of the analysis is to construct indicators retracing a multidimensional conception of inequality. This hypothesis of multidimensionality leads the authors to treat separately seven fields of analysed living conditions (health, resources, property, cultural integration, employment, social relations, housing). One correspondance analysis is performed for each field and the variables which contribute little to the definition of the dimensions are eliminated. But even if the study emphasises (by a synthetic correspondance analysis) the relations between the seven indicators, the purpose is not to build a single indicator of inequality (e.g. by summation of the seven indicators). For Villeneuve (1991), if different fields of inequality are on the same factorial axis, it does not mean that they can be reduced to only one, but simply that the probability of association between these specific inequalities is higher. One will finally notice that, in this approach, the 'monetary resources' dimension is only one field similar to the six others.

Finally, a third category includes several works which adopt an approach turned explicitely towards the construction of a usable measurement scale built from items relating a priori to objective or subjective living conditions (Dickes 1983; Villeneuve 1984; Borkowski 1985; David and Starzek 1987; Lopez 1990). One will first notice that in these studies the proposed indicators are often scales with a low range: for example, the Borkowski index has only three categories, the scales of David and Starzek and of Villeneuve have five categories. This gives the indicators a more qualitative rather than a metric character. Moreover, authors are generally quite suspicious about the use of these indicators in terms of intensity (e.g. David and Starzek prefer to speak about a presumption of greater vulnerability).

In these studies, the link between living conditions and income is assumed without being clearly analysed. For example, for Borkowski (1985) the set 'income and property' constitutes one of the three categories of the indicator (besides health and isolation); in Villeneuve's (1984) indicator, two out of the five retained categories are relating to income (absence of savings; poor guarantee of income in case of illness); in Lopez' indicator (1990), the monetary standard of living is introduced with a five classes variable; finally, in the composite score proposed by Dickes (1983), 11 of the 32 selected items are relating to the received income or to payment difficulties. Although income is not clearly integrated in David and Starzek (1987), the authors analyse the differences of standards of living between sub-groups determined by vulnerability indicators. Finally, the calculation of the correlation between the indicator of living conditions and the monetary standard of living is sometimes used as a validity test of the indicator: a negative but moderate correlation means that the indicator measures a poverty (or precariousness) phenomenon which, however, is not totally identical to strictly monetary poverty (cf. for example Villeneuve 1984).

1.2 Two attempts at methodological confrontation between monetary and non-monetary measures

In previous work (Ray et al. 1991), we have directly approached the question of concordance of measures arising from different methods of poverty measurement by combining three indicators: a monetary standard of living, an indicator of subjective poverty, and a living conditions indicator. First of all, the correlation between the monetary standard of living and the indicator of subjective poverty, which is only -0.30, suggests that the non-monetary indicator measures a specific form of poverty. It is the same with the living conditions indicator, whose correlation with the monetary standard of living is -0.26. Then, thresholds on the three scales have been determined in an empirical and arbitrary way, in order to set up a typology enabling us to show the possible overlap of the three poverty dimensions. It appears that there is a strict concordance of these measures only in 64% of all cases. The arbitrary nature of the thresholds necessitates some caution regarding the conclusions which may be drawn from these results. But these simple statistics invite a deeper comparative analysis of poverty measures.

This type of analysis was extended in Dickes (1992). The author takes a quite similar approach but applies it to a much wider sample (the INSEE survey 'Etude des Conditions de Vie'). The results are quite similar to those of Ray et al. (1991), particularly the correlation between the monetary standard of living and the living conditions indicator which is equal to -0.31. The author avoids the criticism over the arbitrary nature of the thresholds by using a more flexible method which consists of making a hierarchical classification of households along with three poverty indicators. The analysis leads to a typology of seven sub-groups. However, the conclusion from Dickes' work is basically the same as the one obtained by Ray et al. with the threshold method: Dickes numbers two households out of five for which there is no strict diagnostic concordance.

2 The three measures of poverty in the Lorraine household panel

The data used in the empirical part of this paper was provided by the Lorraine household panel study called ESEML (Enquête Socio-Economique auprès des Ménages Lorrains). Lorraine is one of the 22 French administrative regions. There are more than 2.3 million inhabitants in Lorraine and their demographic and socio-economic characteristics are very similar to those observed in France in general (INSEE 1995-96).

The ESEML is a longitudinal study of a representative sample of households in Lorraine. Roughly 2000 households and 7000 individuals were interviewed each year between 1985 and 1990 using detailed questionnaires on socio-economic conditions.[1] This survey is analogous to several carried out in other European countries especially in Luxembourg (Panel Socio-Economique 'Liewen zu Lutzebuerg'), in Germany (Sozio-Ökonomisches Panel), in the United-Kingdom (British Panel of Households Survey), in Belgium (Les conditions de vie des ménages en Belgique). The very recent European Community Household Panel (ECHP) can be considered as a continuation of these national surveys.

2.1 The monetary indicator of poverty

The *monetary indicator of poverty* used in this paper is one of the most simple proposed in the literature. We chose the total income of the household divided by the number of consumption units, calculated with the OECD equivalence scale (known also as the Oxford equivalence scale: the coefficients are respectively 1, 0.7 and 0.5 for the first, the second and the other persons in the households). Despite criticism formulated against this indicator (e.g. Sawhill 1988; Atkinson and Cazes 1990; Ray et al. 1991), it is widely used and sufficient for our purpose. Table 1 shows some descriptive statistics of this indicator in the ESEML.

Table 1
Descriptive statistics of the monetary poverty indicator
(in French francs)

	1986	1987	1988	1989	1990
Number of observations	7553	7342	7380	7096	7480
Mean	4437	5395	4604	4811	5189
Median	3824	4049	4016	4251	4545
Standard deviation	2496	2554	2476	2749	2854

Source: Lorraine household panel (INSEE, Nancy and ADEPS)

When one retains the poverty thresholds generally used, i.e. 50% of the average equivalised household income, the rate of poverty in Lorraine over the considered period has been relatively stable (about 10% to 11%). If, however, we want to place the evolution of the rate of monetary poverty into the macro-economic regional context, for example by comparing it to the evolution of the unemployment rate, it is curious to find that, in the medium term (5 years), monetary poverty has not closely followed the evolution of unemployment: the years of economic recovery 1989 and 1990 have shown a sharp decrease in unemployment, but not of monetary poverty. Looking at the short term economic evolution, a dynamic approach, using poverty transitions from one year to the next one, does not enable us to better understand the link between unemployment and monetary poverty. Considering the regular decrease of unemployment from 1986 to 1990, one could expect that, on the one hand the rate of transitions out of monetary poverty should increase, and on the other hand that the rate of transitions in poverty should decrease. As indicated in Table 2, these two expectations are not fulfilled.

It is interesting to take into account a second dimension of the economic environment: it is the role played by social policy, the 'campaign against poverty'. In the case of France, the second part of the 1980s was marked by the Revenu Minimum d'Insertion (RMI) set up in January 1989. In the case of Lorraine, as well as in the rest of France, the increase in beneficiaries was fast[2] and stabilised during 1990.

Table 2
Unemployment and monetary poverty rates in Lorraine (in %)

	Regional unemployment rate	Monetary poverty rate	Rate of transitions out of monetary poverty	Rate of transitions in monetary poverty
1986	10.5	10.1	-	-
1987	10.6	10.1	40	4.4
1988	10.1	9.8	45	4.8
1989	9.3	11.2	36	5.4
1990	8.4	10.6	41	4.5

Sources: INSEE (1995-96, p. 87); Lorraine household panel (INSEE, Nancy and ADEPS)

In some way, it seems that the effect of this minimum income policy can be found in the rates of transition out of monetary poverty: in 1990 the rate of exit from poverty had clearly increased (from 36% to 41%), whereas the rate of entry into poverty had slowed (from 5.4% to 4.5%).

2.2 The non-monetary indicators of poverty

The construction of the *non-monetary indicators of poverty* was largely inspired by the works of Dickes (e.g. Dickes 1989, 1992; Ray et al. 1991). We first began by collecting the items which were used to measure non-monetary poverty in the questionnaires of the different waves of the study. The number of non-monetary items is not the same each year. For example, there are 27 items in the survey of 1986 but only 2 in the survey of 1989.[3] These items are related to different fields: housing conditions, possession of durable goods, subjective evaluation of living standards, difficulties in coping with certain expenses, leisure, savings, and social benefits (see Appendix for a list of the indicators used in 1986). Since each of these items call upon rather rare situations, their distributions are more or less skewed.

In general, there is some data missing and this can become problematic in analyses based on item combinations. In order to investigate the meaning of non-responses, we performed, for each year, a homogeneity analysis (HOMALS)[4] with non-response as a specific category for each item. After eliminating the subjects with nearly all non-responses, the bi-dimensional solutions yielded very characteristic u-shaped configurations. Such structures are also called horseshoe or Guttman effect in the literature: they indicate the existence of a dimension which orders the item categories according to their magnitude with reference to the measured phenomenon. In our case, this dimension can be interpreted as a poverty continuum. We then assigned the missing data to the nearest category of the variable in the configuration. In the large majority of cases, non-responses were associated with categories indicating non-poverty.

After recoding non-responses, we performed principal components analysis of the non-monetary items, one for each year. In 1986, 1987, and 1988, the results showed a substantial first component which explained between 20 and 28% of the variance. This first component can be interpreted as a general poverty dimension which already appeared in the homogeneity analysis. The scree-test for the number of factors seemed to indicate that two dimensions are sufficient to explain the inter-item correlations. After varimax rotation, the meaning of the two factors was very clear: one delineates poverty in terms of *living conditions* and the other in terms of *subjective evaluations*. It is worth noting that these results were almost the same for the three years studied here despite the items not being identical.

In 1990, there were eight non-monetary indicators of poverty with only two of them pertaining to subjective aspects of poverty. Moreover these two items had some low loadings on the subjective factor of the previous years. Therefore, we prefer to consider only living conditions poverty in 1990. The situation is even more dramatic in 1989 with only two items. Since the correlation between these two items is only 0.03, it is not reasonable to combine the two in a single indicator. One of them, for which a clear factorial meaning was observed in the previous analyses, is however retained in order to provide a rough indicator of subjective poverty in 1989.

The other indicators were obtained by simply adding the items with the highest loadings on the factors.[5] The internal consistency of the measures was verified with Cronbach's α. Two items were eliminated from the living conditions poverty indicator because their correlations wih the total score were too low. The final psychometric characteristics of the indicators are very good for the subjective poverty measure and quite good for the living conditions poverty measure (see Table 3).

As can be seen in Table 2, there are a little more than 7000 respondents in each wave. These are, however, not the *same* 7000 individuals. It is well-known that panel studies suffer from attrition due to death, removals, or refusals to participate: 9545 subjects were interviewed at least one year but only 5396 of them were interviewed each year. Longitudinal analyses are necessarily and unfortunately limited to the latter sub-sample. In order to reduce the loss of subjects, we decided to keep in our longitudinal sample those individuals not interviewed one year but interviewed the year before and the year after. The missing data was replaced by predicted values obtained by linear interpolation for the monetary indicator and by multiple regression for the non-monetary indicators. This procedure finally yields a longitudinal sample of 5535 individuals. The averages of the three poverty indicators calculated with the longitudinal sample are quite identical to those calculated with the cross-sectional samples.

Table 3
Descriptive and psychometric characteristics of the non-monetary poverty indicators from 1986 to 1990

	Subjective poverty indicator				Living conditions indicator			
	1986	1987	1988	1989	1986	1987	1988	1990
No. of observations	7543	7318	7168	7095	7543	7337	7155	7100
Mean	1.78	1.91	2.11	0.50	3.92	1.85	1.65	1.61
Median	1.45	1.60	1.40	0.40	3.75	1.75	1.75	1.50
Standard deviation	1.45	1.45	2.08	0.23	1.67	0.99	0.81	0.78
Theoretical range	13	12	12	1	12	7	6	6
Cronbach's α	0.84	0.83	0.86	-	0.65	0.58	0.58	0.59

Source: Lorraine household panel (INSEE, Nancy and ADEPS)

3 Convergence between the three poverty measures in a static perspective

The convergence between monetary poverty (MP), living conditions poverty (LCP), and subjective poverty (SP) is generally low and many researchers emphasise that they are distinct aspects of poverty. The results obtained in this study confirm the low convergence between the three indicators (Table 4). The correlations[6] are largely similar to those reported with other samples and/or with other items (see for example, Ray et al. 1991 or Dickes 1992).

Table 4
Bravais-Pearson's correlations between the three poverty measures

	1986	1987	1988	1989	1990
MP - SP	-0.35	-0.38	-0.41	-0.49	-
MP - LCP	-0.38	-0.26	-0.27	-	-0.23
SP - LCP	0.22	0.14	0.17	-	-

Notes:
N = 5535; $p < 0.001$ for all the coefficients; MP: monetary poverty; SP: subjective poverty; LCP: living conditions poverty

Source: Lorraine household panel (INSEE, Nancy and ADEPS)

The correlations between MP and SP are negative. They indicate that the subjective feeling of poverty is somewhat higher for the low income individuals. The relations are largely similar when compared from one year to the next, with the exception of 1989. One should remember here that the 1989 SP indicator is very specific because it is obtained with only one item.

As expected, the correlations between MP and LCP are also negative. There is a slight tendency showing that living conditions deteriorate when income diminishes. The decline of the correlations from 1987 onwards should probably be assigned to the parallel decrease of the LCP indicator reliability (see Table 3).

The correlations between SP and LCP are only available from 1986 to 1988. They are lower than the others we have seen. They are positive however, as expected, indicating that a subjective feeling of poverty is slightly more frequent with individuals living in poor conditions.

To summarise, the convergence between the three poverty indicators is relatively low even if the correlations are in the expected directions. Such results are now well-known. It seems that the three indicators convincingly share something in common. But the correlations are not sufficiently high to conclude that they measure the same poverty: each indicator assesses some specific aspect of poverty.

The calculation of poverty thresholds is another way to illustrate the differences between the three indicators. There is much controversy in the literature about the definition of the thresholds (see, e.g. Jeandidier and Kop 1995). Since our objective is not to solve this problem here but to present some descriptive characteristics of the most disadvantaged people, we will use one popular threshold: a household is considered as poor if it's equivalised income is less than 50% of the mean income of the whole sample. In 1986, the monetary poverty threshold was equal to 2216 F per month yielding a monetary poverty rate of 10.1% for 1986. The same rate was also used to dichotomize the distributions of the non-monetary indicators (for example, the 10.1% households with the greatest subjective poverty scores are considered as subjectively poor). The cross-tabulation of the three thresholds is presented in Table 5. As can be seen, the three indicators do not identify the same people: there are only 1.2% of the individuals who are poor according to all three conceptions of poverty.

Table 5
Distribution of the 1986 sample according to a 10.1% threshold for the three poverty indicators (in %)

		Monetary poverty			
		no		yes	
		Subjective poverty			
		no	yes	no	yes
Living conditions poverty	no	76.7	6.0	5.0	1.6
	yes	5.9	1.3	2.2	1.2

Source: Lorraine household panel (INSEE, Nancy and ADEPS), N=5535

If the monetary poor are not the same as the subjective poor who are also not the same as the living conditions poor, what are then the characteristics of these three groups? One way to answer this question is to describe the main features of the households in which poor people are living. For reasons of space, only three criteria will be analyzed here: the age of the household head, the employment status of the head, and a family typology of households (cf. Table 6). These characteristics were chosen because they represent three meaningful aspects: position in the life cycle, economic conditions, and family situation. The reader is referred to Ray et al. (1991) for a much more detailed descriptive analysis of poor households.

When the head of the household is young, the proportion of the monetary poor is relatively low but, interestingly, the proportion of subjective poor and of living conditions poor is relatively high. These are households in which the total equivalised income is not so bad, but the subjective sense of poverty is quite strong (perhaps because they compare themselves with older people) and their living conditions are not yet really satisfactory. The 'young-middle aged' group is characterized by an overrepresentation of subjective poor and an underrepresentation of living conditions poor. For these people, living conditions are quite good and monetary conditions are acceptable, but they express some difficulties in living on their income (perhaps because the consumption level is higher in this group). In the 'old-middle aged' group, the proportion of poor households according to the three indicators is approximatively the same as in the whole sample.

Table 6
Socio-demographic characteristics of the poor households (in %)

	Monetary poor	Subjective poor	Living conditions poor	Total
Age of household head				
≤ 24 years	2.8	9.9	7.0	4.3
25 - 49 years	43.1	61.2	27.7	48.6
50 - 64 years	31.9	26.5	27.7	29.2
65 - 74 years	5.2	0.0	18.7	10.9
≥ 75 years	16.9	2.5	18.8	7.0
Employment status of household head				
Working	45.9	70.4	35.1	63.0
Unemployed	10.5	14.2	6.3	3.4
Housewife	4.4	2.4	4.4	1.5
Retired	31.5	7.1	49.8	29.0
Other inactive status	7.7	5.9	4.4	3.1
Family typology of household				
Single man	2.2	0.0	11.1	4.5
Single woman	21.0	16.5	24.8	9.2
Couple	13.8	7.1	24.1	28.2
Couple with children	47.5	58.8	24.4	47.7
One parent family	10.5	12.9	10.7	6.3
Other households*	5.0	4.7	4.9	4.0

* especially three generation households

Source: Lorraine household panel (INSEE, Nancy and ADEPS), 1986 sample, N=1599

The two older groups stand out in terms of monetary conditions. All of them more often have poor living conditions but it seems that they have adapted to them (the subjective sense of poverty is low). However the 'young-old' group is less often poor in monetary terms and the 'over 75 years' group is more often poor according to the monetary indicator.

When the head of the household is unemployed, a housewife, or has an inactive status (e.g. living most of the time with a disability allowance), the proportion of the poor is higher than in the whole sample according to the three indicators. Such results are not really surprising. In the two other cases, they are perhaps less expected and they illustrate, as was already the case for the age variable, the discriminating features of the three poverty indicators. The 'working-head' households are poor relatively less often according to the monetary and the living conditions indicators. They are more often poor when the subjective indicator is considered. It looks as if the individuals living in such households consider that their income and their living conditions are insufficient in relation to their work. In contrast, the 'retired-head' households are more often poor if we consider the monetary and the living conditions indicators. But it seems that they do not complain about their situation. One interpretation of this finding is that they compare their current situation with their past living conditions which were probably objectively worse.

The 'single woman' households and the 'one parent family' households are more often poorer than the whole sample whatever the indicator. It is also the case for the other households even if the differences are less perceptible. All in all, these results confirm the serious difficulties of single women with or without children. Compared to single women, single men are less often identified as poor than the whole sample for the monetary and subjective indicators. Single men, however, more often live in poor conditions than the whole sample. This result reflects probably the fact that single men are generally young and that they live in apartments with little furniture. In contrast to young single men, single women without children are generally old and widowed. Finally, couples without children are less often poor than the whole sample with respect to all three indicators. The major difference between couples with and without children is that the former more often express a subjective feeling of poverty.

This brief description of poor households was to illustrate the differences between the three indicators of poverty. Monetarily poor individuals often live in households with an old or unemployed head and are often single women with or without children. Poor living conditions individuals often live in households with an old head who is retired; they are often single (young) men or single women with or without children. Finally, the poor individuals identified by the subjective indicator are characterized especially by a young or middle-young head of household who often works; single women with or without children and couples with children also show some of the characteristics of such households.

4 Convergence between the three poverty measures in a dynamic perspective

The conclusion about low convergence between the three poverty indicators fails to take into account the dynamic feature of the poverty phenomenon. One can, for example, lose one's job for just a few months and so have a lower income for a short period without major repercussions in terms of living conditions or subjective feelings of poverty. Such a hypothesis emphasizes the necessity to minimize the weight of temporary hardships. This can be done by considering the whole period of observation rather than one specific year.

In order to test the hypothesis that *low convergence between poverty indicators is due to the impact of temporary hardships whose weight is maximized in the static perspective*, we study the indicators' convergence by taking into account the five years of observation. The simplest way of doing that is to compute the mean of each indicator over the whole period after standardizing the measures to account for the range differences between the non- monetary indicators. The correlations between the longitudinal indicators are shown in Table 7 and they should be compared to the correlations between static indicators reported in Table 4.

As hypothesized, convergence between the three poverty indicators is improved when they are measured over the whole period of observation. It should be noted however that the increase of the correlations is not sufficient to conclude that the three indicators measure the same phenomenon. Moreover, the longitudinal indicators are some kind of aggregated indexes whose reliabilities are greater than that of the static indicators since they take into account more variables. According to psychometric theory (see, e.g. Dickes et al. 1994), the correlation between two measures is dependent upon their reliabilities: all things being equal, a correlation between two measures is higher when the reliabilities of the measures increase. It is then difficult to choose between these two explanations. Perhaps the convergence is better partly because the longitudinal indicators attenuate the impact of temporary hardships and partly because their reliabilities are higher.

Table 7

Bravais-Pearson's correlations between longitudinal indicators and mean correlations between static indicators

	MP - SP	MP - LCP	SP - LCP
Correlations between longitudinal indicators	-0.52	-0.34	0.27
Mean correlations of static indicators (after z transformation)	-0.41	-0.29	0.18

Notes:
N = 5535; p < 0.001 for all the coefficients; MP: monetary poverty; SP: subjective poverty; LCP: living conditions poverty

Source: Lorraine household panel (INSEE, Nancy and ADEPS)

Constructing longitudinal indicators is not the only way to take into account the dynamic phenomenon of poverty. One can also hypothesize that the convergence between the three poverty indicators is low because they are measured at the same time. Indeed, *one can postulate that the relationships between monetary poverty, living conditions poverty, and subjective poverty are not contemporaneous relationships but delayed ones*. Consider for example an individual with a notable decrease in income. The monetary poverty indicator is of course instantaneously affected by this situation. But what about living conditions? It is possible that living conditions remain the same for a certain period. After that the person probably has to sell some belongings and/or to move house. In this simple example, it can be seen that some delayed effects could exist in the relationships between monetary and living conditions poverty.

In order to test this hypothesis, contemporaneous and lagged correlations between the different poverty indicators were computed. Since we have no hypothesis about the causality direction and about the duration of the delayed effect, all possible correlations are reported in Table 8.

The hypothesis is only partly confirmed and the results suggest some more complex patterns. In two cases out of the six considered here, the correlations seem to decrease as the time period increases (see the 'effects' of subjective poverty on monetary poverty[7] and the 'effects' of monetary poverty on living conditions poverty). In two other cases, correlations remain relatively stationary over time (see the 'effects' of living conditions poverty on monetary poverty and the 'effects' of subjective poverty on living conditions poverty). Finally in the last two cases, the hypothesis seems to be corroborated: the delayed correlations are slightly higher than the contemporaneous ones (see the 'effects' of living conditions poverty and monetary poverty on subjective poverty).

Table 8
Contemporaneous and lagged correlations between the different poverty measures

Delayed 'effects' of monetary poverty on subjective poverty (below diagonal) and of subjective poverty on monetary poverty (above diagonal)

	MP_{86}	MP_{87}	MP_{88}	MP_{89}	MP_{90}
SP_{86}	-0.35	-0.30	-0.31	-0.29	-0.27
SP_{87}	-0.37	-0.38	-0.36	-0.33	-0.30
SP_{88}	-0.39	-0.38	-0.41	-0.36	-0.34
SP_{89}	-0.47	-0.47	-0.49	-0.49	-0.46

Delayed 'effects' of monetary poverty on living conditions poverty (below diagonal) and of living conditiond poverty on monetary poverty (above diagonal)

	MP_{86}	MP_{87}	MP_{88}	MP_{89}	MP_{90}
LCP_{86}	-0.38	-0.35	-0.37	-0.35	-0.36
LCP_{87}	-0.26	-0.26	-0.28	-0.25	-0.26
LCP_{88}	-0.24	-0.24	-0.27	-0.23	-0.25
LCP_{89}	-0.22	-0.22	-0.24	-0.21	-0.23

Delayed 'effects' of subjective poverty on living conditions poverty (below diagonal) and of living conditions poverty on subjective poverty (above diagonal)

	SP_{86}	SP_{87}	SP_{88}	SP_{89}
LCP_{86}	0.22	0.20	0.24	0.28
LCP_{87}	0.15	0.14	0.16	0.23
LCP_{88}	0.16	0.17	0.17	0.32
LCP_{89}	0.15	0.17	0.16	023

Notes:
N=5535; p<0.001 for all the coefficients; MP: monetary poverty; SP: subjective poverty; LCP: living conditions poverty

Source: Lorraine household panel (INSEE, Nancy and ADEPS)

Such results, never documented in the literature before as far as we know, are very interesting and suggest some complex mechanisms which contribute to the understanding of the poverty phenomenon. The correlations which decrease over time are contrary to our expectations especially in the case of the hypothetical effect of monetary poverty on living conditions poverty. We have suggested before that living conditions might be affected by income changes only after a certain delay. The results in Table 8 suggest a more immediate effect.

The pattern of correlations between monetary and living conditions poverty on the one hand and subjective poverty on the other hand is congruent with our hypothesis since the lagged correlations are higher than the contemporaneous ones. It means that the subjective feeling of poverty is not immediately related to income or living conditions changes but occurs after some time. One could say that it took some time for the evaluation made by individuals of their standard of living to be altered.

Finally, the observed stationary correlations are probably the most difficult to explain. Perhaps they reflect individual differences: for some people, the changes could occur concurrently and for others, they could be delayed in time. But such correlations may also simply reflect the fact that an effect of living conditions poverty on monetary poverty or of subjective poverty on living conditions poverty is not likely.

In brief, there is somewhat limited evidence in favour of the delayed effect hypothesis. Even if these results suggest some interesting suppositions about the dynamic relations between the three poverty indicators, one should consider them with caution due to the low differences between the correlations.

5 Conclusion

In this paper, we have dealt with the question of different measures of poverty in France. We have noted that in the theoretical French literature, poverty is usually conceived as a multidimensional phenomenon. But in practice, measures of poverty rarely take into account monetary, subjective, and living conditions criteria at the same time. The only studies undertaken from this perspective generally conclude that the convergence between these three poverty measures is rather low.

Using longitudinal data from the Lorraine household panel we have studied firstly the evolution of monetary poverty in relation to the evolution of the economic environment. The evolution of poverty seems partly related to one of the two indicators studied, the minimum guaranteed income, but is not related to the second, the evolution of the unemployment rate. This result perhaps illustrates the fact that the monetary poverty indicator is not adequate to take into account the dynamic complexity of poverty.

Using the same data, we then verified the degree of convergence between the three poverty measures. Convergence is as low as in previous studies and the characteristics of the poor households are not the same regarding the poverty measures used. In order to explore this already known conclusion, we have hypothesized that the low convergence between the measures was due to the fact that time was not taken into account. Two hypotheses were tested. In the first, we assume that a longer period of observation could minimize the weight of temporary hardships that affect the convergence between the measures over a short period of time. In the second, we postulate that some delayed relations may exist between the three poverty indicators.

The results are mixed. Neither hypothesis is clearly rejected by the data, neither is fully supported. It is possible that the empirical part of the study may suffer from methodological difficulties: non-monetary indicators which are limited to the lowest part of a hypothetical poverty-wealth continuum while the monetary indicator covers the whole continuum, inadequate non-monetary indicators in 1989 and in 1990 due to a limited number of available items, use of income before taxes to compute the monetary indicator, use of a too limited period of observation, etc. Such difficulties may explain in part the mixed results. As a remedy for these problems, other studies should be carried out with other longitudinal data. But it is equally possible that a better methodological approach will not substantially increase the convergence between the indicators. This would indicate that even in a dynamic perspective, the three poverty indicators refer to three really different dimensions and that poverty cannot be understood without taking each of these dimensions into account.

Notes

[1] The ESEML is the product of a genuine intensive collaboration between our research team (ADEPS) and the regional delegation of the INSEE. For more information about this survey, the reader is referred to Jeandidier (1992).

[2] In Lorraine, the increase of RMI beneficiaries during the second half-year 1989 was 9%, during the first half-year 1990 it was equal to 8%, but from the second half-year 1990 the increase slowed down at the level of 3%. At the end of 1990, in Lorraine, there were 17,300 people receiving RMI.

[3] There were 19 items in 1987, 18 in 1988 and eight in 1990. In the two last years of the ESEML, and especially in 1989, the questionnaires were substantially reduced due to financial considerations. The first wave of the panel (1985) is not considered in this paper because it was essentially a pre-test administrated to only a sub-sample.

[4] Homogeneity analysis (HOMALS) yields results identical to correspondance analysis (see Tenenhaus and Young 1985).

[5] Factor scores were also calculated. Since the results obtained by weighted and by non-weighted sums are almost identical, only the latter are presented.

[6] Bravais-Pearson's correlations were calculated in order to facilitate the comparisons with previous studies. However, since the distributions of the indicators are skewed, non-parametric correlations should be more appropriate. With Spearman's rank correlations, the correlations are, as expected, slightly higher, but they do not change the substantive conclusions of our analyses.

[7] It can seem puzzling to imagine effects of subjective poverty on monetary poverty. As stated before however, this point refers to the difficult question of the direction of causality (if any) between the different poverty indicators. In the subjective well-being literature, some researchers developed theories called top-down approaches in which subjective well-being is the cause rather than the consequence of certain objective conditions (see, e.g. Veenhoven 1988; Mastekaasa 1994; Kop 1994; Dickes et al. 1996).

References

Atkinson, A.B. and Cazes, S. (1990), 'Mesures de la pauvreté et politiques sociales: une étude comparative de la France, de la R.F.A et du Royaume-Uni', *Observations et Diagnostics Economiques (O.F.C.E.)*, Vol. 33, pp. 105-130.

Borkowski, J.-L. (1985), 'Les inégalités et leurs cumuls parmi les personnes âgées: niveau de vie, santé, isolement', *Archives et Documents*, Vol. 142, INSEE: Paris.

Borkowski, J.-L., Kasparian, E. et al. (1991), *Construire des indicateurs d'inégalité*, Document de travail de la Direction des Statistiques Démographiques et Sociales de l'INSEE, No. F9106, INSEE: Paris.

Croutte, P., Iliakopoulos, A. and Legros, M. (1991), *Panel RMI-CREDOC: point de départ. Présentation des résultats de la première vague d'enquête auprès d'un échantillon représentatif des allocataires du revenu minimum d'insertion*, Document du CREDOC No. 98, CREDOC: Paris.

David, M.G. and Starzek, K. (1987), *Les familles nombreuses, mères isolées: situation économique et vulnérabilité*, Les documents du CERC, No. 85, La Documentation Française: Paris.

Debonneuil, M. (1978), 'Les familles pauvres d'une ville moyenne', *Economie et Statistique*, Vol. 105, pp. 25-37.

Dickes, P. (1983), 'Modèle de Rasch pour items dichotomiques: théorie, technique et application à la mesure de la pauvreté', *Cahiers Economiques de Nancy*, Vol. 11, pp. 72-116.

Dickes, P. (1989), *Pauvreté et conditions d'existence. Théories, modèles et mesures*, Document PSELL No. 8, CEPS/INSTEAD: Walferdange.

Dickes, P. (1992), *Pauvreté en termes de conditions d'existence*, Rapport de recherche pour le compte de la MIRE dans le cadre du programme 'Analyses secondes des données de l'enquête Etudes des Conditions de Vie 1986-87', ADEPS (Université Nancy 2): Nancy.

Dickes, P., Kop, J.-L. and Tournois, J. (1996), 'Modèles d'équations structurales et sens de la causalité dans les études longitudinales: une application au bien-être subjectif', *Bulletin de Méthodologie Sociologique*, Vol. 50, pp. 20-55.

Dickes, P., Tournois, J., Flieller, A. and Kop, J.-L. (1994), *La psychométrie: théories et méthodes de la mesure en psychologie*, Presses Universitaires de France: Paris.

Dupré, J.-P., Hatchuel, G., Pascaud, E. and Simonin, B. (1986), *Pauvreté - précarité. Tentatives de mesure*, Document du CREDOC, CREDOC: Paris.

Euvrard, F., Paugam, S. and Lion, J. (1991), *Atouts et difficultés des allocataires du revenu minimum d'insertion*, Les Documents du CERC, No. 98, La Documentation Française: Paris.

Fénelon, J.-P., Houzelle, Y. and Steinberg, H. (1988), *Pauvreté - Précarité*, Rapport du Secours Populaire Français.

INSEE (1995-96), *Tableaux de l'économie Lorraine*, INSEE: Nancy.

Jeandidier, B. (1992), *Présentation de l'Enquête Socio-économique auprès des Ménages Lorrains*, Document technique, ADEPS (Université Nancy 2): Nancy.

Jeandidier, B. and Kop, J.-L. (1995), *Pauvreté multidimensionnelle en apparence seulement? Concordances ou discordances des évaluations en termes de seuils monétaires, de pauvreté subjective et d'échelle de conditions d'existence*, Les Cahiers de Recherche de l'ADEPS No. 16, ADEPS (Université Nancy 2): Nancy.

Kop, J.-L. (1994), *Le bien-être subjectif: vers une mesure du bonheur*, Thèse de doctorat non publiée, Université Nancy 2: Nancy.

Lopez, A. (1990), *Pauvreté: observation et suivi statistique. Deux monographies locales*, Les Dossiers de l'INSEE Rhône-Alpes, No. 40, INSEE: Lyon.

Mastekaasa, A. (1994), 'Psychological well-being and marital dissolution. Selection effects?' *Journal of Family Issues*, Vol. 15, pp. 208-228.

Paugam, S. (1991), *La disqualification sociale, essai sur la nouvelle pauvreté*, Presses Universitaires de France: Paris.

Ray, J.-C., Dell'era, D., Dickes, P., Jankeliowitch, E. and Jeandidier, B. (1991), *Aux franges du RMI*, Rapport de recherche pour le compte de la CNAF, ADEPS (Université Nancy 2): Nancy.

Sawhill, I.V. (1988), 'Poverty in the U.S.: Why is it so persistent?', *Journal of Economic Literature*, Vol. 26, pp. 1073-1119.

Tabard, N. (1980), *Contribution au rapport sur la pauvreté et la lutte contre la pauvreté*, Document du CREDOC-CGP, CREDOC: Paris.

Tallard, M. and Valetas, M.F. (1981), *Les situations de vie précaires*, Document du CREDOC, CREDOC: Paris.

Tenenhaus, M. and Young, F.W. (1985), 'An Analysis and Synthesis of Multiple Correspondance Analysis, Optimal Scaling, Dual Scaling, Homogeneity Analysis and other Methods for Quantifying Categorical Multivariate Data', *Psychometrika*, Vol. 50, pp. 91-119.

Tran Ap, A. (1992), 'Situations de précarité aux Antilles et en Guyanne', *Economie et Statistique*, Vol. 252, pp. 129-149.

Veenhoven, R. (1988), 'The Utility of Happiness', *Social Indicators Research*, Vol. 20, pp. 333-354.

Villeneuve, A. (1984), 'Construire un indicateur de précarité: les étapes d'une démarche empirique', *Economie et Statistique*, Vol. 168, pp. 93-105.

Villeneuve, A. (1991), *La mesure des inégalités sous son aspect multidimensionnel*, Document de travail de la Direction des Statistiques Démographiques et Sociales de l'INSEE, No. F9105, INSEE: Paris.

Willmott, P., Willmott, P. and Mc Dowell, L. (1978), *Pauvreté et politique sociale en Europe*, Document V/753/1/77-FR, Institute of Community Studies: London.

Acknowledgement

A large part of the analyses on non-monetary indicators of poverty made in this paper was greatly facilitated by the pioneering work of Paul Dickes. The authors take this opportunity to pay tribute to his work. Thanks are also due to David Eckersley for his kind assistance in English.

Appendix List of the individual items used in the 1986 living conditions and subjective poverty indicators

Living conditions

* Do you have hot running water inside your housing (yes / no) ?
* Do you have an indoor flushing toilet (yes / no) ?
* In your household, is there :
    * a telephone ? (yes / no)
    * a dishwasher ? (yes / no)
    * a micro-computer ? (yes / no)
    * a dictionary ? (yes / no)
    * a car ? (yes / no)
* Could you rate your housing on the following scales ?
  Do you think your housing is ...
    * very dark - rather dark - medium - rather light - very light

   * very humid - rather humid - medium - rather protected against humidity - very protected against humidity
   * very noisy - rather noisy - medium - rather quiet - very quiet
   * very contaminated by odours - rather contaminated by odours - medium - rather protected against odours - very protected against odours
* Are there some friends or parents who could give you lodging in case of necessity? (yes / no)

Subjective poverty

* With your monthly income, your household is living ? (with great difficulty - with difficulty - with some difficulty - fairly easily - easily - very easily)
* In the last twelve months, has your household had any difficulties...
   * paying the rent or the mortgage for accomodation ? (no problem - some difficulty - great difficulty - risk of expulsion - needed to move)
   * paying the water bill ? (no problem - some difficulty - great difficulty - needed to ask for a term of payment - discontinuance of the service)
   * paying the gas-electricity bill ? (no problem - some difficulty - great difficulty - needed to ask for a term of payment - discontinuance of the service)
   * paying the heating ? (no problem - some difficulty - great difficulty - needed to ask for a term of payment - discontinuance of the service)
   * repaying the loans? (no problem - some difficulty - great difficulty - needed to ask for a term of payment - experienced a seizure)
   * paying the food ? (no problem - some difficulty - great difficulty - needed to ask for credit - needed help)
   * paying the doctor, the dentist and for prescriptions? (no problem - some difficulty - great difficulty - needed to ask for credit - needed help)
   * paying for clothes? (no problem - some difficulty - great difficulty -could not buy necessary things - needed help)
* Is your household able to make ends meet ? (with great difficulty - with a lot of difficulty - with some difficulty - with not great difficulty - with few difficulties - with no difficulty)
* In the last twelve months, have you had to repay debts from time payment? (yes / no)
* Do you receive social assistance payment ? (yes / no)
* In case of great difficulty, how long could your household live by using its savings? (in months)

Part Three
Using a multidimensional concept of poverty: Results from different countries

Long-term income and deprivation-based poverty among the elderly

Ruud Muffels and Henk-Jan Dirven

1 Introduction

This paper deals with a comparative analysis of the dynamics of income poverty and subjective deprivation in the Netherlands and Germany using panel data from the late 1980s and early 1990s. The focus is not so much on the measurement of poverty per se but on the measurement of long-term poverty and long-term deprivation-poverty. The paper addresses two questions: (1) to what extent did the incidence, distribution and evolution of income inequality and income poverty differ between both countries during the late 1980's, (2) to what extent do the findings on the dynamics of income poverty correspond to the results on subjective deprivation-poverty. To answer the first question we compare the results using five waves of the Dutch and German socio-economic panel-data from the period 1985-1989. For the second, we restrict the analyses to the Dutch situation since we lack data on deprivation and its evolution for Germany. The latter analysis draws on the Dutch data-sets from 1985 to 1991. The analysis is oriented to the development of poverty among elderly persons. Since the socio-economic position of the various generations of the aged is rather different, results will be presented for three age categories of the elderly, 55-65 years, 65-75 years and 75 years and over.

There is reason to belief that between the 1960s and the 1990s an U-shape pattern of income inequality occurred in almost all Western industrialized economies. Since the mid 1980s inequality appears to be increasing at fairly high rates not only among the wage earners but also among social security recipients and the aged. According to recent figures of Statistics Netherlands (SN), based on the income panel study (IPO), the income inequality (net disposable income) according to the Theil-coefficient increased between 1985 and 1991 with 2.1% a year and 13% over the entire period (SN 1994). Using the socio-economic panel data in both countries we found similar results; an average increase in inequality of net disposable income between 1985 and 1989 of 1.7% in the Netherlands and 2.1% in Germany. After 1991 income inequality seems to remain rather stable in the Netherlands, at least for the year 1992, but then rises again in 1993. Because the incomes of the aged are more concentrated in the lower income ranges and the share of the lower incomes decreased due to the rising inequality, the aged shared less in the real income growth in the late 1980s than the young. The anomaly must be attributed to the higher growth rate of earnings compared to benefits in conjunction with the low share of earnings and high share of benefits within the incomes of the elderly. The evidence for both countries also shows that the three age groups differ considerably in terms of real income growth and for that reason presumably also in terms of poverty and deprivation statuses.

These patterns of rising inequality among wage earners and non-wage income earners which show up from the mid 1980s on are the result of two contrasting trends. The first trend is the rising inequality in the earnings distribution due to the recovery of the economy from the mid 1980s on up to the early 1990s, and second the unequalizing impact of welfare state reforms in the Netherlands and Germany. In nearly all Western welfare states during the 1980s and early 1990s, governments pursued retrenchment policies and social security reforms which affected the real level and duration of benefits considerably. Together with the increase of earnings due to the economic growth it has led in all these countries to a widening of the gap between benefit-incomes and earnings. At the same time these reforms caused the share of wage-related benefits to fall in favour of the share of flat-rate benefits. Both trends have offsetting effects on poverty if poverty is defined in absolute terms. Increasing economic growth then leads to decreasing poverty whereas cuts in benefits probably induces a poverty rise. Both trends may strengthen each other when poverty is defined in relative terms. Economic growth may then lead to rising inequality between wage earners and beneficiaries as do retrenchment policies and social security reforms which will also likely result in rising inequality between wage earners and social security recipients and therefore in rising relative poverty. In the paper we will examine how these major trends in the two neighbouring societies work out empirically using socio-economic panel-data and applying various poverty standards.

1.1 The pension systems in Germany and the Netherlands

The pension systems in Germany and the Netherlands reflect the distinction between the selective insurance-based continental (Bismarckian) type of welfare system (Germany) and the universal need-based atlantic (Beveridgian) scheme which in the Netherlands is supplemented by a classical insurance-based occupational system. The German system represents the classical insurance-based pension system financed by payroll taxes (jointly paid by employer and employee) and guaranteeing a pension linked to the average wage income earned over the entire working life. Over time it appeared that the German system converges somewhat to the universal Atlantic system because coverage was extended to include not only workers but also the self-employed and people without an employment record (housewives). If the contribution record of an individual is insufficient to build up even a minimum pension s(he) may draw from the local social assistance agency to receive an additional benefit up to the level of the minimum social assistance benefit ('Sozialhilfe'). The Dutch pension system is grounded on two pillars: the flat-rate statutory old-age pension scheme and the insurance-based occupational pension scheme, both almost entirely financed by proportional payroll taxes. The second pillar, the occupational pension scheme, carried out by sectoral pension funds, guarantees for most of the insured a pension above the minimum up to a level of at least 70% of the final gross earnings.

The question which has to be addressed here is how retrenchment policies and social security reforms with respect to pension schemes lead to a rise in inequality in the incomes of the elderly in Germany and the Netherlands in the late 1980s. The first answer is the widening of the gap between the level of earnings and the level of the lowest pensions. The rise in real earnings due to the economic growth together with the extension of pension rights for a growing number of people in the 1970s and 1980s implied an increase in the levels of occupational pensions, both in Germany and the Netherlands, particularly for the younger generations of the elderly. However, the growth of the lowest old-age pensions did not keep pace with the rise in average earnings due to these retrenchment policies which limited the linkage of benefits to wages. In the Netherlands the level of the statutory old-age benefit has from 1979 on (1980 excluded), until 1990, been frozen at the level of 1979. After 1989 the minimum old-age benefit became annually adjusted to the legal minimum wage level according to a so-called policy-oriented linkage mechanism. For this reason the benefit level stayed behind the minimum wage level to which it was linked formally. Between 1980 and 1995 the purchasing power of these basic statutory pensions, therefore, fell considerably over the entire period.

In Germany more or less similar developments took place. The pensions were, up to 1979, linked to the index of gross-wages calculated over the last 3 years. Between 1979 and 1982 the linkage to the gross-wage index of the last three years was temporarily replaced by a linkage to the gross-wage index of the last year in order to relieve the budgetary problems of the major pension funds. In 1982 the linkage to the wages of the last three years was reestablished but almost immediately, at least temporarily, replaced by the new government-coalition headed by Bundeskanzler Kohl in 1983. The benefits were frozen for 1983 and not adjusted to the wage increases. In 1984 the linkage mechanism was again replaced by a mechanism which linked the pension benefits to the wages of the last year instead of the previous three years. Further retrenchments were taken in the 1980s by limiting the rights to a pension through a reduction in the acccounting periods of contribution payments and a reduction in the building-up of pension rights during unemployment. Since 1992 pensions are now linked to the index of net-wages.

1.2 Hypotheses

From this we can formulate several hypotheses about the performance of the German and Dutch pension system in preventing and relieving poverty:

1. Due to the economic growth during this period the income inequality among the various age groups of the elderly will presumably have increased but more so in Germany than in the Netherlands because the German pension system is more market-oriented than the Dutch one. When a relative poverty line is used it can therefore be presumed that the increase in relative poverty in Germany exceeds that in the Netherlands.
2. The cuts in benefit levels by the German and Dutch governments in the 1980s resulted in a lower real income growth or even a real income loss for pensioners with a low or no occupational pension income. We therefore expect relative poverty to have increased as well. This holds particularly for the eldest generation having low or no occupational pensions and given that a relative income poverty line is used. The increase will likely be stronger in the Netherlands than in Germany while the benefit reductions were more significant in the former than in the latter country. Due to the freezing of the Dutch statutory old-age benefits and the linkage of the German pensions to the index of gross or net wages, the

lowest German employee pensions are less affected by the pension reforms than in the Netherlands.

3. The average level of pensions for the eldest generation will presumably be lower in Germany because of the high share of elderly with no pension or a small occupational pension among this age group. This is due to the fact that Germany lacks a statutory or legal pension scheme operating as a safety net against poverty particularly for the eldest age group with less chances to have an occupational pension income. Because of these lower pensions of the eldest age category compared to younger generations we expect relative income poverty to be higher among the eldest age group in Germany than in the Netherlands.
4. The market conformity of the German system together with the absence of a need-based pension scheme, acting as a safety-net for elderly with no additional occupational pension entitlements such as in the Dutch system, will presumably also lead to higher income mobility and lesser income stability in Germany compared to the Netherlands in this period when seen from a dynamic perspective.
5. The rising inequality among the elderly population is partly the result of increasing economic growth rates in the second half of the 1980s. The increase in economic welfare led to rising pensions for pensioners with occupational pensions. Presumably, poverty rates for the elderly can be shown to have fallen over this period when poverty standards are applied which are less relative and because of that less sensitive to annual income shocks such as the economic deprivation measures. They probably reflect much more the permanent consumption status and living standards of persons and households. This hypothesis with respect to the decline of deprivation can only be examined in the Dutch case since we lack data on deprivation for Germany. For identical reasons we may presume that income mobility is lower and poverty persistence higher when a deprivation standard is used. This is because, if deprivation reflects a more persistent state of low living standards, the likelihood that the deprived will escape deprivation-poverty will be lower.

The paper focuses on the issue of poverty and deprivation in a longitudinal, comparative perspective. We particularly address the question of whether poverty and deprivation are more *temporary* or more *persistent* among the elderly than among the younger age cohorts. This is indeed an important question in poverty research since from a life-cycle perspective we may assume that elderly people, compared to the young, will have less economic resources. This is because they no longer have a relationship with the labour market and therefore are expected to be more prone to poverty.

2 Data, definitions, concepts, and unit of analysis

The data used in this paper are from the Dutch *Socio-Economic Panel (SEP)*, covering six years from 1985 to 1991 and from the *German Socio-Economic Panel* (GSOEP) stretching over the period 1985 to 1989. Each wave of the German and Dutch panels consists of roughly 4.5 to five thousand households and 12 to 14 thousand persons. The definition of income used in the paper is net, annual, after-tax or disposable household income. Between 1985 and 1990 this income is calculated as the sum of 27 income components asked for in the questionnaire of the oral interview. The income concept used includes labour income, capital income, social security income (unemployment, disability, old-age, social assistance) and a limited number of private income transfers.

It should be clarified from the onset that, in the Dutch panel from 1990 on, the *income measurement* from the SEP-panel data has changed. Before 1990 the net monthly income received at the time of the interview was used. The annual net disposable household income has been calculated as the net monthly income multiplied by 12 and summed up with the irregular income receipts. From 1990 on the income definition has changed to the gross annual income in the previous calendar year. This means that the October 1991 wave contains information on the annual income of 1990. To allow for comparisons between the incomes over the entire period these gross incomes are transformed into net incomes by a gross-net algorithm incorporated in a micro-simulation model. However, because of this change in the definition and measurement of income between 1990 and 1991, data on income for 1991 are somewhat different from the ones before.

In the German panel the calendar-year annual income concept has been applied which is similar to the definition used in the Dutch panel for 1991 only. Hence, the comparison of the incomes between both countries for the years before 1991 is hindered because of the use of somewhat different income definitions.

The *unit of analysis* in this paper is the individual and not the household since family well-being changes considerably over time due to the occurrence of household formation events like divorce, (re)marriage, death of the partner or the birth of a child and labour market events, such as losing or acquiring a job, moving to a better or worse paid job, a reduction in working hours or a change in the labour contract. For the aged, the number and type of events during old age will be different from those of the young. Typical for the aged are events like the retirement of the household head or the partner, death of the partner, moving in with the children or moving to an institution for residental care.

For conducting analyses at the individual level we assigned the household income to each adult and child in the household. This means that we consider the household as one undivided consumption unit sharing the household income equally. In reality, this is not necessarily true: some households consist of relatively independent consumption units which only partially share their income with other units within the household. Since we lack information on the intra-household consumption patterns the paper follows the general assumption of equally shared welfare within the household ('joint welfare function').

3 Methodology: Defining income-poverty and deprivation-poverty thresholds

In previous work (Muffels, Berghman and Dirven 1992, 1993; Muffels, Dirven and Fouarge 1995) we have argued that there is no single method which is capable of encompassing and measuring all aspects and dimensions of poverty simultaneously. Each applied methodology has its own strength and weaknesses and reflects in a sense the subjective notions of experts on what a poverty-line should measure and how it should do this. The choice for a multiple set of poverty-standards prevents the academic researcher from making arbitrary and often normative choices for a particular method which can only give a partial view of poverty in the society. From empirical research in a number of countries (Van den Bosch et al. 1993) it became evident that the various poverty line methodologies in terms of incidence and distribution of poverty produce very dissimilar results.

The Dutch panel allows us to use several poverty definitions whereas for the German panel data we lack the information needed to apply these standards. Therefore we can present comparative results only for the so-called European standard which is the half-mean income as applied by the European Commission. To show how the results are affected by the use of different poverty standards we will also give the results for three other poverty-lines for the Netherlands.

The European standard is a statistical measure set at the level of 50% of the country-mean equivalent disposable household income (O'Higgins and Jenkins 1989). This is not an official poverty line of the European Commission but one which has been used in various research projects commissioned by the EC (cf. Muffels 1993). The equivalence scale proposed in a report for the OECD is used here for comparison of both panel-data sets (1 for head, 0.7 for the partner and 0.5 for a child). Since the outcomes prove to be sensitive for the choice of the equivalence scale another less steep scale, proposed by Eurostat, has been used (1, 0.5, 0.3). Furthermore, we applied two other standards on the Dutch data, a subjective standard, the subjective poverty line (Kapteyn, Kooreman and Willemse 1988) and a policy standard. The policy standard is the so-called Dutch social minimum income (SMI) which by and large equals the amounts of the minimum benefits in the social security system, i.e. the social assistance benefits. For a description of these poverty lines we refer to some other papers (Muffels 1993; Muffels, Dirven and Fouarge 1995). Below, a brief description follows.

The *subjective standard (SPL)* has been applied by submitting a question to the respondent about the absolute minimum income s/he for his or her household needs to make ends meet, the so-called minimum income question (MIQ). The level of the poverty line is determined as the average required minimum income level of those people for which the current household income is equal to the necessary minimum income. These people are assumed to be the experts who are best aware of what a household of their size and composition really needs to make ends meet. If the actual income is below this *intersubjectively* assessed minimum income level, which varies according to household size and reference group, the household is considered subjectively poor.

The *Dutch social minimum income* (SMI) threshold is calculated for each household in the sample. According to the social assistance scheme the amounts differ dependent on the family composition and the age of the household members. For each household we determine theoretically the level of the social assistance benefit the household would be entitled to if it had to apply for it. The current income is then compared with this calculated minimum benefit level to determine whether the household is in poverty or not.

All these poverty lines look at poverty in terms of low income or low economic welfare. For that reason we have called these thresholds income-poverty lines. However, poverty is more than lack of income alone. Poverty is also associated with the enforced lack of non-monetary resources, such as good health, adequate housing, enough food, steady employment and a decent social life. Income is without doubt a necessary condition for having a decent life but income alone is not sufficient to guarantee this. For that reason the chosen set of poverty methods is extended with a subjective deprivation-index-method called the subjective deprivation poverty line (SDL) which is developed by Muffels (1993). The deprivation-index method departs from an extended list of deprivation items submitted to the head of households in four waves of the Socio-Economic Panel survey, in October 1985, 1986, 1988 and 1991. The list of items is partly derived from the deprivation-scale of Townsend (1979) and Mack and Lansley (1985). The SDL-method is explained in more detail in section six and Appendix 1.

A deprivation-poverty standard could be calculated directly from the survey-data for 1985, 1986, 1988 and 1991. For the years in between, for which no information is available about deprivation (1987, 1989, 1990), we have tried to fit a logit-model to calculate the probability of being in deprivation-poverty. This is reported in Appendix 2.

4 The evolution of income poverty for the elderly in the Netherlands and Germany

In this section information will be presented on the evolution of income poverty for the elderly in the late 1980s in the Netherlands and Germany. In Table 1, information on Germany and the Netherlands is presented using the European minimum income standard (EMI). In the lines below, information is presented for the Netherlands only but for two other poverty standards, the Dutch social minimum income (SMI) and the subjective poverty line (SPL). To examine poverty figures according to the European minimum income standard we applied two equivalence scales, the original OECD-scale which is a rather steep scale (EMI-OECD) and a modified, less steep scale which has been used by Eurostat in poverty-research (cf. Hagenaars, de Vos and Zaidi 1993) and therefore referred to as EMI-Eurostat (compare Table 1).

According to both versions of the European line the aged do better in the Netherlands and in Germany compared to the total population during the entire period. Contrary to what might be expected, the youngest generation of the elderly had the highest poverty risks at least in the Netherlands, whereas in Germany the eldest generation of the elderly experienced the highest risks except for the years 1985 and 1989. In both countries the middle age group of 65-75 years were less likely to be poor than the youngest and eldest age group.

Table 1
The evolution of poverty for three generations of the elderly according to the European standard in Germany and the Netherlands and according to two other poverty standards for the Netherlands (percentages)

Age class	Poverty standard	1985	1986	1987	1988	1989	1990
55-64	EMI-Germany	3.1	3.1	4.9	2.1	5.1	n.a
	EMI-Netherlands-1	4.3	7.3	6.3	7.0	7.9	4.6
	EMI-Netherlands-2	4.4	7.1	6.7	7.2	8.3	5.5
	SMI	10.0	8.5	8.9	7.9	6.7	8.9
	SPL	18.1	21.0	18.6	18.7	15.7	15.9
65-74	EMI-Germany	1.2	1.1	0.5	1.3	1.1	n.a
	EMI-Netherlands-1	0.9	2.8	5.7	5.2	7.5	3.0
	EMI-Netherlands-2	1.8	3.3	7.1	5.8	8.1	3.3
	SMI	12.7	17.6	15.1	12.7	12.0	5.6
	SPL	24.7	23.4	30.3	39.4	22.8	19.4
75+	EMI-Germany	2.6	12.2	6.2	2.3	2.6	n.a
	EMI-Netherlands-1	1.9	3.3	5.9	4.4	5.5	4.5
	EMI-Netherlands-2	1.9	4.4	6.3	5.3	6.6	5.0
	SMI	11.4	13.3	16.6	18.5	15.5	10.4
	SPL	22.7	31.0	36.8	48.3	25.7	30.4
Total	EMI-Germany	8.8	8.7	9.6	9.3	9.4	n.a
population	EMI-Netherlands-1	6.0	7.2	8.0	7.5	9.2	7.1
	EMI-Netherlands-2	4.2	6.4	6.7	6.3	8.3	6.2
	SMI	6.4	6.4	6.7	6.1	5.4	6.7
	SPL	9.6	11.7	12.8	12.4	9.7	11.0

Notes:
EMI-Germany = European minimum income, OECD equivalence scale (1, 0.7, 0.5)
EMI-Netherlands-1 = European minimum income, OECD equivalence scale (1, 0.7, 0.5)
EMI-Netherlands-2 = European minimum income, Eurostat equivalence scale (1, 0.5, 0.3)
SMI = social minimum income
SPL = subjective poverty line

The observed higher poverty rates for the eldest age group in Germany supports our third hypothesis on the effects of the absence of a legal safety net in Germany for the well above average poverty risks of this age group.

The results further show that particularly in the Netherlands the incidence of poverty among the elderly increased between 1985 and 1989 especially for the youngest and eldest age group. In Germany a much more stable pattern of poverty emerges, where poverty among the elderly is much lower than in the Netherlands except for the eldest age group. This finding contrast to hypothesis 1 on the expected increase in relative poverty in the German pension system, but confirms hypothesis 2. According to this hypothesis Dutch policies freezing the level of the basic pensions will have led to rising income inequality and relative poverty among the elderly. The better position of the younger elderly in Germany is probably associated with the fact that more elderly within the younger generations of the elderly in Germany will have built up a pension which protects them from poverty.

In contrast in the Netherlands, more elderly are dependent on a statutory basic pension which offers no guarantee for staying out of poverty because of the Dutch policies freezing benefits in the 1980s. On the other hand the absence of a publicly provided basic pension in Germany causes more elderly of the eldest generation to fall into poverty than is the case in the Netherlands.

There is reason to believe that the lower poverty rates for the elderly compared to the population have to be attributed to the steepness of the equivalene scale (even the modified scale) which assigns high weights to the costs of children. Since elderly have few children, their income is overestimated. For that reason their poverty status appears more favourable than it in reality is. The results on the other poverty standards for the Netherlands prove this. These results are very different from the findings on the European lines. According to the Dutch policy standard (SMI) and the subjective standard (SPL) it is shown clearly that poverty is more widespread among the aged than among the rest of the population. The eldest generation bears the highest risks and the youngest the lowest. The poverty risks for the aged 65 years and over are twice to three times higher than for the non-elderly. The Table also shows that between 1985 and 1988 the incidence of poverty in the Netherlands apparently increases but after 1988 declines again. The decline is strongest for the subjective poverty line and for the two eldest age groups. Note also the very high subjective poverty risks for the eldest generation in 1988. Almost half of the 75+ elderly consider their income in 1988 too low to make ends meet. After 1988 subjective poverty decreased gradually although, in 1990, still 15% to 30% of the aged over 65 years were subjectively poor.

5 Income mobility and long-term poverty

5.1 Measures for income mobility and poverty persistence

In the next part the interest shifts to the issue of income mobility and poverty persistence among the elderly. The issue is raised whether poverty for the elderly compared to the total population is more temporary or more persistent. To assess income mobility and poverty persistence three measures of income mobility are applied. The first measure is the *n-year income-to-needs ratio* which is a continuous measure for the ratio of the income aggregated over n years of observation to the necessary minimum income aggregated over n years. The level of the minimum income reflects the needs of the household to attain a minimum standard of living. Its level can be derived from the various poverty line definitions which were applied in the study. For that reason the income-to-needs ratio differs according to the different 'needs' or poverty line definitions that were used. The ratio reflects the mean income position of individuals and households over time relative to the mean income level needed to attain the bottom poverty line. According to Sen (1983) the income-to-needs measure can be considered to reflect a relative measure for income deprivation. The second measure is the *number of years in poverty* during the observation period which presents a measure for the frequency of poverty statuses during a certain time period. A third measure proposed by Bane and Ellwood (1986) departs from a *poverty spell* approach where a spell is assumed to start after a transition has taken place from any other initial state in t-1 to the state of interest at time t. The measure is based on the standard life-table approach. Income mobility is here defined in terms of the exit rate out of poverty, conditional on experiencing a poverty spell during one year, two years etc. The survival rates after n years of experiencing a spell provide estimates for the persistence of poverty over time. Income mobility is therefore indicated by the cumulative exit rate which is equal to one minus the survival rate.

According to all three indicators income mobility is defined in terms of movements across certain poverty thresholds.

5.2 Results on the income mobility of the aged

In Tables 2.1 to 2.3 the results on income mobility according to the three aforementioned mobility indicators for the Netherlands and Germany are given. Only the results for the European standard can be compared. For the Netherlands we will also give the results on the spell indicator for the other two poverty lines, i.e. the policy standard (SMI) and the subjective poverty line (SPL).

In Table 2.1 three levels of the income-to-needs ratio are distinguished: the household income is less than 75%, less than 100% or below 125% of the needs level. A first observation is that long-term poverty rates are low both in Germany and the Netherlands for the young as well as for the elderly. This shows the high income mobility in the Netherlands and in Germany. Nevertheless, in Germany more people below 55 years of age are in long-term poverty over a five year period (5.3%) than in the Netherlands (2.3%). Extreme poverty indicated by the number of people having incomes less than 75% of the five year 'needs' threshold hardly exists in either country, not among the young but remarkably also not among the elderly. The proportion of elderly in long-term poverty according to the 100% level is about zero percent in the Netherlands whereas in Germany it is still 3.5%. However, note the increase in the proportion of long-term poor if the threshold itself is assumed at 125% level. It appears that the youngest and the eldest generation then experience long-term poverty. Whereas the proportion of non-elderly and elderly up to 75 years below the 125% threshold is higher in the Netherlands, the proportion of elderly poor of 75 years and over is much higher in Germany, almost 20% compared to 5% in the Netherlands. These figures indicate that because of the high concentration of incomes just above the needs threshold the results are very sensitive for small increases in income.

Table 2.1
Long-term poverty in Germany and the Netherlands according to the n-years income-to-needs ratio European standard, 1985-1989 (percentages)

	Germany			The Netherlands		
	≤ 75%	≤100%	≤125%	≤75%	≤100%	≤125%
≤ 54 years	0.4	5.3	11.8	0.3	2.3	15.3
55-64 years	0.0	0.2	3.4	0.3	0.9	8.2
65-74 years	0.0	0.1	1.7	0.0	0.6	3.2
≥ 75 years	0.0	3.5	19.7	0.0	0.0	4.9

The next Table shows that the picture holds if the analysis shifts to the n-years-in-poverty indicator. Again, the results indicate the higher income mobility among the non-elderly in the Netherlands compared to Germany and the lower mobility among the eldest generation of the elderly. Note that in Germany the proportion of people, who are at least once poor in a five year period, is higher for most age groups, particularly for the non-elderly, compared to the single year figure. Almost 22% of the non-elderly experience poverty at least once in this period whereas only 3 to 7% of the elderly between 55 and 75 years of age belong to this category as do 9% of the elderly over 75 years of age. Particularly in Germany the elderly, who are 75 years and older are more prone to poverty at least once in the five year period.

Table 2.2
Long-term poverty in Germany and the Netherlands according to the n-years in poverty indicator European standard, 1985-1989 (percentages)

	Germany					The Netherlands				
	≥ 1	≥ 2	≥ 3	≥ 4	≥ 5	≥ 1	≥ 2	≥ 3	≥ 4	≥ 5
54 years	21.6	10.5	6.1	3.6	1.5	20.5	7.9	3.7	2.4	0.4
55-64 years	7.2	2.0	0.9	0.1	0.1	18.2	5.5	2.7	1.5	0.0
65-74 years	2.6	1.3	0.7	0.0	0.0	11.5	3.1	1.4	1.1	0.0
≥ 75 years	8.8	7.8	1.5	0.9	0.9	14.9	3.2	0.7	0.7	0.0

Table 2.3
Long-term poverty in Germany and the Netherlands according to the spells-of-poverty indicator, European standard, 1985-1989 (cumulative percentage surviving)

	Germany			The Netherlands		
	After 1 year	After 2 years	After 3 years	After 1 year	After 2 years	After 3 years
≤ 54 years	83.4	43.8	36.6	49.5	37.3	28.1
55-64 years	83.8	30.3	13.9*	46.9	34.3	0.0*
65-74 years	95.7*	95.7*	-	41.8	41.8*	41.8*
≥75 years	100.0*	94.4*	-	25.2	25.2*	0.0*

Notes: The spells-of-poverty indicator equals a life-table estimate of the survivor probability. *) less than 10 cases

In Table 2.3 evidence is presented on the persistence of poverty in both countries using the spells-of-poverty indicator. The results should be considered with caution because of the small numbers involved.

However, from Table 2.3 it is clear that most spells tend to end in the first two years after the spell begins but end sooner in the Netherlands than in Germany. The spell duration is longer in Germany than in the Netherlands corroborating the earlier results showing that income stability is higher and income mobility is lower in Germany particularly among the non-elderly but also among the elderly generations.

Acrosss the generations the findings suggest that the intra-country income mobility among the elderly, particularly the generations below 75 years of age, is higher than among the non-elderly.

Contrary to what might be expected according to hypothesis 4, poverty mobility is lower and poverty stability is higher in the market-oriented German system particularly among the eldest generation. The eldest generation apparently has few chances to escape from poverty in Germany given the absence of a need-based statutory pension system. Because of the non-existence of a safety-net in the pension system the oldest generation has incomes farther below the poverty line than in the Netherlands. Thus only large increases in income will allow an escape from poverty for them. However, the likelihood of large income increases among this age category is expectedly quite low.

Comparing the results across poverty lines the next Table shows how sensitive the findings are for the use of different poverty standards. The figures are for the Netherlands only as a result of lack of data in Germany.

From Table 3 it can be learned that using the poverty spell indicator, the cumulative survival rate of poverty is smaller, and hence the exit rate higher, according to the policy standard (social minimum) than according to the European standard for all spell durations. The survival rate is higher however, and the exit rate lower, in the case of the subjective poverty-line. Hence, the high income mobility we saw from the earlier figures in Germany and the Netherlands must be stressed if a policy standard is used and relaxed somewhat if a subjective standard is used. But even in the case of the subjective standard income mobility is high particularly in the first two years after a spell begins. The highest estimates of persistent poverty are observed for the youngest and the eldest age group of which 27% and 23% respectively, remained subjectively poor even after a stay of four years in subjective poverty.

Table 3

Long-term poverty according to the spells-of-poverty indicator and three poverty-lines, the Netherlands, 1985-1990 (cum. percentage surviving)

	after 1 year	after 2 years	after 3 years	after 4 years
European standard (EMI)				
55-64	37.0	32.8	22.8	0.0
65-74	30.2	12.0	0.0	0.0
75+	32.5	10.5	0.0	0.0
Total population	46.3	28.2	12.3	12.3
Policy standard (SMI)				
55-64	24.4	15.0	2.7	0.0
65-74	25.8	11.3	0.0	0.0
75+	26.8	8.0	0.0	0.0
Total population	28.7	13.9	2.5	0.0
Subjective standard (SPL)				
55-64	53.1	34.8	29.3	26.6
65-74	50.4	29.1	12.5	12.5
75+	54.3	38.2	22.1	22.1
Total population	56.3	39.2	26.1	23.4

Note: For spells-of-poverty indicator see Table 2.3

6 The evolution of deprivation-poverty among the elderly between 1985-1991

6.1 The evolution of deprivation-poverty by age class

In this section the issue is raised whether the use of a less relative poverty-line such as the economic deprivation poverty-line will alter the conclusions with regard to the evolution of poverty and will show that increasing levels of welfare and economic prosperity in this period will likely lead poverty rates to decline (cf. hypothesis 5). Information on the evolution of deprivation-poverty will be given using the so-called subjective deprivation-poverty line (Muffels, 1993; see Appendix 1). In the waves of 1985, 1986, 1988 and 1991 questions were submitted to the respondents about their living conditions. Although the number and wording of some questions changed between the various years for about 20 items the questioning across the years were similar. These 20 items then were used to construct a deprivation index (cf. Appendix 1). In Table 4 the evolution of deprivation-poverty between 1985 and 1991 is given by age group. Table 4 shows that except for 1985 the highest deprivation-poverty risks are observed for the youngest and the oldest age categories whereas the generation of 65 to 74 years bears average risks on deprivation poverty. The figures also show that between 1985 and 1991 the deprivation poverty risks declined for all age groups but particularly for the age group of 50 to 64 years.

Table 4
The evolution of subjective deprivation poverty by age class, 1985-1991 (percentages)

	1985	1986	1988	1991
16-24 years	10.8	11.6	9.7	6.8
25-49 years	9.0	8.7	7.8	5.1
50-64 years	18.5	14.4	11.0	7.7
65-74 years	11.8	8.8	9.3	6.3
75 year	9.2	17.1	21.5	11.3
Total population	10.8	10.4	9.4	6.1

The results seem to confirm what was stated in the fifth hypothesis that poverty rates are likely to decline in a period of economic prosperity given that poverty lines are used which are not entirely relative. Support for this assumption was found in the data since the proportion of people deprived of items gradually declines about 10% on average each year. However, a further look at the data shows that the decline in deprivation-poverty goes back to another factor. It appears that the average level of consumption welfare remains rather stable over the five year period but that the poverty-line itself declined in this period. People seem to become less demanding in terms of what is considered to be a minimum living standard in a growing economy with improving economic perspectives. Although current welfare remained rather stable it was judged better, probably because a future improvement of the living standard was expected.

6.2 *Persistence of deprivation-poverty*

In the last section of this paper we deal with the issue of whether a deprivation-poverty line will show less income mobility and more poverty persistence among the elderly compared to income-poverty lines. If this appears true it is very likely that the former conclusion, with respect to the greater stability in the German pension system, holds a fortiori when poverty is not defined in terms of income but in terms of living conditions or living standards.

Before the data could be used for this purpose we had to impute deprivation-poverty scores for those years where we lack information: 1987 and 1989. The imputation procedure is explained in more detail in Appendix 2. The procedure was to estimate logit models for each of the years for which we had information by regressing deprivation-poverty to a vector of background variables and a lagged deprivation-poverty status variable. Background variables were variables like the number of children, the head's age, the marital status, the head's education level and the housing situation. The parameter estimates were then used to determine the likelihood of being in deprivation-poverty for the missing years.

From the regressions it appears that about 92% of all people were rightly classified in the years for which we had information and 8% were not. This means that about two-third of the observed poverty rates were predicted by the logit models. In Table 5 we present the observed and predicted scores.

Table 5
Observed and predicted levels of subjective deprivation poverty in the Netherlands, 1985-1991 (percentages)

	1985	1986	1987	1988	1989	1990/91
Observed	14.0	13.2	12.5[b)]	11.6	9.3[b)]	8.9
Predicted	9.5[a)]	8.8	7.7	6.7	5.7	4.8

Notes:
a) Based on a model where the deprivation-poverty status variable of 1986 has been included in the model
b) Estimated proportion of people in deprivation-poverty

The estimated proportion of people in deprivation-poverty for the years 1987 and 1989 is based on the average ratio of predicted and observed poverty for the years we had information on. The outcome strongly suggests that, in the late

1980s, deprivation-poverty gradually declined in the Netherlands providing evidence for the last hypothesis about the impact of economic growth. The predicted deprivation-poverty status can then be used to calculate the various measures of income mobility and poverty persistence.[1] In Table 6 the results on the persistence of deprivation-poverty are given.

Table 6
The persistence of subjective deprivation poverty in the Netherlands by age group, 1985-1990/1991

Number of years in subjective deprivation poverty in %	≥1 year	≥2 years	≥ 3 years	≥ 4 years	≥ 5 years	6 years
≤ 54 years	7.1	4.8	2.7	1.8	1.0	0.3
55-64 years	13.4	8.5	5.9	3.1	2.0	1.2
65-74 years	6.6	3.7	0.8	0.0	0.0	0.0
≥ 75 years	11.4	7.2	5.1	3.9	0.8	0.0
Total population	7.8	4.8	2.7	1.8	1.0	0.4
Cumulative percentage surviving	**after 1 year**	**after 2 years**	**after 3 years**	**after 4 years**	**Begin-nings**	**Cen-sored**
≤ 54 years	48.4	29.5	29.5	29.5	272	128
55-64 years	33.0	0.0	0.0	0.0	43	16
65-74 years	49.9	29.8	0.0	0.0	38	19
≥ 75 years	49.1	28.4	28.4	0.0	39	13
Total population	47.8	27.2	27.2	27.2		

The results show that in general the stability of deprivation-poverty is higher than was found using the income-poverty lines, except for the subjective poverty line which shows highest stability. Particularly, the stability of poverty positions for the youngest and the oldest age group which were already more stable according to the income poverty standards appears higher compared to the middle age group. However, the results also clearly indicate that the income mobility among the elderly and even among the oldest age category is still higher than among the rest of the population. Presumably, the stability of poverty positions according to the deprivation-standard would have been higher in Germany than in the Netherlands given that we had data for Germany over the same period. The conclusion made before, that income positions are more stable in Germany, holds therefore even more for the stability of living standards.

In terms of income but even in terms of living standards these results may relax the general assumption that the elderly are more prone to persistent poverty than younger age groups. For the elderly also, there are various gateways to escape from poverty although they are to some extent different from those of the young. Escape from poverty appears related to the occurrence of life events like retirement, changes in living arrangements (moving in with the children or children moving in), changes in work patterns, changes in asset holdings (transforming capital into cash income) and moving to care institutions. It is probably for this reason that the impact of a more market-oriented pension system in Germany on inequality is relatively small since factors like employment or retirement opportunities, patterns of living arrangements and general social policies are probably more decisive for the differences in income mobility and poverty persistence between both countries.

7 Summary and conclusions

In this paper we compare the income, poverty and deprivation situation of three generations of the elderly aged 55 years and older in Germany and the Netherlands. Several indicators for measuring poverty, poverty persistence and poverty mobility have been applied to see how sensitive the results are for differences in methodologies. In particular the paper addresses the question of whether poverty is more temporary or more persistent among elderly than among the younger generations and whether there are striking differences between the two countries. We test some hypotheses about the effects of economic growth and pension policies in both countries on the evolution of relative poverty, income mobility and poverty persistence. We particularly address the question of whether the more market-orientated pension system in Germany (private pensions) leads to more poverty and a higher income mobility than the mixed system in the Netherlands with state provided basic pensions and supplementary private (occupational) pensions.

The figures on income poverty show for both countries that, according to the European poverty line, the elderly (55+) have lower risks of poverty than the younger generations, but this may well be an artefact of the European poverty standard itself. The European standard seems to overestimate the incomes of single persons and elder households because of the presumed high costs for children. If we apply other standards, such as the policy based poverty standard (social minimum income) or the subjective poverty line, poverty risks appear much higher for the elderly (two to three-times higher) than for the younger generations.

We also found that the poverty risks for the oldest age group are much higher in Germany than in the Netherlands, which confirms our hypothesis on the perceived impact of the absence of a statutory basic pension in Germany on poverty. For the presumed higher effect on the evolution of inequality and poverty of the market-orientated pension system in Germany over time we found no evidence. In contrast, we concluded that the more publicly oriented pension system in the Netherlands created more inequality and poverty among the elderly in this period than the market-orientated pension system in Germany. This was particuarly due to Dutch policies freezing the minimum benefits during the 1980s, whereas in Germany the pension benefits remained in nearly all years linked to the index of gross wages. On the other hand it emerged that the absence of a statutory basic pension scheme in Germany resulted in much more poverty among the eldest generation than appeared the case in the Netherlands with a basic pension scheme.

With respect to income mobility and poverty persistence the findings show that income mobility is high in Germany as well as in the Netherlands but more so in the latter than in the former country. Poverty persistence is much higher in Germany particularly among the youngest and eldest age group. The duration of poverty spells is longer in Germany especially for these age groups. In the Netherlands spells tend to end earlier. Hence, contrary to what was expected, poverty mobility is lower and poverty stability is higher in the market- oriented German pension system. Because of the non-existence of a safety-net in the pension system the oldest generation has incomes farther below the poverty line and thus only large increases in income will lead to an escape from poverty (see also Duncan et al. 1993). The results seem to be sensitive to the use of different poverty standards. If we use a policy standard (social minimum income) it appears that the exit rate is even higher than according to the European standard but lower if we use the subjective poverty line. But even if a subjective poverty line is used income mobility is quite high. Highest estimates for persistent poverty are then again observed for the youngest and eldest age groups. About 25% of these groups remained subjectively poor even after a stay of four years in subjective poverty.

In the last section of the paper the hypothesis was examined whether the use of a less relative poverty line than the ones presented earlier would alter the results. For that reason it was assumed that the use of a subjective deprivation standard reflecting not only the income situation of the individual but also the living conditions in other domains of life (health, education, employment, housing situation, social participation) will show that poverty is declining in this period because of the increase in economic welfare. For identical reasons it was expected that income mobility is lower and poverty persistence higher when a deprivation standard is used which is less sensitive to annual income shocks. If deprivation indeed reflects a more persistent state of low living standards the likelihood that the deprived will escape poverty will be lower and hence poverty persistence higher. Firstly, the results show that deprivation-poverty declined strongly 10% on average a year. However, remarkably enough, the reason was not so much the rise in welfare, which remained fairly constant because people in the reference group experienced the same rise in living standards, but the lower demands in terms of living standards that were considered to be the absolute minimum. Although current welfare levels have not changed much people seem to be less demanding because they expect to share future improvements of economic welfare.

The stability of deprivation-poverty appears higher than holds for most of the income poverty lines except for the subjective standard. Particularly the stability of poverty positions for the youngest and the eldest age group appears higher. For that reason it is expected that the stability of deprivation-poverty for these age groups will be higher as well in Germany, indicating again that poverty persistence is more apparent in Germany than in the Netherlands not only in terms of income but also in terms of living standards. Contrary to what was expected initially the impact of the market-orientated German pension system on inequality and poverty appears small probably through the impact of more crucial factors like the design of social policies, the existence of generous retirement gateways, employment opportunities, and the patterns of living arrangements.

A judgement of the German and Dutch pension system, in terms of its performance to reduce (persistent) poverty among the elderly, is hard to make since it depends on what is preferred: a highly mobile pension system with relatively many elderly people prone to transient poverty (the Netherlands) or a somewhat less mobile system with fewer aged persons in transient poverty but more elderly falling into persistent poverty (Germany). The existence of a statutory minimum pension system, such as in the Netherlands, is important to prevent low income elderly becoming persistently poor. On the other hand, a matured universal private pension system, covering a great part of the population and guaranteeing sufficient earnings-related pensions as in Germany, prevents people from moving into poverty at the time they reach retirement or pension age.

Notes

[1] Since we only have information about the deprivation-poverty status of individuals and households and not on the perceived welfare assigned to the current living standard (consumption welfare) we were not able to calculate the first measure of poverty persistence which looks at the average level of consumption welfare over a period of six years and whether this average is below the deprivation-poverty line.

[2] A score of 1 is assigned to each item which the individual is deprived of and a score of -1 to each item which s(he) posses.

References

Bane, M. J., Ellwood, D. (1986), 'Slipping into and out of Poverty: The Dynamics of Spells', *Journal of Human Resources*, Vol. 21, pp. 1-23.

Bosch, K. van den, Callan, T., Estivill, J., Hausman, P., Jeandidier, B., Muffels, R., Yfantopoulos, J. (1993), 'A Comparison of Poverty in Seven European Countries and Regions using Subjective and Relative Measures', *Journal of Population Economics*, Vol. 6, No. 3, pp. 235-259.

Commission of the European Communities (1994), *European Social Policy. A Way forward for the Union*, White Paper, European Commission: Brussels/Luxembourg.

Duncan, G.J., Gustafsson, B., Hauser, R., Schmauss, G., Messinger, H., Muffels, R., Nolan, B., Ray, J.C. (1993), 'Poverty Dynamics in Eight Countries', *Journal of Population Economics*, Vol. 6, No. 3, pp. 234.

Hagenaars, A., Vos, K. de, Zaidi, M.A. (1994), *Patterns of Poverty in Europe*, Paper for the Seminar on the Measurement and Analysis of Social Exclusion, Commission of the EC/Department of Social Security: Bath.

Kapteyn, A., Kooreman, P., Willemse, R. (1988), 'Some Methodological Issues in the Implementation of Subjective Poverty Definitions', *Journal of Human Resources*, Vol. 23, No. 2, pp. 222-242.

Mack, J., Lansley, S. (1985), *Poor Britain*, Allen and Unwin: London.

Muffels, R., Berghman, J., Dirven, H.J. (1992), 'A Multi-Method Approach to Monitor the Evolution of Poverty', *Journal of European Social Policy*, Vol. 2, No 3, pp. 193-213.

Muffels, R., Dirven, H.J., Fouarge, D. (1995), *The Dynamics of Income and Deprivation of Three Generations of the Elderly*, WORC-paper, 95.08.020/2, WORC/TISSER, Tilburg University: Tilburg.

Muffels, R.J.A. (1993), *Welfare Economic Effects of Social Security. Essays on Poverty, Social Security and Labour Market: Evidence from Panel Data*, Series on Social Security Studies, Reports, no. 21, Tilburg University: Tilburg.

Muffels, R., Kapteyn, A., Vries, A. de, Berghman, J. (1990), *Poverty in The Netherlands: Report on the Dutch Contribution to an International Comparative Study on Poverty and the Financial Efficacy of the Social Security System*, VUGA: The Hague.

Nolan, B., Whelan, Chr. T. (1995), *Resources, Deprivation and Poverty*, Oxford University Press: Oxford.

O'Higgins, M., Jenkins, S. (1990), 'Poverty in the EC: 1975, 1980, 1985', in Teekens, R., Praag, B. van (eds.), *Analysing Poverty in the European Community, Eurostat News Special Edition*, 1 - 1990, EUROSTAT: Luxemburg.

Sen, A. (1976), 'Poverty: An Ordinal Approach to Measurement', *Econometrica*, Vol. 44, No. 2, pp. 219-231.

Statistics Netherlands (SN) (1994), *Personele inkomensverdeling 1991-1993 (Income Distribution of Persons* 1991-1993), SDU-Publisher: The Hague.

Townsend, P. (1979), *Poverty in the United Kingdom*, Penguin: Harmondsworth (Middlesex).

Walker, R. (1994), *Poverty Dynamics: Issues and Examples*, Aldershot: Avebury.

Appendix 1 The definition of a deprivation-index and the calculation of a deprivation poverty line

Deprivation is defined as a lack of goods or things from a large list of items representing the average life-style of a community (cf. Townsend, 1979), which the household finds absolutely necessary to have or do. Then a score on the deprivation index is determined for every head of household in the sample.[2] It is defined as the weighted sum of the deprivation score on each consumption item out of a large set of items or indicators of the actual living conditions of people in society (the list of items is given below). The weights are determined differently for necessities and non-necessities. These weights are equal to the proportion of people in the reference group of the respondent having or lacking the item. The more common the possession of a good is in the reference group of the household the higher subjective deprivation is if the household lacks the item (keeping up with the Joneses). On the other hand the less common a good is in the reference group the higher one's subjective welfare is if one possesses the good (status goods).

In the next step, the SDS-index is converted into a deprivation poverty line (SDL) by submitting the following question to the respondents. This question is called the life resources evaluation question, which is asked directly, after the battery of questions, about the actual living conditions (the list of deprivation items): 'If you consider the way in which your household lives at the moment, would you consider your household as poor, or in fact as rich, or as somewhere in between? You may answer by giving a score to your situation. A score of 1 means that you consider your household as being very poor, a score of 10 means that you consider your household as being very rich.' Then, a regression model is estimated in which the scores on the life resources evaluation question, ranging from 1 to 10, are assumed to be determined by a set of variables indicating the consumption welfare (the reverse of the score on the deprivation index), the level of economic resources, and the financial situation. In the final step the deprivation poverty line is then determined as the average consumption welfare level of those households who rate their current living conditions with the school mark 5.5. The 5.5 mark represents the presumed minimum utility level below which a person or household is considered to be living in poverty. The households for which actual consumption welfare is evaluated with 5.5 are assumed to be the experts who are best aware of the minimum needs of the household. As with a school mark in the Netherlands it is assumed that a score of 5.5 indicates the dividing line between a 'satisfactory' and an 'unsatisfactory' score, in this case as regards the evaluation of one's current living conditions.

From the estimation of the regression model, the evaluation of life resources in terms of assigning a school mark between 1 and 10 to the actual living conditions seems to be strongly influenced by the score on the deprivation index, by the marital status of the head, by reference group factors and by financial stress factors. Given the individual scores on these variables for each household and making use of the parameter estimates of the regression model (estimated on the whole sample), the SDL poverty-line can be calculated for every household in the sample.

Table A1.1

Estimation results (GLS) for the joined data sets of 1988 and 1991

Intercept	-3.62
Consumption welfare	1.00
Share of households in the reference group having necessities	0.15
Share of households in the reference group having non-necessities	0.48
Share of non-necessities in all the items people lack	0.01
Net disposable household income	0.03
Negative disposable income (when being self-employed)	0.30
65 years or older	0.07
Divorced	-0.10
Unmarried	-0.02
Household can save	0.10
Household expects the income to improve in the near future	0.02
F	211.96
p	<0.0001
N	8240
R^2	0.221
R^2-adjusted	0.220

The results, given in Table A.1.1, show that the judgement about one's own living conditions is better when the level of the consumption-welfare is higher, the share of households in the reference group possessing necessities is higher, the share of people in the reference group having non-necessities is higher and when the household income is higher. Further, it appeared that having a negative (fiscal) income (when being self-employed) contributes to more positive judgements about one's own living standard and the same holds for the elderly (above 65 years of age). Divorced and unmarried heads of households have a more negative judgement about their living standards than married or widowed people. The judgement is more positive if one can save or expect a clear improvement of the living standard in the nearby future.

Finally, in Table A1.2 the percentages of deprived households for each of the items on the common list of the four years are given.

Table A1.2
Percentage of deprived households, 1985-1991

Item		1985	1986	1988	1991
1	Membership in a social or cultural association	8.9	8.9	6.7	5.0
2	A telephone	2.3	2.0	1.2	1.0
3	Live in a well-maintained area	6.5	6.0	5.0	5.9
4	Live in a well-maintained house	7.3	7.3	6.1	6.0
5	Pay mortgage or rent without problems	4.3	2.8	2.3	1.4
6	Pay gas, water, electr. bill without problems	2.6	1.9	1.4	0.8
7	Regular contacts with family, friends, acquaint.	3.4	3.0	2.9	2.1
8	Good health	13.9	11.8	11.5	13.4
9	Enough bedrooms to give each children of 10 years and older of diff. sex an own bedroom	7.6	7.4	6.0	3.9
10	A refrigerator	0.5	0.6	0.7	1.0
11	A home free of damp	10.7	9.2	10.0	7.7
12	Own WC	0.6	0.7	1.0	0.5
13	A meal with meat, poultry, or fish every 2 days	2.8	2.7	2.0	1.5
14	A washing machine	3.5	3.0	3.3	3.8
15	Evening out once every fortnight (without the children)	14.1	13.8	10.9	8.9
16	A car	4.7	4.7	3.3	3.7
17	Regularly buying new clothes	14.0	12.2	10.2	6.7
18	At least one week's annual holiday away from home (not visit to family)	18.3	16.4	14.2	11.2
19	Having family, friends, or acquaintances for dinner at least once a month	4.6	4.6	3.6	2.7
20	Leisure goods like sportswear or a bicycle for the children	6.6	6.1	4.4	2.4

Appendix 2 Imputation of missing observations on deprivation-poverty by means of logit estimation

As was explained in the paper logit models were estimated in which the deprivation-poverty status variable (taking on the value 0 or 1) was regressed against some background variables which were assumed to be good predictors of deprivation poverty. These variables are listed in Table A.2.1 below. The pseudo R^2 appears to be quite high. Note the significant negative effect of the variable year, which reflects the continuously declining deprivation-poverty rates. Note also the effect of the lagged deprivation-poverty status variable indicating the stability of deprivation-poverty statuses. The results show that about 92% of all observations are correctly classified, but misclassification apparently occurs particularly among the deprivation-poor. For this reason the predicted poverty-rate is on average only two-thirds of the observed poverty rate.

Table A2.1
Logistic regression coefficients of a number of background characteristics on deprivation-poverty status, 1986, 1988, 1991 (N=7,894)

	B	s.e. (B)	exp (B)
Head's age cohort			
- 16-24 years	-0.948	0.290	0.387
- 25-49 years	-0.057	0.142	0.945
- 50-64 years	0.234	0.125	1.264
- 65-74 years	-0.096	0.176	0.908
- 75 years or older	0.867	-	2.380
Head's marital status			
- married	-0.653	0.096	0.520
- divorced	0.999	0.101	2.716
- widow(er)	-0.327	0.124	0.721
- unmarried	-0.019	-	0.981
Number of children living in the household			
- 0	-0.597	0.138	0.551
- 1	-0.102	0.137	0.904
- 2	-0.081	0.144	0.922
- 3	-0.077	0.205	0.926
- 4 or more	0.857	-	2.356
Head's educational level			
- primary education	0.437	0.117	1.548
- secondary: first stage	-0.026	0.120	0.975
- secondary: second stage	-0.278	0.114	0.757
- non-university higher education	-0.079	0.169	0.924
- university	-0.054	-	0.947

	B	s.e. (B)	exp (B)
Number of income recipients in the household			
- 1	-0.262	0.120	0.769
- 2	-0.227	0.119	0.797
- 3 or more	0.489	-	1.631
Main source of income in the household			
- work income	-0.858	0.210	0.424
- pension	-0.620	0.269	0.538
- unemployment benefit	0.146	0.229	1.158
- sickness or disability payment	0.409	0.221	1.505
- social assistance	0.364	0.249	1.439
- student grant	-0.078	0.317	0.925
- alimony	0.162	0.590	1.176
- missing value	0.475	-	1.608
Head's annual property income in Dutch guilders			
- 0	1.187	1.204	3.278
- 1 - 499	0.597	1.208	1.816
- 500 - 999	-0.315	1.251	0.730
- 1,000 - 4,999	0.233	1.223	1.263
- ≥ 5,000	1.037	1.232	2.821
- missing value	-2.739	-	0.065
Housing situation			
- rented house	0.332	4.686	1.393
- subtenancy	1.497	4.695	4.470
- owner occupied house	-0.145	4.686	0.865
- free house	-0.064	4.697	0.938
- missing value	-1.620	-	0.198
Disposable household income (ln)	-1.168	0.110	0.311
Year	-0.123	0.025	0.884
Previous subjective deprivation poverty			
- non-deprived	-0.901	0.052	0.406
- deprived	0.901	-	2.462
Intercept	10.266	4.974	
Pseudo R^2	41.1%		
Correctly classified	92.0%		

Impoverishment and social exclusion: A dynamic perspective on income and relative deprivation in Belgium and the Netherlands

Henk-Jan Dirven and Didier Fouarge

1 Introduction

In various studies conducted for the European Commission's Observatory on National Policies to Combat Social Exclusion (Dirven 1990; Dirven and Jehoel-Gijsbers 1990; Dirven et al. 1992; Kemperman 1994), reviews were made of the conceptualization of social exclusion, poverty, (social) disadvantage, (relative) deprivation and marginalization in the political and scientific debates in the Netherlands. These reviews showed that, in the political debate at the beginning of the decade, the concepts of social exclusion, poverty, (relative) deprivation and marginalization were very uncommon. The concept of (social) disadvantage, on the other hand, was used rather frequently. Within the Dutch scientific community, the concept of income poverty was clearly preferred to other concepts. However, it is widely acknowledged that no definition exists which is capable of taking into account all aspects of the phenomenon of poverty. As a consequence, a large number of poverty definitions and operationalizations are used, often within the same study.

In 1995, with the publication of the Dutch government's report on poverty and social exclusion (Ministry of Social Affairs and Employment 1995, 1997), both concepts have found their way in the political debate. Nevertheless, in the Netherlands, there is no consensus about the concepts of poverty and social exclusion and their relationships with other concepts, such as (relative) deprivation, marginalization and (social) disadvantage. In this contribution, a conceptual framework is used which distinguishes between the concepts of income poverty, relative deprivation, impoverishment and social exclusion (Berghman 1995). This framework is, first of all, based on the distinction between income poverty (i.e., lack of income) and relative deprivation (i.e., bad living conditions). Secondly, it differentiates between static and dynamic perspectives. Starting from this conceptual framework and using data for Belgium and the Netherlands, empirical results are presented on (the dynamics of) income poverty and relative deprivation as well as the interrelationship between impoverishment and social exclusion.

2 The conceptualization of poverty

According to Ringen (1988), poverty can be defined and measured in two ways: directly and indirectly.[1] A direct definition of poverty is one in terms of relative deprivation; poverty is viewed as having a low level of consumption. Such a definition is termed *direct* because it focuses on the actual living conditions of individuals. Measuring poverty using an income poverty line is an indirect method; poverty is determined on the basis of the disposable income of the household. Such a method of measurement is termed *indirect* because it is not the actual living conditions which are being measured but only one of the determinants of those conditions.

The indirect definition of poverty may be termed the *subsistence definition*. According to this definition, people are poor if they do not have at their disposal the minimum amount of resources which is considered necessary in order to achieve a certain level of consumption. This minimum amount of resources is called the subsistence minimum or the income poverty line.

The direct definition of poverty, the *deprivation definition*, states that individuals are poor if their level of consumption (broadly defined) lags behind what is considered as being sufficient within the society. The direct definition is therefore based on a person's actual living conditions, whereas the indirect definition is based on the determinants of these conditions. Research for the Netherlands (Dirven and Berghman 1991) indicates that income poverty is not the sole determinant of relative deprivation; other economic resources, as well as social and cultural resources, appear to have an independent impact as well.

Poverty definitions may thus be classified into (indirect) definitions of income poverty and (direct) definitions of relative deprivation. While the former are based on a one-dimensional perspective on poverty in terms of a lack of income, the latter take a multi-dimensional perspective in terms of people's actual living conditions. Both concepts are used in a static sense, referring to the situation of individuals at a specific point in time. According to Berghman (1995), a distinction should be made between concepts referring to situations and concepts referring to processes. Table 1 displays the four possible combinations of direct and indirect definitions of poverty on the one hand, and static and dynamic definitions on the other hand. The concept of impoverishment may be used to denote the process leading to income poverty, while the concept of social exclusion can be used to refer to a process bringing about a situation called relative deprivation.

Table 1
The conceptualization of poverty

	Dynamic	Static
Indirect	*Impoverishment*	*Income poverty*
Direct	*Social exclusion*	*Relative deprivation*

Source: Berghman (1995: 21)

As processes, impoverishment and social exclusion refer to chains of events causing people's income and living conditions to deteriorate to the extent that a situation of income poverty or relative deprivation occurs. Both processes may be triggered by changes in people's employment status as well as changes in family composition and may be affected by structural features of the labour market and the system of social protection (e.g., (minimum) wage regulations, implicit tax rates and benefit levels). Moreover, due to stigmatization and discouragement effects, previous situations of income poverty and relative deprivation may contribute to the processes of impoverishment and social exclusion.[2]

While the analysis of dynamic aspects of income poverty has seen a growing interest in recent years, the dynamics of relative deprivation have largely been neglected. This contribution takes a dynamic perspective on both income poverty and relative deprivation to study the processes of impoverishment and social exclusion. It should be noted that the analysis presented here is restricted to the extent to which current situations of income poverty and relative deprivation depend on previous situations and should therefore be considered a first step towards a fuller understanding of these processes. Nonetheless, in the remainder, the dynamics of income poverty and relative deprivation are referred to as the processes of impoverishment and social exclusion, respectively.

Impoverishment and social exclusion are not studied in isolation, for there are reasons to expect them to be mutually reinforcing. Due to the availability of longitudinal data on people's incomes and living conditions, it is possible to analyze the strength of the (supposed) relationship between impoverishment and social exclusion. A vicious circle of poverty may exist, in which income poverty increases relative deprivation and relative deprivation contributes to a situation of income poverty.

3 Research questions and hypotheses

This contribution takes a dynamic perspective on income poverty and relative deprivation and seeks to answer the following research questions:

Q.1 What are the dynamics of income poverty and relative deprivation?

Q.2 To what extent are the dynamics of income poverty and relative deprivation interrelated?

Q.3 To what extent are Belgium and the Netherlands different in terms of the dynamics of income poverty and relative deprivation?

The first research question deals with the extent to which people are caught in a situation of income poverty or relative deprivation. It addresses the issues of the persistence of poverty and relative deprivation, transitions into and out of such situations and the permeability of the dividing line between the poor and the non-poor as well as between the deprived and the non-deprived.[3] High rates of mobility would imply little poverty persistence and few barriers to the improvement of one's living conditions (as well as, by the way, little protection against a deterioration). This could be taken as an indication of a high degree of social openness or social fluidity, which was defined by Erikson et al. (1982), in terms of *relative* mobility chances, as the outcome of a competition between persons from different origins for different destinations.[4] Low mobility rates are then indicative of social closure and the formation of an underclass.

While changes in income level and income poverty status are likely to change people's living conditions, it is expected that other resources are brought into action in order to mitigate the negative consequences of income loss. E.g., savings may be withdrawn, social relationships may be used to get (financial) support, courses may be taken in order to increase human capital and, consequently, labour market opportunities, home production may be increased, etc.. Since many other factors besides income provide resources, it is possible to maintain one's living conditions even in case of income loss (see the chapter by Kangas and Ritakallio). Therefore, it is expected that:

H.1 Situations of relative deprivation are more stable than situations of income poverty.

The second research question is about the extent to which the processes of impoverishment and social exclusion are mutually reinforcing. This question deals with the extent to which future risks of income poverty are determined by current living conditions as well as about the extent to which the latter are affected by a (prolonged) lack of income. In this contribution, the mutual reinforcement of income poverty and relative deprivation is seen as a vicious circle of poverty. This view would be supported, if the following hypothesis would be confirmed:

H.2 While situations of relative deprivation increase the risks of becoming income poor, situations of income poverty increase the risks of becoming relatively deprived.

Hypotheses 1 and 2 are tested for Belgium and the Netherlands. The availability of comparable data for these countries enables us to test whether Esping-Andersen's (1990) characterization of Belgium and the Netherlands as belonging to the same world of welfare capitalism, i.e., the social-democratic welfare regime, is reflected in the dynamics of income poverty and relative deprivation. It may be assumed that people's living conditions in social-democratic welfare regimes are more stable compared to liberal and conservative/corporatist welfare regimes, where the impact of the market is stronger (Fritzell 1990; Dirven 1996). Since Belgium and the Netherlands have identical scores on Esping-Andersen's de-commodification index, the observed differences in the dynamics of income poverty and relative deprivation in the two countries should be insignificant:

H.3 In terms of the dynamics of income poverty and relative deprivation, Belgium and the Netherlands are not significantly different.

4 Data, instruments, and methodology

4.1 Data

For the purpose of this contribution, two data sets were used, covering representative samples of the Belgian and Dutch populations. The data are panel data, which means that sampled persons in the first wave are re-interviewed in subsequent waves. The availability of panel data makes it possible to carry out an analysis of the dynamics of income poverty and relative deprivation.

The survey data used for Belgium are from the Socio-Economic Panel and were collected by the Centre for Social Policy in Antwerp. The data for the Netherlands are from the Socio-Economic Panel Survey, collected by Statistics Netherlands (SN). The years covered are 1985 and 1988. In Belgium, the available data for the first wave cover 18,324 persons and 10,757 persons in the second wave; 10,250 persons participated in both waves. The 1985 Dutch data cover 11,432 persons, while 13,770 persons are covered by the 1988 wave; 8,711 persons took part in both waves.[5]

Cross-sectional weights were used to obtain results representative for the total population at the time of interview. For longitudinal analyses, the data have been weighted with longitudinal weights to correct for selective attrition. The panel data can then be considered to be representative for that part of the population in 1985, which did not decease or emigrate between 1985 and 1988.

4.2 Instruments for the measurement of income poverty

The notion of income poverty is generally made operational by defining an income poverty line. For our analysis, three different income poverty lines are used: The European poverty line, the subjective poverty line, and the legal poverty line.

The European poverty line is a purely statistical threshold. It is defined as 50% of a country's median (or, sometimes, mean) equivalent disposable household income. For this contribution, the median was used, because it is less sensitive to extreme values. Equivalent household income is obtained by dividing household income by the household's equivalence scale. The equivalence factors applied in this study are 1 for the first adult, 0.5 for other adults and 0.3 for each child.[6]

The subjective poverty line (SPL) is based on the judgement of heads of households regarding the minimum acceptable level of income for their own household. This does not mean, however, that it is solely the evaluation given by the household head that determines whether the household is poor or not. From the individual judgements, an *average* judgement is derived (after taking into account a number of household characteristics). Hence, this income poverty line is an inter-subjective rather than a subjective standard. Details on the SPL-method can be found in Goedhart et al. (1977), Kapteyn et al. (1988), and Muffels et al. (1990) among others.

While the SPL reflects the views of the population, the legal poverty line can be seen as reflecting a political (official) consensus as regards the minimum acceptable subsistence level in a given country. Although no official income poverty line exists in the Netherlands, the amounts given under the Dutch General Assistance Act can be seen as official minima. The amounts considered to be the minimum according to social security law vary by family type. Besides general assistance benefits, holiday allowances, incidental benefits, child allowances and student grants[7] are also taken into account to determine the official minimum. The exact computation of this line can be found in Muffels et al. (1990). The Belgian legal poverty line equals the guaranteed minimum income under the legal social security system (the Minimex) plus child allowances. The line thus also varies according to family type.

4.3 Instruments for the measurement of relative deprivation

For the determination of relative deprivation, two methods are used: The majority necessity index (MNI) of Mack and Lansley (1985) and the subjective deprivation scale (SDS) of Muffels (1993). Both methods are defined in terms of actual living conditions and allow for a direct evaluation of poverty, in terms of *outcomes*.

Mack and Lansley (1985) introduced the notion of taste into the method of Townsend (1979). Their claim was that differences in consumption patterns between individuals can occur because of differences in tastes as opposed to lack of resources. By way of questionnaires, they asked respondents whether they possessed certain items and if they did not, whether it was because of free will or a lack of income. Only those items which were thought to be necessities by the majority of the population were included in the MNI. Someone was said to be deprived of one of those necessities, if s/he did not have the item for financial reasons.

The point of departure for the construction of the SDS is also a list of items or consumption events included in questionnaires. For each item, household heads are asked whether they find it definitely necessary to have (or do) it. Not having (or doing) a particular item only leads to deprivation if it is considered necessary by the household head.

From the answers to those questions, the SDS can be derived for every household. The SDS is defined as the weighted sum of the deprivation score on each item. The weights are determined by the possession and the necessity of the item in the reference group of the household head, reflecting the assumption that the dis-utility of not having or doing a necessary item is higher if more people in the reference group have or do the item.[8]

4.4 Methodology

The unit of analysis in this contribution is the individual. Household income and poverty status are assigned to every individual in the household. The dynamics of income poverty are analyzed according to the European poverty line, the subjective poverty line and the legal poverty line, while the dynamics of relative deprivation are analyzed using the instruments proposed by Mack and Lansley (1985) and Muffels (1993), respectively. While the results on the stability of income poverty and relative deprivation are largely based on the log-linear analysis of transition tables, structural models were used to analyze the interrelationship of impoverishment and social exclusion. In both panels, the samples included all household members. Since household income and poverty status are characteristics of the household and do not vary across household members, statistical tests are based on the number of households instead of the number of individuals.

5 Income poverty

The income concept used in this contribution is that of (real) disposable household income. Because the income data available in both panels differed slightly, a comparable income definition was applied using only those income components available in both panels.[9] Disposable household income includes labour income, social assistance benefits, unemployment benefits, survivor and old age pensions, sickness and disability payments, child allowances, student grants, alimony and income from letting a room or a house.

Table 2 reveals that, in the Netherlands, the year-to-year poverty rate shows little variation except when based on the European poverty line. According to that line, poverty has increased between 1985 and 1988. This follows the increase in income inequality during the same period. In Belgium, poverty appears to have increased slightly according to the European poverty line, but to have diminished according to the other poverty lines. According to both the European poverty line and the SPL, the incidence of poverty is higher in Belgium than it is in the Netherlands. This result reflects the rather generous level of minimum benefits in the latter country.

Table 2
Poverty incidence according to the European poverty line (EMI), the subjective poverty line (SPL), and the legal poverty line (LEG) in Belgium and the Netherlands (percentages)

	1985	1988
Belgium		
- EMI	4.6	5.0
- SPL	24.8	23.8
- LEG	4.6	3.3
The Netherlands		
- EMI	1.4	3.2
- SPL	16.5	16.7
- LEG	11.4	11.0

6 Relative deprivation

The analysis of relative deprivation is based on a subset of ten common items from the lists of items included in the questionnaires of the 1985 and 1988 waves of the Belgian and Dutch socio-economic household panels. The ten items concern deprivation of home facilities, housing deprivation, recreational deprivation and dietary deprivation.[10] All but one of the items are considered necessary by a vast majority of heads of households in both countries and both years of observation. The one exception is having a car.

In order to compare the incidence of relative deprivation in Belgium and the Netherlands, the ten items were combined into the majority necessity index (MNI) of Mack and Lansley (1985) and the subjective deprivation scale (SDS) of Muffels (1993). Since only those items which are thought to be necessities by the majority of the population should be included in the MNI, deprivation of a car is not taken into account.[11] The SDS is based on the full set of ten items. Using the MNI and SDS, Table 3 presents data on relative deprivation in Belgium and the Netherlands in 1985 and 1988.

Using the MNI, Table 3 shows, first of all, that over 80% of both populations are not deprived of any item included in the index. Moreover, less than 2.5% is deprived of more than one item. Comparing the results between 1985 and 1988, relative deprivation appears to have decreased in the Netherlands, while it remained at a rather stable level in Belgium.[12] In 1988, deprivation in the Netherlands was somewhat lower than in Belgium, while it was the other way around in 1985.

Table 3
Deprivation among the Belgian (Bel) and Dutch (Nld) population according to Mack and Lansley's (1985) and Muffels' (1993) approaches 1985-1988 (percentages)

	1985		1988	
	Bel	Nld	Bel	Nld
The household lacks:				
0 items	84.1	82.3	84.7	87.6
≥ 1 item	15.9	17.7	15.3	12.4
≥ 2 items	2.1	2.4	2.2	1.6
≥ 3 items	0.7	0.5	0.8	0.4
≥ 4 items	0.3	0.1	0.2	0.2
Subjective deprivation (mean value of SDS)	-0.0423	-0.0625	-0.0356	-0.0628

The results according to the SDS do not correspond to those found according to the MNI. Since high values on the SDS imply high levels of deprivation, the results indicate that, in both years, deprivation is lower, on average, in the Netherlands compared to Belgium. Moreover, deprivation appears to have increased in Belgium, while it remained at a rather stable level in the Netherlands.

7 Impoverishment

Table 4 presents data on the dynamics of income poverty between 1985 and 1988 for Belgium and the Netherlands according to the European poverty line, the SPL and the legal poverty line, respectively. In both countries, according to the European poverty line, more than 90% of the population was secure in terms of subsistence in 1985 and 1988. On the other hand, it appears that 1.1% of all Belgians were poor in both years compared to only 0.3% in the Netherlands. Mobility into and out of poverty appears to be more likely in Belgium than in the Netherlands. In Belgium, the odds of being non-poor rather than poor in 1988 for the non-poor in 1985 were 24 : 1, while for the 1985 poor the odds were 3.5 : 1. In the Netherlands, the corresponding odds equalled 46.1 : 1 and 2.3 : 1. The ratio of these odds was equal to 7.0 in Belgium and 19.8 in the Netherlands, suggesting more unequal mobility chances in the Netherlands compared to Belgium.

Similar differences can be observed from the results obtained with the other income poverty lines. According to the SPL, the odds ratios were 10.1 and 20.2 for Belgium and the Netherlands, respectively, while, according to the legal poverty line, the corresponding values were 6.5 and 14.1. Despite these results, the differences proved to be statistically significant in the case of the SPL only. Therefore, it can not be concluded that the degree of social openness of Belgian society is higher than that of Dutch society.

Table 4
The dynamics of income poverty in Belgium and the Netherlands according to the European poverty line, the subjective poverty line and the legal poverty line (percentages)

		Belgium 1988			The Netherlands 1988		
European poverty line		non-poor	poor	Total	non-poor	poor	Total
1985	non-poor	91.3	3.8	95.1	96.9	2.1	99.0
	poor	3.8	1.1	4.9	0.7	0.3	1.0
	Total	95.1	4.9	100.0	97.6	2.4	100.0
Subjective poverty line		non-poor	poor	Total	non-poor	poor	Total
1985	non-poor	66.0	9.8	75.8	78.1	5.3	83.4
	poor	9.7	14.5	24.2	7.0	9.6	16.6
	Total	75.7	24.3	100.0	85.1	14.9	100.0
Legal poverty line		non-poor	poor	Total	non-poor	poor	Total
1985	non-poor	93.4	2.7	96.2	83.8	4.8	88.6
	poor	3.2	0.6	3.8	6.3	5.1	11.4
	Total	96.6	3.4	100.0	90.1	9.9	100.0

Division of the level of disposable household income by the level of the poverty line gives a measure of household income relative to its needs. Such income-to-needs ratios can be ranked and divided into quintiles (5 groups of equal size). Cross-tabulating the quintile position in 1985 and the position in 1988 gives another picture on poverty dynamics between the two years. The transition rates of the income-to-needs ratios for Belgium and the Netherlands based on the European poverty line are presented in Table 5.[13] Similar tables were made using the SPL and the legal poverty line.

Across all income-to-needs mobility tables, it is found that the percentages on the main diagonal are always higher than any other percentage. The highest percentages are found for immobility in the lowest and highest quintiles.

Table 5
The dynamics of income-to-needs according to the European poverty line (percentages)

Quintile position on the income-to-needs ratio		Belgium 1988						The Netherlands 1988					
		1st	2nd	3rd	4th	5th	Total	1st	2nd	3rd	4th	5th	Total
	1st	10.6	4.4	2.6	1.4	1.3	20.4	9.5	6.0	2.6	1.4	0.2	19.8
	2nd	4.5	7.6	4.2	1.9	1.2	19.4	4.3	8.5	5.6	2.0	0.6	21.0
1985	3rd	2.5	4.9	6.2	4.4	1.9	20.0	1.5	4.6	8.0	5.0	1.5	20.7
	4th	1.1	2.2	4.4	7.3	4.4	19.4	1.0	1.6	3.6	8.5	4.7	19.3
	5th	1.4	1.2	2.7	4.7	10.8	20.8	1.0	0.9	1.7	4.0	11.5	19.1
	Total	20.0	20.4	20.2	19.6	19.7	100.0	17.3	21.6	21.6	21.0	18.5	100.0

Moreover, these percentages are, on the whole, higher for the Netherlands than for Belgium. This can be interpreted as meaning that immobility, and in particular immobility for those with a low or a high income-to-needs ratio, is more common in the Netherlands than in Belgium. In both countries, the highest rate of immobility is found for the income-to-needs ratio computed on the SPL.[14] Besides, small changes in the income-to-needs are more likely than large changes.

While in Belgium, the percentage of downwardly mobile persons is higher than the percentage of upwardly mobile people (though only very slightly), the reverse situation holds for the Netherlands, whatever the poverty line used for the computation of the income-to-needs ratios. Furthermore, upward transitions in terms of income-to-needs are more common in the Netherlands than in Belgium. Downward mobility is, however, more common in Belgium than in the Netherlands.

A number of log-linear models for transition tables (Hout 1983; Agresti 1990) were fitted to the data in the income-to-needs mobility tables.[15] The best fitting model proved to be a log-multiplicative full interaction model originally proposed by Xie (1992). Equality restrictions were imposed on the association parameters across poverty lines, while these were allowed to vary by country.[16] The estimated parameters of the model are presented in Table 6. Two remarks can be made. First of all, the saddle-shaped pattern found in the income-to-needs mobility tables is reflected by the association parameters. Secondly, the log-multiplicative comparison parameter for the Netherlands indicates that income positions in the Netherlands are more stable than in Belgium.

Table 6
Estimated parameters of the log-multiplicative full interaction model for impoverishment in Belgium and the Netherlands

				Belgium 1988		
	Quintile	1st	2nd	3rd	4th	5th
	1st	1.46	0.47	-0.31	-0.71	-0.91
	2nd	0.34	0.80	0.20	-0.48	-0.85
1985	3rd	-0.37	0.17	0.43	0.17	-0.40
	4th	-0.77	-0.56	0.01	0.70	0.61
	5th	-0.66	-0.88	-0.33	0.32	1.55

Note: Log-multiplicative comparison parameter for impoverishment in the Netherlands = 1.23

8 Social exclusion

In this contribution, the concept of social exclusion is used to refer to the process leading to a situation of relative deprivation. A first step towards understanding this process is the analysis of the dynamics of relative deprivation. Such an analysis may reveal the extent to which people's living conditions change over time. It may thus give an indication of the persistence of relative deprivation and the opportunities for people to escape such a situation.

Using the majority necessity index (MNI) of Mack and Lansley (1985), Table 7 cross-classifies, for each person in the longitudinal sample and separately for Belgium and the Netherlands, the number of necessary items lacking due to financial reasons in 1985 with the corresponding number in

1988. The results indicate, first of all, that the great majority of the population (76.2% in Belgium and 80.4% in the Netherlands) did not undergo a change in the extent of deprivation between 1985 and 1988. Moreover, while the proportion of the population experiencing an improvement was about the same in both countries (12.2% in Belgium and 12.9% in the Netherlands), increased deprivation appeared to be more common in Belgium (11.5%) than in the Netherlands (6.6%).

Table 7
The dynamics of relative deprivation in Belgium and the Netherlands using Mack & Lansley's (1985) majority necessity index (percentages)

Number of necessary items lacking due to financial reasons		Belgium 1988					The Netherlands 1988				
		0	1	2	≥ 3	Total	0	1	2	≥ 3	Total
	0	73.1	7.8	1.5	1.0	83.4	76.2	4.8	0.6	0.2	81.8
	1	8.9	2.2	0.6	0.5	12.2	9.4	3.6	0.7	0.2	14.0
1985	2	1.4	0.6	0.3	0.1	2.5	0.8	1.4	0.3	0.1	2.6
	≥ 3	0.9	0.3	0.1	0.6	1.9	0.5	0.7	0.1	0.3	1.5
	Total	84.3	10.9	2.5	2.3	100.0	86.9	10.5	1.8	0.8	100.0

The latter result may be the consequence of the overall reduction in the incidence of deprivation observed for the Netherlands in Table 3 as well as in the marginal distributions of Table 7. Naturally, whenever these distributions change, there must be some mobility. In order to arrive at conclusions about the degree of social openness or social fluidity, it is customary in mobility research to control for mobility caused by such marginal changes (structural mobility). Log-linear models may be used to analyze the dynamics of relative deprivation after taking into account changes in the overall distribution of relative deprivation between 1985 and 1988. Moreover, these models can be used to test the differences between Belgium and the Netherlands.

A large number of log-linear and log-multiplicative models were fitted to the data in Table 7. The best fitting model with the fewest parameters appeared to be a log-multiplicative quasi-independence model (Xie 1992) in which the parameters for the cells on the main diagonal were allowed to vary (log-multiplicatively) by country.[17] This model implies that there is a tendency to be immobile, which varies by the number of necessary items lacking due to financial reasons as well as by country, and that, if a change occurs, origin and destination status are independent.

The parameters for the cells on the main diagonal indicate a tendency for immobility which appeared to be highest for those without any item lacking as well as for those with three or more items lacking. The two countries appeared to be different in this respect: In Belgium, tendencies to be immobile were weaker than in the Netherlands. This result implies that, in the Netherlands, situations without deprivation (i.e., no items lacking) as well as with high levels of deprivation (i.e., three or more items lacking) are more stable than in Belgium. Apparently, the degree of social openness is lower in the Netherlands.

The dynamics of relative deprivation was analyzed on the basis of the SDS as well. For that purpose, all sample members were ranked according their score on the SDS in a given year. This was done separately for Belgium and the Netherlands. After making quintiles (20%-groups), a person's position in 1985 was cross-classified with his/her position in 1988. The results are displayed in Table 8. It should be noted that persons in the lowest quintile are the least deprived, whereas persons in the highest quintile are the most deprived. Moreover, the results are affected by structural mobility, because the quintiles were based on the cross-sectional samples. For that reason, and because the observed percentages may be affected by sampling fluctuations and measurement error, log-linear and log-multiplicative models were fitted to the data.

Table 8
The dynamics of relative deprivation in Belgium and the Netherlands using Muffels' (1993) subjective deprivation scale (percentages)

Quintile position on the SDS		Belgium 1988						The Netherlands 1988					
		1st	2nd	3rd	4th	5th	Total	1st	2nd	3rd	4th	5th	Total
	1st	7.1	4.1	3.6	2.9	2.4	20.1	8.1	4.3	3.5	2.6	1.8	20.3
	2nd	4.0	6.4	4.6	3.0	2.1	20.1	4.1	7.3	5.2	2.3	1.8	20.6
1985	3rd	3.2	3.8	5.4	4.2	3.1	19.7	2.6	4.0	6.1	4.7	2.9	20.3
	4th	3.5	3.3	4.0	4.9	4.2	19.9	3.6	2.4	2.4	5.5	3.6	17.6
	5th	2.2	2.4	2.5	4.8	8.3	20.2	1.7	2.4	2.3	4.8	9.9	21.2
	Total	20.0	19.9	20.2	19.7	20.1	100.0	20.3	20.4	19.5	19.9	20.0	100.0

The fixed distance model (Haberman 1979) with specific parameters for the main diagonal of the transition tables appeared to be the best fitting model.[18] According to the fixed distance parameter, large changes in living conditions are less likely than small changes. Moreover, the parameters for the main diagonal cells indicate that immobility is higher in the lower quintiles compared to the higher quintiles. Apparently, the living conditions of the most deprived are more volatile than those of the lesser deprived. Since the differences between Belgium and the Netherlands proved to be insignificant, the degree of social openness in the two countries may be considered equal in this respect.

9 Impoverishment and social exclusion

This section provides a test of the hypotheses on impoverishment and social exclusion advanced in Section 3. First of all, in Subsection 9.1, a comparison is made of the stability of income poverty and relative deprivation. It is expected that situations of relative deprivation are more stable than situations of income poverty. Secondly, in Subsection 9.2, an assessment is made of the extent to which the processes of impoverishment and social exclusion are mutually reinforcing. The hypothesis was that situations of relative deprivation increase the risks of becoming income poor, while situations of income poverty increase the risks of becoming relatively deprived. Thirdly, in both subsections, it is tested whether the differences between Belgium and the Netherlands are indeed insignificant.

9.1 The stability of income poverty and relative deprivation

To compare the stability of income poverty and relative deprivation, log-linear and log-multiplicative models were fitted to the income-to-needs mobility tables and Table 8 on the dynamics of relative deprivation using the SDS.[19] The log-multiplicative full interaction model appeared to give the best fit to the observed mobility patterns. While it was assumed that the parameters for the various combinations of quintile positions on the income-to-needs ratios varied (log-multiplicatively) by country, the parameters for the dynamics of relative deprivation were constrained to be equal in Belgium and the Netherlands. Equality restrictions were also imposed on the parameters of the transition tables referring to impoverishment, reflecting the assumption that the dynamics of income-to-needs did not vary by income poverty line. The model fit proved to be acceptable given the large number of cases and compared to a range of other models.[20] Table 9 displays the parameter estimates of the preferred model.

Table 9
Estimated parameters of the log-multiplicative full interaction model for impoverishment and social exclusion in Belgium and the Netherlands

		Belgium 1988				
	Quintile	1st	2nd	3rd	4th	5th
	1st	1.51	0.47	-0.34	-0.71	-0.93
	2nd	0.32	0.76	0.14	-0.51	-0.72
1985	3rd	-0.35	0.17	0.45	0.16	-0.43
	4th	-0.80	-0.57	0.06	0.74	0.56
	5th	-0.68	-0.83	-0.31	0.31	1.51

Notes: Log-multiplicative comparison parameters: impoverishment in the Netherlands = 1.23, social exclusion in Belgium and the Netherlands = 0.56

The parameter estimates reflect the familiar saddle-shaped patterns of income mobility and deprivation dynamics. More interesting, however, are the log-multiplicative comparison parameters presented in the bottom row of Table 9. These parameters, first of all, confirm the earlier result that changes in income position were less likely in the Netherlands compared to Belgium. Apparently, Dutch society is less fluid in terms of income mobility. Secondly, it appears, rather unexpectedly, that changes in deprivation status are more likely than changes in income position.

At least two explanations may be put forward for the observed high level of change in relative deprivation. First of all, it may be explained from the subjective dimension of the deprivation scale. While the SDS incorporates an objective dimension (i.e., (not) having or doing specific items), subjective feelings of deprivation are incorporated through the construction of a weighting scheme. From the calculation of Pearson rank correlations, it appears that the correlation between the objective dimensions was 0.51 for Belgium and 0.59 for the Netherlands.[21] Implementation of the weighting scheme implied a reduction of these correlations to 0.33 for Belgium and 0.43 for the Netherlands. Apparently, the subjective dimension of deprivation is less stable than the objective dimension.

Secondly, due to unreliability of measurement, high levels of change may be observed while the true deprivation status is rather stable (Hagenaars 1991; Rendtel et al. 1991). Indeed, according to conventional criteria, the reliability of the SDS used in this contribution is modest.[22] If income-to-needs are measured more reliably than deprivation status, the observed level of stability of the former may be higher, while the unobserved or 'true' level of stability is lower.

9.2 The interrelationship of impoverishment and social exclusion

To analyze the extent to which the processes of impoverishment and social exclusion are interrelated, a path analysis (Wright 1934) was made of the correlations between income-to-needs and level of deprivation in 1985 and 1988. In the analysis, both the majority necessity index (MNI) and the subjective deprivation scale (SDS) were used.

Table 10
Impoverishment and social exclusion:
Stability and lagged cross-effects, standardized regression parameters, income-to-needs, and the majority necessity index (MNI)

	Stability				Lagged cross-effects			
	Income-to-needs		Deprivation		Income-to-needs in 1985 → deprivation in 1988		Deprivation in 1985 → income-to-needs in 1988	
	Bel	Nld	Bel	Nld	Bel	Nld	Bel	Nld
European poverty line	0.473	0.600	0.258	0.408	-0.099	-0.074	-0.099	-0.074
Subjective poverty line	0.485	0.626	0.257	0.415	-0.101	-0.065	-0.101	-0.065
Legal poverty line	0.488	0.619	0.257	0.402	-0.096	-0.074	-0.096	-0.074

The preferred model has two dependent variables: income-to-needs and level of deprivation in 1988. While both appeared to depend on income-to-needs and level of deprivation in 1985, it did not prove to be necessary to include an interaction term between the two. The analyses were done separately for Belgium and the Netherlands as well as for the three income-to-needs ratios and the two deprivation indices. Equality restrictions could be imposed on the lagged cross-effects. All models were fitted with LISREL (Jöreskog and Sörbom 1989a, 1989b). While Table 10 displays the results on the MNI, Table 11 presents the results on the SDS.

The results in Tables 10 and 11 indicate that income-to-needs are more stable than levels of deprivation, irrespective of the income poverty line and the relative deprivation index. Also, the stability of income-to-needs and relative deprivation is higher in the Netherlands compared to Belgium, if the lagged cross-effects are taken into account. The latter are statistically significant in both countries. However, they tend to be somewhat stronger in Belgium.

Table 11
Impoverishment and social exclusion:
Stability and lagged cross-effects, standardized regression parameters, income-to-needs, and the subjective deprivation scale (SDS)

	Stability				Lagged cross-effects			
	Income-to-needs		Deprivation		Income-to-needs in 1985 → deprivation in 1988		Deprivation in 1985 → income-to-needs in 1988	
	Bel	Nld	Bel	Nld	Bel	Nld	Bel	Nld
European poverty line	0.469	0.573	0.327	0.416	-0.072	-0.052	-0.072	-0.052
Subjective poverty line	0.484	0.608	0.328	0.413	-0.069	-0.045	-0.069	-0.045
Legal poverty line	0.488	0.586	0.328	0.412	-0.068	-0.061	-0.068	-0.061

These results thus show that low levels of deprivation contribute to a decrease in income-to-needs, while low levels of income-to-needs contribute to an increase in level of deprivation. Apparently, the path analyses support the hypothesis on the interrelationship of impoverishment and social exclusion. The two processes are mutually reinforcing.

10 Conclusions

Starting from a conceptual framework distinguishing between direct and indirect definitions of poverty on the one hand and static and dynamic definitions of poverty on the other hand, this contribution presented results on situations of income poverty and relative deprivation as well as on processes of impoverishment and social exclusion in Belgium and the Netherlands. The main research questions were about the dynamics of income poverty and relative deprivation, about the extent to which the processes of impoverishment and social exclusion are mutually reinforcing and about differences between Belgium and the Netherlands in these respects. It was hypothesized that situations of relative deprivation are more stable than situations of income poverty, that situations of relative deprivation increase the risks of becoming income poor, while situations of income poverty increase the risks of becoming relatively deprived and that Belgium and the Netherlands would not be significantly different.

Unexpectedly, situations of relative deprivation appeared to be less stable than situations of income poverty. Two tentative explanations were suggested for this result. The first explanation was concerned with the definition of relative deprivation. Usually, such definitions include an objective dimension referring to the possession of certain items as well as a subjective dimension referring to feelings of disadvantage. The results in this contribution suggest that the subjective dimension is less stable than the objective dimension. This may be one of the reasons for the rather low level of stability of relative deprivation.

The second explanation was concerned with the measurement of relative deprivation. If measures of relative deprivation are less reliable than measures of income poverty, the observed level of stability of the former may be lower, even if the 'true' level of stability is higher. The majority necessity index and the subjective deprivation scale applied in this contribution have modest reliabilities. This may have produced an underestimation of the 'true' level of stability of people's deprivation status. Clearly, this would call for an improvement of the instrument designed to measure the concept of relative deprivation.

The second hypothesis on the interrelationship between the processes of impoverishment and social exclusion was supported by the data. Significant cross-effects were found of income poverty on the dynamics of deprivation as well as cross-effects of relative deprivation on the dynamics of income. Apparently, the processes of impoverishment and social exclusion are mutually reinforcing, causing a vicious circle of poverty in which income poverty increases relative deprivation and relative deprivation contributes to a situation of income poverty.

The cross-effects of income poverty and deprivation may be explained as follows. On the one hand, income poverty may have a *direct* impact on relative deprivation due to the necessity of financial resources to maintain a standard of living. On the other hand, the impact of income poverty may be *indirect*, through the erosion of other economic resources (e.g., savings) as well as social, cultural and physical resources. Similarly, the impact of relative deprivation on income poverty may be mediated by such resources since these are likely to be affected by unfavourable living conditions and to have an impact on the process of income attainment.

The third hypothesis on the lack of differences between Belgium and the Netherlands in the dynamics of income poverty and relative deprivation was only partially supported by the data. While cross-national differences in the overall stability of relative deprivation appeared to depend on the measuring instrument, the volatility of income-to-needs was consistently found to be higher in Belgium. The latter result may be due to a number of factors. First of all, while Belgium has a lower level of income inequality compared to the Netherlands (Atkinson et al. 1995), changes in income have, on average, similar absolute values (Fouarge and Dirven 1995). As a consequence, Belgium is expected to have higher levels of income mobility (Dirven 1996).

Secondly, although married women's labour market participation has been increasing in the Netherlands, more people live in two-earner households in Belgium.[23] Since two-earner households are more likely to experience labour market events (e.g., unemployment, reduced working hours and/or wage decrease), it can be expected that household incomes are less stable in Belgium. Thirdly, the data used in this contribution indicate that the labour market as well as the marriage market are less stable in Belgium in terms of number of hours worked and marital status, respectively. Given the impact of changes in labour market status and household composition on household income, Belgium is expected to have higher levels of income instability as well. Concerning Esping-Andersen's classification of Belgium and the Netherlands as social-democratic welfare regimes, it may be concluded that, even within the same world of welfare capitalism, people's living conditions may be more stable in some countries than in others.

Notes

[1] Related distinctions were made by Sen (1979) between the direct method and the income method and by Atkinson (1987) between the right to a minimum level of resources and the attainment of a minimum standard of living.

[2] Some authors define (social) exclusion in terms of (social) rights. This approach is not used here for the following reasons. Firstly, definitions such as those proposed by Room (1991) and Gamson (1995) appear to combine processes as well as situations. Secondly, people with similar rights may be exposed to different life events and have different living conditions, while people with different rights may be jeopardized by the same events and live in similar circumstances. Admittedly, both authors do refer to relevant variables operating in the process of social exclusion as defined here. However, (social) rights, or the extent to which these are secured, fall beyond the scope of this contribution.

[3] Permeability refers to mobility across the income/deprivation poverty line taking into account the extent of mobility due to changes in the (marginal) distributions of income poverty/deprivation.

[4] Ultee and Luijkx (1986) argue that relative *inter*generational standard-of-living mobility rates are indicative of social openness or social fluidity. Here, it is maintained that relative *intra*generational mobility rates into and out of income poverty and relative deprivation can be used for the same purpose.

[5] On various occasions, additional samples were drawn by SN causing an increase of the sample size between 1985 and 1988.

[6] Children aged 14 or more get a weight of 0.5. The European poverty line as defined here is a slightly modified version of the poverty line used by O'Higgins and Jenkins (1990).

[7] Dutch students living on their own are considered to be a household separate from their parents. Usually, they are not entitled to assistance benefits, but to student grants at a lower level of benefit.

[8] From the SDS, a subjective deprivation poverty line (SDL; Muffels 1993) can be derived. For doing so, use is made of the life resource evaluation question (LREQ). However, because the Belgian questionnaires do not include the LREQ, the SDL could not be derived for Belgium.

[9] While the European poverty line was based on the comparable income definition, this could not be done for the SPL because of conceptual reasons. To compute the SPL, it is assumed that respondents know about all their income components but that they misperceive their needs. Correction for misperception occurs on the basis of all available income components in the panels. Therefore, it makes sense to include an income definition based on all income components in the regression model for the SPL rather than the less extensive comparable income definition. Because the legal poverty line is based on the level of guaranteed minimum income, it makes no difference for the computation of the poverty line which income definition is used, but it does make a difference for the results obtained.

[10] The following items were used: A telephone, a separate bedroom for children over ten of different sexes, a refrigerator, a damp-free dwelling, exclusive use of indoor WC, a meal with meat, poultry or fish every two days, a washing machine, a car, a week's annual holiday away from home and leisure equipment for the children.

[11] In the 1988 wave of the Belgian panel, the reason for lacking an item was only asked if it was considered a necessity by the head of household. In order to be able to compare the results, the same restriction was applied to the 1985 data as well as to the Dutch data. It should be noted that this restriction was not used by Mack and Lansley (1985), who consider a household to be deprived of an item, even if it does not consider it to be a necessity.

[12] A slight reduction of deprivation was found for Belgium, if the full set of items from the Belgian Socio-Economic Panel was used.

[13] Note that quintiles were computed on the cross-sectional distributions. This explains why the marginal percentages in Table 5 do not equal 20%.

[14] According to the European poverty line, 42.5% of all persons did not change quintile position between 1985 and 1988 in Belgium against 46% in the Netherlands. According to the SPL, these percentages were 44.8 and 50.0 for Belgium and the Netherlands, respectively, while the corresponding percentages for the legal poverty line were 42.2 and 48.5.

[15] All models were fitted with *l*EM (Vermunt 1993). Given the large numbers of observations, the model selection was based on the Bayesian Information Coefficient (Raftery 1986).

[16] The model's L^2 was 82.7 with 79 degrees of freedom (N=6,268).

[17] The model's L^2 was 23.8 with df=13 (N=6,622).

[18] The model's L^2 was 86.7 with df=26 (N=5,940).

[19] The MNI could not be used for that purpose, because over 80% was not deprived of any item and, consequently, calculating quintiles would not have made much sense.

[20] The model's L^2 was 154.8 with df=110 (N=9,243).

[21] These correlations are comparable in size to the correlations between income-to-needs in 1985 and income-to-needs in 1988 (irrespective of the income poverty line).

[22] Cronbach's α for the SDS based on the set of common items ranged from about 0.5 to 0.6, implying a correlation of about 0.75 between the observed/manifest deprivation status and the unobserved/latent ('true') deprivation status.

[23] For Belgium, the proportions of people in two-earner households were 0.35 and 0.36 in 1985 and 1988, respectively, while the corresponding figures for the Netherlands were 0.23 and 0.29.

References

Agresti, A. (1990), *Categorical Data Analysis*, Wiley: New York.

Atkinson, A.B. (1987), 'On the Measurement of Poverty', *Econometrica*, Vol. 55, pp. 749-764.

Atkinson, A.B., Rainwater, L., Smeeding, T. 1995, *Income Distribution in European Countries*, Department of Applied Economics Working Paper 9535, University of Cambridge.

Berghman, J. (1995), 'Social Exclusion in Europe: Policy Context and Analytical Framework', in Room, G. (ed.), *Beyond the Threshold: The Measurement and Analysis of Social Exclusion*, The Policy Press: Bristol .

Dirven, H.J. (1990), *Social Exclusion in the Netherlands: A Feasibility Study*, KUB: Tilburg.

Dirven, H.J. (1996), *Income Dynamics, Persistent Poverty and Welfare Regimes: Evidence from Europe and the United States*, Paper presented at the European Research Conference on 'European Societies or European Society', Blarney, Ireland, 26-31 March 1996.

Dirven, H.J., Berghman, J. (1991), *Poverty, Insecurity of Subsistence and Relative Deprivation in the Netherlands: Report 1991*, KUB: Tilburg.

Dirven, H.J., Jehoel-Gijsbers, G.J.M. (1990), *Social Exclusion in the Netherlands: First Annual Report, 1990*, IVA: Tilburg.

Dirven, H.J., Jehoel-Gijsbers, G.J.M., Serail, S. (1992), *Dutch Policies to Combat Social Exclusion: Consolidated Report, 1990-1991*, IVA: Tilburg.

Erikson, R., Goldthorpe, J.H., Portocarero, L. (1982), 'Social Fluidity in Industrial Nations', *British Journal of Sociology*, Vol. 33, pp. 1-34.

Esping-Andersen, G. (1990), *The Three Worlds of Welfare Capitalism*, Polity Press: Cambridge.

Fouarge, D., Dirven, H.J. (1995), 'Income Dynamics Among the Elderly: Results of an International Comparative Study', *Actes des XVe Journées de l'Association d'Economie Sociale*, Berger-Levrault GTI: Nancy.

Fritzell, J. (1990), 'The Dynamics of Income Distribution: Economic Mobility in Sweden compared to the United States', *Social Science Research*, Vol. 19, pp. 17-46.

Gamson, W.A. (1995), 'Hiroshima, the Holocaust, and the Politics of Exclusion', *American Sociological Review*, Vol. 60, pp. 1-20.

Goedhart, T., Halberstadt, V., Kapteyn, A., Praag, B. van (1977), 'The Poverty Line: Concept and Measurement', *Journal of Human Resources*, Vol. 12, pp. 503-520.

Haberman, S.J. (1979), *Analysis of Qualitative Data*, Academic Press: New York.

Hagenaars, J. (1991), *Examplifying Longitudinal Log-linear Analysis with Latent Variables*, Department of Sociology Working Paper Series, KUB: Tilburg.

Hout, M. (1983), *Mobility Tables*, Sage: Beverly Hills.

Jöreskog, K.G., Sörbom, D. (1989a), *LISREL 7 - A Guide to the Program and Applications, Second Edition*, SPSS Publications: Chicago.

Jöreskog, K.G., Sörbom, D. (1989b), *LISREL 7 Users Reference Guide*, Scientific Software: Chicago.

Kapteyn, A., Kooreman, P., Willemse, R. (1988), 'Some Methodological Issues in the Implementation of Subjective Poverty Definitions, *Journal of Human Resources*, Vol. 23, pp. 222-242.

Kemperman, M.H. (1994), *Social Exclusion in the Netherlands: Rearranged Consolidated Report 1994*, IVA: Tilburg.

Mack, J., Lansley, S. (1985), *Poor Britain*, Allen and Unwin: London.

Ministry of Social Affairs and Employment (1995), *De Andere Kant van Nederland: Over Preventie en Bestrijding van Stille Armoede en Sociale Uitsluiting*, Ministry of Social Affairs and Employment: The Hague.

Ministry of Social Affairs and Employment (1997), *De Andere Kant van Nederland: Voortsgangsnota. Nieuwe Stappen tegen Stille Armoed en Sociale Uitsluiting*, Ministry of Social Affairs and Employment: The Hague.

Muffels, R. (1993), *Welfare Economic Effects of Social Security. Essays on Poverty, Social Security and Labour Market: Evidence from Panel Data*, KUB: Tilburg.

Muffels, R., Kapteyn, A., Berghman, J. (1990), *Poverty in the Netherlands: Report on the Dutch Contribution to an International Comparative Study on Poverty and the Financial Efficacy of the Social Security System*, VUGA: The Hague.

O' Higgins, M., Jenkins, S.P. (1990), 'Poverty in the EC: Estimates for 1975, 1980 and 1985', in Teekens, R., van Praag, B. (eds.), *Analysing poverty in the European Community*, Eurostat: Luxembourg.

Raftery, A.E. (1986), 'Choosing Models for Cross-classifications (Comment on Grusky and Hauser)', *American Sociological Review*, Vol. 51, pp. 145-146.

Rendtel, U., Langeheine, R., Berntsen, R. (1991), *Mobilitätsprozesse und Einkommensarmut: Erfragtes und errechnetes Haushaltseinkommen im Vergleich*, Paper presented at the International Conference on Social Science Methodology in Trento, Italy, 22-26 June 1992.

Ringen, S. (1988), 'Direct and Indirect Measures of Poverty', *Journal of Social Policy*, Vol. 17, pp. 351-366.

Room, G. (ed.) (1991), *National Policies to Combat Social Exclusion: First Annual Report*, Commission of the European Communities: Brussels.

Sen, A., (1979), 'Issues in the Measurement of Poverty', *Scandinavian Journal of Economics*, Vol. 81, pp. 285-307.

Townsend P. (1979), *Poverty in the United Kingdom*, Penguin: London.

Ultee, W., Luijkx, R. (1986), 'Intergenerational Standard-of-living Mobility in nine EEC Countries: Country Characteristics, Competitive Balance and Social Fluidity', *European Sociological Review*, Vol. 2, pp. 191-207.

Vermunt, J.K. (1993), *lEM: Log-linear and Event History Analysis with Missing Data using the EM Algorithm*. WORC Paper 93.09.015/7, WORC: Tilburg.

Wright, S. (1934), 'The Method of Path Coefficients', *Annals of Mathematical Statistics*, Vol.5, pp. 161-215.

Xie, Y. (1992), 'The Log-multiplicative Layer Effect Model for Comparing Mobility Tables', *American Sociological Review*, Vol. 57, pp. 380-395.

Acknowledgements

The authors wish to thank Jos Berghman for his helpful comments and suggestions.

Poor Swedes, poor Britons: A comparative analysis of relative deprivation

Björn Halleröd

1 Introduction

This chapter represents an attempt to compare the prevalence of deprivation and poverty in Sweden and Great Britain in the early 1990s. To begin with it is necessary to discuss the two basic concepts: deprivation and poverty. Townsend argues, in an often quoted passage, that: 'People can be said to be deprived if they lack material standards of diet, clothing, housing, household facilities, working, environmental and locational conditions and facilities which are ordinarily available in their society, and do not participate in or have access to the forms of employment, occupation, education, recreation and family and social activities and relationships which are commonly experienced or accepted' (Townsend 1979, p. 413). Townsend did not argue that the experience of deprivation in itself is poverty. People are only poor if they lack the necessary resources to obtain these conditions and if they for that reason are unable to fulfil their role as a member of society (Townsend 1987, p. 140). Thus, poverty is related to a specific cause, namely lack of economic resources (for a discussion of this matter see Mac Cárthaigh 1994). This means that people can be deprived without being poor, but they cannot be poor without being deprived. This argumentation is the basic rational for Townsend's, often criticised, strategy of discussing the outcome of poverty in terms of deprivation while measuring poverty as lack of economic resources.

The concept of deprivation and deprivation indices have been widely applied since Townsend's path breaking work. However, the distinction between poverty and deprivation has usually been dropped in later studies. Instead of defining people as poor if their economic resources fall under a certain poverty line, they have been classified as poor if they suffer from a particular degree of deprivation (Heikkilä 1991; Halleröd 1991, 1995, 1996; Callan et al. 1993; Muffels et al. 1992; Nolan and Whelan 1996). Thus, the poverty line has been fixed at a certain level on a deprivation index. This study will basically follow this line but it will take it one step further by abandoning the use of a poverty line. The analysis will instead focus on the degree to which certain sections of the population suffer from deprivation. Hence, the chapter will not focus on how many people live in poverty in Sweden and Britain. Instead, the degree to which people are deprived will be the focus of attention. Or to put it in another way, what will be studied is if people that live under specific circumstances are more or less poor, not if they are poor or not poor on a dichotomized scale.

How to compare poverty and deprivation in different countries

The most common way of comparing poverty among countries is to classify households with an income under a certain proportion of the median income, usually 50 per cent, as poor (Mitchell 1991; Förster 1994; Duncan et al. 1993; Van den Bosch et al. 1993; Ritakallio 1994; McFate et al. 1995). However, the comparability of such an exercise can be questioned. Fifty per cent of the mean or median income is a totally arbitrary figure and we do not know if the social meaning of having an income below the poverty line is the same in different countries. Other income based approaches used in comparative studies are more sensitive to specific conditions in different countries. The consensual poverty line method (sometimes referred to as the subjective poverty line method) has been used in some comparative analyses (Saunders et al. 1994; Deleeck and Van den Bosch 1992; Van den Bosch et al. 1993). Another approach based on existing minimum levels within the social security systems has been developed by Gustafsson and Lindblom (1993). However, there are also more general problems connected to the measurement of economic resources.

It has recently been shown in a number of studies that there is a substantial mismatch between poverty measured indirectly as low income and poverty measured directly as observed deprivation. A large proportion of those classified as poor because of low income are not deprived and vice versa (Ringen 1987; Heikkilä 1991; Halleröd 1991, 1995; Deleeck and Van den Bosch 1992; Callan et al. 1993; Muffels et al. 1992; Mayer 1995; Nolan & Whelan 1996). There are several reasons for these results. The cost of making ends meet differs among individuals and households, as does the ability to make ends meet with a given sum of money. People can also have access to a wide range of non-monetary economic resources. In the case of comparative research, we can add, among other things, differences in the financing of social insurance systems and the supply of free services, for example free health care. Diversity in the relative price structure can also result in differences in the actual experience caused by low income.

Another reason is that we cannot entirely trust income data. The income that people report is not always the same as the income they actually have. It can also be shown that the way income data are collected influences the result (Halleröd 1993, 1995). The possibilities to conduct comparative research on income distribution and economic poverty have been largely improved during the last decade and the Luxembourg Income Study represents the most developed attempt to create a harmonised income data base. However, there are still substantial problems to overcome. National survey samples are derived in different ways. The coverage of the populations differ. Information about incomes is sometimes gathered from official tax registers and sometimes from survey questionnaires. Most countries use annual income, but some countries use incomes that cover shorter periods. The effects of taxes and transfers are sometimes imputed and the imputation differs among countries etc. (Whiteford 1995). All these problems complicate comparative research on poverty and question the reliability of the results.

Another strategy for analysing poverty is to study to what degree people actually suffer from hardship and deprivation, not how much money we believe that they possess. A precondition for such a comparison is that deprivation can be measured against a standard that has social relevance in each country involved in the study. That is, deprivation must be measured as *relative deprivation*. Relative deprivation here refers to Townsend's objective interpretation of the concept, that is, people are deprived when they cannot 'participate in the activities and have the living conditions and amenities which are customary, or at least widely encouraged or approved, in the society to which they belong' (1979, p. 31). The strategy used here to measure relative deprivation builds on Mack and Lansley's (1985) direct consensual definition: deprivation and poverty are defined as *an enforced lack of socially perceived necessities*. The method will be described in some detail later in this chapter.

2 Why are some people more deprived than others?

To explore differences in the prevalence of deprivation between countries is of course important and will result in greater awareness about differences in living conditions. It will also make it possible to rank countries according to people's abilities to achieve a decent standard of living. However, such information says very little about why there are differences between countries. To reach greater insights we have to move further and analyse the conditions within each country that produce deprivation, and finally explore how they differ between countries. The data used in this study makes it possible to examine some of these conditions and they are briefly discussed here. The actual operationalisation of the independent variables will be described later.

People's material standard is decided in the balance between their access to economic resources and their needs. Hence, it is obvious that the overall income level and the distribution of incomes are crucial in explaining the prevalence of deprivation within countries and the differences between countries. Compared with other developed countries, Sweden turns out the be among the ones with the most equal income distribution. Britain is more of a middle range country (Mitchell 1991; Fritzell 1991; Whiteford 1995). The picture is largely reproduced if one looks at economic poverty. The fraction of households with a disposable income below 50 per cent of the mean income in Sweden increased from about 5 per cent in the early 1980s to nearly 9 per cent in the beginning of the 1990s (Gustafsson 1994). The corresponding figures in Britain were about 10 per cent up to 1985, and then rised sharply to reach about 20 per cent in the early 1990s (Nolan & Whelan 1996, p. 31).

It is likely that the more uneven income distribution and the higher incidence of economic poverty in Britain will have an impact on the prevalence of deprivation. However, all the problems that are connected with income as an indicator of poverty remain when it is used as a predictor of deprivation. We can, therefore, not expect income to suffice as the sole predictor of deprivation.

There are numerous studies that confirm the connection between poverty and unemployment. One obvious reason why the unemployed often are poor is that they earn less money than others. However, income data are often limited to annual income or even shorter periods and are sensitive to temporary fluctuations. It is reasonable to assume that many households have the capability to adjust to such fluctuations by using savings and avoiding expenditure. Long term low income has more far-reaching effects that lead to the fundamental erosion of the economic resources of households (Nolan and Whelan 1996). The real problems of deprivation occur, not at the very moment that income falls under a certain level, but when all savings are depleted and when the need for new clothes, maintenance of the car, the house, etc. can no longer be neglected. Unemployment, and especially long term unemployment, can therefore be seen as a supplement to income as a predictor of deprivation, capturing more far-reaching aspects of income stress than income itself.

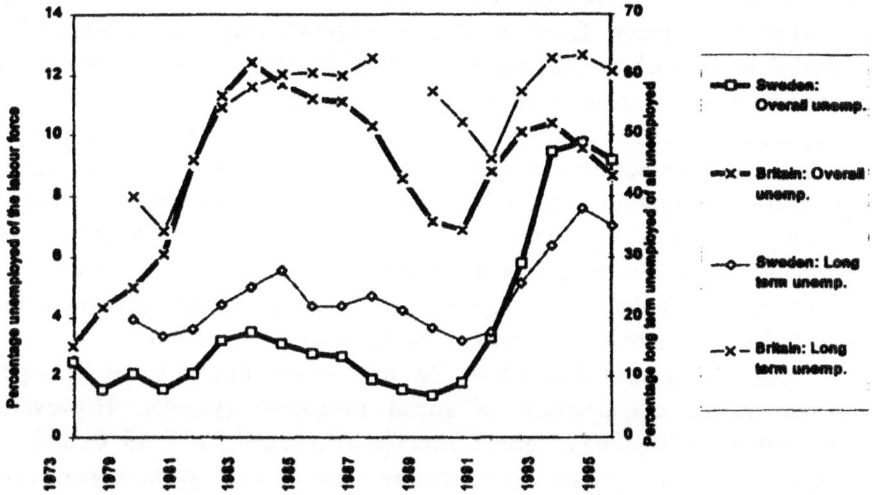

Figure 1 Unemployment rate and long term (> six month) unemployed as percentage of all unemployed in Sweden and Britain

Source: OECD Employment Outlook September 1986, 1987 & 1988; July 1989, 1994 & 1996; OECD Main Economic Indicators March 1995

There is, as is shown in Figure 1, a marked difference between Sweden and Britain when it comes to unemployment. Britain, as many other European countries, experienced a rapid increase of the unemployment rate in the late seventies and early eighties. Sweden managed, in contrast to most European countries, to keep unemployment at a very low level throughout the 1980s. However, unemployment rose rapidly in the beginning of the 1990s and by the year 1995 the unemployment rate in Sweden was somewhat higher than in Britain. Another striking difference between the countries is the long term unemployment rate. During the 1980s about 20 per cent of the unemployed in Sweden were unemployed more than six months. The increase in unemployment in the early 1990s resulted in a rise in long term unemployment to close to 40 per cent of all unemployed. The situation in Britain is markedly different. During the past ten years long term unemployment in Britain has varied from about 50 to 60 per cent of the unemployed. The difference in the unemployment rate will almost certainly be a cause of differences in the prevalence of deprivation in the two countries at the beginning of the 1990s.

It has often been argued that the main goal of the welfare state is to abolish poverty and the existence of poverty can of course be related to features in the social security system. There are, as is well known, important differences in the Swedish and British welfare states. The British social security system has been based on a flat rate national minimum income level since the 1940s. The obligation has been to meet all citizens basic needs and guarantee that no one be left in want and squalor. The need for supplementary social security insurance has gradually grown and the British system of today is a mix of basic income security programs and various private forms of social security systems, particularly employment-based benefits provided by companies. The development has also meant a gradual abandonment of the universal principle and a growth of means tested programs (Lawson 1987, 1990).

After the Second World War, Sweden seemed to follow the same path as Britain in its construction of social insurance systems. However, the development in Sweden diverged from the British path in the 1950s and the flat rate social security system was transformed into an income maintenance system (Lindqvist 1990; Edebalk 1994). The Swedish income security system therefore is not based on citizenship but largely restricted to those who are or were employed. Thus, it is predominantly a welfare state for income earners. The cornerstone of this model is the active labour market policy that has kept unemployment at a very low level. There are nevertheless sections of the population that are not covered by the social insurance system (Marklund and Svallfors 1986; Salonen 1993). There are also parts of the population that cannot support themselves on their labour market income. The social insurance programs are therefore supplemented by means tested income support programs.

Those receiving means tested benefits in Sweden and Britain can be seen as the part of the population defined by welfare state praxis as the worst off. The treatment of this group is decisive for the occurrence of deprivation and poverty. Again it can be argued that the fact that people receive means tested benefits is only an additional indicator of income since only low income earners receive them. However, there are reasons to believe that means tested benefits indicate something more than lack of income and, for that matter, something more than unemployment. Making ends meet in the household economy is by all means a complicated equation that can hardly be captured by a few one-dimensional variables. The various causes that finally lead to a household being dependent on means tested benefits are often highly complex, covering both individual and structural features of human life that make up the complex fabric of a society (Halleröd 1991; Salonen 1993). Dependence on means tested benefits can, therefore, be seen as an indicator of structural problems, expenditure pressure, as well as an infinite number of individual features. The relationship between means tested benefits and poverty is also relevant from another point of view. Means tested benefits are supposed to step in when the other income security systems fail. In addition, its fundamental purpose is to prevent poverty. The relationship between means tested benefits and poverty should, therefore, be weak if this purpose is fulfilled.

Income, unemployment and social security are factors that relate to the households' supply of economic resources. However, access to economic resources has to be related to the needs that are to be met. Large households need more resources than small households to make ends meet. This is usually taken into account by adjusting the disposable income according to household size. However, this is not a completely satisfactory solution. All the problems connected with the income variable are, of course, still present, and now we have to add the question of equivalence scales. The difficulties of choosing an equivalence scale that reflects the needs of different households in a correct way are well known (Buhman et al. 1988; Bradbury 1992). To rely entirely on the equivalence scale means that we accept the scale as correct without any test. It is therefore favourable to incorporate household composition as an independent variable in the analysis even though income is adjusted for household size (Nolan and Whelan 1996).

Both income and household composition are related to people's age. It can nevertheless be assumed that age has an independent effect on deprivation that is mainly associated with differences in needs over the life cycle. Young people who are about to establish an independent household have not yet accumulated resources and they have had less time to establish an economic buffer. We can therefore suspect that they have an increased risk of being deprived. Older people can also be assumed to have an increased poverty risk. One obvious reason for this is the decrease in income among the retired part of the population. However, the elderly can also suffer from an increased probability of being poor because of an increase in their needs. Economies of scale disappear if one of the spouses dies. We can also suspect that some elderly people will have increased costs for health care and medicine, transportation, food, etc.

The expression 'feminization of poverty' refers to the fact that women make up an increasingly larger share of the poor. The development is connected with changes in household structure in Western societies, resulting in a larger share of single parent households, households that predominately are headed by females (Kamerman 1995). An additional problem is women's weaker position on the labour market. However, the debate is heavily influenced by the situation in the United States and there is less evidence of a feminization of poverty in European countries (Wright 1992). The hypothesis will nevertheless be tested in this study.

Income, unemployment, dependence on means tested benefits, household type, age, and gender are all conditions that can be assumed to have an impact on the prevalence of deprivation and poverty. These conditions have been pointed at as decisive for the presence and distribution of poverty in numerous studies. Thus, their inclusion in this study is not at all arbitrary. That is not to say that they are the only relevant ones. It would, among other things, have been desirable to analyse poverty in relation to occupational class. However, a satisfactory analysis of class cannot be done because of lack of reliable British data.[1]

3 Data and definitions

The Swedish data set used here is the Swedish Standard of Living Survey (SLEV). The data were collected in 1992 and are based on an initial sample of 1075 individuals representative of the total population aged between 20 and 75. The field work was conducted by Statistics Sweden. Face to face interviews were completed with 74 per cent of the initial sample, yielding a final working sample of 793 households. The data are representative of the population with respect to gender, age, household composition, and occupational class. There is, however, a bias regarding income, and low income earners are underrepresented in the working sample. The working sample has therefore been weighted according to income (Halleröd 1994a).

The British data are from the 1990 Breadline Britain Survey (BBS). A quota sample of 1319 adults aged 16 and older were interviewed during the summer of 1990. Additional field work among households living in particular deprived areas was carried out later the same year with 512 quota interviews. Quotas were based on sex, age, and working status. All interviews were conducted face to face. Aggregated data are weighted by age, household type, tenure, and ACORN housing type to be representative of the population of Great Britain (Gordon and Pantazis 1995, p. 204). In this study the BBS has been restricted to the same age spectrum as was used in SLEV. The working sample consists of 1551 cases representing the British population. Both BBS and SLEV are, at least partly, replications of the 1983 Breadline Britain survey (Mack and Lansley 1985). Thus, the national data sets are related but there are, nevertheless, several problems that have to be solved to make a comparison possible (for additional information about SLEV see Halleröd et al. 1993 and Halleröd 1994a, for BBS see Gordon and Pantazis 1995).

3.1 Relative deprivation and poverty

The direct consensual definition of poverty was originally formulated by Mack and Lansley (1985). The approach is based on two steps. First, what constitutes necessary consumption is determined. Second, those who have to do without these necessities because of lack of economic resources are identified. The first step is conducted with the help of a list that contains an extensive number of consumption items. The respondents are asked the following question: 'Please would you indicate... the living standards you feel all adults should have in Sweden/Britain today. For each item indicate which you think is necessary, and which all adults should be able to afford and which they should not have to do without'. In the next step the respondents are confronted with the same list of consumption items and asked which items they actually have. Items that they do not have are classified into two groups. The first is *do not have and do not want* and the second is *do not have and cannot afford*. The aim of providing these response alternatives is to sort out the impact of taste and to isolate shortage of money resources as the specific reason for lacking consumption (Mac Cárthaigh 1994).

The purpose of the direct consensual definition of poverty is to relate the measurement of deprivation to the prevailing lifestyle in the society in question and to provide a socially relevant measurement of deprivation. However, the method makes comparisons between countries a relatively complex task. Disparities in cultural patterns, lifestyles, climate, etc. create differences that are bound to be reflected in the list of consumption items used in a particular country. To present an identical list of items in two different countries would be to throw out the baby with the bath water. The data would in one sense be truly comparable but they would tell us very little about deprivation as a social phenomenon.

There are 36 items that are used as indicators of the consumption of goods and services by adults in both surveys. Eighteen of these are the same in SLEV as in BBS and they are listed in Table 1.

Table 1
Percentage of the population that regards consumption item as necessary and percentage of the population that cannot afford consumption item (SWE n=793, GB n=1551)

Consumption item	*Necessary, everyone should be able to afford*		*Would like to have but cannot afford*	
	SWE	*GB*	*SWE*	*GB*
Telephone	95.8	55.2	0.9	7.1
Householders' comprehensive insurance	95.7	88.7	1.1	9.8
Washing machine	92.8	74.0	2.9	3.2
Modern dwelling (bath/shower, WC, central heating, stove, and refrigerator)*	84.4	85.8	1.5	2.7
New, not second hand clothes	73.8	65.5	7.0	3.6
A hobby or leisure activity	73.8	67.5	5.8	6.9
TV	70.0	56.2	0.8	0.6
Presents for friends and family at least once a year	70.1	67.0	1.4	5.1
A holiday away from home for one week a year, not with relatives or friends	54.4	54.8	16.2	20.8
Car	46.7	27.3	6.9	16.7
Celebrations on special occasions	44.0	73.2	5.4	3.9
A 'best outfit' for special occasions	44.1	54.0	3.8	7.8
Save at least 500 SEK (£10) each month	28.9	67.8	31.2	28.4
A special meal once a week	24.6	63.3	6.3	5.9
Friends/family for a meal once a month	23.1	36.8	13.1	10.0
A night out once a fortnight	18.4	41.4	14.7	14.1
Dishwasher	11.7	4.4	11.5	18.4
VCR	6.6	12.8	7.5	9.5

* The responses to this question are, in the case of Britain, derived from four separate questions: a) heating to warm living areas of the home if it's cold, b) refrigerator, c) indoor toilet, not shared with other households, d) bath, not shared with other households. 85.8 per cent of the population indicate that all of these four items are necessary and 2.7 per cent say that they cannot afford at least one of the items

Column one and two in Table 1 show that the ranks of preferences differ between Swedes (SWE) and Britons (GB). Thus, the social meaning of not being able to maintain a specific type of consumption differs between the countries. Column three and four show the proportion that cannot afford the consumption items. There are three items that a larger proportion of Swedes report that they want but cannot afford while there are ten items that a larger shares of Britons want but cannot afford. The remaining five items show only marginal differences between the countries.

A comparison of *relative* deprivation requires a deprivation index that takes account of the differences in preferences in the two countries. A *proportional deprivation index* (PDI) has therefore been used (Halleröd 1994a, 1994b; Halleröd et al. 1995).

Each item on the list in Table 1 is given a weight based on the proportion of the population that regards it as necessary. Thus, those who want but cannot afford a TV will get a deprivation score of 0.70 in Sweden and 0.56 in Britain. The reflection of public opinion is further strengthened by adjustments of the item weights according to significant differences in preferences between men and women, age groups, household types and, in Sweden but not in Britain, geographic regions. For example, about 18 per cent of the Swedes regard *a night out each fortnight* as a necessity. However, this mean value is not representative for the whole population since nearly 30 per cent of those under the age of 30 but only about ten per cent of those over the age of 65 regard this activity as a necessity. The corresponding figures for Britain are about 45 and 30 per cent. The weight of the item has therefore been adjusted to reflect differences between age groups within each country as well as the difference between the countries. It is important to acknowledge that the weight assigned to each item is not connected to a subjective evaluation of a particular household but to the average rank of preferences within the relevant reference group. This procedure will establish an inter-personal and non-subjective rank of preferences of the consumption items. The specific feature of the PDI makes it suitable for use in comparative research since a specific PDI value will express the same degree of *relative deprivation* in Sweden as in Britain. The PDI values can therefore be seen as comparable between countries.

Two PDI were initially constructed. One was based on the eighteen items presented in Table 1 and the other covered all 36 consumption items used in SLEV and BBS. The latter one is, then, not based on the same items in Sweden as in Britain.[2] It can nevertheless be argued that the use of the complete list of items will provide a better basis for comparisons. The aim of the lists of consumption items is to capture consumption that is central and basic in both countries. If we assume that this goal has been attained than we also can assume that the PDI gives an accurate and comparable measurement of deprivation in both countries.[3] It can also be noted that the correlation (Pearson's r) between the 18-item PDI and the complete 36-item PDI is 0.96 in Britain and 0.92 in Sweden, indicating that they can be looked upon as interchangeable. The complete 36-item PDI will therefore be used in the following analysis.

3.2 *The poverty line and method*

The purpose of poverty research is usually to establish a poverty line that divides the poor from the non-poor. If poverty is defined and measured as lack of economic resources, the poverty line represents a certain minimum income regarded as necessary to maintain an acceptable standard of living. If poverty is defined and measured in terms of deprivation, then the poverty line has to be fixed on a certain score on the deprivation index. The use of a poverty line definitely serves a purpose if poverty is measured as lack of economic resources. The poverty line could then be related to different social policy programs and minimum income levels at the labour market. However, the value of a poverty line can be questioned when poverty is defined and measured as deprivation. The rational for such a poverty line should be the existence of a qualitative difference between the poor and the non-poor and that difference could be located at a certain level of the deprivation index (Halleröd 1994a, p. 19). Several attempts have been made to derive a more or less objective poverty line from a deprivation index (Townsend 1979; Mack and Lansley 1985; Muffels and Vreins 1991; Nolan and Whelan 1996). These attempts are more or less successful and they are all to some degree based on pragmatic or/and normative decisions. In some cases the use of a poverty line has been motivated by only methodological considerations (Halleröd 1996).

It is argued here that the PDI produces a comparable measurement of relative deprivation. The most ideal strategy is therefore to compare the distribution of PDI scores using the PDI as a metric variable. However, the PDI is far from normally distributed in the population, a feature that complicates the statistical analysis. Most methods aimed at analysis of continuous variables have the normal distribution as a precondition and can therefore not be applied here. However, the PDI can be looked upon as a censored variable that represents an underlying unobserved variable with a normal distribution. The basis for this assumption is that the list of consumption items on which the PDI is based theoretically can be increased by an infinite number of items (or at least as many items as there are things to consume). The point is that it is plausible that a PDI based on a substantially increased number of consumption items would be more or less normally distributed. However, such a strategy is not possible in practical survey research, where the number of items on a list is usually restricted. The number of items is therefore limited to measure the conditions among the most deprived. The PDI used here can therefore be seen as capturing the upper tail of a variable that in theory is normally distributed. It is therefore possible to analyse the PDI as a metric variable using a TOBIT regression model. The TOBIT model produces coefficients that represent the effects of the independent variables on a latent (unobserved) normally distributed dependent variable (Y*). Y* is equal to the observed dependent variable (Y) if Y* exceeds a certain constant (in this case zero). The estimated TOBIT regression coefficients are interpreted in the same way as the regression coefficients produced by an OLS regression model.

3.3 Operationalisation of the independent variables

Income The British income data are derived from a question in the BBS. The respondents were asked to indicate their household's total income per week after deductions for tax and national insurance. The answers were to be placed in one of eighteen income groups starting with under £50 per week and ending with over £600 per week.

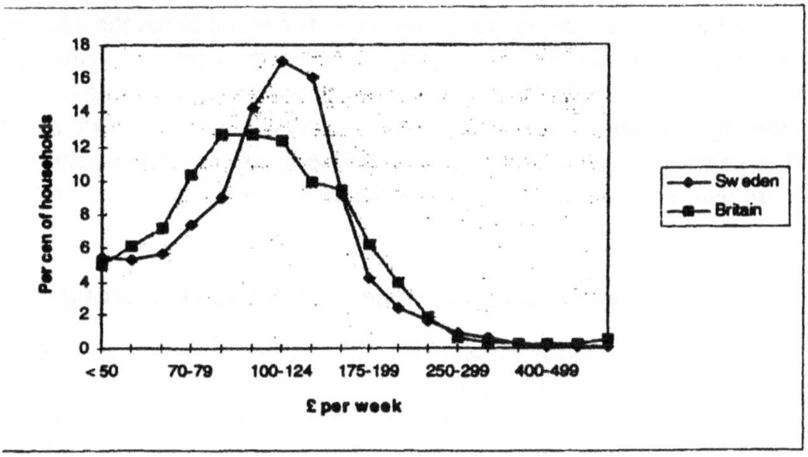

Figure 2 Distribution of equivalent disposable household income in Sweden (SLEV) and Britain (BBS). Incomes adjusted by purchasing power parities standard

The income data in SLEV was gathered from the official tax register and was first deflated to the money value of 1990 and thereafter recalculated into British pounds per week using the purchasing power parity standard. It was then divided into the same groups used in the British BBS (For additional discussion of the income data see Appendix). Figure 2 shows the income distribution in the two countries. The so-called OECD equivalence scale was used to adjust the income to household size.[4]

A higher proportion of the British households is found in the lower end of the income distribution. However, it is worth noting that there are equal proportions of households with incomes below £50 a week in both countries. British households are also slightly overrepresented in the upper end of the distribution while Swedes are in majority in the middle range. The Figure reproduces the well-established picture of Sweden as the country with the more equal distribution of incomes.

Unemployment The respondents were in both surveys asked if they were unemployed at the time of the interview. In the BBS the respondents were also asked about their experience of unemployment during the past ten years. From this information, a variable that discriminates three groups has been derived: (a) not unemployed, (b) short term unemployed (STU), that is, unemployed one year or less during the past ten years, and, (c) long term unemployed (LTU), comprising the group that have been unemployed for more than one year during the past ten years. The question used in SLEV asked about the number of weeks the respondent had been unemployed during the past five years. The derived variable discriminates among those who are: (a) not unemployed, (b) STU, referring to those who have been unemployed six months or less during the past five years, and, (b) LTU, referring to the group that have been unemployed more than six months during the past five years.

Table 2
Unemployment in Sweden and Britain (percentages)

	Unemployed at the time of data collection	*STU: Unemployed 6 (12) months or less during the past 5 (10) years*	*LTU: Unemployed more than 6 (12) months during the past 5 (10) years*
Sweden	4.7	10.1	5.6
Britain	11.7	15.2	20.2

The differences in unemployment are clearly revealed in Table 2. Close to five per cent of the respondents in the Swedish sample were unemployed at the time they were interviewed. The corresponding figure for Britain was more than twice as high. The other figures in Table 2 are not strictly comparable. However, they do indicate the magnitude of the differences between the countries, especially regarding long term unemployment.

Means tested benefits Those who received means tested benefits from at least one of the following systems: income support, family credit, housing benefit or/and community charge/poll tax benefit, are defined in the BBS as one group, here labelled as recipients of means tested benefits (RMTB). Sweden has two important means tested income support systems. Social assistance is a last resort income support system that can, despite dissimilarities, be equated with income support and family credit. There is also a system of housing allowance that can be equated with housing benefit. Those receiving any of these will be classified as RMTB.[5]

In Sweden 18.1 per cent of the households were RMTBs. The corresponding figure in Britain was 15.9 per cent. The size of the RMTB group depends on the incapacity among parts of the population to maintain an income and on the generosity of the means tested programs. The fact that the group is larger in Sweden than in Britain can probably be explained by the generosity factor. The mean income among the Swedish RMTBs was about £80-89 per week, and among Britons about £50-59 per week. Thus, there are reasons to suspect that RMTBs in Britain are worse off than Swedes in the same group.

Age, gender, and household composition. The three remaining variables discussed above are household composition, age, and gender. Age and gender are based on the respondent in each household. Households are divided into four categories: single without children, single parent, couple without children, and couple with children. However, there is an additional category in the British data consisting of an unspecified group labelled '*others*'. This group comprises about 14 per cent of all households in the BBS and can not be neglected as a marginal response error group. The group '*others*' will therefore be included in the analysis of British data.

4 The prevalence of deprivation in Sweden and Britain

In Table 3, the distribution of the PDI in Sweden and Britain is compared. The first thing to note is that the mean PDI value is 1.23 in Sweden and 2.33 in Britain. Thus, there is a higher degree of overall deprivation in Britain. The differences between the countries are most evident in PDI decile nine and ten, especially decile ten where the mean PDI value is twice as high as in Sweden. In Sweden, slightly more than 40 per cent of the total sum of deprivation is found in decile ten. The corresponding figure for Britain is about ten percentage points higher. Finally, the number of items missing among the most deprived is also much higher in Britain than in Sweden. Thus, the problem of relative deprivation is more severe among Britons than among Swedes and, deprivation is distributed more unevenly in Britain than in Sweden. This result is an important finding in itself. However, the question is why are Britons more deprived than Swedes?

Table 3
Mean PDI value, percentage of deprivation, and mean number of missing items in each PDI decile

PDI decile	Mean value PDI SWE	% of deprivation SWE	No. of missing items SWE	Mean value PDI GB	% of deprivation GB	No. of missing items GB
1-3	0.00	0.0	0.0	0.00	0.0	0.0
4	0.10	0.9	1.2	0.00	0.0	0.0
5	0.26	3.7	1.5	0.12	0.9	1.1
6	0.47	5.1	1.9	0.48	3.6	1.6
7	0.81	9.9	2.8	0.91	6.3	2.7
8	1.17	14.6	3.8	1.76	12.9	4.5
9	1.87	23.3	5.6	3.31	24.0	7.4
10	3.47	42.6	9.0	7.18	52.4	13.5
All	1.23	100.0	2.5	2.33	100.0	3.1

4.1 Income and deprivation

What the exact relationship between economic resources and deprivation looks like has been a topic of debate within the field of poverty research for a long time. The central assumption, emanating from Townsend (1979) is that there exists a 'threshold', or a break in the curve, at which deprivation increases disproportionately as income decreases. As shown in Figure 3, this assumption holds for Britain, but not for Sweden.

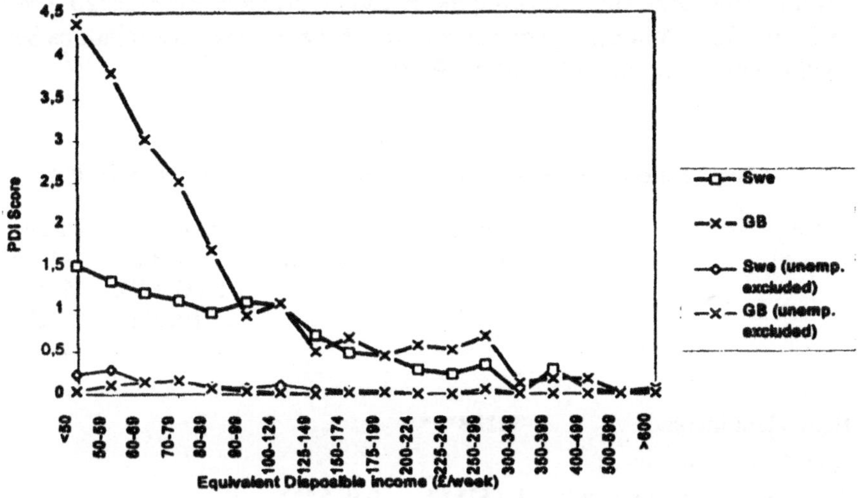

Figure 3 The relationship between equivalent household income and PDI scores in Sweden and Great Britain

In Sweden there is an almost linear relationship between income and the PDI score. The PDI value increases as income decreases but there is no sign of a threshold. The curve for Britain shows a different picture and there is a clear increase in deprivation as the equivalent household income falls under £90 a week. The question of course is what is it that creates this difference. There seems to be an easy answer to this question. The two curves at the bottom of Figure 3 describe the relationship between income and deprivation when all those who had been unemployed at some time during the past five (Sweden) or ten (Britain) years are excluded from the sample. First, the overall level of deprivation is markedly decreased when the unemployed are excluded. Second, the differences between the two countries disappear. Thus, it seems as if deprivation is mainly a dilemma for people suffering from unemployment.

4.2 Multivariate analysis of deprivation

The analysis now proceeds with a multivariate analysis investigating the effects of the independent variables presented above. The analysis is conducted in several steps, basically following the so called 'effect change design' (Hellevik 1992, pp. 70). Column two in Table 4 shows the bivariate associations between each independent variable and the PDI.

Table 4
Regression coefficients for estimated PDI scores (Sweden)

Independent Variables	Bivariate Estimate	Cont.Var: Income	Cont.Var: Income, STU, LTU, RMBT	Cont.Var: Income, STU, LTU, RMBT, household type
Equivalent income	-0.188***	-		
[Ref. Not unemployed]				
Short term unemployment (STU)	1.157***	0.915***	-	
Long term unemployment (LTU)	1.181***	1.067***	-	
Recipients of means tested benefits (RMTB)	1.144***	0.895***	-	
[Ref. Couple without children]				
Single parent	1.311***	0.964***	0.698**	
Single without children	0.988***	0.838***	0.700***	
Couple with children	0.271*	0.004	0.067	
Other				
[Ref. Age 55-64]				
Age 20-24	1.638***	1.248***	1.054***	0.817***
Age 25-34	1.256***	1.050***	0.860***	0.925***
Age 35-44	0.634***	0.453*	0.343	0.440*
Age 45-54	0.165	0.151	0.127	0.169
Age 65-74	0.356	0.201	0.227	0.135
Gender [women]	0.197	0.164	0.118	0.146

Significance levels: *** = p<0.001, ** = p<0.01, * = p<0.05

The dummy variables within each category are analysed simultaneously. Thus, the coefficients for STU and LTU in column two show, for example, the deviation from the *not unemployed.* In the second step the analyses are repeated, but this time income is included as a control variable for each of the other independent variables. This step will test the hypothesis that all the other independent variables influence deprivation via income. Thus, the coefficients in column three show what remains when we have controlled for the impact of income.

Table 4 (cont.)
Regression coefficients for estimated PDI scores (Great Britain)

Independent Variables	Bivariate Estimate	Cont.Var: Income	Cont.Var: Income, STU, LTU, RMBT	Cont.Var: Income, STU, LTU, RMBT, household type
Equivalent income	-0.567***	-	-	
[Ref. Not unemployed]				
Short term unemployment (STU)	0.593	0.916**	-	
Long term unemployment (LTU)	3.468***	2.765***	-	
Recipients of means tested benefits (RMTB)	3.963***	2.881***	-	
[Ref. Couple without children]				
Single parent	4.422***	3.393***	1.777***	
Single without children	1.598***	1.096**	0.523	
Couple with children	1.286***	1.191***	1.030***	
Other	0.796*	1.297***	1.014***	
[Ref. Age 55-64]				
Age 20-24	1.245**	1.522***	1.113**	0.713
Age 25-34	1.194**	1.748***	1.596***	1.298***
Age 35-44	0.497	0.897*	1.117***	0.787**
Age 45-54	0.282	0.588	0.826*	0.538
Age 65-74	0.401	-0.217	0.552	0.624
Gender [women]	0.733*	0.501*	0.604**	0.398*

Significance levels: *** = p<0.001, ** = p<0.01, * = p<0.05

It was argued above that unemployment and RMTB can be seen as additional indicators of income, capturing more far-reaching aspects of the households' economic resources. Therefore, in the third step STU, LTU, and RMTB are used together with income as control variables. The hypothesis is that these three variables together will capture the effects of each one of the remaining independent variables. The analysis is thereafter proceeding with a fourth step that includes household type as a control variable for age and gender, testing the possibility that these two remaining variables are related to deprivation via their relationship with household type.

Looking first at the results for Sweden. All independent variables, except gender and the two oldest age categories, have bivariate effects on the PDI. All these effects decrease when income is used as a control variable, but they all, except the effect for couples with children, remain significant. Hence, couples with children in Sweden are more deprived than couples without children because they have lower equivalent incomes. Low income also explains parts of the PDI values among the unemployed, recipients of means tested benefits, people living in single households, and the younger sections of the population.

However, these groups also receive relatively high PDI scores for other reasons than low annual income. In the third step, LTU, STU, and RMTB are used together with income as control variables. This leads to additional decreases of the effects among the household and age categories but they mainly remain significant.

Finally, in the fourth step, the household categories are added to the control variables when analysing age and gender effects. This leads to a further decrease in the coefficient for the youngest age group, but to a small increase in the coefficient for the two following age groups, indicating the existence of interaction effects.

The bivariate estimates for Britain to a large degree replicate the pattern shown by the Swedish data. However, there are some important differences. Short term unemployment and the effect of age group 35-44 are not significant in Britain. Gender has a significant effect and the result shows that British women tend to be more deprived than British men. Important differences between the two countries are also shown by the absolute size of the coefficients. LTU, RMTB, and single parents have in Sweden an estimated PDI value that is about one unit above the reference groups. The corresponding values for Britain range between 3.5 for LTU, 4 for RMTB, and nearly 4.5 for single parents. Thus, the Britons in these groups are clearly more deprived than their Swedish counterparts. Also the coefficient for income differs between the countries and income has a substantially larger impact in Britain, reflecting the more uneven income distribution.

Controlling for income leads, as one can see in column three to a clear decrease in the coefficients for LTU, RMTB, and single parents. However, even though the effects for these three variables decrease, they are still significant and the absolute size of the coefficients are still large. Some of the other results in this step of the analysis indicate problems in the specification of the model. The coefficients for STU, the household group 'other' and all age groups under the age of 55 increase instead of decrease when they are controlled for the effects of income. A result that indicates the existence of interaction effects. The most plausible interpretation of this outcome is that a combination of these variables and low income leads to a high degree of deprivation.

The third step includes STU, LTU, and RMTB as control variables. We can now observe an additional decrease in the coefficients for the household variables. The decrease is especially apparent for single parents. Thus, very much of the extreme degree of deprivation in this group is attributable to the fact that they have low income, are unemployed and that they are dependent on insufficient means tested benefits. The results are more difficult to interpret when it comes to the age groups. There is, in both countries, a decrease in the effects for the two youngest groups. However, in Britain there is an increase in the two following age groups. In Britain, there is also an increase in the coefficient for gender. Hence, we once again have to acknowledge the existence of interactions effects. In the fourth, and last step, household type is introduced among the control variables. We can now see that the youngest age group loses its significance. Thus, the deprivation among this group in the end seems to be attributable to the type of household in which they live. The effect for gender is also decreasing but the coefficient remains significant.

Finally, in Table 5 the complete regression model for both countries is presented. The models include all the variables discussed earlier. Additional models including different kinds of interaction effects have been estimated but they are not presented here because of the simple fact that the interactions did not have any significant impact.[6]

In both countries it is clear that low income, unemployment, STU as well as LTU, and RMTB increase the PDI score. This result was of course expected and indicates similarities when it comes to basic processes behind the existence of poverty. However, it is again important to notice the differences when it comes to the size of the coefficients.

Table 5
Regression coefficients for estimated PDI score

Independent Variables	Sweden		Great Britain	
	Estimate	Std. Error	Estimate	Std. Error
Equivalent income	-0.123***	0.022	-0.332***	0.040
[Ref. Not unemployed]				
Short term unemployment (STU)	0.567**	0.177	0.809**	0.287
Long term unemployment (LTU)	0.786***	0.226	2.084***	0.236
Recipients of means tested benefits (RMTB)	0.616***	0.143	2.089***	0.265
[Ref. Couple without children]				
Single parent	0.602*	0.273	1.068*	0.469
Single without children	0.509***	0.145	0.449	0.325
Couple with children	-0.304*	0.152	0.532	0.323
Other	-	-	0.893**	0.310
[Ref. Age 55-64]				
Age 20-24	0.837***	0.241	0.676	0.410
Age 25-34	0.954***	0.191	1.259***	0.371
Age 35-44	0.469*	0.202	0.765*	0.372
Age 45-54	0.193	0.196	0.515	0.372
Age 65-74	0.147	0.203	0.608	0.378
Gender [women]	0.188	0.105	0.359	0.197
Constant	0.294	0.280	0.217	0.494
Log Likelihood	-1081.778		-2285.610	
McFadden Pseudo R^2	0.093		0.096	
N	789		1176	

Significance levels: *** = $p<0.001$, ** = $p<0.01$, * = $p<0.05$

The impact of low income on the PDI is larger in Britain than in Sweden, reflecting the fact that Britain has a more uneven income distribution. There is a substantial difference when it comes to the LTU: the coefficient is more than twice as large in Britain compared with Sweden. There are two likely explanations for this result. Firstly, the social security system for the unemployed is more generous in Sweden and it is, therefore, more effective when it comes to the prevention of deprivation among the unemployed. Secondly, one has to be aware of the possibility of differences in the unemployment duration among the long term unemployed. All we know is that they have been unemployed for more than six months during the past five years (Sweden) or more than twelve months during the past ten years (Britain). We do not know if they have been unemployed for one year, five years or ten years. However, a look at labour market statistics shows that the long term unemployed in Britain are unemployed for longer periods than their Swedish counterparts (OECD 1995, p. 219).

Low income is a precondition for being entitled to means tested benefits. The fact that the effect of means tested benefits remains significant in all models clearly indicates that there is more connected with this situation than low income. The problem is that the group that receives means tested benefits is a very heterogeneous mixture of individuals and it is impossible to say exactly what it is that makes them poor, aside from the fact that they have low incomes. What we can suspect is that a combination of high expenditure pressure and more or less unique individual circumstances leads to a high degree of deprivation. Probably important, but not possible to test here, is the length of the period during which the households receive the benefits. However, it is clear from Table 5 that RMTB in itself has a more negative impact on peoples' standard of living in Britain than in Sweden.

When looking at household composition, the first thing to note is that being a single lone parent tends to significantly increase the PDI score in both countries. It is difficult to interpret this as anything else than an effect of special needs since not only income, but also the additional indicators of low income, STU, LTU, and RMBT, are controlled for in the models. It is simply quite expensive to be a single parent. However, the effect is once again much stronger in Britain, a fact that probably can be related to differences in labour market and social policy. In Sweden, earnings from salaried work are viewed as the fundamental source of family income also among single parents. There are no specially designed benefits for single parents who are outside of the labour force. The effect is that the labour force participation in this group is exceptionally high. In Britain, single parents have the right to means tested benefits (income support) until the youngest child is 16 years of age. There is no pressure to undergo training or take a job (Kamerman 1995, p. 245). Thus, the circumstances under which single parents have to earn a living differ markedly between the countries. It clearly looks as if the Swedish strategy to include single parents in the labour market and the general social policy system is to be preferred.

When looking at one person households without children and couples with children we can notice two substantial differences between the two countries. (Observe that the estimates from the last step in Table 4 differ from those in Table 5 because gender is included in the latter model.) Firstly, single persons without children deviate significantly from the reference group in Sweden but not so in Britain. To understand why this is the case must remain a task for future research since no plausible explanation is offered here. Secondly, Swedish couples with children have, other things being equal, lower scores on the PDI compared with couples without children. There is no such effect in Britain. It is likely that this difference can be explained by differences in family policy. The extensive Swedish family support system, including not only money transfers but also extensive child care, makes life easier for both the children and their parents. It is finally worth noting that the final regression models generate no significant estimates for gender in both countries. This result was clearly expected in the case of Sweden since the estimates for gender were not significant in every step of the analysis. The situation was different in Britain where gender was significant in every step except in the final regression model. Thus, British women are more deprived than British men because of low income, unemployment problems, dependence on means tested benefits, their household situation and, finally, because they are exposed to age, or cohort, related problems.

5 Conclusions

This chapter represents an attempt to compare relative deprivation in Sweden and Great Britain and, to relate the prevalence of deprivation to other social conditions. The measurement of relative deprivation is related to prevailing living conditions in the two countries with the use of a proportional deprivation index. One main result, even though expected, is that deprivation and poverty are clearly more prevalent in Britain than in Sweden. Thus, Britons are more deprived according to British standards than Swedes are according to Swedish standards.

The central question is why this is the case. An important finding is that the mechanisms that generate deprivation and poverty seem to be largely the same in both countries. Low income households, the unemployed, recipients of means tested benefits, and single parents suffer from an increased probability of being poor in both countries. It is also shown in the multivariate analysis that that these conditions influence the likelihood of being poor independently of each other.

The fact that deprivation is less severe in Sweden can be seen as a confirmation of the success of the 'Swedish model'. Active labour market policies, low unemployment, an extensive redistribution of income, and an income maintenance system covering the major part of the population has clearly succeeded when it comes to the prevention and alleviation of deprivation and poverty. One obvious conclusion is therefore that bringing the British welfare state closer to the 'Swedish model' would solve a great deal of the poverty problems in Britain. However, in reality the reverse seems to be happening. The results from the analysis are based on data collected in 1990 in Britain and 1992 in Sweden. Since then, major changes have occurred in Sweden. The unemployment level has risen at an unforeseen rate. Full employment, the cornerstone of the hitherto successful income maintenance system, is crumbling, and mass-unemployment is now also a reality in Sweden. The state budget deficit and a huge state debt make it almost impossible for the state to preserve the same level of income maintenance. Major cuts in the welfare provisions have already been undertaken, and there is probably more to come. Sweden now has to find new polices to adjust to an increasingly global world economy. Unless such policies can be found the results presented here indicate that current developments in Sweden will increase the prevalence of deprivation and poverty in the future. No one can claim to have been taken by surprise if, in a few years, we find ourselves living in a more 'British' society. We know where we are headed because others before us have walked the same path.

Notes

[1] In the British survey the respondents are asked about the 'social class of the head of the household'. There are five response alternatives: class AB: professional and managerial occupations, class C1: other non-manual workers, class C2: skilled manual workers, class D: semi-skilled and unskilled manual workers, and class E: social security recipients. This categorisation is clearly problematic since it combines two different classification systems. Classes AB to D are based on occupational status that follows traditional theories of class while class E is based not on occupational status but on the position in the social security system. Any analyses of class will therefore be blurred.

[2] The items used in SLEV are presented in Halleröd (1994a, 1995) and the items used in BBS are presented in Gordon and Pantazis (1995).

[3] A precondition for this argument is that the indices used are based on the same number of items, as is the case in this study. The PDI must otherwise be adjusted to be comparable.

[4] The OECD equivalence scale assignes the value of 1 for the first adult, 0.7 for each additional adult and 0.5 for every child.

[5] There is no Swedish analogy to community charge/poll tax benefit.

[6] The following interactions terms have been specified and tested:
a) income * age,
b) income * age 20-24,
c) income * age 25-34,
d) income * age 35-44,
e) income * STU.
None of the interaction effects have significant effects on the Swedish data. Looking at the British data, interaction terms a, c and e had no effect on the PDI whatsoever. Interaction terms b and d had significant impact on the PDI when they were entered into the basic model one by one. However, none of them remained significant when entered together into the model. It might be worth mentioning that the interaction terms showed that low income in combination with age 35-44 resulted in a high PDI value. However, low income together with age 20-24 resulted in a lower PDI value. At first this result might be regarded as odd. The explanation seems to be that almost all young people have low incomes, but those with the lowest income are still dependent on their parents and do not yet have the total responsibility for the task of making ends meet.

References

Bradbury, B. (1992), *The Welfare Interpretation of Family Size Equivalence Scales*, SPRC Discussion Papers, No. 37, University of New South Wales, Sydney.

Buhman, B., Rainwater, L., Schmaus, G. and Smeeding, T.M. (1988), 'Equivalence Scales, Well-Being, Inequality and Poverty: Sensitivity Estimates Across Ten Countries Using the Luxembourg Income Study (LIS) Database', *Review of Economic and Wealth*, Vol. 34, pp. 115-42.

Callan, T., Nolan, B. and Whelan, C.T. (1993), 'Resources, Deprivation and the Measurement of Poverty', *Journal of Social Policy*, Vol. 22, pp. 141-172.

Deleeck, H. and Van den Bosch, K. (1992), 'Poverty and Adequacy of Social Security in Europe: A Comparative Analysis', *Journal of European Social Policy*, Vol. 2, pp. 107-120.

Duncan, G.J., Gustafsson, B., Hauser, R., Schmauss, G., Messinger, H., Muffels, R., Nolan, B. and Ray, J.-C. (1993), 'Poverty Dynamics in Eight Countries', *Journal of Population and Economics*, Vol. 6, pp. 215-234.

Edebalk, P.G. (1994), 'Möllermodellen, svensk socialförsäkring 1944-51', *Socialvetenskaplig tidskrift*, Vol. 1, pp. 21-44.

Fritzell, J. (1991), *Icke av marknaden allena: Inkomstfördelningen i Sverige*, Almqvist & Wiksell International: Edsbruk.

Förster, M.F. (1994), *Measurement of Low Incomes and Poverty in a Perspective of International Comparison*, OECD/GD(94)10 Labour Market and Social Policy Occasional Papers No. 14.

Gordon, D. and Pantazis, C. (1995), *Breadline Britain in the 1990's*, A report to the Joseph Rowntree Foundation.

Gustafsson, B. and Lindblom, M. (1993), 'Poverty Lines and Poverty in Seven European Countries, Australia, Canada and the USA', *Journal of European Social Policy*, Vol. 3, pp. 21-38.

Gustafsson, B. (1994), *Ekonomisk fattigdom i Sverige sedan mitten av 1970-talet*, Working Paper, Department of Social Work, University of Gothenburg.

Halleröd, B. (1991), *Den svenska fattigdomen: en studie av fattigdom och socialbidragstagande*, Arkiv: Lund.

Halleröd, B. (1993), *Tillförlitliga inkomstdata? En jämförelse på individnivå mellan inkomstuppgifter hämtade från intervjuer och register*, Working Paper, Department of Sociology, Umeå University.

Halleröd, B. (1994a), *Poverty in Sweden: A New Approach to the Direct Measurement of Consensual Poverty*, Umeå Studies in Sociology, No. 106, Umeå University.

Halleröd, B. (1994b), *A New Approach to the Direct Consensual Measurement of Poverty*, Discussion Paper No. 50, Social Policy Research Centre, University of New South Wales.

Halleröd, B. (1995), 'The Truly Poor: Indirect and Direct Measurement of Consensual Poverty in Sweden', *Journal of European Social Policy*, Vol. 5, pp. 111-29.

Halleröd, B. (1996), 'Deprivation and Poverty: A Comparative Analysis of Consensual Poverty in Sweden and Great Britain', *ACTA Sociologica*, (in Press).

Halleröd, B., Bradshaw, J. and Holmes, H. (1995), 'Adapting the Consensual Definition of Poverty', in Gordon, D. and Pantazis, C. (eds.), *Breadline Britain in the 1990's*, A report to the Joseph Rowntree Foundation, pp. 161-182.

Halleröd, B., Marklund, S., Nordlund, A. and Stattin, M. (1993), *Konsensuell fattigdom - en studie av konsumtion och attityder till konsumtion*, Umeå Studies in Sociology No. 104, Umeå.

Heikkilä, M. (1991), 'Poverty and Accumulation of Welfare Deficit', in Juhani, L. (ed.), *Deprivation, Social Welfare and Expertise*, Research Report No. 7, National Agency for Welfare and Health: Helsinki.

Hellevik, O. (1992), *Introduction to Causal Analysis*, Scandinavian University Press: Oslo.

Kamerman, S.B. (1995), 'Gender Role and Family Structure Changes in the Advanced Industrialized West: Implications for Social Policy', in McFate, K. Lawson, R. and Wilson, J. W. (eds.), *Poverty, Inequality and the Future of Social Policy*, Russell Sage Foundation: New York, pp. 231-256.

Lawson, R. (1987), *Contrasting Approaches to Social Security: Comparison Between Britain and Sweden*, Working Paper, Department of Sociology and Social Administration, University of Southampton.

Lawson, R. (1990), *'Social Citizenship', Work and Social Solidarity: Historical Comparison Between Britain and Sweden*, Working Paper, Department of Sociology and Social Administration, University of Southampton.

Lindqvist, R. (1990), *Från folkrörelse till välfärdsbyråkrati*, Arkiv: Lund.

Mac Cárthaigh, S. (1994), *Resources, Deprivation and Poverty*, Working Paper, Department of Social Policy and Social Work, University College: Dublin.

Mack, J. and Lansley, S. (1985), *Poor Britain*, George Allen & Unwin Ltd.: London.

Marklund, S. and Svallfors, S. (1986), 'Välfärd efter prestation - om arbetstvång inom socialförsäkringen', *Nordiskt sosialt arbeid*, No.4, Årg 6, pp. 17-32.

Mayer, S. (1995), 'A Comparison of Poverty and Living Conditions in the United States, Canada, Sweden, and West Germany', in McFate, K., Lawson, R. and Wilson, J. W. (eds.), *Poverty, Inequality and the Future of Social Policy*, Russell Sage Foundation: New York, pp. 109-152.

McFate, K., Smeeding, T. and Rainwater, L. (1995), 'Markets and States: Poverty Trends and Transfer System Effectiveness in the 1980s', in McFate, K., Lawson, R. and Wilson, J. W. (eds.), *Poverty, Inequality and the Future of Social Policy*, Russell Sage Foundation: New York, pp. 29-66.

Mitchell, D. (1991), *Income Transfers in Ten Welfare States*, Avebury: Aldershot.

Muffels, R. and Vreins, M. (1991), *The Elaboration of a Deprivation Scale and the Definition of a Subjective Deprivation Poverty Line*, Paper presented at the Annual Meeting of the European Society for Population Economics, 6-8 June, Pisa.

Muffels, R., Berghman, J. and Dirven, H-J. (1992), 'A Multi-Method Approach to Monitor the Evolution of Poverty', *Journal of European Social Policy*, Vol. 2, pp. 193-213

Nolan, B. and Whelan, C.T. (1996), *Resources, Deprivation and Poverty*, Clarendon Press: Oxford (forthcoming).

OECD *Employment Outlook*, various editions.

OECD (1995), *Main Economic Indicators*, March 1995.

Ringen, S. (1987), *The Possibility of Politics*, Clarendon Press: Oxford.

Ritakallio, V.-M. (1994), *Finnish Poverty: A Cross-National Comparison*, LIS Working Paper No. 119: Luxembourg.

Salonen, T. (1993), *Margins of Welfare*, Hällstad Press: Kristianstad.

Saunders, P., Halleröd, B. and Matehson, G. (1994), 'Making Ends Meet in Australia and Sweden: A Comparative Analysis Using the Subjective Poverty Line Methodology', *Acta Sociologica*, Vol. 37, pp. 3-22.

Townsend, P. (1979), *Poverty in the United Kingdom*, Penguin Books Ltd.: Harmondsworth

Townsend, P. (1987), 'Deprivation', *Journal of Social Policy*, Vol. 16, No. 2, pp. 125-146.

Van den Bosch, K., Callan, T., Estivill, J., Hausman, P., Jeandidier, B., Muffels, R. and Yfantopoulos, J. (1993), 'A Comparison of Poverty in Seven European Countries and Regions using Subjective and Relative Measures', *Journal of Population and Economics*, Vol. 6, pp. 235-259.

Whiteford, P. (1995), *Is Australia Particularly Unequal?* Paper presented to the Public Policy Network Conference at the ANU, 2-3 February 1995, Canberra.

Wright, R.E. (1992), 'A Feminization of Poverty in Great Britain?', *Review of Income and Wealth*, Vol. 38, pp. 17-25.

Appendix

There are three problems concerning the comparability of the income data. Firstly, the British data are based on weekly income, while the Swedish data are based on annual income. The British data are, therefore, more vulnerable to short term income fluctuations. Secondly, data for Britain are derived from interviews while the Swedish data are from the official tax register. It is hard to know the exact impact of this difference. What we do know from SLEV is that the non-response rate is higher among persons living in low-income households. The fact that register income is obtainable, not only for the working sample, but also for the total initial sample means that we can weight the working sample and thereby counter-balance the biased non-response rate. This is not the case with the British data. The third problem is that the internal non-response rate on the income question in BBS is 23.8 per cent. The response rate is low among professionals and people with low values on the PDI. The unemployed and people dependent on means tested social benefits are, on the contrary, less reluctant to answer the income question. Thus, we can draw the conclusion that the internal non-response rate leads to an underestimation of incomes in the BBS. It is important to bear in mind that incomes are underestimated in relation to the total working sample. We do not know how the incomes reported in the BBS sample differ from the British population because of the possibility of an initial biased non-response rate. These remarks about the income data make it evident that we cannot use the BBS and SLEV for an accurate comparison of economic poverty. It is also apparent that the income variable must be used with caution.

Part Four
Applying the dynamic approach

Long-term recipiency of social assistance in Germany: The eighties versus the nineties

Petra Buhr and Andreas Weber

Introduction

Long-term poverty and long-term recipiency of social assistance are usually regarded as serious social problems which may lead to dependency and psycho-social distress. From this point of view it is important to analyse the causes of long-term poverty and social assistance and to identify those groups which are most at risk to remain in poverty or social assistance for many years. This kind of information is necessary for policy makers and social workers in order to target special programs and to prevent long-term poverty or social assistance.

In the USA, the dynamics of poverty and social assistance have been analysed since the end of the seventies based on longitudinal data sets like the Michigan Panel Study of Income Dynamics (cf. Duncan 1984; Bane and Ellwood 1986, 1994). In Germany, however, until recently, reliable data on the extent of short-term and long-term poverty were not available, and the dominant public image of poverty was long-term. It was not before the end of the eighties that dynamic research on poverty and social assistance in Germany was initiated by the Bremen longitudinal study on social assistance (cf. Leibfried 1987; Buhr 1995; Leibfried et al. 1995; Ludwig 1996; Buhr and Weber 1996). Since then a dynamic approach has been implemented by several other research projects based on various data sources like the German Socio-Economic Panel (cf. Heady et al. 1990; Rendtel and Wagner 1991; Krause 1994) and the Bielefeld data bank on social assistance (cf. Samson 1992; Andreß 1994).

The new dynamic approach has challenged traditional assumptions about poverty and social assistance: The extent of long-term poverty and long-term receipt of social assistance is not as high as assumed by public opinion and suggested by poverty studies on the basis of cross-sectional data. For most people poverty and social assistance are only short phases in the life-course, and only a minority of people stay on social assistance for many years. Moreover, qualitative research has shown that long-term receipt of social assistance does not inevitably lead into a vicious circle of hopelessness and passivity (cf. Buhr 1995; Ludwig 1996).

This does not mean, however, that we can withdraw our attention from long-term poverty or long-term receipt of social assistance. As the number of long-term recipients accumulates over time, the proportion of long-term recipients is higher in the current caseload than among new recipients, and, with rising numbers of recipients of social assistance as in Germany, the absolute number (not the proportion) of long-term recipients will rise, too.

We also have to keep in mind that duration of poverty or social assistance may change over historical time. Thus, a widespread assumption in Germany is that the extent of long-term receipt of social assistance has increased during the eighties, e.g. due to changes in labour market conditions. The sparse empirical evidence, however, points into a different direction: According to Andreß (1994) and Samson (1992) duration of social assistance has decreased continously since 1977. And Hagen and Hock (1995) report only little change in time on assistance between 1988 and 1992 in a small town in South-West Germany.

In this paper we use data from the Bremen longitudinal study on social assistance to analyse the impact of social change on social assistance. Previous research has shown that about half of all people whose first spell of social assistance in Bremen began in 1983 ('1983 cohort') already left social assistance within the first year. Long-term recipiency was more common among single parents, the elderly, and people with low qualifications (cf. Buhr 1995; Leibfried et al. 1995).

Since 1983, however, the structure of recipients and duration of social assistance may have changed as socio-economic conditions have changed, too. Here we will concentrate on three possible sources of change: immigration, labor market and employment conditions, and social policy.

All in all, we expect more 'German immigrants' and refugees among new recipients of social assistance at the end of the eighties.[1] The effect on time on assistance, however, is different for both groups of immigrants: Increasing numbers of German immigrants, on the one hand, may result in a shortening of duration because most of them are entitled to social insurance benefits (mostly unemployment benefits and old age pensions) and thus will leave social assistance quickly after a short period of waiting for the first payment of these transfers.[2] Increasing numbers of refugees, on the other hand, may lead to longer duration as refugees usually stay on assistance continously for quite a long time until they are granted political asylum or are deported to their home countries.[3]

As unemployment rates decreased between 1983 and 1989,[4] we expect fewer unemployed people entering social assistance in the second half of the eighties. The decrease in unemployment and long-term unemployment [5] may also result in a shortening of time on assistance as it might be easier to find a new job and remain in employment.

However, due to the Employment Promotion Act of 1985 ('Beschäftigungsförderungsgesetz') we also expect an increase in discontinous employment careers and higher proportions of people with insufficient unemployment benefits at the end of the eighties. This may in turn result in higher proportions of unemployed people who are in need of supplementary social assistance and may lead to longer - probably discontinous - careers of social assistance. Employment schemes for recipients of social assistance, on the contrary, will probably shorten duration. These programmes only provide temporary jobs. However, most participants will not have to reapply for assistance because they are entitled to unemployment benefits afterwards and have improved their chances to find a job on the 'normal' labour market.

To clarify if it is more difficult to leave social assistance in the nineties as compared to the eighties and to identify the impact of social change we compare the 1983 cohort which was observed until 1989 with a more recent cohort: new recipients of 1989 observed until 1994.

In the first step, we compare the structure of the two cohorts and the causes for receiving assistance. In a second step, we analyse time on assistance in the 1983 and the 1989 cohorts using different concepts for measuring duration. Do social assistance careers last longer in the new cohort due to social, economic, and political changes? Afterwards we ask for the determinants of leaving social assistance in the two cohorts. Is, for example, age as important for explaining long-term recipiency of assistance in the nineties as in the eighties?

The data base is the Bremen 10% Longitudinal Sample of Social Assistance Files (LSA), which was carried out by the Department of Women, Health, Youth, Social Affairs, and Environment, Bremen, in colloboration with the Centre for Social Policy Research and the Special Research Center 186 at the University of Bremen (cf. Buhr et al. 1990). Our analysis of time on assistance is limited to people who receive maintenance benefits ('Hilfe zum Lebensunterhalt'). That is, we excluded those people from the analysis who only received benefits for special needs ('Hilfe in besonderen Lebenslagen'), the second branch of the German social assistance system. Our unit of analysis are files or applicants for social assistance, respectively.[6] The 1983 cohort consists of 586 files or applicants, in the 1989 cohort the number of new recipients has increased to 922.

The observation window for both cohorts is 69 months: The 1983 cohort was observed until the end of September 1988, the 1989 cohort until the end of September 1994.[7] In the 1983 cohort, 18.3% of the recipients were still (or again) receiving social assistance at the end of the observation period ('right censored cases'), in the 1989 cohort, it was 14.3%. This already points towards a shortening of social assistance careers.

1 Structure of recipients and causes of recipiency

The socio-demographic structure of the two cohorts indeed differs in one important point (see Table 1).

Table 1
Residence status groups in the 1983 and the 1989 cohorts

Groups	Cohort			
	1983		1989	
	n	%	n	%
Native Germans	475	81.1	428	46.4
Resident foreigners	63	10.8	65	7.0
	538	91.8	493	53.4
German immigrants	24	4.1	260	28.2
Refugees	24	4.1	169	18.3
	48	8.2	429	46.5
Number of cases	586	100	922	100

Source: Bremen Longitudinal Sample of Social Assistance Files; Dep. of Women, Health, Youth, Social Affairs and Environment, State of Bremen; Center for Social Policy Research and Special Research Center 186, University of Bremen

In the 1989 cohort, nearly 30% of the recipients are immigrants of German origin from Eastern Europe, the former Soviet Union, and the German Democratic Republic (we call them 'German immigrants'); in the 1983 cohort it was only 4%. The proportion of refugees, e.g. applicants for political asylum, also increased from 4% to 18%. The proportion of native Germans, on the contrary, decreased from 81% to 46%, and the proportion of resident foreigners, that is foreigners who have already lived in Germany for many years, from 11% to 7%. Moreover, even the absolute number of native Germans and resident foreigners has decreased in the 1989 cohort.

All in all, according to our expectations, unemployment has lost some of its importance as a cause for social assistance in the 1989 cohort. This holds for the total population and for the subgroup of residents. The proportion of recipients who enter social assistance because of unemployment decreased from 57.5% to 54.4% and from 59.5% to 56.8%, respectively (see Table 2).

Table 2
Causes for beginning social assistance (percentages)

Causes for entering	All cases		Residents[a]	
social assistance	1983	1989	1983	1989
Unemployed, waiting	32.2	*37.4	32.5	*26.6
Unemployed, not waiting	25.2	*17.0	27.0	30.2
Other causes, waiting	4.1	6.1	3.2	5.3
Other causes, not waiting	38.4	39.5	37.4	37.9
Waiting total	36.4	*43.5	35.7	31.9
Unemployed total	57.5	54.4	59.5	56.8

Notes:
a) Native Germans and resident foreigners
* Difference between cohorts significant at the 5% level. Deviation from 100% is due to rounding errors

Source: See Table 1

However, we have to differentiate between different groups of the unemployed: Overall, due to the increase in the number of German immigrants, the proportion of 'waiting' unemployed cases, that is unemployed people who are just waiting for unemployment benefits to be paid, is higher in the 1989 cohort as compared to the 1983 one, while the proportion of recipients with no or insufficient benefits has decreased. In the subgroup of native Germans and resident foreigners, however, there is an opposite trend: The proportion of 'waiting' unemployed cases decreased, while the proportion of unemployed recipients who are not waiting and have to supplement insufficient or lacking unemployment benefits with social assistance increased. This may indicate an increase in insecure and irregular patterns of employment following the Employment Promotion Act of 1985 in combination with changes in the eligibility rules for unemployment benefits.

2 Time on assistance

If we want to measure duration of social assistance we have to take into account that people may have several spells of social assistance, interrupted by shorter or longer periods of independence. Thus, by referring only to single spells or first spells total duration of assistance is underestimated. We will first look at a descriptive measure of total duration: 'gross duration' - the time period between the first and last payment including interruptions. Afterwards we will analyse the duration of the first spell and the determinants of having multiple spells.

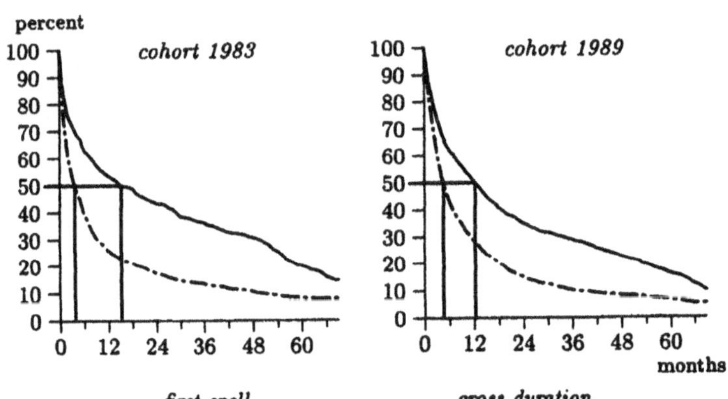

Product-Limit estimation with the programm TDA (Rohwer 1994)

Figure 1 Duration of social assistance in the 1983 and the 1989 cohorts: First spell and gross duration

Source: See Table 1

Figure 1 shows the survivor functions according to the first spell and gross duration in the two cohorts. This function expresses the probability that a person remains in social assistance until time t.

All in all, recipients in the new cohort do not stay longer on social assistance. On the contrary, short-term recipiency is even more common in the nineties than in the eighties. However, the differences between the two cohorts are minimal: As to the first spell, the median increased from four months in the 1983 cohort to five months in the 1989 cohort. The proportion of social assistance careers lasting up to 12 months decreased from 74% to 72%, those lasting longer than 60 months decreased from 8% to 6%. As to gross duration, the median decreased from 15 months in the 1983 cohort to 12 months in the new cohort. The proportion of social assistance careers lasting up to 12 months increased from 47% to 50%, those lasting longer than 60 months decreased from 19% to 16%.

Thus, in contrast to public opinion, social assistance careers do not last longer in the nineties as compared to the eighties. We should note, however, that the proportion of recipients with an extremely short period of recipiency (up to two months) is lower in the 1989 cohort.

How can we explain the decrease in total duration between the two cohorts? One possible explanation is that opportunity structures, e.g. the chances to find a new job have changed since 1983. As mentioned above, since the mid-eighties the situation of the labour market in Germany has slightly improved.

Another possible explanation for the decline in duration is the observed change in the socio-demographic structure of the recipients. Changes in the structure of recipients may, in turn, have consequences for time on assistance as duration of assistance differs by social groups.

German immigrants usually have short spells of assistance, because they are just waiting for other social transfers to be paid, such as unemployment benefits or old age pensions. In this group in the 1989 cohort, median duration of the first spell is three months (all cases: five months) and median gross duration six months (all cases: 12 months). Refugees, too, are often short-term cases, because they were quickly moved to other federal states or because they were deported to their home countries relatively soon after they had applied for assistance in Bremen. In the 1989 cohort, median duration of the first spell is six months for refugees and gross duration is eight months.

If we exclude German immigrants and refugees from the analysis, time on assistance is slightly longer in the new cohort, while it decreased in the total population: As to gross duration, the proportion of recipients who already have left assistance after one year decreased from 45% in the 1983 cohort to 41% in the new one, and the proportion of long-term recipients increased from 21% to 22%.

As to the first spell, the proportion of recipients who have already left assistance after one year decreased from 74% to 70% in the new cohort. The proportion of recipients with long-term assistance, lasting longer than 60 months, is in both cohorts 8%.

Thus, if immigration had not become such an important cause of social assistance in Germany, the number of new recipients would have decreased and we would find lower proportions of short-term and higher proportions of long-term recipiency among new recipients of social assistance.

The decrease in short-term recipiency among native Germans and resident foreigners is mainly induced by changes in the causes of social assistance: In the subgroup of residents in the 1989 cohort there is a lower proportion of 'waiting' cases, that is recipients who leave social assistance quickly after a short period of waiting for other social transfers to be paid (see again Table 2).

3 Determinants of leaving social assistance in the 1983 and the 1989 cohorts

What are the determinants of long-term recipiency and have these determinants or their relative causal weight changed over time?

Duration of social assistance may be influenced by various factors: social and economic factors such as labour market conditions or social policy; characteristics of the social assistance program such as benefit levels; life events and/or immediate causes of entering social assistance such as loss of a job, divorce, or birth of a child; socio-demographic variables such as nationality, gender, age, or type of household.

In this paper we concentrate on the influence of immediate causes and socio-demographic variables on duration of assistance. In previous publications (cf. Buhr 1995) we have shown that it is difficult to explain or predict total duration by socio-demographic variables and causes of assistance measured at the beginning of the first spell of social assistance. One reason is that total duration is made up of several aspects of time: number and duration of single spells and time off assistance until the next spell begins. Thus, instead of estimating models for gross duration, in this paper we concentrate on the determinants of leaving the first spell and having a second spell of assistance ('multiple spells').

3.1 Determinants of ending the first spell of assistance

To identify the determinants of leaving the first spell, we estimated a log-logistic hazard-rate model with (time-constant) covariates measured at the beginning of the spell. The 'hazard rate' or 'exit rate' describes the 'risk', or more precisely, the conditional probability of terminating social assistance recipiency within a short time interval, assuming that there was no change prior to the beginning of this interval (cf. Blossfeld and Rohwer 1995).

Table 3
Determinants of ending the first spell of social assistance in the 1983 and 1989 cohorts (regression coefficients)

Variables	Cohort			
	1983		1989	
Constant	-1.7764*	(0.1470)	-1.6678*	(0.1106)
Resident foreigners	0.1509	(0.1852)	-0.0647	(0.1608)
German immigrants	0.4951	(0.2658)	0.4481*	(0.1013)
Refugees	-1.5110*	(0.3139)	-0.4154*	(0.1162)
Up to 20 years	-0.3016*	(0.1599)	-0.4581*	(0.1130)
50 years and over	-0.9197*	(0.2210)	-0.7181*	(0.1486)
Vocational qualification	0.8245*	(0.1253)	0.2513*	(0.0945)
Children under three years	-0.1777	(0.2567)	-0.5627*	(0.1540)
Single parents	-0.5856*	(0.2444)	-0.6404*	(0.1469)
Couples with children	-0.1280	(0.2230)	-0.0548	(0.1450)
Single women	-0.2538	(0.1907)	-0.0631	(0.1417)
Single men	0.1915	(0.1462)	0.2886*	(0.1059)
ln(p)	0.2329*	(0.0358)	0.3692*	(0.0282)
Log likelihood H_1	-1734.19		-2850.06	
Log likelihood H_0	-1909.34		-3096.98	
χ^2 (df = 11)	350.30		493.84	
Number of cases	586		922	

Model specification: Log-logistic model with time-constant covariates, reference-groups: resident Germans, 20-50 years of age, no vocational qualification, no children under three years, all other households. Statistically significant *$p < 0.005$, standard errors in brackets. The likelihood ratio test (χ^2) follows a *Chi*^{2}-distribution. Estimated with the programm TDA (Rohwer 1994)

Source: See Table 1

The following covariates were included in the model: residential status (resident foreigners, German immigrants, refugees, reference group: native Germans); age (below 20 years, over 50 years, reference group: 20-50 years); vocational qualification (reference group: recipients without vocational qualification); presence of a child under age three in the household (reference group: no child under age three); type of household (single parents, couples with children, single women, single men, reference group: all other households).

A positive sign of a coefficient indicates better chances to leave social assistance and accordingly shorter duration as compared to the reference group. A negative sign, in turn, indicates worse chances to terminate assistance and longer spell duration.

Table 3 shows the determinants of leaving the first spell in the 1983 and 1989 cohorts for the total population. In the 1983 cohort, refugees, young people, the elderly, and single parents stay significantly longer on assistance. Recipients with vocational qualification, on the contrary, leave social assistance more quickly than other groups.

In the new cohort, residential status, age, vocational qualification, and being a single parent also exert an influence on the duration of the first spell. Some effects, however, are not as strong as in the 1983 cohort. In the new cohort there is also a significant positive effect for single men and German immigrants, while households with small children stay significantly longer on social assistance than in the 1983 cohort. Thus it has become more difficult to leave social assistance for recipients with small children over time, while single men and German immigrants have improved their position relative to other groups.

If we include the causes of entering social assistance in the model, as expected, we find a strong positive effect of 'waiting for other transfers' in both cohorts. That is, recipients who are just waiting for other social benefits to be paid have significantly shorter durations. However, as the causes of social assistance are correlated with socio-demographic variables, they partly suppress the effect of other covariates on the exit rate, especially residential status and type of household.

3.2 Determinants of having a second spell of assistance

So far, we have only looked at the first spell of social assistance. However, social assistance careers often are composed of several spells: In the 1983 cohort, nearly 40% of the recipients had two or more spells. In the new cohort there is a lower frequency of multiple spells, as the proportion of recipients with multiple spells decreased to 31%. This decrease in discontinuous recipiency, which is partly responsible for the decrease in total ('gross') duration mentioned above, is again due to the different composition of the two cohorts according to residence status: If we exclude German immigrants and refugees from the analysis, the proportion of recipients with multiple spells decreased only slightly from 41% to 38%.

Nearly 30% of all new spells begin within three months, more than 40% within six months and more than 60% within one year after the end of the first spell.[8] This leads to the question of why some recipients have to reapply for assistance after a shorter or longer period while others manage to stay off assistance permanently after they have finished the first spell. An answer to this question is important for policy makers and administrators to identify candidates with multiple spell careers at an early stage and target special services for them.

Like duration multiple spell careers may differ by socio-demographic variables such as age or type of household. The risk of having a second spell may also vary among recipients who leave social assistance for different reasons. Some routes out of assistance may lead to permanent selfsufficiency while others may not.

We estimated a log-logistic hazard-rate model, for the total population, to identify the determinants of having a second spell as compared to not having to reapply during the observation period of 69 months, and therefore to remain off assistance. We measured the time without social assistance, after the first spell has ended. As in the model for the first spell, we controlled for residential status, age, vocational qualification, presence of a child under age three, and type of household. We also tested the impact of the causes for ending the first spell (work, other benefits/social security, reference group: other causes for ending).

All in all, it is more difficult to explain multiple spell careers than the duration of the first spell (see Table 4). While there is only one significant effect in the 1983 cohort, socio-demographic variables gain importance in the new cohort.

In both cohorts, German immigrants and refugees seldom have to reapply for assistance which is indicated by the negative sign of the coefficients. For young people and for households with small children it is more difficult to leave social assistance permanently at the end of the eighties than at the beginning. In contrast the elderly, and to a lower degree single parents and couples with children have a lower risk of having a second spell in the new cohort as compared to the 1983 cohort.

Table 4
Determinants of having a second spell after the end of the first spell of social assistance in the 1983 and 1989 cohorts (regression coefficients)

Variables	Cohort			
	1983		1989	
Constant	-8.1453*	(0.3446)	-8.0461*	(0.3418)
Resident foreigners	0.3145	(0.3755)	-0.3465	(0.4190)
German immigrants	-2.1917*	(0.8195)	-0.8304	(0.2995)
Refugees	-1.3551	(0.8258)	-2.2572*	(0.4110)
Up to 20 years	0.5185	(0.3268)	0.8572*	(0.2965)
50 years and over	0.1022	(0.4677)	-0.9422*	(0.4779)
Vocational qualification	0.0404	(0.2692)	0.1749	(0.2581)
Children under three years	-0.3361	(0.4888)	0.6360	(0.4064)
Single parents	0.8292	(0.4948)	0.0863	(0.4110)
Couples with children	0.5009	(0.4601)	0.1719	(0.3904)
Single women	-0.0066	(0.4071)	-0.4825	(0.3826)
Single men	0.3517	(0.3146)	0.2444	(0.2911)
Causes for ending:				
Employment	0.5364	(0.3375)	-0.1508	(0.3185)
Other benefits	0.3958	(0.2867)	0.0196	(0.2905)
ln(p)	-0.3433*	(0.0571)	-0.3946*	(0.0526)
Log likelihood H_1	-1972.84		-2507.47	
Log likelihood H_0	-2022.85		-2594.29	
χ^2 (df = 13)	100.04		173.64	
Number of cases	537**		862**	

Notes:
* Significant at the 5% level
** Cases with right-censored first spell are not used; Model specification see Table 3

Source: See Table 1

What about the causes for ending social assistance? In the 1983 cohort, recipients who leave based on employment have a high, albeit not significant risk of having a second spell. In the new cohort, however, leaving via a job does not increase the risk of having multiple spells.[9] This could mean that due to the better conditions on the labour market employment careers are more stable in the nineties with the result that fewer recipients have to reapply for assistance.

All in all, the results show different routes to long-term recipiency. German immigrants mostly have only one short spell. The elderly, refugees, and to a lower degree single parents tend to have few, but longer spells. Young recipients and to a lower degree households with small children, finally, tend to have multiple and long spells.

4 Concluding remarks

We have compared two cohorts of new recipients of social assistance in order to assess the impact of social change on social assistance. Has time on assistance increased over time as often assumed in the public debate on social assistance? What are the determinants of long-term recipiency in the nineties as compared to the eighties?

The empirical evidence does not point towards longer lasting social assistance careers in the nineties as compared to the eighties. On the contrary, total time on assistance has decreased for the new cohort. This decline in duration is mainly due to the different composition of the two cohorts according to residence status: In the 1989 cohort there is a much higher proportion of immigrants and refugees. If such high numbers of immigrants had not appeared among the new recipients of 1989 - invited by politicians -, the number of new recipients would have been lower and total ('gross') duration would have increased slightly.

The determinants of ending the first spell and having a second spell of assistance have also changed over time. Some covariates such as old age have lost importance while some groups, especially recipients with small children, and young people, seem to have more difficulties in leaving social assistance permanently in the nineties as compared to the eighties.

All in all, the differences between the two cohorts are minimal. Few signs indicate that recipients of social assistance are more inclined to 'settle in' in the nineties as sometimes claimed by right-wing politicians.

Notes

[1] The number of 'German immigrants', i.e. immigrants from the German Democratic Republic and of immigrants of German origin from Eastern Europe and the former

Soviet Union increased from less than 50,000 in 1983 to more than 700,000 in 1989. The number of refugees and applicants for political asylum rose, too, from about 20,000 in 1983 to about 120,000 in 1989 and a peak of more than 400,000 in 1992 (cf. Statistisches Bundesamt 1990, 1995).

[2] In 1990, however, entitlement to unemployment benefits was changed for German immigrants.

[3] Until 1991 refugees were not allowed to work at all. Since then they can obtain permission to work which may also have an effect on time on assistance.

[4] The rate of unemployment in Germany increased from 3.8% in 1980 to 9.1% in 1983 and 9.3% in 1985. Since then the situation on the labor market has slightly improved as indicated by a decrease of the rate to 7.9% in 1989 and 6.3% in 1991. During the nineties, however, the rate has increased again to 9.2% in 1994.

[5] Long-term unemployment, defined as unemployment lasting more than one year, strongly increased during the eighties to a peak of about one third of all unemployed in 1988. Since then the proportion of long-term unemployed has decreased continuously to about 26% in 1993. In 1994, however, long-term unemployment rose again to 32.5%.

[6] In the case of married couples, the applicant is usually the husband. Besides the applicant, several other persons in a family may receive social assistance from the same file.

[7] For the comparison, the observation period had to be cut to 69 months.

[8] This corresponds to the situation in the USA (cf. Blank and Ruggles 1994).

[9] This effect is especially strong and significant for the subgroup of residents.

References

Andreß, H.J. (1994), 'Steigende Sozialhilfezahlen. Wer bleibt, wer geht und wie sollte die Sozialverwaltung darauf reagieren? Eine Analyse der Bezugsdauer von Sozialhilfe mit Hilfe der Bielefelder Datenbank "Sozialhilfe-Statistik"', in Zwick, M. (ed.), *Einmal arm, immer arm? Neue Befunde zur Armut in Deutschland*, Campus: Frankfurt a.M./New York, pp. 75-105.

Bane, M. J. and Ellwood, D. T. (1994), *Welfare Realities*, Harvard University Press: Cambridge/ London.

Bane, M. J. and Ellwood, D. T. (1986), 'Slipping into and out of Poverty: The Dynamics of Spells', *The Journal of Human Resources*, Vol. 12, pp. 1-23.

Blank, R. M. and Ruggles, P. (1994), 'Short-term Recidivism among Public-Assistance Recipients', *American Economic Review* (Papers & Proceedings), Vol. 84, pp. 49-53.

Blossfeld, H. P. and Rohwer, G., (1995), *Techniques of Event History Modeling*, Lawrence Erlbaum: Hillsdale, New Jersey.

Buhr, P. (1995), *Dynamik von Armut. Dauer und biographische Bedeutung von Sozialhilfebezug*, Westdeutscher Verlag: Opladen.

Buhr, P. and Weber, A. (1996), *The Impact of Social Change on Social Assistance. Two Cohorts of German Welfare Recipients Compared*, Sonderforschungsbereich 186 (Sfb 186 Working Paper No. 31), Universität Bremen: Bremen.

Buhr, P., Ludwig, M. and Priester, T. (1990), *Die Bremer 10%-Stichprobe von Sozialhilfeakten*, Zentrum für Sozialpolitik (ZeS Working Paper No. 1), Universität Bremen: Bremen.

Duncan, G. J. (1984), *Years of Poverty, Years of Plenty*, The University of Michigan, Institute for Social Research: Ann Arbor, MI.

Hagen, C. and Hock, B. (1995), *Die Dynamik von Armut in einer hessischen Kleinstadt. Sozialhilfeverläufe und -karrieren*, Universität Frankfurt, Fachbereich Gesellschaftswissenschaften (unpublished thesis): Frankfurt/Main.

Heady, B., Habich, R., Krause, P. (1990), *The Duration and Extent of Poverty - Is Germany a Two-Thirds-Society?*, Wissenschaftszentrum (Working Paper No. P90/103): Berlin.

Krause, P. (1994), 'Zur zeitlichen Dimension von Einkommensarmut', in Hanesch, W. et al. (eds.), *Armut in Deutschland. Der Armutsbericht des DGB und des Paritätischen Wohlfahrtsverbands*, Rowohlt: Reinbek, pp. 189-206.

Leibfried, S. (1987), 'Projektantrag: Sozialhilfekarrieren - Wege aus der und durch die Sozialhilfe und ihre sozialstaatliche Rahmung', in Heinz, W. (ed.), *Statuspassagen und Risikolagen im Lebensverlauf*, Universität Bremen: Bremen, pp. 801-861.

Leibfried, S., Leisering, L., Buhr, P., Ludwig, M., Mädje, E., Olk, T., Voges, W. and Zwick, M. (1995), *Zeit der Armut. Lebensläufe im Sozialstaat*, Suhrkamp: Frankfurt a.M.

Ludwig, M. (1996), *Armutskarrieren. Zwischen Abstieg und Aufstieg im Sozialstaat*, Westdeutscher Verlag: Opladen.

Rendtel, U. and Wagner, G. (eds.) (1991), *Lebenslagen im Wandel: Zur Einkommensdynamik in Deutschland seit 1984*, Campus: Frankfurt a.M., New York.

Rohwer, G. (1994), *TDA (Transitional Data Analysis) Working Papers*, Universität Bremen: Bremen.

Samson, R. (1992), 'Analyse der Bezugsdauer von Hilfe zum Lebensunterhalt anhand der Abrechnungsdaten der Stadt Bielefeld', in Johrendt, N. and Schneider, H. (eds.), *Computergestützte Sozialberichterstattung und Sozialplanung, BDS-Schriftenreihe*, Vol. 11, Bielefeld, pp. 109-119.

Statistisches Bundesamt (Federal Statistical Office) 1990, 1995, *Statistisches Jahrbuch für die Bundesrepublik Deutschland*, Metzler & Poeschel: Stuttgart.

Poverty risks and the life cycle: The individualization thesis reconsidered

Hans-Jürgen Andreß and Katja Schulte

1 Introduction

What are the ways into and out of poverty? A cursory review of the literature shows at least three hypotheses: the assumption of poverty persistence (the persistence hypothesis), the assumption of cyclically changing entry risks and exit chances (the life cycle hypothesis), and the assumption of individually varying poverty profiles with different developments that cannot be described by the classical socio-demographic variables (the individualization hypothesis).

The *persistence hypothesis* can be found most prominently in the work of Oscar Lewis about a culture of poverty (Lewis 1966; Goetze 1992; Rommelspacher 1989). According to Lewis, living in poor neighbourhoods creates an independent subculture whose main characteristics are transferred from one generation to the next by socialization processes within the family. Implicitly, the persistence hypothesis is included in many other approaches: e.g. in Heinze's and his coworkers' work explaining poverty risks by labor market segmentation (Heinze et al. 1981), in marxist theories (e.g. Chassé 1988), in theories of marginal groups (e.g. Chassé et al. 1992), and in recent welfarization research, which assumes that the welfare state is (re)producing its own clientele (Leisering and Voges 1992; Voges, Buhr and Zwick 1996). The basic assumption of all these theories is a sort of reinforcing process: individual, institutional, and social consequences of poverty are at the same time the causes of its persistence. These mutually enforcing factors include 'counterproductive' attitudes and behavior, social control and social exclusion, (spatial) segregation and intergenerational transmission of poverty by socialization deficits.

The *life cycle hypothesis* dates back to the work of Benjamin Seebohm Rowntree published in 1901 in his study of the 'wage-earning classes in provincial towns'. He found that they live in poverty only during certain phases of their life, namely when they are the bread-winner of a family and when they retire from their active working career (Rowntree 1980, p. 137). Many recent research has also shown that poverty risks change during the life course of individuals as labor market participation and household composition change. Critical life course transitions during which poverty risks are high include the transition from school to work for young adults, the birth of the first and following children, divorce and death of the partner, and finally the retirement phase. 'Poverty within the life cycle' means that besides the classical vertical inequalities additional temporal disparities exist. In certain phases of family life, when entering the labor market, and after retiring from active work poverty risks are much higher than in other parts of the life cycle.

The *individualization thesis* has been formulated in Germany most prominently by Ulrich Beck (1986): Because traditional norms and regularities, classical stratification processes, etc. loosen their hold on the individual, life styles and biographies become much more open and diverse and depend increasingly on individual decisions. The 'prescribed' or so-called 'normal' biography turns into a biography that is chosen by the individual. One of Beck's coworkers, Peter Berger, applies this idea to the analysis of poverty: 'On the one hand, the ways into poverty will be multiplied and will be less tied to the standard risks of capitalistic industrial societies including unemployment, illness, and old age. [...] On the other hand, with this development the often noted heterogeneity of the poor population increases making it more and more difficult to understand poverty as a collective problem and to reduce it to one dominant or at least a few and therefore easily contested causes. [...] Finally, the transition from normal to chosen [...] biographies points to a new dimension of inequalities that could characterize at the same time a new aspect of poverty: If the assumption of extended decision possibilities is true, then the absence of important biographical options, wrong decisions, missed opportunities, and status passages passed too quickly or too slowly can be characteristics of a "modernized" poverty' (Berger 1994, pp. 26). According to the individualization hypothesis, it has become more and more difficult to distinguish typical poverty profiles. Anything goes and the classical causes of poverty -- labor market, family, welfare state -- are pushed to the background. Instead, 'subjective perceptions and competences' (Berger 1994, p. 39) to surmount biographical demands become more and more important.

With these three hypotheses in mind we want to interpret the poverty profiles that we find in panel survey data. We use them as general orientations, not as testable hypotheses in a strict statistical sense. For statistical testing, these hypotheses are much too rough and imprecise. Nevertheless, they give our research questions a specific direction:

1. How do people become poor?
2. Is poverty for them a transitory or a permanent status?
3. What is the role of the labor market, the family, and the welfare state when a person overcomes the poverty status?

In order to describe the ways into and out of poverty, we need longitudinal information. For that purpose we use data from the German Socio-Economic Panel (GSOEP, cf. Projektgruppe Panel 1993), a representative survey for West and East Germany including about 5900 households in the West and nearly 2200 in the East. Since we wanted to follow the poverty status of German households over the longest possible period, we used only the West German sample for which longitudinal information was available since 1984. The Eastern panel was started shortly before the currency transfer (Währungsunion) in 1990.

Panel and survey data are used routinely for poverty analyses. However, given our hypotheses and the specific methods used in this paper two qualifications need to be noted. First of all, it should be stressed that representative population surveys hardly capture all marginal groups. The practice of survey research -- at least in Germany -- implicitly assumes that each target person has a permanent lodging. People living in institutions and in common lodging-houses (Gemeinschaftunterkünfte) are explicitely excluded from the sample design of German survey research institutes, the so-called ADM-Design (see Schnell (1991) for a thorough discussion of the excluded groups in German population surveys). It is therefore questionable whether we can really test the persistence hypothesis, which predominantly applies to marginal groups that are either by definition (e.g. the homeless) or in practice excluded from survey research (e.g. interviewer selectivity, compliance and intellectual capacities of the respondents).

The second qualification concerns the way we make use of the panel information. The GSOEP contains information about socio-economic characteristics of persons and households over time. We want to use this information not only to describe the ways into and out of poverty, but also to infer from it statements about the intentions and purposeful actions of individuals. In other words, we are not only interested in the ways out of poverty, but also in the coping strategies that people use to overcome this status. If, for instance, in a panel household the husband becomes unemployed and one year later his wife finds a job, then we interpret this as a reaction to the income loss of the husband, although the data do not tell us anything about the intentions of the wife. Since we have only very little information about the motives and intentions of the respondents in the panel data, assumptions based on common sense are necessary. In some cases these may be misinterpretations (e.g. the wife wanted to start working anyway). In order to minimize such misinterpretations, we decided to take a very close look at the raw data using interpretative methods to develop a model of coping with poverty 'grounded' on the panel data. More specifically, we use case studies of a cohort of households falling into poverty to analyze, (a) which persons and households are afflicted by income poverty, and (b) what kind of behavior can be observed within these households over time.

The chapter is organized as follows: In section 2 we present a model of labor-oriented coping strategies that guided our interpretations of the 'cases' and their behavior over time. Coping is modeled as the result of resources, restrictions, and subjective evaluations of each household member. The operationalization of these theoretical constructs with the GSOEP data is shown in the Appendix. Section 3 describes the selection of poor households from the data base and the methods used to interpret the raw data. The results of our analysis are discussed in section 4. In the first step, we look at the income information alone and distinguish three kinds of income profiles. Taking into account the other variables besides income we develop a typology of poverty profiles and their causes. Low education is prevalent in most groups with one exception, the escapers from poverty. This leads to the hypothesis of a risk-filled life cycle for those characterized by having a low education. It can be stated as follows:

H1: Individuals with lower education have a higher probability of entering poverty several times during their life. This higher risk of recurrent poverty goes hand in hand with the traditional family cycle characteristic of this group.

The validity of this assumption compared to the individualization hypothesis is discussed in the last section 5.

2 Ways out of poverty: How to model them theoretically

Models of individual behavior have been formulated by different scientific disciplines. While the economic model describes how a rational human being optimizes the use of scarce resources given his or her preferences (cf. e.g. Becker 1976), the psychological model stresses cognitive and evaluative perceptions of the situation (appraisal) by the individual that may lead to different adaptive reactions (coping), which are not necessarily identical with the (rational) reactions predicted by the economic model (cf. e.g. Lazarus and Folkman 1987). Our model is quite close to the economic model. However, instead of viewing preferences as fixed, we conceive them as a variable that may change in time.

Coping with poverty bears many similarities with other reactions of families to external and internal crises. The family stress theory has developed process models to describe the coping behavior following a stressful event. According to these models, coping behavior depends on the resources available to the family members and on evaluations of the stressor by the family members (one of the first models is Hill's 1949, extensions can be found in McCubbin and Peterson 1983). In the following 'coping', 'resources', and 'evaluations' will be used as purely descriptive categories. From the economic model, we have added the term 'restrictions' indicating that resources are not always freely available, as is often the case with poor households.

Implicitly, we are assuming that a situation of financial scarcity - especially when intensified by critical life events (Filipp 1981) - generates a certain tension that leads to coping behavior of the individual and all the others living together with him or her in the household. Here, we are especially interested in activities that either improve the financial situation of the individual and the corresponding household or that adjust the behavior of the individual and the household to the reduced income. Often this environmental challenge is accompanied by cognitive processes in which the individual evaluates relevant personal goals ('What is at stake for me?') and appraises his or her possibilities in improving the troubled person-environmental relationship ('Can I control the outcomes?'). It should be noted that the psychological model negates that certain actions must necessarily follow financial pressures and - if they occur - that they must necessarily eliminate the problem. For instance, evasive coping behavior may result from changing personal goals, and this does not alter the problem of financial scarcity. We have analyzed more general types of coping behavior elsewhere with our own survey (Andreß et al. 1996;

Salentin 1996), but with the data of the GSOEP it is impossible, because the necessary psychological information is missing.

Besides that, we can analyze only a selection of so-called problem-oriented coping strategies with the GSOEP data. We shall focus on work-related strategies, especially increases in labor supply that improve the income position of the household. In addition to gainful employment, the economic situation of a household depends also on its size and composition, but we do not have any information whether household members strategically vary these parameters: for instance, by deferring the wish for another child or by marrying a better-off partner. Of course, a financially precarious situation can be bridged by take-up of social security and welfare payments, but our empirical analyses showed that government transfers only play a secondary and compensatory role. Lastly, we miss any information about economic adjustments to decreased incomes in the GSOEP data: e.g. the economization of current consumption, the delay of large purchases, the liquidation of assets, indebtedness, and the like. These activities do not change the current income position. Basically, they transfer past or future incomes into the present time or they adjust current consumption to decreased income. In this sense, the following model is a description of strategies that change the current income position by gainful employment, by one's own actions, so to speak, and not through the interventions of others and the welfare state.

As shown by Figure 1, decisions about employment can be modeled as a two-stage process: First, it is decided within the household whether an employable person should enter the labor market. If he/she decides to do so, it then depends on the labor market situation whether this labor supply finds its corresponding demand. Given this two-stage process there are in principle two possibilities of not being gainfully employed: economists call these possibilities 'voluntary' and 'involuntary' unemployment. It can be assumed that the factors deciding in the second stage whether a certain labor supply finds its demand may also influence the first decision (cf. e.g. discouragement). However, a positive decision in the first stage presupposes that there are unused manpower reservoirs in the household. Therefore, we have constructed our model as a two-stage process, in which we examine in the first stage the manpower resources of the household given the (time) restrictions of its members. A typical time restriction would be e.g. children in the household that have to be taken care of. From the resources available within given restrictions we then derive certain options for the household and its members. Depending on their subjective evaluations of their financial situation we can observe a certain coping behavior, in our case a given labor supply in the labor market.

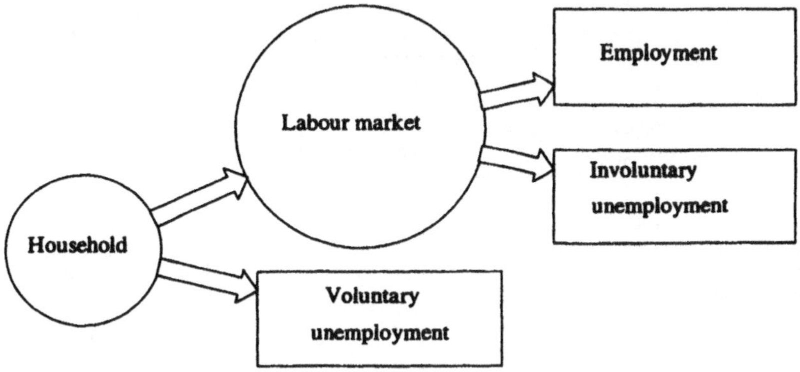

Figure 1 A sequential model of labour supply

Whether this coping behavior leads to successful adjustment, i.e. a successful overcoming of the 'objectively' measured poverty status, depends on factors that act on the second stage of the process model. Besides the development of the labor market (the macro level), we are especially interested in the characteristics of the people looking for a job (the micro level). Whether their labor supply finds the corresponding demand, depends, among other things, on restrictions of their human capital. We call these restrictions 'risk factors' to distinguish them from restrictions of time that are decisive in the first stage of the model, e.g. how many (additional) hours of work are to be supplied in the labor market. A typical risk factor would be the old age of a person. It does not really restrict the time resources, but it influences (via the macro level) the chances of a successful labor supply.

Thus, risk factors are restrictions at the second stage of the process model that determine whether a person is employed or remains involuntarily unemployed. Time restrictions in a more narrow sense determine at the first stage whether the person supplies labor at all or remains voluntarily unemployed. Of course, the assumption of a sequential decision process is a simplification, because people will evaluate their chances and risks on the labor market when considering whether they have time to supply (additional) labor. Nevertheless, for the interpretation of poverty profiles a stepwise procedure makes sense: First, we ask whether a household has unused manpower reserves. Then, we observe whether, dependent on subjective evaluations of need, additional labor is supplied. Finally, we determine whether this supply is successful given certain risk factors. Figure 2 summarizes this stepwise procedure.

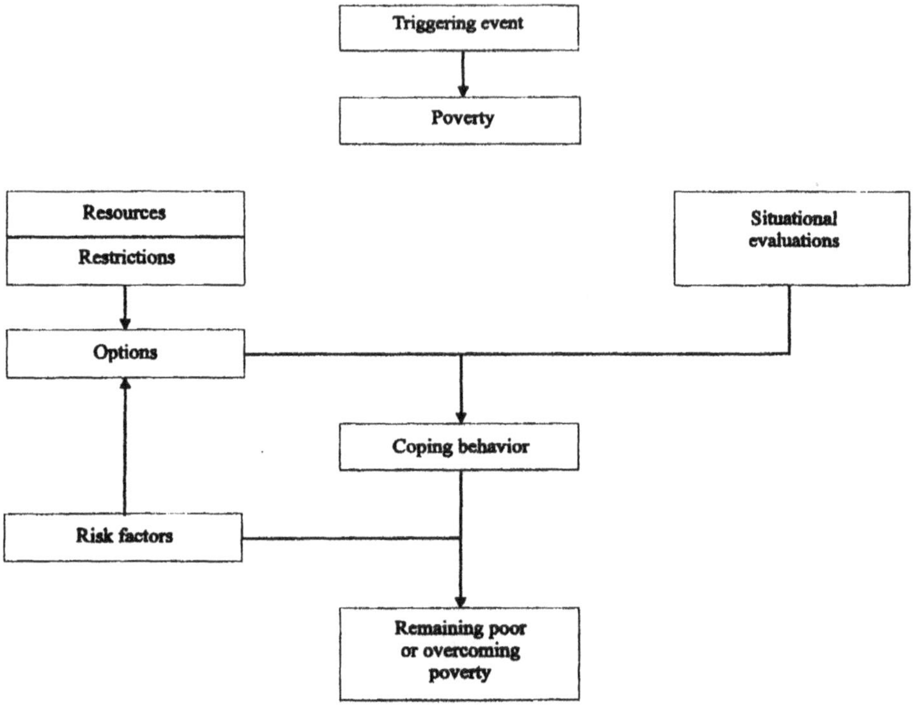

Figure 2 A model for the interpretation of work-related coping processes

We start with an event affecting the economic position of the household - for instance, the dissolution of a partnership, the birth of a child, or the entry into unemployment by one household member, all of which may cause a longer or shorter spell of poverty. The model then tries to disentagle the following coping behavior of the household and its members. When looking at the possible labor market activities of the household, the term 'resources' means employable household members not working full-time. Restrictions, on the other hand, comprise children that have to be taken care of, members of the household needing permanent health care, health impairments of employable household members, and the like. Given the resources available on the one hand and the restrictions of the household on the other hand certain labor options can be inferred. We call these the manpower reserve or the manpower capacity of the household. Besides that, it is equally important to recognize the subjective evaluations of the household members, that is, whether they perceive the 'objectively' measured poverty subjectively as problematic. The actual behavior of each household member, whether he or she in fact uses his/her manpower capacity, results from the options at hand and the subjective evaluations of the household members. Whether these activities lead to a successful way out of poverty, depends in the end on the aforementioned risk factors of the household members. These include among other things their level of education and qualification, their age, the duration of their unemployment and/or welfare use. Risk factors influence the chances of escaping poverty independently of the actual behavior of the individual. In most cases, risk factors cannot be changed by the individual, at least in a short-term perspective. For instance, a 55-year old unemployed male can try to find a new job (we would call this his 'behavior'), but the chances that he finds a new job are relatively low, because of his high age (the 'risk factor').

All these components have to be analyzed for each household member and for each point in time. The model itself serves as an interpretative tool for the observed changes in each household's income position and the accompanying work-related activities of the household members. As already mentioned, our interpretations will very often rely on common sense assumptions, since information about intentions and purposes is not available for the acting individuals. Also, the assumption of sequential decisions is questionable. Feedback mechanisms and bidirectional effects cannot be neglected. For instance, the question whether to supply work, i.e. the coping behavior, will depend on the individual's perceptions of his or her risk factors. Despite these objections the model is a valuable tool for interpretative methods. It structures the amount of longitudinal information, and it constructs a meaningful connection for the activities observed. Besides that, it can be easily operationalized with the GSOEP (see Appendix).

3 Data and methods

From the German Socio-Economic Panel (GSOEP) we selected all households with a German head that became poor in 1985. Thus, we analyze an entry cohort of 'new' poor households instead of a cross-section of poor households from a certain year that always includes a mixture of households with long and short poverty spells. Our sample has the advantage that all households investigated have a common starting point in poverty. The year 1985 was chosen for two reasons: firstly, to have some information about possible causal events by comparing data from 1984 (the first wave of GSOEP) and 1985, and secondly to yield as much possible longitudinal information as possible (i.e. until the year of 1992).

The income information comes from a question answered by the household head: the so-called income screener. It measures total monthly household income after taxes including government transfers and subsidies. For practical reasons, we chose a poverty measure which is frequently used in German poverty research: It is the European Community (EC) definition classifying households as poor whose household equivalent income is lower than 50% of the average household equivalent income. The equivalence scale used corresponds to the regulations for social assistence payments in Germany after July 1990 assigning a weight of 0.8 for each additional adult and weights between 0.5 and 0.9 for children depending on their age. After checking several other selection criteria like the availability of plausible income data and longitudinal information for at least five years, we came up with a sample of 49 households including about 170 persons within the observation period from 1984 to 1992.

In an earlier quantitative analysis (Andreß 1996; Andreß et al. 1996) with all the longitudinal information from 1984-92 (not only the 1985 entry cohort), we were able to replicate the findings of other researchers showing the economic risks of labor-related and demographic events (Berntsen 1992; Headey et al. 1990). Moving downward into poverty occurs very often in connection with an exit from the labor market, an increase in household size (in most cases a child birth), the death of the partner, or the dissolution of a partnership/marriage. At the same time however, these quantitative analyses left some questions unanswered. First of all, it was very difficult to measure precisely the temporal ordering of certain events in the panel without referring to the raw data, and this is a prerequisite for distinguishing events and following reactions of the individuals. It was especially difficult to operationalize the take-up of social security and welfare payments. In sum, all programmed analyses remained rather coarse and left many observed changes unexplained. Before going on with testing specific hypotheses, we really wanted to 'understand' the data. Therefore, the following analysis uses interpretative tools instead of standard statistical procedures. As we will see later on, this explorative approach yields well-grounded results of its own. But we want to give some explanations first, of why we deliberately refrained from using quantitative techniques although the data are of a quantitative nature.

First of all, using elaborated statistical procedures presupposes precise hypotheses. We do not deny that such hypotheses exist (e.g. for human capital theory), but the scope of these hypotheses is often specific (e.g. the analysis of unemployment spells), they focus on the individual person, introduce the household context in a rather ad-hoc fashion, and fail to model reciprocal effects between different variables, different time points, and the individual level and the household context. We decided that we should 'learn' from the data in the first place, and therefore, we used the data in a very descriptive format to derive our interpretations.

Secondly, it follows from our process model that the changes of certain variables in time have to be considered very carefully when analyzing the coping processes of poor households. Changes in household structure and employment status of its members are examples of that kind. However, we have not seen many convincing examples of quantitative analyses taking these changes into account. All too often they relate simple status change variables from the previous period t-1 to certain events in the present period t. As already mentioned, many panel data are not precisely enough measured to infer the exact temporal ordering of events, and even if this would be the case, it is difficult to distinguish between anticipation and reaction, both empirically and theoretically. Again, before assuming away this uncertainty, we decided to have a look at the data first.

Thirdly, it is obvious that a process model like the one just discussed implies the analysis of many different variables for all household members at the same time. Given the small number of poor households in all population-wide representative surveys, we very quickly run out of cases when using multivariate techniques.

Fourthly, all social science data include measurement error, and especially with panel data we have more possibilities to detect these errors, because we can compare the same variables across time. If we detect, for instance, an extraordinary income change within a household, we can crosscheck this with changes in the household and employment structure of the same case. Given a constant household and employment structure, such a change does not appear very plausible (and we found several such unplausible income values, when looking at the GSOEP data individually). Therefore, serious statistical analyses with panel data need a lot of data-editing and the inclusion of measurement models.

Basically, data-editing consists of looking at single cases and interpreting what plausible and unplausible data values are. We took one step further and said, if we need to do this data-editing anyway, we can have a look at the same time at the total household information available and try to give an interpretation of that household's poverty coping behavior. Our data material consisted of a data sheet for each of the 49 households plotting all relevant variables from our model for the household and each household member across time.

Because of privacy regulations we are not allowed to publish single cases, but to illustrate our data, the following Table 1 shows a fictional household with the corresponding longitudinal information from the first three years of our observation period. Similar information is available for the years after 1986 until 1992.

The aim of our analysis was to derive a realistic as possible picture of poverty processes in an exploratory fashion. The procedure used borrows many ideas from the procedure developed by Uta Gerhardt originally for an analysis of patients' careers ('Idealtypische Strukturanalyse', Gerhard 1986a,b, 1991a,b). We modified and extended it in several ways for the analysis of quantitative panel data (for the details see Schulte 1995).

More specifically, we tried first to capture the multitude of single poverty profiles within the sample by using data-sheets, case histories, and case contrasts. A data-sheet as shown in Table 1 includes all relevant raw data for the household and each household member in a longitudinal format. Case histories summarize the main characteristics of the household and its members after editing the raw data and eliminating inconsistencies and implausible values. Case contrasts are simply comparisons of cases histories across different dimensions, for instance across poverty causes, across income profiles, etc. Since we are interested in ways into and out of poverty, the income information proved to be the most important dimension. In the second step of our analysis, we therefore reduced the variety of single cases into a typology of income profiles which consists of a group of continuously poor, a group of upward movers, and a group of discontinuously poor. Finally, when looking at the coping behavior we could differentiate this typology even further. Several 'Idealtypen' (Weber) were found and described in more abstract terms. With this (finer) typology we intend to detect more general structures and processes. It was cross-validated with a second entry cohort from the year 1986. The results of this validation show that our typology can be replicated in more than half of the households in the 1986 sample.

Table 1
A data sheet of a fictional household

observation period	1984	1985	1986
household composition	husband(27) wife (26)	husband (28) wife (27) son (0)	husband (29) wife (28) son (1)
gainful employment	husband: working fulltime as a mechanic, no overtime wife: working fulltime, no overtime	husband: working fulltime as a mechanic, no overtime wife: not working	husband: working fulltime as a mechanic, no overtime wife: not working
income	2,100 DM	1,400 DM	1,500 DM
relative income class	0.95	0.48	0.49
sources of income	h: wage (12x) w: wage (8x)	h: wage (12x) w: -- children/housing allowance	h: wage (12x) w: -- children/housing allowance
resources		wife: capable of working	wife: capable of working
restrictions		1 child	
options		w: restricted option to work	w: restricted option to work
situational evaluations		h: satisfaction with household income (6), some worries about financial situation w: satisfaction (5), some worries ab. financial situation	h: satisfaction (7), some worries about financial situation w: satisfaction (5), some worries ab. financial situation
coping behavior		h: wants to work fulltime w: wants to work in the future	h: wants to work fulltime w: wants to work in the future
risc factors		w: low qualification	w: low qualification + more than one year without job
changes	birth of child wife quits job children/housing allowance		

4 Results

4.1 Income profiles

First of all, we wanted to detect different income profiles in the sample. Through various case contrasts three different patterns of profiles could be finally distinguished.

The diagrams in Figure 3 give an impression of the income profiles of the 49 households for the three groups. One line represents the income development of one household. Because of missing income data some lines are interrupted. The thicker dotted lines indicate the 60% and 50% poverty line. The abscissa shows the observation period, i.e. the years between 1984 and 1992. The ordinate shows the relative income class of each household. The relative income class equals the ratio of the household's equivalent income and the average household equivalent income. For example, a value of 1 indicates an average household equivalent income, and a value be- low 0.6 indicates a household equivalent income below the 60% poverty line (upper dotted line). Since all households enter poverty in 1985, the lines in all diagrams show a sharp decrease for this year.

The first diagram in Figure 3 shows the first group of households, which can be characterized by long-term constant poverty. Therefore, they are called 'continuously poor households'. This type comprises 19 out of 49 cases (= 39%). The households belonging to this type either continuously receive social assistance payments during the observation period or their (relative) income position remains continuously below the 60% poverty line (except for some cases). When classifiying the income profiles, we did not adhere strictly to the 50% poverty line. We used it only for selecting the sample. However, a broader procedure was applied when classifying individual cases, since all (income) poverty lines include some kind of arbitrariness. More specifically, we used a rather liberal demarcation line of 60% as well as interpretations of the data when the income information seemed to be implausible in some cases. Because of this, there are also points above the 60% poverty line in the diagram of the continuously poor households.

The second diagram shows the second group of 'upward movers', which has about the same size as the first one. Altogether 22 households (= 45%) belong to this group. After a short period with low household income, these households apparently overcome their poverty status. In the last two years of the observation period nearly all of them command an income which is above the 60% poverty line.

Continuously poor households

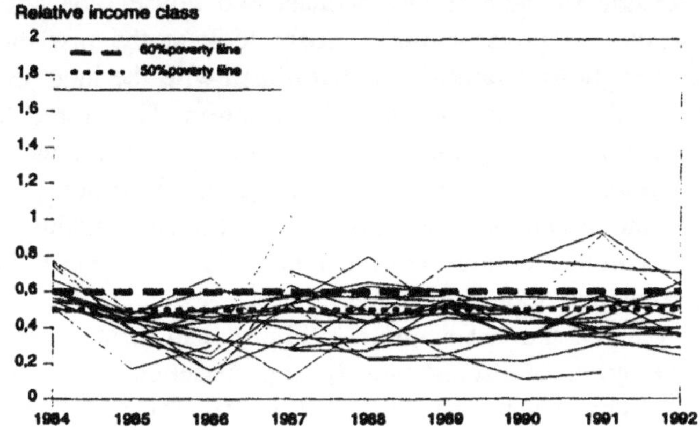

Upward movers

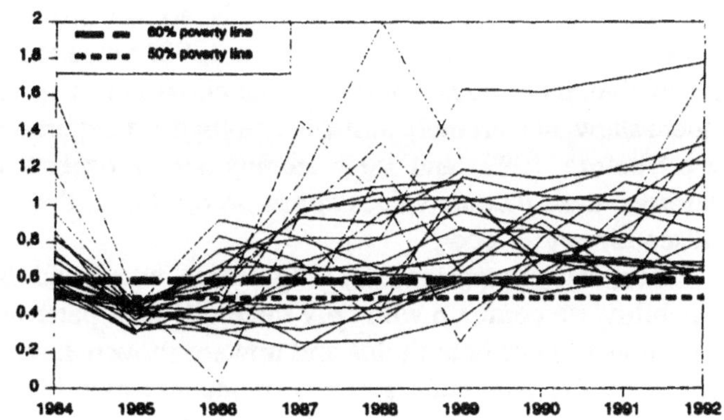

Discontinuously poor households

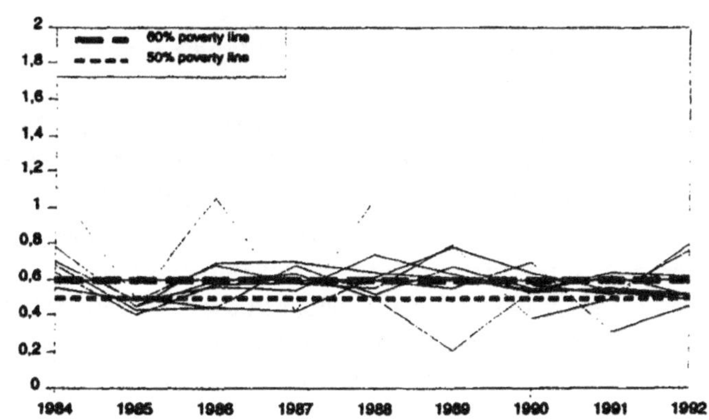

Figure 3 Income profiles

According to their income values, two households still seem to be in the proximity of poverty, but a closer look at the raw data shows that these surprisingly low values do not conform with the income development before 1991 and the other household information. Therefore, these two households were classified as upward movers, although their income data do not agree with the typical income profile of this group. It should be noted that (quick) quantitative analyses very often neglect such 'sensible' interpretation of the data within the household context. This is clearly an advantage of our interpretative approach.

Finally, the last diagram in Figure 3 illustrates the remaining and much smaller group of discontinuously poor households. Only 8 of all 49 households (= 16%) have been assigned to this group. Their income profiles show several increases above the 60% poverty line, but all of them fall back into their former poverty status. Again, three households do not strictly fit into this group according to their pure income data in 1992. Since they are above the 60% poverty line, these households could be classified as upwardly mobile. But all of them show an extremely unstable employment pattern within the observation period before 1992, and their employment prospects are rather negative. Therefore, their income values appear as outliers and we have classified them as discontinuously poor.

Thus, by comparing carefully single cases and including aspects of plausibility we come up with only three different patterns of income profiles. Continuously poor households and upward movers have about the same size. They form the two main patterns of income mobility. Compared to these, 'really' discontinuously poor households as a third pattern occur only very rarely.

4.2 A typology of poverty profiles and their causes

In the next step of our analysis we developed a typology of poor households with respect to the probable *causes* of their poverty profiles. Now we looked at the strategic variables of our theoretical model that are available in the GSOEP data (cf. the Appendix). Using this model as an interpretative guide line, we differentiated our three income groups into eight typical poverty profiles, which we call 'Idealtypen' (Weber), because they describe typical ways into and out of poverty. Before discussing the main features of this typology, we want to explain one idealtype in greater detail to illustrate the interpretative method used. We have called this idealtype the 'traditional family with older children'. It is a subgroup of the upward movers and consists of eight households. Again, these subgroups were formed by contrasting the case histories of single households across the strategic variables of our model. In the following, we describe the idealtype with an 'idealized' case history. This history includes characteristics of several empirical cases illustrating the distinct features of the idealtype in 'ideal' form. We call our 'traditional family with elder children' the Meyers.

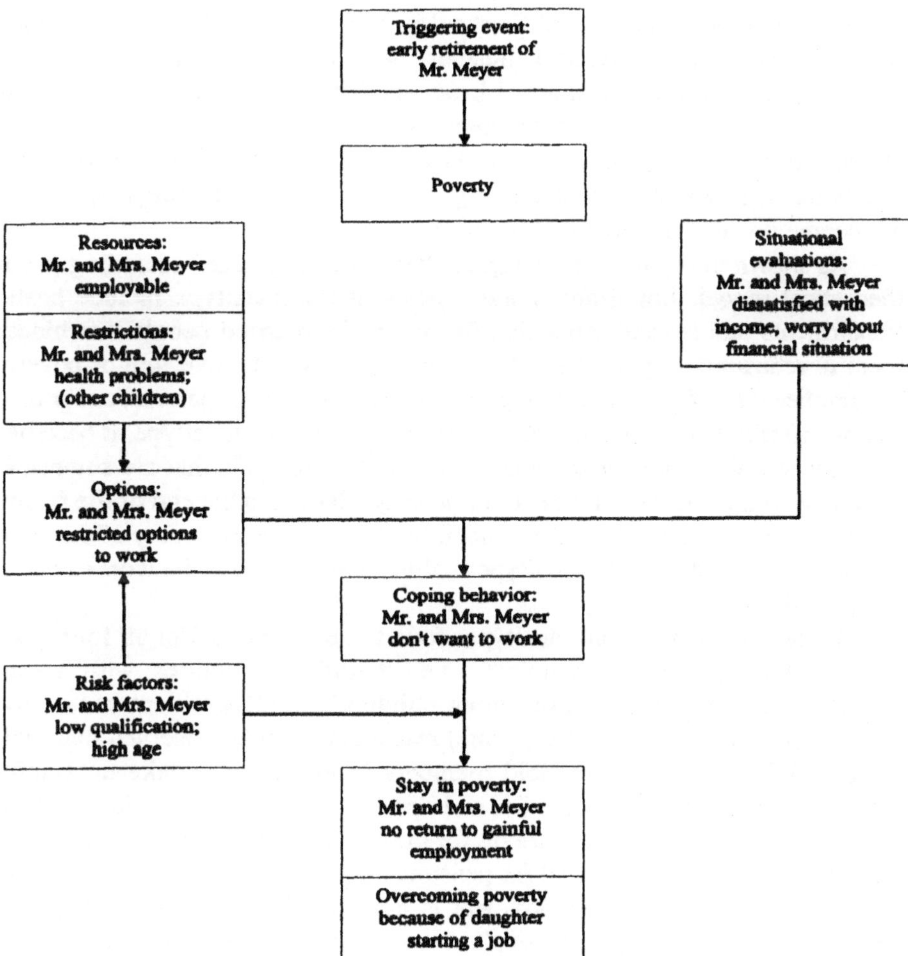

Figure 4 Our model including the data of the Meyer's

In 1985 Mr. and Mrs. Meyer are both 51 years of age and live together with two daughters, age 15 and 18. Until one year ago, Mr. Meyer was working as a bricklayer, now he has retired early on health grounds, and because of his missing earned income the family is relatively poor. Mrs. Meyer has not been gainfully employed since 1970, before that time she was employed as a childcare worker. The older daughter currently is completing an apprenticeship as a hairdresser, while the younger daughter still goes to school. Both, Mr. and Mrs. Meyer, are dissatisfied with their living standard and worry about their financial situation. Since both of them suffer from health problems, they are not looking for new jobs anymore. Besides their health impairments, their low qualifications and their ages are risk factors. They leave their poverty status indirectly when their younger daughter enters the labor market. At the age of 19, she starts a vocational training at a bank, and since her income adds to the family income - albeit in the beginning not dramatically - the Meyer's achieve an income position above the 60% poverty line.

As shown in Figure 4 these figures have been organized according to our theoretical model. Important characteristics of this idealtype include health impairments and several other risk factors of the married people that hinder them in returning to gainful employment. The 'upward move' out of poverty occurs, because of a child entering the labor market. Both parents, as far as it can be inferred from the data, remain passive. From this idealtype, it becomes apparent that there are certain phases within the life cycle that are somewhat favorable with respect to moves out of poverty. Here, it is the end of the family phase that allows upward financial mobility. After a short summary of the main characteristics of the other 'Idealtypen', this observation will be worked out in more detail.

Table 2 summarizes all idealtypes found in the sample. For all four types of continuously poor households - i.e. 'traditional families with young children', 'single mothers with young children', 'multi-problem cases' and 'pensioner households' - certain (time) restrictions can be observed that limit the possibilities of the household members to extend or to take up gainful employment: for traditional families and single mothers, the restrictions include children that have to be taken care of; for the 'multi-problem' households, they include health impairments; and for pensioner households, because of their age, the possibility of gainful employment is not a practical alternative anyway. Depending on their subjective evaluations of their financial situation, these household members are more or less ready to look for new jobs. Especially unemployed 'multi-problem' cases strive for gainful employment. The fact that they are not very successful in this respect during the observation period is un-

Table 2
A typology of poverty profiles

Income Profiles	Idealtypes	Typical characteristics (in1985)
continuously poor households	'traditional family with young children' (N=2)	couple; man: employed fulltime; woman: not employed; at least 1 child under 10; low qualifications
	'single mother with young child' (N=2)	single mother; not or part-time employed; at least one child under 10; low or middle qualifications
	'multi-problem case' (N=4)	single person, couple without children, single mother; between 50 and 55 years old; unemployed; low qualifications; health impairments
	'pensioner household' (N=7)	recipients of a pension; no children; at least 60 years old; low or middle qualifications
upward movers	'job beginner' (N=8)	household head under 30 years and in apprenticeship or studying; no children; low, middle or high qualifications
	'traditional family with older children' (N=8)	couple; man: employed fulltime; woman: not employed; all children at least 12 years old; low qualifications
	'transition into retirement' (N=2)	single person or couple; no children; no more fulltime employed; at least 56 years old; low qualifications
discontinously poor households	-- (N=7)	typical characteristics cannot be specified for this group
no typical income profile	'self-employed' (N=7)	household head: self-employed; low middle or high qualifications

derstandable because of the accumulation of risk factors within this idealtype. Typically, they have only low qualifications, have been unemployed for a long time, and are 50 years of age and older.

Also, in the case of the upward mobile households the theoretical model helps us to understand, why these households successfully overcome their poverty status. The 'job beginners', which are younger people entering the labor market in the observation period, are the only individuals in the sample that neither show any restrictions nor any risk factors (except low qualifications in some cases). Therefore, they succeed in overcoming poverty via the labor market more or less directly after finishing their education. Compared to this group, 'traditional families with older children' as well as those observed at the 'transition into retirement' show health impairments and some risk factors (e.g. a relatively high age in addition to low qualifications). Probably because of this - and in agreement with their partially positive evaluations of their financial situation - they are no longer prepared to work. They overcome poverty not based on efforts of their own: either along the traditional family cycle like the Meyer family or by going along the welfare path as with retirement.

The idealtype of the 'self-employed' comprises households that have only one thing in common: the employment status of the household head. Obviously, this type of employment can cause different income profiles: continuous and discontinuous poverty as well as leaving poverty permanently. Therefore, this idealtype is not a subgroup within the three income groups. When looking at the *cause* of the income profile in each case it turned out that it is the employment status of the household head that involves high poverty risks leading in some cases to persistent and in other cases to temporary poverty. Thus, this idealtype cannot be integrated into our typology of income profiles, although it identifies an important cause of poverty. Other discontinuously poor households besides the 'self-employed' differ very much from each other. Because of this heterogeneity a meaningful typology cannot be found for them. When looking at the strategic variables of our model, one will notice that they share some characteristics with the continously poor households in some phases of their career, but similarities with the upward mobile households can be observed in other phases.

4.3 Education and risks within the life cycle

When looking at the differences between successful escapers from poverty and the continuously poor households, it becomes clear that both groups can be distinguished more or less precisely according to life cycle. Obviously, there are favorable and unfavorable phases in the life cycle when the escape from or the persistence of poverty is highly probable. However, in a closer look it seems to be also necessary to distinguish different levels of education. For instance, individuals with higher education can only be found within the idealtype of 'job beginners' and (less often) within the 'self-employed'. In a life cycle perspective this means that quite generally there exists only one risky phase within the lives of higher educated individuals. This is the end of their educational career and their transition into the labor market. Given a successful mastery of this critical phase, additional poverty risks can hardly be observed for them, at least within the period covered by our data and as long as they do not start their own business.

However, for individuals with lower qualifications (a lower secondary school at maximum), several risky as well as favorable phases within their lives can be observed. This becomes evident when looking at the continuously poor and upward mobile idealtypes 'traditional family with young children', 'job beginner', 'traditional family with elder children', and 'pensioner'. Phases with high poverty risks seem to be childhood, the family phase (especially with a traditional division of labor between the spouses) and sometimes also the retirement phase. Favorable phases exist after entering the labor market from school (this is in analogy to the individuals with higher education) and at the end of the family phase. Thus far, there seems to be an association between poverty and life cycle or more precisely, between poverty and family cycle. Poverty (with a certain automatism) appears to be recurrent or more precisely: poverty risks vary cyclically within the life course, which does not necessarily mean that it affects the same individuals and households (remember that we cannot analyze the same households and individuals at different life phases within an observation period of only nine years).

Even if the remaining idealtypes - especially the 'single mother with young child' or the 'self-employed' - refer to poverty risks apart from the family cycle, our results suggest that observations made at the beginning of this century by the British poverty researcher Rowntree (1980) are still valid today for certain parts of the population. As mentioned in the introduction, Rowntree found that British working class men were not poor their whole lives, but only in some phases: as a child, as young parents, and as pensioners. In other phases of their lives they lived in comparative plenty. Thus periods of poverty and prosperity alternate. On the basis of the results of our study and in analogy to Rowntree, one could therefore draw a sort of present-day poverty cycle, which would apply for individuals with low qualifications living the traditional family cycle.

5 Discussion

Some people, most prominently the followers of the individualization thesis, may object that the traditional family cycle, as such, diminishes while alternative forms of living, for instance single-parent families, increase. However, evidence from recent research on the sociology of the German family casts doubts on the general validity of these changes. The results indicate that the distribution of 'traditional' and 'alternative' forms of living varies with respect to social structure. According to Strohmeier (1993), individuals with low education make up the core of traditional life styles - in his terms: the traditional marriage with a housewife and a working husband (similar results based on qualitative milieu studies are reported by Burkart and Kohli 1992). For instance in 1989, 84% of all persons 30-34 years old with lower secondary school certificate were married, 75% had a least one child and about 44% practiced a traditional division of labor in the household. For the corresponding persons with higher education all of these percentages are about 20 or 30 percentage points lower. Strohmeier interpretes these data as the result of a polarization process between a more or less stable family sector on the one side and an individualized non-family sector on the other side. According to Strohmeier, this polarization develops on the basis of still existing vertical inequalities, i.e. differences with respect to education.

While our results show clear effects of the family and the employment cycle on poverty risks, this does not necessarily exclude explanations that refer to the individualization thesis. Both phenomena may coexist and some poverty processes may result from cyclically changing risks and chances, while others result from 'individualized' forms of living. But in order to examine the individualization hypothesis, its implications for poverty risks have to be spelled out more explicitly. At least two postulates can be formulated (cf. e.g. Leisering 1995, p. 71, p. 73):

1. Poverty is a temporary phenomenon.
2. Poverty has no social demarcation.

Our results neither confirm the first nor the second thesis in their totality. According to the income profiles observed, we could distinguish two groups of households: continuously poor households and escapers from poverty, both of about the same size. Discontinuously poor households are only a small minority. Especially when looking at the GSOEP income data in more detail on a case-by-case basis, one gets the impression that temporal heterogeneity may be a result of cursory quantitative analyses not controlling for measurement error (see also Rendtel, Langeheine and Berntsen 1992). Furthermore, if one interprets the results in connection with the concept of the family cycle, the life of some social groups appears as a roller coaster with ups and downs depending on the family cycle they happen to be in. This is especially true for people with low education. Besides their risk factor 'low education' and the corresponding unskilled jobs, they also 'choose' the more risk-filled life cycle: a traditional family with a housewife and an employed husband.

References

Andreß, H.J. (1996), 'Analysen zum unteren Einkommensbereich - Auf- und Abstiege, Ereignisse, Reaktionen und subjektives Wohlbefinden', in Zapf, W., Schupp, J., Habich, R. (eds.), *Lebenslagen im Wandel: Sozialberichterstattung im Längsschnitt*, Campus: Frankfurt, New York, pp. 321-347.

Andeß, H.J., Burkatzki, E., Lipsmeier, G., Salentin, K., Schulte, K., Strengmann-Kuhn, W. (1996), *Leben in Armut: Analysen der Verhaltensweisen armer Haushalte mit Umfragedaten*, unpublished research report for the German National Science Foundation: Bielefeld.

Beck, U. (1986), *Risikogesellschaft. Auf dem Weg in eine andere Moderne*, Suhrkamp: Frankfurt.

Becker, G.S. (1976), *The economic approach to human behavior*, University of Chicago Press: Chicago.

Berger, P. (1994), 'Individualisierung und Armut', in Zwick, M. (ed), *Einmal arm, immer arm? Neue Befunde zur Armut in Deutschland*, Campus: Frankfurt, pp. 21-46.

Berntsen, R. (1992), *Dynamik in der Einkommensverteilung privater Haushalte*, Campus: Frankfurt.

Burkart, G., Kohli, M. (1992), 'Liebe, Ehe, Elternschaft. Die Zukunft der Familie', in Chassé, K.A. (ed.) (1989), *Armut nach dem Wirtschaftswunder*, Campus: Frankfurt.

Chassé, K.A., Drygala, A., Schmidt-Noerr, A. (eds.) (1992), *Randgruppen 2000: Analysen zu Randgruppen und zur Randgruppenarbeit*, KT-Verlag: Bielefeld.

Filipp, S.H. (ed.) (1981), *Kritische Lebensereignisse*, Urban und Schwarzenberg: München.

Gerhardt, U. (1986a), 'Verstehende Strukturanalyse: Die Konstruktion von Idealtypen als Analyseschritt bei der Auswertung qualitativer Forschungsmaterialien', in Soeffner, H.-G. (ed.), *Sozialstruktur und soziale Typik*, Campus: Frankfurt, pp. 31-83.

Gerhardt, U. (1986b), *Patientenkarrieren: Eine medizinsoziologische Studie*, Suhrkamp: Frankfurt.

Gerhardt, U. (1991a), 'Krankheits- und Patientenkarieren', in Flick, U. et al. (eds.), *Handbuch qualitativer Sozialforschung*, Psychologie Verlags Union: München, pp. 312-316.

Gerhardt, U. (1991b), *Gesellschaft und Gesundheit. Begründung der Medizinsoziologie*, Suhrkamp: Frankfurt.

Goetze, D. (1952), 'Culture of Poverty - eine Spurensuche', in Leibfried, S., Voges, W. (eds.), *Armut im modernen Wohlfahrtsstaat*, Sonderheft 32 der Kölner Zeitschrift für Soziologie und Sozialpsychologie, pp. 88-103 .

Headey, B., Habich, R., Krause, P. (1990), *The duration and extent of poverty - is Germany a two-thirds-society*?, Arbeitspapier P90-103 der Arbeitsgruppe Sozialberichterstattung am WZB: Berlin.

Heinze, R.G., Hohn, H.W., Hinrichs, K., Olk, T. (1981), 'Armut und Arbeitsmarkt. Zum Zusammenhang von Klassenlagen und Verarmungsrisiko im Sozialstaat', *Zeitschrift für Soziologie*, Vol. 10, pp. 219-43.

Hill, R. (1949), *Families under stress*, Harper & Brothers: New York.

Lazarus, R.S., Folkman, S. (1987), 'Transactional theory and research on emotions and coping', *European Journal of Personality*, Vol. 1, pp. 141-169.

Leisering, L. (1995), 'Zweidrittelgesellschaft oder Risikogesellschaft? Zur gesellschaftlichen Verortung der "neuen Armut" in der Bundesrepublik Deutschland', in Bieback, K.J., Milz, H. (eds.), *Neue Armut*, Campus: Frankfurt, pp. 58-92.

Leisering, L., Voges, W. (1992), 'Erzeugt der Wohlfahrtsstaat seine eigene Klientel? Eine theoretische und empirische Analyse von Armutsprozessen', in Leibfried, S., Voges, W. (eds.), *Armut im modernen Wohlfahrtsstaat*, Sonderheft 32 der Kölner Zeitschrift für Soziologie und Sozialpsychologie, pp. 446-472.

Lewis, O. (1966), 'The culture of poverty', *Scientific American*, Vol. 215, pp. 19-25.

McCubbin, H.I., Patterson, J.M. (1983), 'The family stress process: The double ABCX model of adjustment and adaption', in McCubbin, H.I., Sussman, M.B., Patterson, J.M. (eds.), *Social stress and the family. Advances and developments in family stress theory and research*, The Haworth Press: New York, pp. 7-37.

Projektgruppe Panel (1993), 'Das Sozio-Ökonomische Panel (SOEP) nach zehn Jahren', *Vierteljahreshefte zur Wirtschaftsforschung* 1-2, pp. 27-42.

Rendtel, U., Langeheine, R., Berntsen, R. (1992), *Mobilitätsprozesse und Einkommensarmut. Erfragtes und errechnetes Haushalseinkommen im Vergleich*, Deutsches Institut für Wirschaftsforschung, Diskussionspapier Nr. 56: Berlin.

Rommelspacher, T. (1989), 'Kultur - Subkultur - Kultur der Armut?. Kritische Überprüfung einer Konzeption', in Breckner et al. (eds.), *Armut und Reichtum: Erscheinungsformen, Ursachen und Handlungsstrategien in ausgewählten Großstädten der Bundesrepublik*, Germinal: Bochum, pp. 93-110.

Salentin, K. (1996), 'Niedrigeinkommen: Psychische Belastung und Bewältigung', *Soziale Probleme*, Vol. 5, No. 1/2, pp. 31-59.

Schnell, R. (1991), 'Wer ist das Volk? Zur faktischen Grundgesamtheit bei "allgemeinen Bevölkerungsumfragen": Undercoverage, Schwererreichbare und Nichterreichbare', *Kölner Zeitschrift für Soziologie und Sozialpsychologie*, Vol. 43, pp. 106-137.

Schulte, K. (1995), *Wege aus der Armut - eine qualitative Analyse quantitativer Längsschnittdaten*, Unveröffentlichte Diplomarbeit an der Fakultät für Soziologie der Universität Bielefeld: Bielefeld.

Seebohm, R.B. (1980), *Poverty. A Study of Town Life*, Garland Publishing: New York, London.

Strohmeier, K.P. (1993), 'Pluralisierung und Polarisierung der Lebensformen in Deutschland', *Aus Politik und Zeitgeschichte* B17, pp. 11-22.

Voges, W., Buhr, P., Zwick, M. (1996), 'Einmal drin - immer drin? Sozialhilfebezug von Familien', in Behrens, J., Voges, W. (eds.), *Kritische Übergänge - Statuspassagen und sozialpolitische Institutionalisierung*, Campus: Frankfurt, New York, pp. 285-322.

Appendix Operationalization of the model with data from the German Socio-Economic Panel (GSOEP)

Components	Operationalization with GSOEP
Triggering event	*Events between panel waves (asked retrospectively):* Birth of a child Marriage Child left household Death of partner Separation from partner Partner moves into household Divorce *Changes in household/employment structure and income sources:* - *Household structure:* Household size Type of household Sex of household members Age of household members Family relation to household head Family status of household members - *Employment structure:* Employment status of household members Secondary activities of household members Further training of household members - *for employed household members:* job occupational status hours working over time - *for unemployed household members in working age:* unemployment - *Duration and net amount of all income sources (asked retrospectively):* Child allowance Housing allowance Assistance in special situations

	Assistance for continuous subsistence Income from rent Capital income Salaries and wages Income from self-employment Income from secondary activities Pensions/rents Education allowance Maternity benefits Unemployment benefits Private transfers
Poverty	Household income after taxes (screener) Relative income class (see text)
Resources	See employment structure above
Restrictions	Children in the household Household members needing permanent health care Reduction of earning capacity of household members (not asked 1990) Subjective evaluation of own health status (not asked 1988-1991)
Options	Does the household have mainpower reserves? (inferred from resources and restrictions)
Subjective evaluations	Satisfaction with household income Worries about financial situation of the household
Coping	- *for employed household members:* Wants to work how many hours - *for unemployed household members of working age:* Wants to get a new job When to start new job Wants to work how many hours
Risk factors	*for employable household members (see options):* Schooling, vocational training Reduction of earning capacity/subjective evaluation of health status (see above) Age/sex Earlier employment experiences Year of last employment Hours worked Cause of unemployment

Part Five
Problems of poverty research: Lessons from Italy and Russia

The expansion of poverty as a social cost of transition: A challenge for Russia

Vladimir Mikhalev

1 Introduction

The phenomena of inequality and poverty, to which even the most prosperous Western societies are not immune, have acquired a particular significance in the former centrally-planned economies which are now undergoing an unprecedented transition to a market economic system. Although the existence of poverty was acknowledged in the former Soviet Union and other East European countries as the crisis in their economies intensified by the end of 1980s, the radical transformation initiated in the early 1990s has been associated with an heretofore unknown increase in inequality and poverty. A deterioration in welfare caused by the economic collapse was exacerbated by austerity programmes introduced to achieve macroeconomic stabilisation. At the same time the processes of privatisation, the elimination of price controls, and the liberalisation of wage policies speeded up the process of income differentiation, introducing sharp contrasts between expanding poverty and concentrating wealth in the hands of only a few.

The severity and scope of problems related to the growth in poverty are possibly greatest in Russia, the largest economy in transition. The crisis of welfare here is complicated by the disintegration of the former Soviet Union associated with enormous economic and social costs. The complexity of these problems is also due to the large size of the country, which has extremely diverse regional economic and social conditions to contend with and a particularly hard situation in a number of large and economically depressed territories. The emergence of substantial poverty and the deterioration of social welfare present a serious challenge to the economic reforms and the process of democratisation. To date there has been an insufficient policy response in this regard.

It has proved extremely difficult to combine measures of financial stabilisation and structural reforms with the development of new welfare institutions. The old social security system has been eroding at too fast a rate for it to be replaced by a new one. Severe budget constraints and a high rate of inflation determined the priorities of monetary stabilisation over social protection, and therefore did not allow sufficient resources to be allocated to restore adequate levels of welfare. Adequate social policy responses are absolutely necessary to ensure the continuity of transition. In addition, a considerable amount of inconsistency in Russian policy-making - rendered even more complex by the confused relationship between the federal and local governments - has frequently disrupted the implementation of social policies. The lack of an effective safety net capable of alleviating the social hardships of the transition has been an important cause of growing popular disappointment, despair and even giving rise to the danger of social unrest. The results of the December 1995 parliamentary elections in Russia (where the communists won a majority of votes) and the collisions in the course of the presidential election campaign in 1996 provided a vivid evidence of the gravity of political backlashes against the reforms.

Research on poverty in Russia has recently attracted considerable attention from Russian governmental and academic institutions, and international organisations, primarily the World Bank (Word Bank 1995; Milanovic 1995). However, various poverty assessments demonstrate substantial differences in approaches and findings. In addition, new evidence being constantly introduced by rapid social changes, along with the appearance of new social survey data require further in-depth study. This paper analyses new available evidence with the aim to provide additional input for the understanding of the nature and dimensions of poverty in Russia as well as to the discussion on the available social policy options.

The analysis begins in Section 2 by reviewing the major trends in real incomes and inequality. Section 3 considers poverty thresholds applied as instruments of poverty measurement in Russia. Section 4 analyses evidence on the incidence of poverty and regional variations in its level. The final Section 5 focuses on the composition of poverty, with an attempt to identify who the poor are in Russia as well as what are the main causes that bring them into poverty.

2 The change in real incomes and growth in inequality

The economic collapse and difficulties of adjustment in Russia has had well-known consequences taking the form of a massive drop in industrial output and the appearance of unemployment. Combined with the effects of wage and price liberalisation, accompanied by high inflation, these adverse developments have resulted in a considerable fall in individual and household incomes. In the Russian case the erosion of incomes in general and of wages in particular has been aggravated by the unwillingness of the state to sustain the minimum wage and pay levels of the state budgetary sector employees.

Given the decentralisation of wage-setting, the official minimum wage has retained a very limited instrumental function and serves as a rigid benchmark only for that sector of the economy which is financed directly from the state budget. In addition, it is used to scale the level of several social benefits: family allowances, minimum unemployment benefits, social pensions (paid to those who have never worked), and disability pensions. The adjustment of the minimum wage has been irregular: from every three to four months in 1992-93 to once in seven months in 1994-95, and it has lagged well behind the rate of inflation. As a result, in real terms the minimum wage in 1995 amounted to only 20% of its 1991 level and was equal to only 7% of the average wage.

Since wage movements in the state budgetary sector comprising the government administration of the central and local levels, research, education, health care, and cultural services were determined by changes in the minimum wage, real wage levels there experienced an equally sharp decline. Correspondingly, the welfare of people depending on cash transfers scaled by the minimum wage were also similarly affected.

On average, however, the nominal wage level did not depend on the minimum wage trend as much as in the budgetary sector. In the privatised and newly emerging private sector wages were adjusted more frequently - approximately every two months. Nevertheless, the average real wage also declined quite significantly. Following price liberalisation of January 1992 the average wage fell to less than half its purchasing power of late 1991. Subsequently, real wages saw some recovery throughout 1992-93, attaining their highest levels at the end of each of the two years. However, these gains were neutralised significantly at the beginning of each subsequent year (1993 and 1994). In 1994 real wages barely kept up with inflation, so that by the end of 1994 they were still roughly half of their 1991 level. On the other hand, real GDP also declined considerably in this period of time. In 1995 the real wage experienced a further decline by nearly one quarter against the level of the previous year, so by early 1996 it was only worth about 40% of its level of the pre-reform time.[1]

Moreover, actually paid wages are even lower due to widespread wage arrears which amount to nearly one third of the overall wage bill, totalling some 4 billion dollars by early 1996. Only about 40% of workers are reported to be paid fully and on time. Wages paid in arrears varying in duration from two to six months, are not indexed, and so lost significantly in their value particularly since monthly inflation was running up to 20% in some months.

Profound changes in the process of wage formation since the beginning of the economic reforms have resulted in extremely diverse wage movements by sector, industry, and occupation, contributing greatly to an unprecedented increase in wages inequality (Mikhalev and Bjorksten 1995). The most striking phenomenon is that of the very low wage levels in the state budgetary sector, notably in education, research, social, cultural and health care services. The gap between wages in industry, on the one hand, and those in education, research, culture, and health care, on the other, increased from 1.4 times in 1991 to 1.7-2.3 times in 1992. Despite a subsequent narrowing of this difference, in 1995 earnings in the budgetary sector still amounted to no more than 60% of those in industry.[2] At the other extreme, earnings in the banking and insurance sector, a rapidly expanding area of new private entrepreneurship, are very high. Salaries there are about three times higher than in education or health services and twice the economy-wide average.

Within the industrial sector, wage differentials related to variations in enterprise economic performance or to the extent of monopolisation in the product markets are no less significant. The oil, gas, coal, and energy supply industries - which have the strongest market power - pay the highest wages. For example, the leading gas industry pays wages which are 3.3 times higher than the industrial average and 7.2 times higher than the currently depressed light manufacturing industry.[3] Workers in the transport and communications sector are also relatively better off, contrary to the troubled agricultural sector and engineering and textile industries. Unable to cope with massive inefficiencies and suffering from the drastic fall in demand, the latter three sectors have experienced a profound decline in output. Wages there are only half of the average in industry and are as low as those in the budgetary sector. The newly developing private sector generally pays much higher wages. However, it is also characterised by considerable instability, particularly in the small scale trade sector.

Another striking development of the transition is that professionals and engineers (who were traditionally underpaid in Russia) have suffered even more. Their wages have fallen to levels on average 1.2-1.3 times lower than those of low-skilled workers, due particularly to the very low earnings of teachers and medical staff. The majority of professionals are employed in the budgetary sector, which has the lowest pay levels. However, even in the private sector professionals do not earn much more than blue collar workers, reflecting the tradition of underpayment for high skills. Top managers form a group which has profited the most from economic independence, granted by the new status of their enterprises, both state-owned and privatised. Managers' salaries are on average 2.5-4 times higher than the wages of their employees.

The generally depressed wage level has stimulated the emergence of other sources of personal incomes, which have become available with the development of new forms of economic activity. Statistics show that real per capita monetary incomes are increasing faster than real wages. The share of wages in overall personal incomes decreased from 82% in 1992 to 60% in 1993, and to 47% in 1994 and 45% as estimated for 1995.[4]

In 1995 about 16% of the personal incomes in Russia originated from pensions, stipends, and other social benefits, which for the most part do not apply to the employed labour force; 38.5% of the total incomes is provided by entrepreneurship, dividends and interest earnings where the share of employed workers is presumably not very high compared to the entrepreneurial class (VCIOM 1994, No. 6, p. 33). Only about 5% of that amount is represented by the incomes of self-employed individuals, which in a number of cases may include some additional activities of the employed population. Probably more important for the workers is the expansion of secondary employment, which in 1994 was reckoned to be available to 12-15% of the work force, compared to 3.5% in 1991 (Commander et al. 1993; Mozhina et al. 1995, p. 55). It is important to bear in mind that those other sources of incomes besides cash wages can be underestimated by statistics as they are very difficult to monitor. Their real significance may be even higher than that shown by the above figures.

However, incomes from secondary employment are also distributed very unevenly. They constitute a twice larger share for those employed in the private sector as compared to the public sector employees (VCIOM 1994, No. 6, p. 33). Consequently, employees of the budgetary sector having the lowest wages are also disadvantaged in their access to secondary employment. All this evidence shows that despite the development of new multiple forms of economic activities generating alternative incomes, wages still account for the bulk of income for the majority, largely determining the overall change in living standards.

Incomes originating from major social benefits have not seen any increase in inequality, contrary to wages and other sources of incomes. The amount of public transfers available to individuals, on the contrary, moved closer to flat rates along with their devaluation by inflation. Old-age labour pensions form the core of the Russian social security system, determining social conditions for 80% of the total of 36 million pensioners, i.e. for 19.5% of the Russian population. This type of pension takes over half of all the expenditure on safety nets, the rest going on child allowances, sick pay, and other social benefits (Mikhalev 1996). The inability and unwillingness of the government to sustain the level of pensions and other benefits against the high inflation resulted in a sharp fall of their real value, while the increases in the statutory minimum pension were no more than one third of the rate of inflation. The difference between the minimum and maximum pension diminished while the proportion of pensioners on a higher pension decreased. In 1994 80% of pensioners received pensions which were equal to 1.0-1.5 times the minimum pension. During the first reform years most pensioners experienced a clear deterioration of their position relative to those in employment. The level of the average pension has declined from 39% of the average wage in 1990 to 35% in 1992-94, falling in certain periods to 25% of the average wage. Only in 1995 did this proportion regain its pre-reform level of 39% due to indexation of pensions.[5]

The considerable differentiation in income earning opportunities which has affected both money wages and other incomes has resulted in a sharp increase in incomes inequality. Although a certain amount of inequality was not unknown in Russia under the Soviet regime, the economic transition has seen income differentiation accelerate at a speed which is unprecedented, not only in Russia but also in most developed market economies. The structure of the income distribution stabilised only in 1995 when it had already acquired a very unequal configuration. Evidence available on the extent of inequality differs but all sources show a steep rise throughout 1992-1994. Gini coefficients calculated from Goscomstat data are 0.35 for 1992, 0.40 for 1993, 0.41 for 1994 and 0.39 for 1995 showing a dramatic increase up from 0.26 for 1990.[6] Although measurements based on the Goscomstat data may have well-known drawbacks, including an incomplete account of certain forms of incomes, e.g. from various informal economic activities, they underestimate rather than overstate the extent of inequality. It is primarily the highest incomes that statistics are unable to monitor properly.

Thus, although the measures of inequality for the pre-reform period may well have been understated, it quite likely applies to the current situation even more as sources for unreported high earnings have multiplied. This assumption is confirmed by alternative calculations, for example by the Russian Longitudinal Monitoring Survey (RLMS) and the Russian Centre for Public Opinion Research (VCIOM) survey results which show higher rates of income inequality than those given by Goscomstat.[7] RLMS data yielded a Gini coefficient of 0.49 as of the end of 1993 while in the VCIOM sample it was 0.46 for March 1994 (World Bank 1995, p. 30). These measures of income inequality fall within the range of countries characterised by a strongly unequal income distribution, such as Argentina or the Philippines, and are much higher than levels in Western Europe.

The above evidence may be supported by data on the distribution of income between deciles. The ratio of the first and the ninth deciles, the decile coefficient, increased from 2.82 in early 1992 to 4.69 in 1993 (McAuley 1994, p. 23). The gap between the top tenth decile and the bottom first has increased even more dramatically: from 3.4 times in 1991 to 4 in 1992 and 14.3 times in 1994 decreasing somewhat to 13.5 in 1995.[8] These indicators of general income inequality are closely interrelated with the increased disparity between social and occupational groups originating from the differentiation of wages and other incomes by sector, industry and occupation as described above. In addition, it is important to mention here that economic inequality has a significant regional dimension.

There was also a dramatic increase in differentiation in per capita income levels by region. This has been largely determined by the greater inter-industry wage differentials, primarily because of high earnings in the oil and gas industry dominating the economic structure of certain regions, for instance Tumen oblast in Northwest Siberia. In contrast there are depressed regions affected by industrial decline. Among these are Ivanovo and Vladimir oblast in Central Russia and the Republics in the Volga region -Chuvashia, Mordovia, and Mariy-El dominated mainly by light and engineering industries as well as by agriculture, which all have the lowest wage levels. Predominantly agricultural areas like Stavropolsky krai, the Tambov and Bryansk oblasts as well as Northern Caucasus Republics are also among the poorest.

Local price levels and the general cost of living do not always match the level of wages, such disparities contributing to greater gaps in regional per capita real incomes. The ratio of real per capita income between the richest and the poorest regions increased from 8.36 in 1992 to 42 in 1994 (World Bank 1995, p. 31). Due to diverse wage and price movements the regions of the North, Siberia, and the Far East, which used to have the highest nominal incomes because wages there were increased by special regional coefficients applied to compensate for harsh climatic conditions, nowadays show a significant diversity in real income levels. For example, regions such as Magadan, Kamchatka, and Yakutia (Saha), or Krasnoyarsky krai and Komy Republic fall within the richest group while the Chitinskaya, Amurskaya oblasts, and Primorsky krai - which are geographically in the same or similar area - have the lowest income levels.

The tremendous drop in incomes combined with their much more uneven distribution has resulted in an expansion of massive poverty. However, poverty measurements and the identification of categories of the poor present a serious theoretical and practical problem which is complicated by rapid social change, instability of incomes and difficulties in their monitoring. Thus drawing an appropriate poverty line as both an analytical and political instrument acquires particular significance.

3 The poverty line definition

The need for adequate policy responses has stimulated considerable activity on poverty research in Russia. Due to the sharp fall in incomes and the severity of extreme poverty this research as well as practical policy making were mainly based on an approach focusing on the absolute rather than relative concept of poverty. One of the first results of those efforts has been the introduction of a new poverty line - the subsistence minimum, which has replaced the old minimum consumption budget of pre-reform times (Popkin, Mozhina and Baturin 1994). The core of this forms a basket of food items corresponding to the WHO and the FAO nutritional recommendations. This basket differs for children, the able-bodied and pensioners. On average the subsistence minimum provided for 57% of individual income to be spent on food, which is much higher as compared to poverty lines applied in other countries.[9] For pensioners this proportion was 73% of their income.

The official subsistence minimum regarded by the Russian Ministry of Labour as a poverty line has a number of advantages as an instrument for empirical poverty research. It is regularly published by the State Committee of Statistics (Goscomstat) with a monthly adjustment to the rate of inflation. Thus it is the most easily available and convenient indicator for calculating the headcount poverty index, i.e. the proportion of the population below the poverty line. The latter is also regularly published by Goscomstat and is based on their monitoring of household incomes.[10]

It is important to bear in mind that poverty lines and measurement can never be entirely objective and value-free. The official poverty line in Russia is criticised as inadequate from several points of view: for instance, for being too low (with the share of income spent on food too high), or, on the contrary, too generous. The subsistence minimum was calculated as a temporary definition designed for the conditions of acute economic crisis. It was expected to be used for about one year to help to overcome the initial most difficult stage of transition. As the economic situation did not radically improve, the subsistence minimum remained as both a statistical and a political instrument for much longer. Meanwhile, the subsistence minimum allowed a clearly insufficient proportion of personal income to be spent on clothes, footwear, medicines and services, and virtually nothing on consumer durables. Of course it was absolutely inadequate, especially in a situation when prices for these goods were soaring. People affected by poverty were forced to refrain from purchases of most non-food consumer items. If they were able to survive through the first reform year of 1992, the perpetuation of such a situation through 1993-95 has made their position much worse, and the need for warm clothes and other essential goods has become more acute. Moreover, the sale of housing and public utilities at market prices has raised the share of rent as well as that of bills for water, electricity, and the telephone from the earlier 3-5 to 15-20% of an average family budget, with particularly adverse effects on the poor. The Government's plan is to eliminate completely housing and utility subsidies by 1998. The population will then have to pay the full market cost of housing rents and utilities.

Another limitation of the use of the aggregate official subsistence minimum lies in the wide regional differences in the cost of living. From this perspective empirical research is facilitated by regionally adjusted subsistence minimums which are estimated by the regional governments. In doing so most regions follow a uniform Ministry of Labour methodology which simplifies interregional comparisons. Nonetheless some regions (oblast), for example, Moscow, have departed from this recommended methodology and adopted standards that are twice as high. In the case of Moscow this is justified by the much higher costs of many essential goods and services. For instance, a monthly ticket for urban transportation (metro, buses, trams, etc.) costs 180,000 rubles, or 37% of the January 1996 country-wide monthly subsistence minimum of 485,000 rubles. Thus for certain regions not only should the cost of the uniform minimal basket of consumption items be adjusted to local price levels; its composition should also be revised in accordance with specific territorial conditions.

Another objection to the use of the subsistence minimum as an instrument of poverty measurement relates to the role of household assets in real consumption. It is understood that in the particular case of Russia, money income does not give a complete measure of real consumption. While it is true that the majority of households, even those affected by poverty, have some accumulated assets which help them to survive, money income still seems to be an adequate indicator of current trends in poverty. Household assets have depreciated considerably over the past five years, during which time the poor have been unable to replace them. In addition, markets allowing those assets to be sold or leased, and thus to help a family make ends meet, are still underdeveloped. Savings were also wiped out by inflation unless people kept them at home in foreign hard currency. However until 1992 to keep foreign currency was illegal and also practically difficult to get and exchange, so such cases were relatively rare.

The above consideration is closely related to the issue of economies of scale in household consumption. It is widely believed that it costs less than twice as much to support two individuals as it does to support one. However, since the cost of common goods (such as rent, heating, and so on) in the budget of poor families in Russia is small, neglecting economies of scale in consumption for the purposes of poverty research may not introduce a great distortion (McAuley 1994, p. 33).

More important is to take into account various non-money forms of support or incomes from informal activities available to many families. There is good reason to expect that this part of real incomes is not adequately captured by statistics. To overcome this difficulty it would be useful to look at household expenditures as a measure of real consumption. Such data have become available from the Russian Longitudinal Monitoring Survey initiated by the World Bank. According to these reports household expenditure exceeds reported income, so, where possible, it would be useful to compare the RLMS expenditure data with the income statistics. Furthermore, the RLMS has examined the extent of private inter-household transfers as a means of an informal safety net (Cox, Eser and Jimenez 1995). Such estimations may be useful to make adjustments to the incidence of poverty obtained through the Goscomstat income statistics.

Dissatisfaction with the official poverty line has also stimulated attempts to design alternative poverty lines, some of which have been based on individuals' subjective measures of poverty, i.e. have been similar to the Leiden School approach (Hagenaars and van Praag 1985). In Russia the subjective approach is used for surveys of public opinion, particularly those carried out by VCIOM (the Russian Centre for Public Opinion Research). The results of such surveys are heavily influenced by the specific situation of Russia where the average income has fallen sharply against a rapidly growing income disparity and the emergence of wealthy groups of the population. In their individual perceptions of a sufficient income, people naturally refer to standards typical of their previous rather than their current circumstances as well as to the living standards of the newly prosperous elites. A sensitivity analysis of this type, accounting for individual perceptions of how much income is needed to provide for a minimum subsistence, yields a subjective poverty line which is 1.5-2 times higher than the official subsistence minimum.

Where the poverty line is drawn is largely a question of policy, and for the design of policy responses an approach based on the official poverty line is appropriate. From a political perspective any decision to move the poverty line up or down, even slightly, would imply including or excluding a significant number of Russians from being poor and, hence, from being the target of social assistance. Meanwhile the proper targeting of the group affected by poverty - as that in most acute need of aid - is a key issue for the design of adequate safety nets. Drawing the poverty line too high, e.g. by including more than half of the population, actually means refusing to implement realistic poverty-relief programs. If the official poverty line is too high from the point of view of feasibility of social assistance, it is useful to look at that group in desperate need whose income is half or less than half the official subsistence minimum.

4 The incidence of poverty

Much evidence suggests that the incidence of poverty in Russia has increased since the beginning of the economic transition in 1992. However, the various approaches and poverty lines applied yield different estimates of the number of people affected by poverty. An assessment based on the official Ministry of Labour methodology (average subsistence minimum poverty line) and published by the Russian State Committee of Statistics (Goscomstat) offers the longest available time series. The headcount poverty index more than doubled in 1992, immediately after the initiation of price liberalisation.

A further trend in the headcount poverty ratio throughout 1992-1995 is more difficult to ascertain due to the considerable variations caused by substantial fluctuations in the monthly rate of inflation. Quarterly aggregates show a still higher number for 1993 as compared to 1992, and a decrease in 1994 with a subsequent sharp rise in early 1995 followed by a downward trend further throughout the year (Table 1). An estimate for the end of 1995 yields roughly 20% of the population or about 30 million individuals with incomes below the official subsistence minimum.[11]

Table 1
Quarterly poverty rates

Year	Headcount ratio (per cent)				Number (millions)			
	Q 1	Q 2	Q 3	Q 4	Q 1	Q 2	Q 3	Q 4
1992	26.8	23.9	18.9	15.7	39.9	35.5	28.1	23.3
1993	33.0	29.0	34.0	28.0	49.0	43.0	50.4	41.6
1994	25.3	25.1	23.1	21.4	37.5	37.2	34.4	31.8
1995	30.4	28.5	24.0	20.3	45.1	42.2	35.6	30.2

Sources: *Izvestia*, 14 February 1996; *Informatsionniy statisticheskiy bulleten N 13* (Informational Statistical Bulletin No. 13), Moscow, Goscomstat, November 1995, p. 30; *Obzor economki Rossii, III, 1994* (Review of the Russian Economy, Third Quarter 1994), Moscow: Working Centre for Economic Reform under the Government of the Russian Federation, 1994, p. 81

It is typical of the Russian press as well as of Russian and western academic experts to express scepticism towards the Goscomstat numbers on the incidence of poverty. A common line of argument claims that the Goscomstat statistics underscore the real incidence of poverty for at least two reasons. Firstly, the applied minimum of subsistence is inadequate and needs to be adjusted to changes in consumer price structure. i.e. to the relative increase in the cost of essential non-food consumer goods and services including medicines, housing rents, utilities, and transportation among other things, which used to occupy only a small share of household expenditures.

Secondly, there are doubts about the representativeness of the sample of the family budget survey from which Goscomstat derives its estimates. It is alleged that the sampling frame and the methods through which the sample was drawn biased the average income upwards. Such a bias originates from a disproportionate inclusion of higher income groups into the sample (Braithwaite 1994, p. 8). Indeed, in a situation where the highest quintile of the income distribution receives half of all income, two thirds of that amount going to the top 10% of income earners, the average per capita income does not correspond to a real living standard of the majority. If the top 20% of incomes were excluded from the sample, the average income of the remaining 80%

would be 1.5 times lower. This consideration, however, is only relevant to the ratio of the incomes of the poor to the average per capita income, implying that the real median income groups of the population are poorer than shown by statistics.

Another common argument against the subsistence minimum on which Goscomstat bases its headcount poverty index is that it contrasts sharply with the population's perception of how much income a family needs to live on. Respondents in the June 1995 VCIOM survey suggested an amount of 367,000 rubles a month (US $ 80.9 at the prevailing exchange rate), i.e. 1.5 times higher than the official poverty line of 277,400 rubles (US $ 61).[12] In June 1994 the same difference was more than twice (194,000 rubles against 92,000 rubles; World Bank 1995, p. 18). These poverty rates based on subjective estimates are therefore much higher than Goscomstat figures. Based on nine surveys by VCIOM realised in 1993, Tatyana Zaslavskaya estimated the incidence of poverty in Russia as high as 54% of the population (VCIOM 1994, No. 2, p. 5.). A later study by VCIOM in 1994 revealed 58% of the respondents in the sample living in conditions of poverty (VCIOM 1994, No. 4, p. 25.). A 1995 VCIOM survey yielded a number exceeding 80% of the population.[13] Although useful for a general assessment of the social situation, such estimations cannot provide a meaningful guide for social policy-making.

An opposite line of criticism against the Goscomstat estimates of the poverty rate maintains that the family budget survey on which those calculations are made do not fully account for the supplementary incomes available to households, or that they underestimate economies of scale in household consumption. Survey data reveal that only about one in five Russian households relies solely upon the wage at the main job or on transfers received from the system of social protection. Over 80% of families undertake additional activities to improve their well-being. A 1994 survey 'Family and Society' carried out by the Research Institute on Family, the Ministry of Social Protection, and the Russian Peace Fund revealed that only 17.6% of Russian families do not undertake any additional activities to earn a supplementary income; 12.6 of respondents had a permanent second job, 23.4% took on occasional supplementary jobs, 35.7% sought various forms of self-subsistence, and 53.7% gained incomes in kind from their country plots.[14] These subsidiary incomes are not properly accounted for by the Goscomstat in the family budget survey.

It is worth mentioning, however, that, as becomes clear from the above data, a stable source of secondary income is still available to a minority. Most activities in the informal sector represent poorly remunerated jobs located mainly in the service sector. Only for 7% of respondents with a second job in a VCIOM survey did it provide more than half of the household income (World Bank 1995, p. 29), while in 6% of the poor households the breadwinner worked at two jobs still being unable to raise his family income above the poverty line (VCIOM 1994, No. 4, p. 25). For poorer households it is more typical to rely on various forms of self-support in kind, which may alleviate rather than radically improve their position.

According to the RLMS, even with access to a private plot a household is only 7.3% less likely to be poor, which implies that for an absolute majority home food production cannot offer a way out of poverty (World Bank 1995, p. 32). A survey by the Moscow Institute of Socio-Economic Studies of the Population (abbreviated in Russian as ISEPN) conducted in 1992 in four Russian cities found out that for an average household in an urban area, where three in four Russians live, income gained from a country plot in kind forms only 4.3% of the family income (Mozhina et al. 1994, p. 18). For the majority these recently acquired tiny plots of 600 square meters require substantial effort and investment rather than generating any significant income. According to the second October 1993 round of the ISEPN survey, the cost of inputs into such country plot production averaged 42.5% of the total value of the output. The cost of travel (let alone time spent) to a 'dacha' (the Russian word for a summer house), particularly significant in large metropolitan areas due to longer distances (up to 150-200 km), should also be taken into account.

Thus the actual significance of the income gained from a plot becomes at least two times smaller than even the modest proportion shown by the above ISEPN survey figure. It is also worth mentioning that this kind of food production cannot at all be regarded as efficient, nor is it a rational way of adjustment to economic hardships. It looks rather like an archaic means of self-subsistence through naturalisation of consumption, which is hardly consistent with the very essence of market-oriented transition. The above consideration would challenge this bias for overstating the importance of country plots for consumption of Russian households, which is common to publications of many Western experts. Moreover, a commonly available means of self-support would hardly compensate for the loss of income induced by the massive delay in wage payments, the effect of which is not properly accounted for by Goscomstat either.

Private transfers through family networks or from friends and neighbours make up another source of aid available to many poor households. In Russia, as in many other countries, private safety nets act as the most important means of poverty relief. Although such transfers do not go exclusively to lower income families, they benefit such vulnerable groups as new households, elderly pensioners, female-headed households with many children, the disabled, and those affected by unemployment. According to the RLMS data, private transfers averaged 40% of the recipient households income and brought poverty rates down 10 percentage points as compared to households which were not involved in private safety networks (World Bank 1995, p. 51). Intra-family transfers are much more important than assistance based on non-family ties. Although transfer behaviour tended to persist during the difficult reform years despite high inflation, the decline in incomes, and the rise in inequality, its pattern is now undergoing changes. In the pre-reform years transfers were typically received by younger families from their better-off parents. Nowadays it has became more common for elderly pensioners to get support from their children, including especially those engaged in new private businesses. In the latter case particularly, the recipients of such transfers are much less likely to represent a low income or vulnerable group.

In addition to the supplementary incomes, means of self-support, and private transfers underestimated in Goscomstat statistics, there are possible economies of scale in household consumption which are not captured in the MOL subsistence minimum used as a poverty line. Substantial economies in consumption may occur as the size of the household increases. For poorer households, however, significant economies of scale are less likely because their consumption pattern is largely dominated by foodstuffs, but this factor may become more meaningful with a further increase in housing and utility prices.

To make up for the above deficiencies the RLMS approach suggested using household expenditures as a better measure of living standards rather than reported nominal incomes. However, the RLMS expenditure-based headcount poverty index for individuals does not prove to be too different from the pattern emerging from Goscomstat estimates. Moreover, the RLMS expenditure data yields an incidence of poverty which is even higher than Goscomstat numbers: 26.2% for July-September 1992, 36.9% for June-September 1993 and 30.9% for October 1993 - February 1994. Hence this evidence does not confirm the hypothesis that Goscomstat overstates the rate of poverty or that the real consumption of the poor is higher than shown by income statistics. For all this, the Goscomstat per capita income data may be regarded as an acceptable approximation for the purpose of estimating poverty rates.

The Goscomstat poverty rates can also be compared with those given by Milanovic, who sets the poverty line used for international comparisons at US $ 120 a month multiplied by the 1990 local currency purchasing power parity

(PPP). This method is used to obtain the local currency poverty line equivalent for 1990. That number is then adjusted to the country's cost of living to obtain poverty lines for the subsequent years. The poverty line acquired by such a method for Russia is slightly higher than the Russian MOL subsistence minimum. According to this PPP methodology, the poverty rate in 1993 was 21%, or well below the Goscomstat number (31%) (Milanovic 1995, p. 15-16). A similar estimate for the pre-reform period of 1987-88 reveals only 2% of the population in poverty. Thus the PPP poverty rate estimates offer a much more optimistic picture differing from all other estimations based on different methods. It is also worth mentioning that the same approach yielded surprisingly low poverty rates for several other countries in transition (data for 1992-93): 17% in Romania, 16% in Poland, 12% in Ukraine (to compare with 41% in Belarus where conditions in the same period were not too different), 2% in Hungary, 1% in Slovakia, less than 1% in the Czech Republic and 0% in Slovenia, the latter known for a high level of unemployment (Milanovic 1995, p. 16). Discrepancies of the above figures with the other available evidence may thus call into question the validity of the PPP methodology for poverty rate estimates.

As has been mentioned in Section 2, living standards differ widely in the geographically extensive and diverse Russian regions. This differentiation becomes more evident in the course of the transition due to the growing disparity in regional economic and social conditions. A sample survey by the Ministry of Social Protection (MOSP) undertaken in October 1994 - February 1995 revealed drastic variations in the incidence of poverty, ranging from 72% for Astrakhan oblast to 17% for Magnitogorsk city in the Urals region. The poverty rates are highest in the mainly agricultural regions followed by regions dominated by light manufacturing, machine building, and armaments industries. Poverty is much less acute in regions rich in natural resources, particularly in those producing oil and gas.[15]

Sharp contrasts in living standards and poverty rates exist not only between large regions but are essentially associated with type of residence: large cities, small towns, or rural areas. The incidence of poverty in smaller towns was higher than in the regional centres in five out of the nine regions in the MOSP survey. Higher incomes increasingly concentrate in the largest cities which become major centres for the development of new private businesses, the commercial and banking sectors, while the transformation of the economic structures in smaller settlements is impeded by the underdevelopment of a necessary infrastructure. Smaller towns suffer more from the decline of local industrial enterprises which are unable to adjust to new economic conditions as there are significantly fewer opportunities in the regional labour markets compared to large metropolitan areas, while labour mobility is hindered by many economic and social factors, not least by the lack of available housing and the housing market. The ISEPN 1993 survey of four Russian cities revealed that in the small town of Vyazniki a second job was available to 5% of the local labour force, while in the metropolis of St. Petersburg and the medium-sized regional centres of Petrozavodsk and Astrakhan secondary employment extended to 20% of all workers (Mozhina et al. 1995, p. 43).

Rural residents in general found themselves considerably disadvantaged in the new economic situation. The cuts in subsidies to the agricultural sector combined with the strongly negative effect of price liberalisation on inefficient farming led most farmers to particularly difficult financial straits. Price increases for energy, agricultural machinery, and industrial inputs considerably raised the cost of agricultural products and undermined their competitiveness. The terms of trade changed dramatically in favour of urban residents. Agricultural producers faced demand constraints and intense competition from imports on the product markets. The incomes of farmers and farm employees fell more sharply in comparison with industrial workers. Economic hardships do not allow outdated machinery and farm equipment to be replaced. For all these reasons many regions experienced a profound decline in farm production. Some regions have considerable hidden unemployment in agriculture, resulting in a loss of wage income for the affected farm workers. Rural areas are also disadvantaged in possibilities for alternative employment and hence sources for additional incomes. Thus opportunities for the rural population to improve their well-being are extremely limited. In addition, there is a widespread collapse of infrastructure and social services in rural areas, which has always been far inferior to those of the cities. Rural poverty, however, is less acute in fertile regions which are used for intensive farming, allowing household food production to provide adequate food products for rural families. This is a case evident from the survey data on Oryol oblast (located in the fertile Black Soil area) where the incidence of rural poverty was nearly twice as low than in the oblast centre city of Oryol. Such self-subsistence virtually does not produce any cash income, so the livelihood of households in such regions may consist entirely of consumption of the harvest collected from private plots.

The headcount incidence of poverty, although extremely high in a number of regions, does not give a full picture of the severity of the problem as it does not say anything about the depth of poverty. Russian statistics also offer estimates of the poverty gap ratio with the intention of showing how deep poverty runs. The poverty gap is defined as an aggregate deficit of the income of the poor, needed to bring them up to the poverty line. It is expressed as a percentage of total income. There are also estimates of poverty shortfall as a percentage of GDP (Table 2).

Table 2
The poverty gap

Year	Poverty gap as per cent of income	Poverty gap as per cent of GDP
1991	2.03	0.53
1992	5.80	1.50
1993	8.40	3.10
1994	3.70	2.50
1995	5.40	3.30
Jan. 1996	4.00	...

Sources: Braithwaite 1994, Tab. 1; *Socialno-economcheskoye polozhenie Rossiiskoi Federatsii v yanvare-iyune 1995 goda* (The Economic and Social Situation of the Russian Federation in January-June 1995), Moscow: Goscomstat, 1995, p. 139.

The country-wide poverty gap more than doubled in 1992 and nearly doubled again in 1993. The intensity of poverty fell markedly in 1994 but this improvement was not maintained since in 1995 the poverty gap grew again. The end of 1995 and the beginning of 1996 demonstrated new signs of improvement, showing an overall decline in the gap.

The above estimates of the poverty gap may question the view suggested by Milanovic that poverty in Russia is 'shallow'. Milanovic asserts that despite the high numbers, the poor in Russia, as in other East European countries, do not represent a clear 'underclass' as, for instance in Latin America (Milanovic 1995, p. 27-28). The income of an average poor person in the transition economies is some 20% below the poverty line, while in Latin America it is 40% below the poverty line. Milanovic rightly points out that the poor still possess substantially high educational levels, reasonable dwellings, and household assets, and enjoy access to major social services, including schooling for children and health care, all of which does not differ them too much from the rest of the population. The decline in their income is still recent and looks as though it is a transitory shock.

There are doubts, however, that economic growth may easily provide 'trickle down' effects to pull large numbers of the poor up above the poverty line. Growth may not necessarily yield a desirable effect, allowing adequate levels of welfare to be restored. In Poland - which has had growth for three years - the poverty rate has remained the same and levels of inequality have increased. Poland's experience may be particularly instructive for Russia. Milanovic has made an attempt to distinguish factors that have contributed to the increase in poverty, specifying an overall decline in output and income, a rise in inequality, and demographic change (Milanovic 1995, p. 20). It appears that for Russia the major cause of the increase in poverty has been the rise in inequality, which has proved to be more than twice as significant as the fall in income. This analysis suggests that economic growth alone in Russia will not be sufficient to achieve a reverse trend in the incidence and intensity of poverty.

If it takes too long for output to recover or growth is not accompanied by a decrease in inequality, the welfare of the poor is unlikely to improve. When poverty persists over a longer time span the poor may lose their human capital and gradually acquire characteristics which differ from the rest of the population and which will make their path out of poverty still more difficult. The likelihood of such a prospect presents a particularly serious challenge to social policy-makers. Appropriate income distribution policies and social safety nets are vitally necessary. The success of their design and implementation largely depends on how they address the major determinants of poverty and take into account the social and demographic composition of the population affected by it; this is the subject to which we will turn in the next section.

5 The composition and determinants of poverty

The expansion of massive poverty in Russia has been largely induced by new factors which were unknown in the times of Soviet rule. Poverty - which in the pre-reform period was limited to certain vulnerable categories of the population - has extended to social groups which used to be securely protected against the principal social risks. At the same time poverty among the traditionally poor groups has also intensified.

During the Soviet period for a household with two working family members there was virtually no risk of poverty. However, the income of only one working adult was often inadequate to support a family due to low wage levels and the official income levelling policy. This situation put at particular risk single-parent families or large families with more than three children or with other dependants (for instance, a disabled family member) as well as mainly young families where one of the parents was temporarily not working (often on maternity leave). Social benefits designed for these disadvantaged categories of the population, including maternity and child care allowances, disability pensions and certain forms of assistance provided to single-parent and large families, were barely sufficient to raise living standards up to the level of subsistence. Of these categories young families with small children normally found themselves in temporary difficulty only and they frequently received support from their parents. These difficulties were usually overcome with the resumption of regular employment, which was facilitated by the widespread provision of pre-school child care.

Pensioners on a low pension living alone were another high risk category as such pensions were unable to provide for a minimal level of subsistence. This risk was also high for people on disability pensions as in most cases those were relatively low. This group, however, represented a smaller number among pensioners since the majority had either a larger pension, or lived together with their children, being supported by them, or remaining employed and receiving both a pension and a salary.

Some families were also comprised of wage earners in poorly-paid occupations, including employees in the retail trade, primary education, some branches of light industry as well as lower-skilled medical staff and cultural (for instance, library and social club) workers. These branches of the economy were mainly occupied by women, so the low pay level did not necessarily cause poverty in dual-parent families with a male-household head earning a sufficient income. However, there was a higher risk of poverty for female-headed single-parent households. Finally, there has always been a small group of homeless and recently institutionalised population with the highest risk of poverty due to significant disadvantages for them in finding jobs which would provide them with housing.

The above groups of the so-called 'old poor' have found themselves in an even more disadvantaged situation under the new circumstances. They constitute a substantial part of those affected by poverty, as can be seen from evidence on the demographic and social composition of the poor, for both individuals and households (Table 3). In October 1993 the total amount of the poor were formed by children (28.4%), working age adults (52.5%, among them 17.4% women aged 30 to 55, 17.7% young adults aged 16 to 30, and 17.4% men aged 30 to 60), and individuals of pensionable age (19.8%). According to the 1995 MOSP regional survey data, 60 to 90% of the poor by household were represented by families with children, while the share of families comprised of pensioners varied by region between 7 to 32%, the remaining 5-10% belonging mainly to working age singles or childless families. These data show that although the share of pensioners representing a group of the old poor is substantial, children and working-age adults form the bulk of the poor, rather than pensioners.

Understanding that apart from family breakdown child poverty is mainly related to the low income of their working-age parents implies that massive poverty is caused by economic problems encountered by the economically active population. This is confirmed by evidence on the composition of the poor by the labour force status of the household head.

Table 3
The composition of the poor by demographic group, as of October 1993

	Persons living in families with per capita income less than poverty line		Persons in given demographic group	Share of demografic group in poverty
	million	per cent	per cent	per cent
Children				
- 6 years	4.5	9.9	7.8	38.7
6 - 16 years	8.4	18.5	14.3	39.6
Adults				
16 - 30 years	8.0	17.7	18.5	29.2
Women				
30 - 55 years	7.9	17.4	19.1	27.9
> 55 years	6.9	15.2	15.8	29.5
Men				
30 - 60 years	7.6	17.4	19.1	27.9
> 60 years	2.1	4.6	6.1	23.4
Total population	45.5	100.0	100.0	30.6

Source: McAuley 1996

In the 1993 RLMS data, 67% of the poor were employed and only 5% unemployed, 21%% were represented by pensioners, 5% by disabled persons, 1% by students and 1% by mothers on maternity leave (World Bank 1995, p. 19). The prevailing number of the working poor and the appearance of the unemployed in poverty are clearly new phenomena associated with the difficulties of the transition. These groups of the 'new poor' outnumber the old. The change in the social composition of the poor indicates new determinants of poverty working in combination with traditional factors. Their significance can be revealed by the evaluation of poverty risks in different demographic, social, and occupational groups.

As shown in Section 2, wage earnings failed to keep up with inflation, so the fall in real incomes appeared to be the most important new determinant of poverty. A normal family with one or two children and with both spouses employed which was very unlikely to be poor in the pre-reform period, formed the most numerous category of the new poor, occupying a 40% share of the total population below the poverty line (Mozhina et al. 1994, p. 23). In addition to traditionally low-paid occupations, a substantial number of earlier higher paid employees fell into poverty. This can be seen from data on the composition of the working poor grouped by professional status obtained form VCIOM surveys (Table 4). Skilled workers and professionals there accounted for the largest shares of respectively 50% and 21%. A high incidence of poverty among previously higher paid professionals can be explained by the predominating share of currently low paid budgetary-sector workers among professionals. In early 1995 an estimated 15 million budgetary sector employees were paid wages below the level of subsistence minimum.

Table 4
The working poor by professional status, March 1994

	Per cent of total population	Per cent of the poor
Managers	9	6
Professionals	23	21
Government officers	15	12
Skilled workers	43	50
Unskilled workers	10	11

Source: VCIOM 1994, No. 4, p.26

This situation reflects the grave problems of such sectors of the economy as education, research, health care, and cultural services as well as the military industrial complex. Poverty has widely affected the most qualified part of the working class and the so-called former middle-class, which in the Russian context comprises high professionals and intellectuals. It has extended to employees of such sectors as science and higher education, which have never had similar problems in any developed market economy or even in a developing country. As a result, Russia is witnessing a rapid erosion of its highly developed research base and university education that has been built over the years. As for skilled workers affected by poverty, this is largely a result of the steep industrial decline and respective fall in real wages, particularly in such industries as machine building or light manufacturing. August 1995 wage levels averaged only 95% of the subsistence minimum in the health care sector, 81% in agriculture, 77% in education, 76% in the light manufacturing industry, and 74% in culture and arts.[16] This explains the high concentration of the working poor in the above sectors of the economy.

Apart from the erosion of nominal wages, the situation in large areas of the economy is aggravated by widespread wage arrears, contributing greatly to the expansion of poverty among employees of several industrial branches, and the population of whole regions where this problem is particularly acute. Massive delays in wage payments can be regarded as a specific new poverty factor.

The large number of poor children indicates that the weight of dependants continues to be an important determinant of poverty. The risk of becoming poor for an average family significantly increases with the number of dependants in a household. This traditional factor causing poverty in large and single-parent families grew in significance due to the sharp rise in the cost of living and the erosion of social transfers available to such families, primarily child allowances. The incidence of poverty among the RLMS households for the period of October 1993 - February 1994 was 28% for those with one child, 36% for those with two children, and 50% for those with three or more children (World Bank 1995, p. 17). Although the average family size in Russia is 3.2 - which is not large - families with three and more children form a significant minority of 8% (about 2 million families) with a high probability of becoming poor (Mozhina 1995, p. 89).

Child allowances, in existence in Russia since 1990, have been unable to prevent child poverty due to the fact that they are so low: they have been allowed to be devaluated by inflation to a greater extent than the other social transfers. The amount of child benefit was fixed at the level of 60% of the minimum wage, so that its real value has shrunk together with the minimum wage due to poor indexation. At the end of 1994 the level of child allowance was equal to only 18% of the minimum subsistence for a child,[17] so it contributed no more than 8% to the budget of an average poor household (Mozhina et al. 1995, p. 95). Such a low level of child benefit may be regarded as an additional cause of poverty in large and single-parent families. Moreover, evidence available suggests that despite formally universal coverage, households having no members with regular jobs tend to be excluded from family support schemes. This situation is created by the bureaucratic problems of their distribution. They are normally paid through the place of employment, so access is more difficult for parents who have become unemployed as well as for the self-employed and those engaged in the informal sector. The provision of these benefits at the place of residence, although theoretically a possibility, has often faced difficult practical problems of bureaucratic and financial nature. In addition, as with other social transfers, there may be considerable delays in payment of child allowances. As a result about 20% of all families were either excluded from child benefits or did not receive them regularly (Mozhina et al. 1995, p. 95).

Single-parent households, which are more widespread than large families, are more likely to be poor than a two-parent family. They form about one third of all families with children and about 36% of them are poor (Mozhina et al. 1995, p. 88). These are predominantly female-headed households where women bear the burden of being the breadwinner for the family. This status extended to 44% of all female respondents in the VCIOM survey. Such families have particular difficulties in adjusting to their circumstances and for this reason require high priority social assistance.

Unemployment has become a new and important determinant of poverty. Loss of work is linked to a very high risk of becoming poor. In the RLMS data the presence of an unemployed family member exposes such a household to twice as high a poverty risk (43.2%) than the average of all the households in the sample (24.3%; Braithwaite 1995, p. 26). Reductions in employment in Russia have been much lower than output falls. In 1995 registered unemployment was no more than 3% of the work force. Estimates for total unemployment, including those unregistered, come to 8%.[18] However, job status has changed for a much larger proportion of workers. Nearly 10% of these were obliged to take involuntary unpaid leave and over 6% have been subjected to shorter working hours with a corresponding drop in earnings (OECD 1995, p. 126). This is a strategy to which many enterprises resort instead of inflicting mass dismissals. The registered unemployed on unemployment benefit (1,854 million of the 2,228 million total of registered people, or 83% as of November 1995) are a one third minority of the total number of unemployed, most of which do not receive any relief in the form of social transfers.[19] But even for people on unemployment benefit this relief is absolutely insufficient, as on average it amounts to only one tenth of the average wage and to one third of the subsistence level minimum (OECD 1995, p. 197).

Retirement pensions - which took the largest share of expenditure on social transfers in Russia - were in general better adjusted to inflation compared to other social benefits. This meant that any further expansion of poverty among pensioners was prevented. The average pension in late 1995 was equal to 107% of the subsistence minimum for pensioners. However the minimum pension was only about half of the subsistence minimum. Poverty thus could not be avoided unless there was additional support.[20] On the whole, pensioners are at no higher risk of poverty than the population of working age. The incidence of poverty among them is slightly lower than for the population as a whole. There are, however, wide variations in the positions of different groups of pensioners.

Pensioners who are still employed (about 20% of their total number) run virtually no risk of poverty. This risk is also significantly lower for the elderly who live in larger households together with their children. The situation is more difficult for households comprised purely of pensioners; however, two pensioners living together are less likely to be poor even compared with households comprised of two incomes and one child. Pensioners living alone are at the highest risk, and this increases further with age. There is also a gender difference among the elderly. For elderly females the poverty rate is nearly twice as high as that of males (44% against 22.5% by RLMS data; World Bank 1995, p. 21), the latter representing less than a third of all the pensioners due to the considerably lower male life expectancy in Russia.

The ISEPN survey of the four cities revealed the proportion of high risk categories among pensioners. These include single pensioners (12 to 30%, varying by city), the elderly over the age of 80 (6 to 12.6%), and pensioner household-heads having dependants: children continuing education, grandchildren, single or divorced daughters on maternity leave or unemployed (8 to 16%; Mozhina 1995, pp. 114-115). The position of these categories, comprising from 26 to 58% of all pensioners depending on the region, is of particular concern with regard to adequate social assistance. Rural pensioners also have specific problems due to inadequate access to medical facilities and major social infrastructures. Their food consumption could be supplemented by a harvest from a private plot, but to farm a plot may be physically impossible for the elderly women living alone, now representing a major proportion of the residents of Russian villages. Weak health may also become a particularly serious problem for rural pensioners, precluding them from commonly available means of self-subsistence. In addition to caring for food procurement by farming their plot, they also have to keep up the house, provide it with water and fuel, look after a cow, goats, hens, or whatever animals are in the household. All this is not easy for those of advanced age, even when they are in good health.

In certain periods the poverty among pensioners was aggravated by the considerable delays in paying out pensions caused by the financial difficulties of the Pension Fund. More than any other category, pensioners depend on their small current income, so even a short delay in the payment of a pension causes serious hardship. The timely payment of pensions in Astrakhan, Petrozavodsk, and Vyazniki in autumn 1993 would have decreased the poverty rate among pensioners by 4-5% (Mozhina et al. 1995, p. 136). The low level of pension provision causing poverty among the elderly is also related to the deficiencies in calculating entitled pensions. Universal federal standards are applied to pension entitlement regardless of the difference in the cost of living and social conditions of each region. Thus pensioners living in regions with a higher cost of living find themselves considerably disadvantaged and may have much higher poverty rates. This consideration highlights the need for adjustment within the pension system, to take into account inter-regional diversity. Although poor pensioners are in general fewer in number compared to the working age categories of the poor, there is much more limited means of adjustment and self-support available to them. For working age adults poverty is more likely to be a temporary phenomenon, while for pensioners in poverty this status is very likely to become permanent. In this perspective poor pensioners represent a long-term priority target of social policy.

Disability is another determinant of poverty not only for the handicapped person but also for the household where he (she) lives. Disability pensions range from the level of the minimum pension to two thirds of it (depending on the invalidity category), and so are in all cases well below the subsistence minimum. The presence of a disabled family member significantly raises the chance for such a family to be poor (from 25.2 to 35.4% according to the RLMS Oct. 1993 - Feb. 1994 data; World Bank 1995, p. 17).

Student scholarships have devaluated in real terms probably more dramatically than any other benefit, currently amounting to 10-12% of the subsistence level minimum, hence creating difficulties for young people in higher education. It is indeed an important cause of poverty among the young. In addition, youth unemployment is aggravated by the considerable disadvantages in finding a job for new labour force entrants, particularly in economically depressed regions. Also the difficulties for young families with small children, often associated with poverty, increase due to a loss of wage income of one of the spouses while caring for a child.

Some specific categories of the poor such as the homeless and the deinstitutionalised population, have increased in number only as the hardships of the transition have become more acute. 60,000 homeless children have been reported in Moscow (UNICEF 1995, p. 76). This group of homeless has been augmented by the inflow of about four million (since 1992) migrants and refugees caused by the disintegration of the Soviet Union and the armed conflicts in Chechnya and the 'near abroad'. This migration is likely to continue on a substantial scale in the coming years. The number of new migrants was over 800,000 in 1994, over 650,000 in 1995.[21] Many of them need shelter and emergency social assistance. They have also joined the pool of those seeking jobs.

Another specifically poor group is composed of people with deviant behaviour. In the Russian context, poverty in some cases may be related to poor life-style choices (in particular, alcoholism) which also contribute to the deterioration of such welfare indicators as health, and male life expectancy (declined from 65 years in 1987 to 59 in 1995). The heavy drinking of a household head maybe a major reason for the poverty of his whole family, in which case it probably renders ineffective the provision of a cash benefit as a means of assistance.

The above analysis of the composition and determinants of poverty has far-reaching implications for social policy-making. The large numbers of the 'new poor' - comprised mainly of wage-earners and the unemployed - have radically changed the nature of poverty and thus require a substantial modification of the system of social assistance. The distinction between the 'old poor' and the 'new poor' corresponds by and large to the difference between the poverty of the 'weak' and that of the 'strong' (Gordon 1995, pp. 132-141). The traditionally socially vulnerable groups (the 'weak'), comprising about 10% of the population, which considering the size of Russia yields a vast number of people, remain the primary target of social assistance. The safety net caring for 'the weak' obviously needs to become more effective, targeted and specific to particular categories of the poor. The way to improve the well-being of the working-age majority of the poor, among which are a part of the most active and qualified workers and intellectuals (the 'strong'), lies rather in a general economic recovery, industrial restructuring, active labour market policies, the promotion of private initiative, particularly in small business development, as well as in a more vigorous income distribution policy.

6 Conclusion

The severe welfare crisis experienced by Russia, like that of almost all countries in transition, has many dimensions, among which a high incidence of poverty persisting through the fifth year of the market reforms. Evidence from other countries suggests that a radical transformation of economic systems would not be possible without high welfare costs. The crisis of social welfare in Russia does not originate from the dislocations of transition alone, but has deeper roots in economic and welfare losses inherent in the deficiencies of the previous economic system. Underinvestment in industrial and social infrastructures, the depletion of essential resources by wasteful industrial production and high military expenditures, deep structural distortions created by pervasive price controls accompanied by massive shortages and suppressed inflation were among the most significant causes of welfare deterioration. The ultimate collapse of the old system and the difficulties of the creation of a new one would only add impetus to the crisis.

The fall in incomes and the expansion of poverty in the Russian case, however, have been exacerbated more than elsewhere by the spread of inequality. The formation of large private properties did not come about only as a result of the redistribution of natural resources and productive assets through the privatisation of state property, to which most ordinary people have never had real access. It also occurred as a result of an alienation of part of the population's consumption fund by depressing their wage levels as well as by monopolisation of consumer prices. Hence, the capitalisation of the national wealth has also removed that part of it which used to be at the disposal of the working population (Gordon 1995, p. 115). Such a development pattern in the Russian context is favoured by the weakness of the new democratic institutions, in general, and of labour unions, in particular.

A very unequal new pattern of development has been aggravated by the government's move to carry out reforms by a primarily technocratic approach, where the major hardships deriving from the transition were placed on the shoulders of the working population. In spite of frequent declarations on the importance of social policy, in the reality of reforming Russia it has been given a subordinate role to that of monetary stabilisation. Adjustment of the minimum wage and social benefits to the rate of inflation has been regularly delayed, so that social security and social provision bear the main burden of the tight monetary policies. The resulting pattern of development and reform policies largely explains the appearance of great numbers of a new working poor who have dramatically changed the composition and the overall incidence of poverty.

The above analysis has revealed different causes of poverty specific to particular social and demographic groups, and their considerable variation in range and combination by region and type of settlement. The scope of social assistance provided to socially vulnerable groups in poverty is limited mainly to emergency type relief measures. The analysis shows that this whole system in Russia is far from satisfactory and needs considerable and immediate improvement. It is important not to allow poverty and deprivation to become a permanent condition of a substantial part of the population, thus forming a new underclass within the society. The danger is that the persistence of poverty may be accompanied by fundamental changes in cultural attitudes and behavioural patterns of the affected groups, which will make a way out of poverty for them still more difficult. Further neglect of social policies or the inability to implement them properly can only reinforce the emerging social exclusion (Procacci 1996). Utmost care in this regard should be given to children in poverty - which means an immediate improvement in the system of child allowances, the provision of pre-school education and checks on secondary school attendance since this is undermined by the need to earn money for the family at an early age.

Social policy in a wider context cannot ignore the needs of a wider group of the new poor, comprising a large fraction of economically as well as politically active citizens, among which figure skilled workers, professionals, and intellectuals. The political attitudes of these groups largely determine the outcome of elections and the political scene in general. Their support is thus crucial for the continuity of the reform. The utilisation of their skill and intellectual potential through adequate remuneration and employment in accordance with qualification is also essential for the success of the transition and the acceleration of economic development. In other words, they should not be left to survive by taking odd jobs or resorting to whatever means of self-subsistence are available. An adequate living standard for the Russian middle class is equally important to maintain the levels of education, culture, research, and technology development, which themselves provide key investments in the human capital and are therefore indispensable for the eradication of poverty. These considerations highlight the importance of coherence in social policies where assistance to the very poor (primarily children and the elderly) is unlikely to be efficient without active labour market policies, sound regulations for a more equitable income distribution (among which is the improvement of the budgetary sector wages), and the development of other areas of welfare, most importantly housing, education, and health care provision.

Notes

[1] *Izvestia* (News), 23 January 1996.

[2] *Informatsionniy statisticheskiy bulleten No 13* (Informational Statistical Bulletin N 13). Moscow: Goscomstat, November 1995, p. 24.

[3] Ibid.

[4] *Birzhevye vedomosti* (News of the Exchange), No. 47, November 1994, p. 7; *Izvestia*, 14 February 1996.

[5] *Informatsionniy statisticheskiy bulleten No 13* (Informational Statistical Bulletin N 13). Moscow: Goscomstat, November 1995, p. 15.

[6] *Informatsionniy statisticheskiy bulleten No 13* (Informational Statistical Bulletin N 13). Moscow: Goscomstat, November 1995, p. 18; *Obzor economki Rossii, III, 1994* (Review of the Russian Economy, Third Quarter 1994). Moscow: Working Centre for Economic Reform under the Government of Russian Federation, 1994, p. 80.

[7] The Russian Longitudinal Monitoring Survey was undertaken by the World Bank in collaboration with the Russian Goscomstat. It is a nationally representative survey of approximately 17,000 individuals in 6,500 households.

[8] *Statisticheskoye obozrenie*, No. 11, 1995, p. 59.

[9] In 1995 this proportion was adjusted by the Russian Ministry of Labour from an earlier 68.3 % to take into account higher price increases for clothes and other non-food consumer goods.

[10] Since the 1950s Goscomstat has regularly carried out a family budget survey covering households' income and expenditure. The sample comprised 47,000-49,000 families in the late 1980s and early 1990s and was claimed to be representative. There are doubts however about the representation of the lower part of the income distribution in the survey.

[11] *Izvestia*, 14 February 1996.

[12] *Izvestia*, 26 January 1996.

[13] Ibid.

[14] *Izvestia*, 23 December 1994.

[15] This discussion owes much to the input by Lilia Ovcharova.

[16] Calculated from *Statisticheskoye obozrenie* (Statistical Review), No. 11, 1995, p. 61.

[17] *Izvestia*, 10 January 1996.

[18] *Statisticheskoye obozrenie*, No. 11, 1995, p. 64.

[19] *Socialno-economcheskoye polozhenie Rossiiskoi Federatsii v yanvare-iyune 1995 goda* (The Economic and Social Situation of the Russian Federation in January-June 1995). Moscow: Goscomstat, 1995, p. 131.

[20] *Statisticheskoye obozrenie*, No. 11, 1995, pp. 62,63; *Russian Economic Trends. Monthly Update. 15 December 1995*. Moscow: Working Centre for Economic

Reform under the Government of Russian Federation and Russian European Centre for Economic Policy, 1995, tab. 9.

[21] *Statisticheskoye obozrenie*, No. 11, 1995, p. 8.

References

Braithwaite, J.D. (1994), *The Old and New Poor in Russia*, The World Bank (mimeo): Washington, DC.

Commander, S.L., Liberman, L. and Yemtsov, R. (1993), *Wage and Employment Decisions in the Russian Economy. Analysis of Developments in 1992*, The World Bank: Washington, DC.

Cox, D., Eser, Z. and Jimenez, E. (1995), *Family Safety Nets During Economic Transition: A Study of Inter-Household Transfers in Russia*, The World Bank: Washington, DC.

Faith, G. (1995), *Family Support Policies in Transitional Economies: Challenges and Constraints*, UNICEF, International Child Development Centre: Florence.

Gordon, L. (1995), *Oblast vozmozhnogo. Varianty socialno-economicheskogo razvitiya Rossii I sposobnost rossiiskogo obshestva perenosit tyagoty perekhodnogo vremeni* (The Range of Possible: Variants of Economic and Social Development of Russia and the Ability of the Russian Society to Overcome the Hardships of the Transition), The Russian-American Foundation for Trade Union Research and Education and the Institute of World Economy and International Relations: Moscow.

Haagenars, A.J.M. and van Praag, B. (1985), 'Synthesis: Poverty Line Definitions', *Review of Income and Wealth*, Vol. 31, No. 2, pp. 139-153.

McAuley, A. (1994), *Social Welfare in Transition: What Happened in Russia*, The World Bank: Washington, DC.

McAuley, A. (1996), 'Russia and the Baltics: Poverty and Poverty Research in the Changing World', in Oyen, E., Miller, S.M. and Samad, S.A. (eds.), *Poverty: A Global Review. Handbook on International Poverty Research*, Scandinavian University Press: Oslo, Copenhagen, Boston.

Mikhalev, V. (1996), 'Social Security in Russia under Economic Transformation', *Europe-Asia Studies*, Vol. 46, No. 1, pp. 5-25.

Mikhalev, V. and Bjorksten, N. (1995), *Wage Formation during the Period of Economic Restructuring in the Russian Federation*, OECD: Paris.

Milanovic, B. (1995), *Poverty, Inequality and Social Policy in Transition Economies*, The World Bank: Washington, DC.

Mozhina, M.A. et al. (1994), *Izmeneniya v urovne zhizni I socialniye problemi adaptatsii naseleniya k rinku* (The Change in Living Standards and the Social Problems of the Population's Adjustment to the Market), Institute for the Economic and Social Studies of the Population: Moscow.

Mozhina, M.A. et al. (1995), *Uroven zhizni gorodskogo naseleniya Rossii I socialniye problemi reform* (The Living Standard of the Urban Population in Russia and the

Social Problems of the Reform), Institute for the Economic and Social Studies of the Population: Moscow.

OECD (1995), *OECD Economic Surveys. The Russian Federation 1995* (Economicheskie obzory OESR. Rossiskaya Federatsiya 1995), OECD: Paris.

Popkin, B., Mozhina, M.A. and Baturin, A.V. (1994), 'Metodi obosnovaniya prozhitochnogo minimuma' (The Method of Subsistence Minimum Definition), in Mozhina, M.A. et al. (eds.), *Bednost: vzglyad uchenikh na problemu* (Poverty: Scholars' Views), Institute for the Economic and Social Studies of the Population: Moscow.

Procacci, G. (1996), *Poor Citizens: Social Citizenship and the Crisis of Welfare. Paper for the European Forum Conference 'Social Citizenship in a World of Migration'*, European University Institute, Florence, Italy, 22-24 February 1996 (mimeo).

UNICEF (1995), *Poverty, Children, and Policy for a Brighter Future*, UNICEF, International Child Development Centre: Florence.

VCIOM (The Russian Centre for Public Opinion Research), *Economicheskiye I socialniye peremeni: monitoring obshestvennogo mneniya* (Economic and Social Change: Monitoring of the Public Opinion), various editions.

Volkova, G.N. and Migranova, L.A. (1994), 'Nekotoriye problemi bednikh semei I puti ikh socialnoi zashiti. Po materialam sociologicheskikh obsledovanii' (Problems of Poor Families and the Way for their Social Protection), *Uroven zhizni naseleniya regionov Rossii N 12* (The Living Standards of the Population in Russian Regions, Bulletin No. 12), The Russian Centre for Living Standards Studies under the Ministry of Labour: Moscow.

World Bank (1995), *Poverty in Russia: An Assessment*, The World Bank: Washington, DC.

Urban poverty and local policies against social exclusion in Italy: The north-south divide

Yuri Kazepov

Introduction

The aim of this contribution is to present some of the main features of the *Italian model of poverty* and, in particular, to show how it is characterised by a strong urban and regional bias due to the joint effect of highly fragmented social policies and divergent socio-economic contexts. Both these aspects, and the lack of a national income maintenance scheme aimed at equalising living conditions in the country, contributes to the reproduction and consolidation of the existing inequalities. After presenting in the first section a qualitative overview of urban poverty patterns in Italy and their regional context, I attempt to verify empirically the outlined scenario and particularly the persistence (despite the ongoing transformations) of the north-south divide which underlies the model. The second section introduces the problem of the availability of data for poverty research in Italy, showing the intrinsic difficulties in this task and the need to understand the interplay between institutional intervention and poverty patterns. This need derives from the fact that the way in which institutions intervene contributes, together with the socio-economic context, to this territorial divide by pre-structuring the profiles of the poor in the two parts of the country. Following on from this, the third section describes the institutional framing of social assistance in a selection of Italian cities and regions and their fragmented schemes as an example of Italian welfare benefits for people in a condition of economic need. The fourth section integrates this description by showing how the main characteristics of people living below the poverty line, defined by the Italian Government Poverty Commission, are linked to the patterns of social policy. Both these last two sections illustrate the overall coherence of the *Italian model of poverty* by looking at it from different but complementary perspectives.

1 An overview of urban and regional poverty patterns in Italy

In the last two decades poverty has undergone a deep structural change and became increasingly widespread within the social fabric in most of the metropolitan areas in industrialised countries (Mingione 1996; McFate et al. 1995; Morris 1995). A set of extremely complex factors underlie this change and its diffusion. On one side, we have a shift in the occupational structure connected with de-industrialisation, a decline in jobs in big industries, and a tertiarisation of employment leading to the polarisation of work conditions between high-income and highly skilled jobs and low-income and unskilled jobs (Sassen 1991, 1996; Esping-Andersen 1993). On the other side, we observe great socio-demographic changes like the ageing of the population, brought about by the lengthening of the average life span and the decline in births (Golini 1994). These factors have worsened the structural crisis of all welfare states in the industrialised countries, thereby showing the inadequacy of the protection schemes which have in the last few decades been trying to cope with the changes that these societies are undergoing.

When we look at the Italian case in the light of this set of conditions, we find some interesting peculiarities that can be linked mainly to the wide socio-economic, demographic, and even institutional differences between the north and the south of the country. For instance, although more affected by de-industrialisation (Turin, Genoa) and by occupational polarisation within the advanced tertiary sector (Milan) than those situated in the south, northern Italian cities have suffered less than other western metropolitan areas from the impact of the recent transformation processes involving working conditions. The dense network of small and medium-sized firms, which characterises the main metropolitan areas in the north (e.g. Milan, Bologna), has helped to make the production system more flexible, allowing it to absorb in most cases a substantial part of the 'excess labour force' arising also in the production-oriented tertiary sector. Furthermore, the amount of self employment has increased. Both these counter-trends have contributed, at least until the beginning of the nineties, to keeping the processes of marginalisation and impoverishment under control.

In the cities of the South (or Mezzogiorno), on the contrary, efficient and diversified local industrial systems are in most cases lacking and, as a consequence, the disadvantages like concentration of long-term unemployment[1] and precarious jobs cumulate (Inchiesta 1993). The interruption to industrial development in the second half of the seventies led to the consolidation of an economy based on clientelism[2] and welfare dependency (Giordano 1992) and to growing unemployment. The drop in industrial employment did not occur as a consequence of the externalisation of tertiary functions, as in most northern Italian cities, but because of both the downsizing of the metropolitan industrial systems and the reduced commitment of state-run enterprises (Morlicchio and Spanò 1992), which in the mid sixties accounted for nearly 80% of production in the Mezzogiorno. The generally weak job guarantees that this situation implies has to be added to the poor state of basic public services (schools,[3] vocational training, social security and assistance), crucial in determining life opportunities for low-income households.[4] The family is the only efficient mechanism of solidarity, but it is overburdened by social problems within a context of more limited institutional resources.

The persistence of the economic crisis in the first half of the nineties seems to have contributed to a change in both halves of the country. In the cities of the north, the particularly high cost of living, together with the re-emerging structural crisis is triggering off new patterns of deprivation. The increase in badly paid and poorly guaranteed *McJobs* also in the large cities of the north and the chronic housing crisis (Mingione and Zajczyk 1992) are worsened by the general inefficiency of the Italian public welfare system. The structural aspects of the occupational crisis will presumably change these patterns and poverty will no longer remain a limited phenomenon but also affect the social standing of population groups which until a few years ago seemed to be strongly guaranteed. In the cities of the Mezzogiorno (Sidoti 1989; Morlicchio and Spanò 1992) the problem is different. In this context of persisting negative indicators the question is how long family, kin, and community will be able to compensate for the chronic scarcity of resources.

Both in northern and southern urban areas, primary social institutions of reciprocity have maintained a crucial role in influencing living conditions, probably more than in any other industrial society. This role differs according to the regional context. In the north-eastern regions of Italy and in Lombardy, where self-employment, familial entrepreneurship, and small and medium-sized firms are far more widespread, mixed figures of worker-artisans and worker-entrepreneurs provide the local productive system with a high degree of flexibility and smooth adaptation to the new organisational patterns of production. The externalisation of productive functions and of production-oriented services has increased the number of local units and diminished the average size of firms, but it has not substantially lowered overall employment. In this context, the wide use of early retirement schemes has been sufficient to guarantee the exit of older less qualified workers from the labour market. Unemployment rates for the young in the north are very low compared to the national average and to the south.[5] In short, more favourable structural conditions in the north have positively interacted with the social networks to reduce the risk of impoverishment.

In the Mezzogiorno none of this has happened. On the contrary, the family has often appeared as an element of risk apart from being a place of compensation for conditions of need. Its greater size[6] and often the presence of only one breadwinner, in the context of high youth unemployment, the structural weakness of the labour market, and the lesser dynamism of familiar entrepreneurship, has prevented southern Italy from performing as well as the north. Informal activities only partially compensate for this weakness, because earnings are neither high nor regular throughout the year and do not contribute to the acquisition of particular skills so that it is impossible in the long run to build up a professional career with which to enter the regular labour market and have access to its benefits.

Nevertheless in both cases the social networks have helped to compress poverty allowing the development of alternative or complementary strategies to the market and to state assistance. In this sense, the new forms of poverty cannot be fully understood without considering these networks, particularly in the case of young people who depend, in most cases for many years, on help from their family of origin and kinship networks (Paci 1992). In fact, in Italian cities the young are the group most at risk of poverty. The family breadwinner, who was extremely well protected until the beginning of the nineties, is now beginning to encounter more flexible and less protected labour market regulating mechanisms. This entails several important problems for subjects at risk because the period of benefit has been reduced and more and more people are left without any kind of protection, although access to the same schemes has been widened (partly also to some small firms). The changes described above therefore interact with two very different regional contexts, from both a socio-economic and a socio-demographic point of view, giving rise (as we will see in the second section) to the concentration of urban poverty mainly in the cities of the Mezzogiorno. In southern Italy live 36.3% of the population, but also 72.9% of the Italian poor (CIPE 1996a, 1996b). In the centre-north, on the contrary, the extent of poverty is limited: 27.1% of the Italian poor live there, against 63.7% of the population.

In the long run we should take into account that this spatial cleavage may be accompanied by others, for instance immigration flows from less developed countries also need to be considered. The phenomenon is still too recent to allow the identification of pockets of chronic poverty and marginalisation.[7] The living conditions of immigrants are often even worse than those of the Italian poor but their living strategies view these bad conditions as an, at least in the short term, acceptable first step in upward mobility (Mingione and Zajczyk 1992). In all events, this situation bears a high risk of poverty for this group, because of the lasting economic crisis and given their weak position both on the labour market and from an entitlements standpoint. Poverty in Italy, however, is not structured according to ethnic and cultural membership, as in the United States (Wilson 1987, 1991, 1996; Mingione 1996b), but rather along the lines of the social and geographical north-south division.[8] In the long run, however, the extent of the immigration flow could create pockets of ethnic segregation, especially among those without a regular residence permit, the case of most recent immigrants.

2 Poverty research in Italy: Data availability and policy constraints

It is not possible to verify empirically the picture outlined in the previous section at the urban and regional level because there are no comparable data sources available allowing us to analyse localities and regions directly. This is due to the fact that existing data for poverty research have a very different statistical significance depending on the territorial area of reference.

On one side there are no comparable administrative data on recipients of social assistance benefits (*Minimo Vitale*) either at the local or national level. Also, data on the distribution of available incomes are unreliable because figures based on income tax returns are distorted by the high level of tax evasion. On the other side survey data are not statistically significant at the local or even at the regional level: the sample is too small. Therefore, a picture which takes also the territorial dimension into account can be built up only using ad hoc case studies or data at the macro-regional level.[9] Table 1 shows which sources of information are available in Italy, at which territorial level and which characteristics of the population of reference are identified.

As far as administrative data are concerned, the lack of a homogeneous institutional framework on the national level and the heterogeneous criteria of access to welfare benefits impede the comparability of locally produced data on social assistance recipients (columns 1-4 in the Table).

Table 1
Data sources available in Italy for poverty research

Source of data	Social Assistance Statistics (USL) [1]	Social Assistance Statistics (Municipalities) [2]	Social Assistance Statistics (INPS) [3]
Characteristics of poverty a) considered b) not considered	a) Income, social security benefits, health, socio-demographic indicators, housing (...); b) Social integration (only qualitatively), intervention outcomes (...).	a) Income, education, social security benefits, housing, health, socio-demographic indicators, (...); b) Self-provisioning, non-monetary benefits (...).	a) Income (before pension) (...); b) Housing, education, consumption, health, self-provisioning (...);
Groups at risk a) identified b) not identified	a) Benefit recipients (also long-term) (...); b) Hidden poverty (non-take-up), homeless (if not off. resident) (...).	a) Benefit recipients (...); b) Hidden poverty (non-take-up), homeless (if not officially resident) (...).	a) Benefit recipients (mainly elderly) (...); b) Hidden poverty (non-take-up), homeless (...).
Regional level	Local-Health-Unit districts*	Municipal, city districts, zip codes	Provincial, regional, national, zip code
Method	Archives with individual files on all benefit recipients; unpublished data	Archives with individual files on all benefit recipients; unpublished data	All recipients of INPS (National Social Insurance Institute) pensions (social and minimum pensions); not published in an official journal
Availability/Publications	Appearing on an ad hoc basis (not comparable)	Appearing on an ad hoc basis (not comparable)	'Sistema previdenziale', a monthly review of INPS, publishes some data

Source: Own calculations on available sources; Banca d'Italia (1989, 1991, 1993, 1995), Brandolini (1993), CIPE (1996a, 1996b), ISTAT (1995a, 1995b), Eurostat (1996), Kazepov (1996a)

Third sector (no profit) [4]	European Household Panel (Eurostat/ISTAT) [5]	National Familiy Budget Survey (ISTAT) [6]	National Income Survey (Bank of Italy) [7]	Italian Government Poverty Commission [8]
a) Income (not always), education, housing, health (...). Data vary very much according to the groups considered; Caritas standardises the data collection	a) Income (family and individual), housing, health, labour market, education, social security benefits, subjective poverty (...); b) Social integration (...)	a) Consumption, family income (aggregated), housing, health (only expenditure), labour market, self-provisioning; b) Social integration, social security benefits	a) Family and individual income, savings, health (since 1995), housing (...); b) Non-monetary benefits	a) Consumption, family income (aggregated), housing, health (only expenditure), labour market, self-provisioning; b) Social integration, social security benefits
a) Private assistance recipients, who are to a great extent homeless.	a) Long-term unemployed, long-term poor (...); b) foreigners, homeless (...).	a) Youth, elderly, large families b) long-term poor, unemployed, benefit recipients, foreigners, homeless.	a) Long-term unemployed, long-term poor (panel section); b) foreigners, homeless (...).	a) as in [2], homeless and foreigners only through ad hoc research; b) as in [2]
Municipal, parish, deanery.	National macro-regions at NUTS level**.	National and macro-regions	National and macro-regions	National and macro-regions
Archives with individual files on all recipients (but not all organizations have it).	Panel on a sample of 8,000 families (18,000 individuals >16) out of 60,000 households in Europe selected from the population register; annual waves	Survey on a sample of about 24,000 families (until 1996 36,000) selected from the population register	Survey on a sample of about 8,000 families (4-5,000 until 1986) including 25,000 individuals	Ad hoc calculations on ISTAT data (see [6]); contextual data from ad hoc thematic surveys/ analyses, qualitative and quantitative methods.
Appearing on an ad hoc basis (not comparable).	First report in press, expected for spring 1997.	'I consumi delle famiglie Italiane', Notiziario Istat (Suppl. of ISTAT bulletin).	Supplemento al 'Bollettino Statistico', since 1991 new series (every 2 years).	Series of 'Quaderni' (published not periodically but frequently).

Notes:

* In some regions Local-Health-Units (USL) are integrated with social services

** NUTS = Nomenclature of the Regional Statistics of the European Union

The fragmentation of policies and the absence of guidelines for data collection impact very negatively on the management of information at the local level. If we consider the way in which information is managed as an indicator of the capability of welfare systems to produce knowledge useful for assessing its own interventions as well as influencing the policy-making process, we have to admit that the situation in most Italian municipalities is very bad, both quantitatively and qualitatively. There are of course some exceptions (e.g. Turin is one of the best examples, but also Bologna and Trent), but the general situation is one in which the municipalities have no informational system for monitoring policies and targets. The few that do have systems produce different data, depending on the differences both in the policies design and the local monitoring systems.[10] This means that the municipalities really don't know exactly how many welfare recipients they have, who they are, and what kind of problems they have. They do have of course a general idea of the situation, but this rests in most cases only on qualitative information from social workers and their *case-by-case* perspective. In small municipalities the situation is more under control. At the regional level the situation is, on the contrary, very problematic, because municipalities also within the same region have different policies and produce different data. In most cases there is of course information on expenditures, but at a very aggregate level without any (or only few) socio-demographic data on recipients. Data on recipients remain mainly unexplored in the individual records of the single services (columns 1, 2 and 3). A consequence of this complex situation is that numbers cannot be used as comparative indicators of the seriousness of social problems at the local level. High numbers of recipients can be both an indicator of a socially deprived area as well as of an area where good access to benefits is to be found. On the other hand, low numbers of recipients can be an indicator of an unproblematic situation, of a low level of entitlements, as well as of an unreliable monitoring system. In short what we lack are homogenous criteria, and they are lacking precisely because the policies are very different one from another.

To these basic problems we have to add all the methodological limitations of these data: not all poor people will be considered, only those who are entitled to some benefits. The non-take-up of entitled people also distorts the picture just as low benefits reduce the number of potential claimants.[11] This means that data on recipients have to be looked at in context and not considered as a direct quantitative indicator of the number of the poor. On the contrary, they should be considered an indicator of the performance of social policies and part of the process of *the social construction of poverty*.

For all these reasons, apart from a few exceptions, there is no research tradition which systematically studies poverty issues by considering welfare state performance at the local level.[12] For the same reasons, however, it is important to understand the institutional embeddedness of poverty patterns and its implications, particularly when we want to understand their regional differences. As far as survey data are concerned, the European Household Panel (Eurostat, column 5), the Family Budget Survey (ISTAT, column 6) and the National Income Survey (Bank of Italy, column 7) are significant only at the national and the macro-regional level. The Italian Government Poverty Commission uses data from the Family Budget Survey to draw an overall picture of poverty in Italy (column 8). Like data on recipients, however, survey data also have some methodological drawbacks which can lead to misconceptions if not correctly interpreted. For instance, they underestimate[13] the poor population in the sample and the relative measures and calculations which are based on these figures show the typical problems of all measures based on the *International Standard of Poverty Line*,[14] i.e. they measure inequality rather than poverty. The perverse effect of considering poor all persons whose budget is below the average, is that a decrease in average expenditure can bring about a drop in the incidence of poverty in the population, even when the living conditions of those below the poverty line have worsened. This is explained by the fact that the consumption level of poor families is relatively rigid and less receptive to the market fluctuation of prices than that of middle class families, whereas a contraction in the consumption level of the middle and upper classes lowers average consumption.[15]

Given this widely varying data availability and its significance at the different territorial levels (municipalities, local health units, regions, macro-regions), we have to take different sources into consideration in order to paint a more accurate picture of poverty patterns in Italy, and to make the underlying model of poverty explicit. On one hand, we have to know how the interventions of institutions influence the phenomena. On the other hand, we have to use this institutional perspective to frame the information that emerges from survey data. In this way we can try to grasp the overall coherence underlying the different sources, recognising how both perspectives give us two pictures which reinforce one another and partly explain the north-south divide, further articulating it at the local level.

3 The regulatory frameworks for social policy in Italy[16]

The importance of taking social policies and their regulatory frameworks into account in the analysis of poverty lies in the fact that they structure the context of risks within which poverty arises. This happens mainly through the establishment of specific rules which address the flows of resources aimed at overcoming these situations of risk. Different access criteria, different definitions of need (who is to be considered needy), different amounts, and different accompanying measures change the direction of the resources and impact the conditions of need attached to the risks in a very differentiated way. This determines specific conditions of inclusion and exclusion, which will be analysed in this section, considering in particular the social assistance measures existing in Italy which are aimed at granting minimum living conditions to people in economic need. The social function of these measures, however, cannot be fully understood if they are not embedded in the wider structure of the Italian welfare system which frames their social role. Let us, therefore, introduce its main features briefly.

As has been pointed out by several scholars (Ferrera 1984; Ascoli 1984; Mingione 1988; Esping-Andersen 1990; Paci 1989), Italy's welfare system is characterised by the fact that eligibility for welfare benefits depends mostly on one's labour market position. In practical terms, this means that persons are entitled to specific benefits, for instance family allowances, only if they have a job. The consequence of this overall framework is that the greatest protection is assured to those who run the least risk, i.e. those who have relatively secure jobs. The prevailing logic is, in fact, that of preserving differences in acquired status. From the functional point of view this structure of entitlements provides a strong protection to the *breadwinner*, whose task it is to maintain an adequate family income within a contributory system. The structure of labour-related policies clearly reflects this and male adults are seldom unemployed. However, entitlements are highly fragmented and there is no general scheme. Persons who were supposed to lose their job because of a structural crisis of the enterprise (the potentially unemployed) received benefits for long periods of time, in some cases more than ten years. Up to 1991 and particularly during the eighties, the *Cassa Integrazione Guadagni* (CIG), a kind of 'temporary' unemployment benefit, essentially guaranteed 80% of a worker's gross wage for many years.[17] This scheme, often misused as a social buffer during industrial restructuring or general economic crisis, was limited to workers employed in large and medium-sized industries. The long periods of benefit, not entirely legal for what is supposed to be a temporary measure, were due to the fact that regular unemployment benefits, until the end of the eighties, were only around 800 Lira a day (approx. 50 US Cents). The temporary benefit therefore fulfilled the function of a regular benefit, at least for some of the people at risk of impoverishment. In recent years the inequitable nature of this measure has become evident because more and more people have been excluded from any protection. For these reasons, in 1991 the regulations were changed (National Law No. 223/91): regular unemployment benefits have been increased up to about 25% of the salary for 180 days and temporary benefits have been reduced to two years for northern regions and three years for southern regions. Smaller firms and different sectors can now also apply for the temporary benefit. However, in extending coverage to more people, the new regulations have reduced the overall institutional guarantees for persons at risk of poverty because of long-term unemployment. This is particularly true as there is no real means-tested minimum income in the event of need and poverty: the long-term unemployed will not have access to any supportive measures after they have exhausted their contributory entitlements.[18] As we will see, social assistance is, within this picture, a residual measure delegated essentially to the regions. The basic welfare unit remains the family. However, compared to other countries where the *subsidiarity* principle (e.g. Germany, partly France) is adopted, Italy does not have an adequate system of support for the family if none of its members has a job.[19] The state intervenes only when the family becomes incapable of fully providing for its members without, however, supporting the able-bodied jobless who are not entitled to labour-related benefits. As a consequence, the familial and kinship systems are often overburdened with responsibilities and the risk of individuals being dragged down into poverty depends on the capacity to mobilise alternative resources and support them in their condition of need.

Given these more general features, the existing urban and regional differentiation shows a very contrasting picture. Turin, Trent, Bologna, and Milan, for instance, have compared to other Italian cities a long-lasting tradition of relatively efficient social services. Southern cities like Naples, Bari, Cosenza, or Catania present, on the contrary, a very desolate picture, characterised by inefficiency, lack of regulation, and a high degree of discretion. By international standards, however, even the social assistance systems of the north Italian cities appear to be weak and inadequate, particularly in periods of profound and rapid change. This weakness emerges clearly when we consider the overall structure of social assistance in Italy, the existing local differences and the resulting diverging degree of protection provided by institutions for the different groups at risk of poverty in different places. In this respect, Italy (together with Greece, Portugal, and Spain) is comparatively speaking one of the few countries in Europe without a national law on social assistance. Like Spain, it has both innovative and advanced social policies (e.g. for specific groups in Bologna, Trent, Turin) and more socially stigmatising and traditional services (mainly concentrated in the south).

3.1 The fragmented rights in the Italian context: The importance of the locality

Since 1977, in line with the Presidential Decree 616, the state has transferred competence for social assistance to the regions and the municipalities. This change can be seen as one of the great *lost opportunities* of Italian social policy against poverty. The regions and the municipalities inherited the assets and functions of a series of charitable bodies (which partly still exist and are funded), which intervened according to category and group instead of the condition of need per se. However, the state gave no clear guidelines for establishing homogeneous access criteria building up a coherent system of social security able to guarantee a last safety net for people in a condition of economic need. This lack of a framework law left both the regions and the municipalities in a *vacatio juris,* the negative effects of which are still being felt.

In the meantime many regions, while waiting for the national framework law, have approved a regional framework law on social assistance. This process began in the early eighties and is still going on. Some regions (e.g. Piedmont) have already introduced their second framework law (1982 the first and 1995 the second). This has brought about some problems. First of all, not every region has a regional framework law; secondly in approving these laws, the regions have not co-ordinated their efforts so that now we have different access criteria to social benefits in different regions. There are of course similarities, but more on the level of stated principles than of concrete measures. In fact, the implementation guidelines, which were intended to make the principles concrete, have contributed to differentiating the policies at the local level to an even greater extent, increasing the variability and heterogeneity of the overall picture. Within this picture the municipalities have added a further level of heterogeneity, by designing specific implementation rules for specific groups and/or categories at risk. Since 1990, as a consequence of National Law No. 142 on decentralisation and re-organisation of all regulatory criteria, this situation has been slowly changing. Some municipalities are setting up unified criteria for accessing social services. However, this process is still under way and does not solve the problem of inter-municipal differences, not to speak of the fact that it touches only the formal aspects and not the practices which are still categorising claimants and recipients.

The consequence of this situation is the consolidation of a differentiated system of social citizenship, framed by very different legal contexts within which *citizens* are entitled to different sets of rights, related not so much to their condition of need, but to the specific features of entitlements and to the specific way in which social services are organised in the places where they live. This heterogeneity is one of the greatest problems facing the Italian welfare system in this period of deep socio-economic and socio-demographic transformation (described in section one), which is increasing the overall social vulnerability. This problem can be partially solved only by a national framework law aimed at setting down homogenous access criteria to guarantee minimum standards. The social policies adopted by most of the municipalities already have several aspects in common. Some of these are, for example:

a) similar thresholds for receiving social assistance benefits (*Minimo Vitale)* (usually the state minimum pension of 650,000 Lira per month);
b) similar formally stated procedures to determine the benefit which is supposed to be the difference between the real income of the household and the threshold for that specific household, but this is not always the case;
c) similar obligations for the family which has to contribute to the well-being of its members (relatives up to the first degree have to take care of other members in case of need);
d) similar budgetary constraints which can limit benefits.

Apart form these similarities, which are not necessarily implemented everywhere and which are not necessarily positive, we have also numerous differences. Even where similar measures are called by different names, the categorisation of claimants (e.g. single mothers, minors, adults, disabled, elderly) often persists and still determines the flow of resources to more or less protected groups in a very differentiated way. Connected to this aspect we find many features which vary from context to context without necessarily depending on the mere condition of need. In order to determine a more adequate threshold, in some cases the effective housing costs are added to the basic amount (the minimum INPS-National Insurance pension), in other cases these costs are standardised; they may or may not include heating and other costs (there are no general regulations which specially entitle the person in a condition of need to have housing costs included in the determination of the benefit). Also the benefit paid varies consistently and is not necessarily the amount resulting from the difference between the official threshold and the household's real income; it is often lower. The duration of payments is limited and does not always last as long as the condition of need; in this respect, there are once again great differences amongst groups of claimants and recipients.

All the above-mentioned differences create a fragmented picture within which long-lasting benefits are granted only to the elderly (aged above 60 or 65), the disabled, and minors, i.e. categories (or groups) for whom there is already legislation covering most of their problems both at the regional as well as at the national level.[20] What has been carried over from the debate on the *deserving/undeserving poor* is clear. The best protected are those who are not responsible for their condition, those who are considered able to work (despite possible structural unemployment) have to cumulate the conditions of need in order to receive benefits.

Table 2
Equivalence scales in some Italian cities used to determine the family threshold and the amount of social assistance (Minimo Vitale) according to the number of household members

	TO	TN	MI	BO	PC	FI	AN	PS	CT	CIPE
1 person	100	100	100	100	100	100	100	100	100	100
2 persons	70	75	65	89	70	59	50	50	25	66
3 persons	40	50	47	82	50	46	33	33	35	56
4 persons	40	50	42	82	50	37	24	24	15	50
5 and more	40	20	39		50	37	24	24		46
Single		120								

The cities are: TO = Turin, TN = Trent, MI = Milan, BO = Bologna, PC = Piacenca, FI = Florence, AN = Ancona, PS = Pesaro, CT = Catania; CIPE is the scale of the Poverty Commission

Source: Kazepov (1996a)

Another important aspect influencing differences between municipalities are the *equivalence scales* used to determine the family's threshold. They differ for no rational reason from context to context. The differences shown in Table 2 have many implications. For example, given the same condition of need and the same available income of 1 million lire, the entitlement of a family to the minimum benefit will depend also on these scales. Bologna has one of the most generous, while Catania is relatively *punitive*. If we consider that in both cities the threshold for a single person is the minimum state pension (1996: about 650,000 Lira), in Bologna a family of three will have a threshold of 1,761,500 Lira compared to 877,500 Lira in Catania. This means that in Bologna the family will be formally entitled to a benefit at an income twice as much as in Catania. What happens in practice, however, makes things even more complicated: both in northern as well as in southern municipalities, the family will be entitled to benefits only if there are other conditions of need which cumulate with economic deprivation, for instance the presence of a minor or a dependent elderly member. In case of mere economic need, most municipalities do not grant automatic access to the benefits and the degree of discretion is generally high. It is even higher in the case of adults, who are almost everywhere partially excluded from substantial access to benefits. This under-representation of adults has to be related to the strong protection of the *male family breadwinner* mentioned previously. Although his position is still better protected than that of adults who have never entered or who have long since left the labour market, changes in both labour market conditions and in the regulatory mechanisms increase the importance of social assistance schemes.

3.2 Some basic problems

The cumulative effect of all the differences briefly described makes it difficult to understand how the mechanisms at the very basis of local social policies work and what are the implications for the persons in a condition of need. This gives rise to some basic problems which affect the possibility of investigating the extent of poverty through social policy indicators. I have already mentioned the important consequences on data availability in section two of this chapter.

A second problem, which was already pointed out in the first section, is the high concentration of poverty in the south. Its problematic nature is also confirmed from an institutional point of view: both regions and municipalities have developed a weak structure of entitlements and services. The benefits last for shorter periods, some groups (single adults) are totally excluded from any benefit, and social services are chronically under-staffed. Access to benefits is more restrictive and there is a much higher degree of discretion. In many cases regulations are not implemented and there are practically no monitoring systems. In the municipalities of the north the situation is better but not as much as one would expect when looking at the regional framework laws, in which the principles are layed down.

A third problem is related to the fact that despite the differences there is also a worrying convergence in the way the social assistance (*Minimo Vitale*) is regulated: the categorisation of recipients is being maintained. In order to receive an economic subsidy, as we have seen above, an individual has often to qualify his/her condition of need since mere economic poverty is not considered enough due to the budgetary constraints faced by municipalities. This means that people who fulfil means-tested conditions are not automatically entitled to a monetary subsidy. Their right depends, in most cases, on the limits of the municipality's budgetary constraints. More or less resources at its disposal determine the regulatory context of the social assistance. This means that it is budgetary constraints that determine how many persons in a condition of need are entitled to a subsidy, and not their condition of need. It is self-evident that such a social policy can easily end up being strongly influenced by the economic cycle and giving rise to dangerous pro-cyclical trends. A situation of crisis creates, on one side, a socio-economic context with increasing risks of impoverishment (e.g. loss of a job) and on the other side increasingly tighter budgetary constraints. This implies that in a situation of growing need there are less and less available resources while in a period of economic well-being, when the condition of need is less widespread, available resources increase. The consequence of such a situation is that besides having an insufficient income a person has often to also demonstrate some other conditions of deprivation, for instance having dependent members in the household, or minors facing judicial proceedings or in care of the court, or any other situation that limits household autonomy. The implementation guidelines specify that social workers are to intervene only in cases of households with qualified needs combined with an insufficient income. The conceptual problem related to this implementation rule is the fact that it tends to categorise interventions around specific states of cumulative deprivation without considering that social intervention should encompass the situation of mere need. Its implications are particularly negative for adults who are not covered by any other program (for instance labour related policies). Mothers with children are relatively well protected (but with a high level of discretion in the amounts paid) and the elderly are the best protected group, but it depends on the locality. This does not mean, of course, that coverage is adequate (particularly when they are no longer autonomous), but only that the benefit is paid automatically in the event of their income being below the minimum pension (INPS) threshold.

4 Structural profiles: Who are the groups most at risk?

Identification of the poor and tracing their profile has always been a controversial topic and in fact different methods and sources often lead to different results. The data availability, presented in section two, makes it difficult to verify empirically the picture outlined, particularly at the urban and regional level. Nevertheless, the description of the institutional settings helps to embed the scenario presented in section one and will allow us to understand better the macro-regional data that will be presented in this last section. In fact, the concentration of the poor mainly in the south is intimately related to the role played by social policies in the reproduction of the socio-economic inequalities between northern and southern Italy. In particular, this persistence can be seen as an indicator of their inadequacy and ineffectiveness in compensating for existing urban and regional disparities. More specifically, institutions contribute to structuring the risks of becoming poor and in this way influence the emerging profiles of the poor.

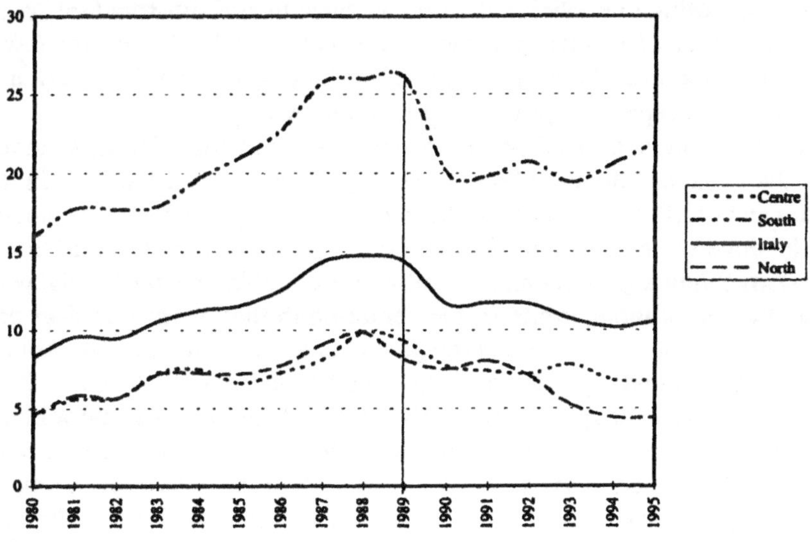

Figure 1 Population living below the poverty line, 1980-1995 in macro-regions

Source: Own calculations from CIPE (1996a, Tables 4, 6-9; 1996b, Table 2)

This becomes evident from the description of the existing poverty patterns according to the data drawn from the Family Budget Survey (CIPE 1996a, 1996b).[21] This data confirms the overrepresentation of the south (72.9% of the Italian poor live there) and shows how the gap between the northern and southern regions widened since the eighties from a difference of 10.2 percentage points in 1983 to 17.8 in 1989 and, after a short interruption (1991: 11.2), increasing again to 17.5 percentage points in 1995 (see Figure 1). This suggests that, to a great extent, the typologies and the main tendencies of the phenomena are influenced by trends typical of southern regions.

It is possible to question this overrepresentation of the poor in the south by arguing that the cost of living is lower than the national average and that potential self-provisioning is higher. This would entail a readjustment of the relative poverty line downwards so that the poor in the south would be less numerous. Although there is some truth in this argument, it does not consider that a large part of the population living below the 60% threshold is more and more concentrated in cities and metropolitan areas, where the cost of living is not significantly lower than the national average and where self-provisioning is more difficult (Mingione 1996a). To this we have to add sub-standard social services, which are less efficient and less effective and this implies fewer institutional resources (both in terms of in-kind and cash benefits) and opportunities to escape from poverty (see section two).

Given the aforementioned premises, data from the Family Budget Survey confirm the territorial divide, allowing us to identify great differences in the typologies and profiles of the poor in the two areas of the country. In the south, economic poverty is prevalent within large households (with 5 or more members) involving a growing number of minors (in 1995 one third of the poor in the south were minors, while in the centre-north they were less than one fifth). In the centre-northern regions the picture is reversed and poverty affects more single households (particularly the elderly) and elderly couples. Poor people above 65 years of age represent slightly less than 30% of all poor in the north, while in the south they represent about 15%. In fact about 80% of poor minors are concentrated in the south, but *only* 57% of the elderly poor (above 75 years of age). Particularly in the north, between the eighties and the mid nineties, the incidence of economic poverty amongst the elderly decreased (-3.8 percentage points, cf. Table 3 on the following pages) as a consequence of the indexation of social and minimum state pensions. In general the policies in favour of the elderly were to the advantage of the north, where their incidence is higher, and this, together with the high increase of poverty amongst large families in the south (+12.9 percentage points), explains the divergent tendencies of the last few years.

These data could give the impression that in the southern regions we have more *traditional* forms of poverty related to the marked presence of rural activity and economic backwardness and in the northern regions more forms of *new poverty*.[22] However, the economic poverty that characterises the life style of nearly one quarter of the actual population of the south has nothing to do with the rural poverty of the fifties (Braghin 1978). As we have seen in section one, at the very basis of contemporary Italian poverty patterns lie the same occupational transformation processes (e.g. tertiarisation, unstable jobs, insecure careers, high long-term unemployment, untypical forms of work) which characterise the increase of social vulnerability in all industrialised countries. For these reasons the traditional aspect of poverty is more related to the role of the southern family system in facing poverty and compensating for its effects. The southern family is not, in fact, overwhelmed by increasing instability and heterogeneity as occurs in most industrial countries and also, to some extent, in the centre-northern regions. However, being overburdened with social costs, the over-proportional number of children born and growing up in deprived social contexts, and the fact that women are shunted to the margins of the labour market are part of a complex mix of cultural traditions, low expenditure levels, and strong social control. These are then embedded in general socio-economic backwardness, which strengthens family ties within chronically depressed areas.[23] Family members are less inclined to break reciprocity networks also because stress-inducing economic events (like unemployment) are more widespread and, therefore, not functioning as mechanisms of social isolation or discrimination in relation to the community of belonging (Mingione 1994).

To this high concentration of poverty (and low consumption) in the southern regions corresponds the high concentration of unemployment mentioned in section one (see Figure 2 and Table 3). The trend of both phenomena has in the south followed the same pattern from the early eighties to the mid nineties: the highest levels of economic poverty correspond to the highest levels of unemployment, despite the fact that between 1987 and 1989 there was no recession. As Pugliese (1993) and Mingione (1996a) point out, however, there is no mechanical relation between the two phenomena. We have seen in section two that the unemployed in the south are mainly young people, who do not receive any benefit and are cared for by their family of origin.

Table 3
Incidence of poverty according to household size, age, gender, occupational status, and macro-regions in Italy, 1980-1995 (in %)

	1980				1987			
	North	Centre	South	Italy	North	Centre	South	Italy
Hh. size								
1 person	12.1	5.5	16.1	11.9	11.6	9.2	29.4	16.3
2 persons	5.4	5.7	17.6	8.9	11.2	10.0	30.7	16.7
3 persons	1.2	2.5	8.5	3.4	5.4	6.5	21.3	10.1
4 persons	2.2	3.7	12.9	6.0	6.5	6.0	20.5	11.7
5 or more	5.3	6.2	23.0	13.8	12.4	10.6	28.8	20.6
Age[1]								
< 35	2.4	2.8	13.6	6.6	4.7	6.4	21.3	11.3
36 - 45	2.3	3.4	15.2	6.8	6.2	5.0	20.1	10.9
46 - 55	2.4	2.6	14.5	6.3	6.3	6.3	22.3	11.2
56 - 65	3.1	3.7	12.9	6.1	7.3	7.8	23.7	12.6
> 65	12.0	10.3	23.8	15.2	18.6	14.1	39.7	24.0
Sex[1]								
Male	3.4	4.4	15.9	7.7	7.7	7.5	24.8	13.8
Female	10.4	5.1	17.0	11.4	12.0	10.8	30.4	16.9
Status[2]								
Blue collar	2.9	4.0	20.3	8.8	7.6	9.1	28.2	15.2
White collar	0.8	1.6	6.5	2.8	3.0	3.5	9.7	5.3
Self-empl.[3]	1.9	3.2	10.6	5.2	5.6	4.1	20.5	11.0
Unemployed	*	*	*	*	*	*	*	*
Retired	10.3	8.8	22.7	13.7	13.6	12.3	34.3	19.2
Other	6.2	4.2	15.6	9.3	13.3	13.3	38.4	22.0
Total	4.6	4.5	16.0	8.3	9.1	8.1	25.8	14.4

Notes:
1) Characteristics of the reference person in the family
2) Working position of the reference person
3) National data for 1995 include also entrepeneurs, managers, professionals
* not available

Source: Own calculations from CIPE (1996a, 1996b), based on the Family Budget Survey, ISTAT, 1980-1995

1995				△ 1980-1995			
North	Centre	South	Italy	North	Centre	South	Italy
5.6	6.6	19.4	9.6	-6.5	+1.1	+3.3	-2.3
4.2	9.6	22.6	10.6	-1.2	+3.9	+5.0	+1.7
3.1	4.2	16.5	7.1	+1.9	+1.7	+8.0	+3.7
3.1	4.4	16.7	8.5	+0.9	+0.7	+3.8	+2.5
8.3	10.9	35.9	23.1	+3.0	+4.7	+12.9	+9.9
2.2	3.6	18.2	8.1	-0.2	+0.8	+4.6	+1.5
3.4	5.8	19.6	9.6	+1.1	+2.4	+4.4	+2.8
2.9	3.4	18.9	8.1	+0.5	+0.8	+4.4	+1.8
3.4	6.3	20.1	9.0	+0.3	+2.6	+7.2	+2.9
8.2	11.6	29.3	15.8	-3.8	+1.3	+6.0	+0.6
3.7	6.1	21.4	10.3	+0.3	+1.7	+5.5	+2.6
6.2	8.8	23.7	11.7	-4.2	+3.7	+7.7	+0.3
3.8	5.6	25.4	11.7	+0.9	+1.6	5.1	+2.9
1.3	3.1	11.5	5.3	+0.5	+1.5	+5.0	+2.5
2.3	4.3	14.9	8.1	+0.4	+1.1	+4.3	+1.7
13.7	10.9	40.0	28.3	*	*	*	*
6.1	8.0	25.4	11.5	-4.2	-0.8	+2.7	-2.2
7.5	14.7	30.0	18.1	+1.3	+10.5	+14.4	+8.8
4.4	6.8	21.9	10.6	-0.2	+2.3	+5.9	+2.3

Similarly, among the population living below the 50% threshold (60% for single persons), the unemployed do not necessarily account for the majority of cases; we also observe households with multiple incomes who are in a condition of poverty (see Table 4).

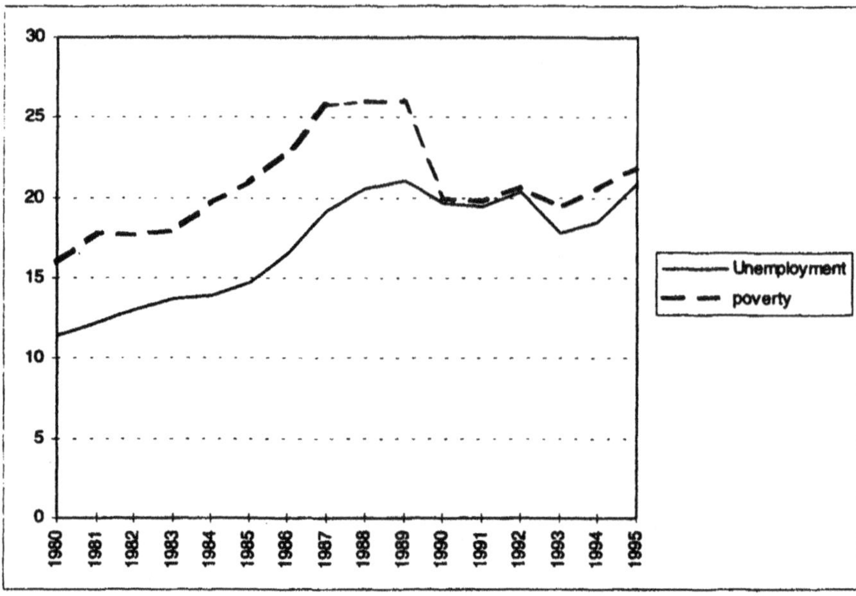

Figure 2 **Unemployment rates and incidence of poverty in the south of Italy 1980-1995**

Source: CIPE (1996a), Istat, Quarterly Bulletin (1995)

Table 4
Incidence of poverty according to some family typologies north and south (1995) (in %)

Selected typologies	North	South	Italy	North/South
Single person aged > 65	8.8	25.8	14.2	+17.0
Ref. person without education	11.1	38.7	28.1	+27.6
Ref. person university degree	0.8	4.6	2.3	+3.8
Single parent with 1 child	7.8	20.4	13.2	+5.4
Family (couple) with 1 child	2.9	14.9	6.4	+3.5
Family with > 2 children	8.5	33.7	24.0	+15.5
Family without empl. pers.	7.7	30.4	16.1	+22.7
Family with > 3 empl. pers.	3.7	20.2	6.5	+16.3

Source: Own calculation from CIPE (1996b: 8, Table 2, 5, and 12)

This situation can be explained by the fact that these incomes are often low pensions[24] or low wages of precarious workers, keeping these persons at the subsistence level. The great majority of the unemployed are not the families' household heads, but mainly young people who are not looking for a job on the labour market because they are discouraged by the unfavourable conditions of labour demand. This is the reason for their low participation rate.[25] Among them we find the apparently paradoxical situation that young males coming from the lower social classes are less affected by unemployment than their middle-upper class counterparts, but this is due to the fact that they cannot afford to be unemployed for longer periods of time and have to accept precarious and underpaid jobs (Ires-Cgil 1992; Pugliese 1993). It is, however, more short-term unemployment, typical for instance among workers in the construction sector, as well as the lack of stable and adequate job opportunities that influence the poverty patterns of the southern population. One of the consequences of the structural occupational crisis is the de facto exclusion of many households from all labour-related social policies (e.g. family allowances). Another consequence is the exclusion of women[26] from the labour market and paid employment and the persistence of a high number of large families relying on one source of income. The high incidence of poverty amongst large families in the south is not so much a demographic problem, but the consequence of social and macro-economic conditions which characterise the general context together with high drop-out rates of school, bad health and social services, deficits in the public transportation and in the system of care (Negri and Saraceno 1996; Kazepov 1996a). In these circumstances, women's domestic work is more than needed to overcome these negative conditions.

In the centre-northern regions the poverty patterns are quite different. As can be seen from the data of the Poverty Commission (CIPE 1996a, 1996b), the concentration of the poor is among singles (mainly elderly women) and elderly couples who have remained the largest group. Nevertheless, since the early eighties they have been constantly on the decline and, as a consequence, we have a medium- to long-term tendency which is independent from short-term contingent economic factors and characterised by increasing poverty amongst most age groups with the exception of the elderly (>65 years of age). The groups at risk are, however, much more differentiated than in the southern regions and are more associated with the difficulty of managing critical passages in the life cycle, such as retirement, long-term health problems, or a condition of social and familial isolation (Laffi and Micheli 1995; Kazepov et al. 1995). The family's sheltering capacity is being weakened more in the northern than in the southern regions (e.g. higher divorce and separation rates, more single households). Nevertheless, also in the centre-northern regions single-parent households are less represented amongst the poor than elsewhere in the industrialised world.[27] This is explained not only by the fact that single-parenthood is less widespread in Italy in general, but also by the fact that children born out of wedlock are not so common also amongst the lower strata of the population. As we have seen in section four, social policies for this target group are also better developed. Data from the Family Budget Survey is, however, insufficient[28] to show the greater heterogeneity of poverty profiles in the north, where it is more a cumulative process of conditions of deprivation (Laffi and Micheli 1995; Kazepov 1995b) leading to poverty than more widespread homogeneous structural effects. This does not mean that poverty does not exist, but that its specific characteristics make it more difficult to observe since they are strongly interrelated with the institutional mechanisms of regulation, and also highly fragmented and individualised.

5 Conclusion

From the point of view of social policies, the consequences of the described characteristics of the *Italian model of poverty* are particularly worrying because they bear a high potential for social conflict, due to persisting inequalities and increasing social vulnerability. The social security system established in the post-war period characterised by high economic development was *more or less* sufficient to cover the whole population at risk and prevent, at least in the north, the formation of pockets of poverty. Now, in a period of persistent long-term unemployment and flexibilisation of labour relations, this system has become increasingly obsolete. The number of well-protected workers is constantly shrinking and although male adults still show low levels of unemployment,[29] the *institutional pre-conditions* for the development of downward mobility paths are emerging more and more also in the northern cities and regions of the country. This is increasing the importance of social assistance schemes, but the institutional differences described in section three have consolidated a system of regional inequality, which is not able to guarantee the right to similar minimum living conditions throughout the whole country and particularly in the south. The particularistic and fragmented nature of the locally existing schemes is therefore increasingly becoming a powerful barrier to social participation and citizenship since it reinforces the socio-economic gap between Italy's northern and southern regions, instead of counteracting it from an institutional standpoint.

Notes

[1] In 1991 the unemployment rate was 25.1% in Bari, 33.5% in Catania, 42.7% in Naples, and 34.8% in Palermo. These high rates are even more of a problem because of the low activity rates, ranging between 37.3% in Catania and 39.3% in Naples (Source: Census 1991, Istat). Most of the unemployed (nearly 70%) are long-term unemployed, with a high concentration of young people below 25 years of age (nearly 60%). Unemployment is highest among young females (14-25 of age) at over 80% (!) in most of the cities of the south. In January 1995 the youth unemployment rate in the Mezzogiorno was 63,3% (Source: Istat, Labour Force Survey). For the Italian model of unemployment see Pugliese (1993).

[2] Together with the lack of a proper unemployment and an income maintenance scheme, one of the consequences of clientelism is the distribution of invalidity pensions to unemployed people. This took place implicitly as a functional substitute for the missing protection schemes and on the basis of patronage. Not by chance the ratio of invalidity pensions to old age pensions can even reach ten to one in the south compared to the north. In Lombardy there are 21.7 invalidity pensions for every 100 old age pensions, in Molise 213 and in Sardegna 198.1 (INPS 1993: Figure 1.3.6).

[3] In the south there are double and even triple shifts, larger classes and higher drop-out rates also during compulsory education. The differences persist also at the level of secondary schools. In terms of school attendance, for instance, in the twenty years from 1972 to 1993 the difference between the north and the south increased from about 5% to 6.2%, versus an increase of the national school attendance rate from 41.8% to 75%. Also the dropping-out rate reveals the north-south divide: 7.1% in the north as against 10.1% in the south dropped out of secondary school (Unpublished source: calculation of CISEM on Istat data).

[4] The per-capita income differences (1991) are very high: while Bologna has a per-capita income of 26,8 million Lira, and Milan of 26,7, in the south Naples has 13,8 and Catanzaro 12,7 or Enna 12,6 (Source: Istituto Tagliacarne).

[5] In the north-eastern regions and in Lombardy the unemployment rate for young people (below 25 years of age) is on average about 10% (lowest in Trentino: 8.3%). In southern regions (e.g. Calabria, Sicily, and Basilicata) the rate is more than 50% (highest in Campania: 60.1%). For this reason the national average (31.8%) can be misleading, because the deviation from the mean is very high: a difference of 51.8 percentage points between the highest and lowest level for the youth unemployment rate. For adults the deviation is 15.3 percentage points for men and 26.2 percentage points for women (Source: own calculations on 1994 data, Eurostat 1995a).

[6] In Naples, for example, half of the families living below the poverty line are composed of 5 or more persons. These families (a sample of 576 families) live mainly in two-room apartments with no hot water and no proper bathroom (Morlicchio and Spanò 1992). See last section of this chapter.

[7] At the end of 1994 there were (estimated by Caritas 1996) around 1.25 million foreigners in Italy, both legal and illegal. Other sources estimate the total number of foreigners around 1.5 millions of whom 922,706 legal (Source: Ministry of Interiors).

Milan and Rome are the cities with the highest density. The data show, however, that the numbers (% of the resident population) do not reach the levels of other European metropolitan areas, like Frankfurt/M. (27%), Amsterdam (29%), Liege (20%), Paris (16%, not including naturalised immigrants). Greater London has a higher ethnic minority population (Census 1991: about 20%) than the whole of Italy. In Milan the figure for legal foreigners is about 4.7% (estimation: about 6%) of the resident population, in Rome about 4.3% (estimation: about 5.6%) including EU citizens.

[8] The Autonomous Province of Bolzano is an exception. The risks of impoverishment are concentrated amongst the Italian-speaking population.

[9] The most common macro-regions to which the National Statistics Bureau refers are: the north, the centre (Tuscany, Umbria, the Marches, and Lazio) and the south (including islands). The north and the south are sometimes split, the north into north-east (Trentino-Alto Adige, Veneto, Friuli Venezia Giulia, and Emilia Romagna) and north-west (Piedmont, Valle d'Aosta, Lombardy, and Liguria) and the south into mainland south (Abruzzo, Molise, Campania, Puglia, Basilicata, and Calabria) and islands (Sicily and Sardinia).

[10] Some municipalities, for instance, are monitoring the number of payments, others recipients. The data may refer to the household, the recipient, or the reference person. The kind of additional information (socio-demographic, labour-market-related information, etc.) considered in each context varies widely. The cases may be organised into centralised or decentralised (in each district) archives, on paper, or machine-readable form. In most cases there is no annual statistical report at all.

[11] For an overview of the methodological problems implicit in the use of data on recipients see among others Sen (1981), Øyen (1992), Hanesch (1990), Zajczyk (1995).

[12] Hence we have only a series of case studies not comparable to one another for a few cities: Bologna (Guidicini and Pieretti 1988, 1992), Ravenna (Guidicini and Pieretti 1989), Modena (Sarpellon 1991), Milan (Kazepov and Laffi 1993, 1994; Mingione and Zajczyk 1992; Kazepov 1995a), Turin (Berzano 1992), Parma (Scivoletto and Zani 1989), Rome (Labos 1987; Calza Bini and Mirabile 1995), Naples (Morlicchio 1993, 1996; Morlicchio and Spanò 1992), Matera (de Bernard 1992).

[13] This underestimation is due to a technical aspect. Low income families have the highest non-response rate. Non-response, up to 40-45% among all families, and the substitution process, alters the randomness of the sample, whose representativeness is granted only for sex, age, and size of the municipality. For an overview of the sampling problem see Fabbris (1989).

[14] According to the *International Standard of Poverty Line* a family of two persons has to be considered poor if its consumption level is below the average consumption for a single person. This amount corresponds to 60% of the average income threshold for individuals living alone and 50% of the average income threshold for individuals living in larger households.

[15] In Italy, between 1992 and 1993, the incidence of poverty (the number of people with an expenditure level below half than the average) decreased from 11.7% to 10.7% However, this happened more as a result of the decrease in average monthly

expenditure from 1,041,651 to 1,024,973 Lira than to the poor being better off (own calculation on CIPE 1996a).

[16] Section 3 is based on the results of a pilot study co-ordinated by the author on *Local Policies against Social Exclusion*. The study has been carried out for the Italian Government Poverty Commission (Kazepov 1996a) in 14 Italian cities, located in 11 regions and covering 14.7% of the Italian population. The cities can be considered as representative of the territorial disparities existing from the institutional point of view between the centre-north and the south of the country. Many thanks go to Chiara Saraceno who accompanied the project for the Poverty Commission.

[17] The law fixes a maximum amount payable and this reduces the nominal 80% of the gross wage to a real 65%.

[18] For an overview of the institutional changes in the Italian labour market see Dell'Aringa and Samek Lodovici (1996); for a reconstruction of the Italian welfare state see Ferrera (1984, 1993); for an overview of all social policies against poverty in a broader sense, see Negri and Saraceno (1996). Since January 1997 a Governmental Commission has been established to propose an overall welfare reform aimed at overcoming the existing structural fragmentation and inequality.

[19] Italy has no real measure to support families with children. Italian family allowances are more a particularistic and means-tested labour-related income support for salaried workers and pensioners. The presence of children is relevant only in terms of household size for the calculation of the family threshold. It is not by chance that Italy has one of the lowest percentages of expenditure on social protection devoted directly to the family (1993: 3.3% compared to a 6.6% EU average). Conversely it has, with Greece, the highest percentage of expenditure on social protection devoted to the elderly (51.8% compared to a 36.7% EU average). Own calculations from Eurostat (1995b).

[20] In this ranking the handicapped and the elderly are the best off, at least from the formal point of view. The latter, for instance, are entitled to the INPS social pension, which is regulated at the national level and granted automatically to all people above 65 years of age as soon as their income is lower than the threshold (1996: about 550,000 Lira). However this subsidy is lower than the INPS minimum pension (1996: about 650,000 Lira) that is considered in most municipalities to be the minimum amount needed in order to lead a decent life. In this case the municipalities supplement the pension up to the limit of the threshold.

[21] The Poverty Commission adopts the *International Standard of Poverty Line* using data from the Family Budget survey carried out by Istat every year. This amount corresponds to 60% of the average income threshold for single persons and to a 50% threshold for families (see Table 2 for the equivalence scales used). I thank Enzo Mingione for his insights on this section of the chapter.

[22] In Italy the debate on the *new forms* of poverty arose during the mid eighties, but was not related to the increase in unemployment as elsewhere in Europe. It was more influenced by the debate on post-material and relational needs. Here, however, I refer to the increase in unemployment (with its novel aspects in mind) to show the new patterns of poverty.

[23] It would take us too far to go into the underclass debate and its relationship with the question of the 'culture of poverty'. What has to be said, however, is that the vagueness of Lewis' concept (1959) and its misuse by conservative politicians and scholars (e.g. Gladwin 1961) hindered its diffusion. Only situationalists (e.g. Valentine 1968; Gans 1962) built upon it by developing a critical perspective according to which cultural elements are not transmitted by socialisation but are determined by the structural and material conditions of the society. The poor do not necessarily have different values, but they do have restricted options. For the connection with the underclass debate see Mingione (1996b), Morris (1994), Wilson (1987, 1996). For the culture of poverty debate see Ghezzi (1996).

[24] Pensions in the south are up to 40% lower than in the north and mostly around the minimum pension's threshold (INPS 1993: Figure 1.3.7).

[25] Activity rates for young people (14-29 years of age) are comparatively low in the cities of the south: Naples (14.1%), Palermo (17.2%), Catania (20.2%). In the northern cities these rates are three times higher: Milan (43.5%), Turin (41.2%), Bologna (50.9). Considering that their secondary school and higher education attendance is lower [Naples (27.1%), Palermo (28.6%) and Catania (27.7%)] compared to the north [Milan (39%), Turin (33.8%) and Bologna (37.2%)], the situation is really worrying (Source: Census 1991).

[26] If we consider the 25-30 years of age group, the activity rate for women in the centre-north is more than 50%, while in the south it is less than 25%. If we take male adults (between 30 and 40 years of age) we can see that in the northern cities less than 10% are unemployed or badly employed, while in the South the figure is nearly 40% (Source: Census 1991).

[27] Data of the Poverty Commission (CIPE 1996a: Table 4) show that single-parent households constitute only 6.1% of all poor families in the north, compared to 6% of *all* single-parent households. This means that they are slightly over-represented compared, for instance, to families with 3 or more children who constitute 8% of the resident population and 18% of the poor in the south.

[28] This insufficiency derives directly from the heterogeneity of the potential paths of impoverishment and is related to the fact that the same income threshold is not necessarily adequate for the satisfaction of the basic needs of all persons. Therefore it is not income per se, but adequacy in maintaining *ones own* capabilities in relation to a standard of living considered acceptable in a given context (Sen 1992) which should be taken into consideration.

[29] In the European Union, Italy is one of the countries with the lowest male unemployment rates. In some regions such as Trentino Alto Adige (1994: 3.1%) and Lombardy (1994: 4.5%) their unemployment is at a frictional level (Eurostat 1995). As far as young people are concerned the question is different. The high level of protection of male adults contributed to a deficit of occupational mobility and a kind of *frozen employment*, i.e. a situation in which there is no turnover, impeding entry to the labour market. Italy is, together with Spain, the country with the highest youth unemployment rates in Europe. In the Campania region, for instance, it is over 60% (1994). In some contexts young female unemployment rates even surpass 80%.

References

Ascoli, U. (ed.) (1984), *Welfare state all'italiana*, Laterza: Bari.

Banca d'Italia (1989), 'I bilanci delle famiglie italiane nell'anno 1987', *Supplementi Bollettino Statistico*, Vol. XLII, No. 5.

Banca d'Italia (1991), 'I bilanci delle famiglie italiane nell'anno 1989', *Supplementi al Bollettino Statistico. Note metodologiche e informazioni statistiche*, New series, I, No. 26, 8th October 1991.

Banca d'Italia (1993), 'I bilanci delle famiglie italiane nell'anno 1991', *Supplementi al Bollettino Statistico. Note metodologiche e informazioni statistiche*, New series, III, No. 44, 14th July 1993.

Banca d'Italia (1995), 'I bilanci delle famiglie italiane nell'anno 1993', *Supplementi al Bollettino Statistico. Note metodologiche e informazioni statistiche*, New series, V, No. 9, 10th February 1995.

Berzano, L. (1992), *Uomini senza territorio*, Il Segnalibro: Turin.

Braghin, P. (1978), *Inchiesta sulla miseria in Italia*, Einaudi: Turin.

Brandolini, A. (1993), *A Description and an Assessment of the Sample Surveys on the Personal Distribution of Incomes in Italy*, The Microsimulation Unit, Discussion Paper No. MU 9303, University of Cambridge, UK: Cambridge.

Calza Bini, P. and Mirabile, M. L. (eds.) (1995), 'L'esclusione sociale fra politiche pubbliche e percorsi individuali. Il caso di Roma', *Ires Materiali*, Rome, No. 7, July.

Caritas di Roma (1996), *Immigrazione '95. Dossier Statistico*, Anterem: Rome.

CIPE (Commissione di Indagine sulla Povertà e l'emarginazione) (1995), *Verso una politica di lotta alla povertà. L'assegno per i figli e il minimo vitale*, Collana della Commissione Povertà, Istituto Poligrafico dello Stato: Roma.

CIPE (1996a), *La povertà in Italia 1980-1994*, Collana della Commissione Povertà, Istituto Poligrafico dello Stato: Roma.

CIPE (1996b), *La povertà in Italia 1995*, Collana della Commissione Povertà, Istituto Poligrafico dello Stato: Roma.

De Bernard, M. (1992), *Matera trent'anni dopo*, Esi: Naples.

Dell'Aringa, C. and Samek Lodovici, M. (1996), 'Policies for the Unemployed and Social Shock Absorbers: the Italian Experience', Paper presented at the MIRE conference on *Comparing Social Welfare Systems in Southern Europe*, Florence, 22-24 February.

Esping-Andersen, G. (1990), *The three Worlds of Welfare Capitalism*, University Press: Princeton.

Esping-Andersen, G. (1993), *Changing Classes: Post-industrial Mobility Regimes*, Sage: London.

EUROSTAT (1995a), *Basic Statistics of the European Union*, 32nd edition, European Commission: Luxembourg.

EUROSTAT (1995b), *Social Protection Expenditure and Receipts 1980-1993*, Theme 3, Population and Social Conditions, European Commission: Luxembourg.

EUROSTAT (1995c), *Annuario '95. Visione statistica dell'Europa 1983-1993*, European Commission: Luxembourg.

EUROSTAT (1996), *The Household Panel Newsletter*, Theme 3, Series B, 2.

Fabbris, L. (1989), *L'indagine campionaria: metodi, disegni e tecniche di campionamento*, NIS: Rome.

Ferrera, M. (1984), *Il welfare state in Italia. Sviluppo e crisi in prospettiva comparata*, Il Mulino: Bologna.

Ferrera, M. (1993), *Modelli di Solidarietà. Politica e riforme sociali nelle democrazie*, Il Mulino: Bologna.

Gans, H. (1962), *The Urban Villagers*, MacMillan: New York.

Ghezzi, S. (1996), *The 'Culture of Poverty' Debate in the Sixities. Stigma and Prejudice during the 'War on Poverty'*, University of Toronto, Department of Anthropology, mimeo.

Giordano, C. (1992), *Die Betrogenen der Geschichte. Überlagerungsmentalität und Überlagerungsrationalität in mediterranen Gesellschaften*, Campus: Frankfurt/M.

Gladwin, T. (1961), 'The Anthropologist's View of Poverty', *The Social Welfare Forum*, pp. 73-86.

Golini, A. (ed.) (1994), *Tendenze demografiche e politiche per la popolazione*, Il Mulino: Bologna.

Guidicini, P. and Pieretti, G. (eds.) (1988), *I volti della povertà urbana*, Franco Angeli: Milan.

Guidicini, P. and Pieretti, G. (eds.) (1989), *Tra marginalità e povertà. Uno studio sulle politiche di intervento pubblico a Ravenna*, Franco Angeli: Milan.

Guidicini, P. and Pieretti, G. (eds.) (1992), *Le radici dell'impoverimento*, Franco Angeli: Milan.

Hanesch, W. (1990), 'Armut und Armutsberichterstattung in Kommunen', in: Ott, H.-U., Karsten, M.-E. (eds.), *Sozialberichterstattung. Lebensräume gestalten als neue Strategie kommunaler Sozialpolitik*, Juventa: München, pp. 58-76.

Inchiesta (1993), 'Modelli regionali di disoccupazione', XXII, 99, January-March.

INPS (Istituto Nazionale per la Previdenza Sociale) (1993), *Le pensioni domani. Primo rapporto sulla previdenza in Italia, promosso dall'INPS*, Il Mulino: Bologna.

ISTAT (Istituto Nazionale di Statistica) (1995a), *Indagine campionaria sui consumi delle famiglie anno 1994*, Serie 4, Foglio 41, XVI, No. 8, December 1995.

ISTAT (Istituto Nazionale di Statistica) (1995b), 'I grandi comuni: Milano. 13.', *Censimento Generale della Popolazione e delle Abitazioni*, 20 October 1991.

IRES-CGIL (Istituto per la Ricerca Economica e Sociale) (1992), *Caratteristiche e tipologia della disoccupazione in Italia: sperimentazione di strumenti di analisi e valutazione*, Research Report, mimeo: Rome.

Kazepov, Y. (1995a), 'Ai confini della cittadinanza: il ruolo delle istituzioni nei percorsi di esclusione a Stoccarda e Milano', *Polis*, 1/95, pp. 45-66.

Kazepov, Y. (1995b), 'I nuovi poveri in Lombardia. Sistemi di welfare e traiettorie di esclusione sociale', *Quaderni Regionali di Ricerca*, No. 1, Regione Lombardia: Milan.

Kazepov, Y. (1996a), *Le politiche locali contro l'esclusione sociale*, Istituto Poligrafico dello Stato: Rome.

Kazepov, Y. (1996b), 'La legge non è uguale per tutti. Assistenza economica e istituzionalizzazione dei rischi a livello locale', *Assistenza Sociale*, Vol. 52, pp. 115-134.

Kazepov, Y. and Laffi, S. (1993), 'Povertà e servizi: contesti e percorsi negli utenti dell'Ufficio Adulti in Difficoltà di Milano', *Marginalità e Società*, Vol. 22, pp. 19-28.

Kazepov, Y. and Laffi, S. (1994), 'Sguardi sulla povertà a Milano', *Ricerca*, Vol. 2, pp. 17-27.

Kazepov, Y. and Mingione, E. (eds.) (1994), *La cittadinanza spezzata. Il dibattito teorico e metodologico su esclusione sociale e povertà*, Armando Siciliano editore: Messina.

Kazepov, Y., Mingione, E. and Zajczyk, F. (eds.) (1995), *Povertà estrema: istituzioni e percorsi a Milano*, Franco Angeli: Milan.

LABOS (Laboratorio per le politiche sociali) (1987), *Essere barboni a Roma*, Ter: Rome.

Laffi, S. and Micheli, G. (eds.) (1995), *Derive. Stati e percorsi di povertà non estreme in una survey nel veneto*, Franco Angeli: Milan.

Lewis, O. (1959), *Five Families*, New York.

Mc Fate, K., Lawson, R. and Wilson, W.-J. (eds.) (1995), *Poverty, Inequality and the Future of Social Policy*, Russel Sage Foundation: New York.

Mingione, E. (1986), 'La povertà familiare nelle città meridionali', *Inchiesta*, Vol. XVI, No. 73, pp. 53-61.

Mingione, E. (1988), 'Problems and Prospects of the Welfare State in Italy', in: Brown, K. M. (ed.), *Remaking the Welfare State. Retrenchment and Social Policy in America and Europe*, Temple University Press: Philadelphia.

Mingione, E. (1994), 'Life Strategies and Social Economies in the Postfordist Age', *International Journal of Urban and Regional Research*, Vol. 18, No. 1, pp. 24-45.

Mingione, E. (1996a), 'I soggetti della povertà', *Assistenza Sociale*, Vol. 52, pp. 71-86.

Mingione, E. (ed.) (1996b), *Urban Poverty and the Underclass. A Reader*, Blackwell: Oxford.

Mingione, E. and Morlicchio, E. (1993), 'New Forms of Urban Poverty in Italy: Risk Path Models in the North and South', *International Journal of Urban and Regional Research*, Vol. 17, No. 3, pp. 63-79.

Mingione, E. and Zajczyk, F. (1992), 'Le nuove povertà urbane in Italia: modelli di percorsi a rischio nell'area metropolitana milanese', *Inchiesta*, Vol. XXII, No. 97-98, pp. 63-79.

MISSOC (Mutual Information System on Social Security) (1995), *Social Protection in the Member States of the Community*. Situation on July 1st, 1994 and evolution, Commission of the European Communities, DG V: Brussels.

Morlicchio, E. (1993), 'Povertà ed emarginazione nel Mezzogiorno', *Marginalità e Società*, Vol. 22, pp. 64-77.

Morlicchio, E. (1996), 'Exclusion from Work and the Impoverishment Processes in Naples', in: Mingione, E. (ed.), *Urban Poverty and the Underclass. A Reader*, Blackwell: Oxford, pp. 325-342.

Morlicchio, E. and Spanò, A. (1992), 'La povertà a Napoli', *Inchiesta*, Vol. XXII, No. 97-98, pp. 80-89.

Morris, L. (1994), *Dangerous Classes. The Underclass and Social Citizenship*, Routledge: London.

Morris, L. (1995), *Social Divisions. Economic Decline and Social Structural Change*, UCL Press: London.

Negri, N. and Saraceno, C. (1996), *Le politiche contro la povertà in Italia*, Il Mulino: Bologna.

Øyen, E. (1992), 'Some Basic Issues in Comparative Poverty Research', *International Social Science Journal*, Vol. XLIV, No. 4, pp. 615-626.

Paci, M. (1989), *Pubblico e privato nei moderni sistemi di Welfare*, Liguori: Naples.

Paci, M. (1992), *Il mutamento della struttura sociale in Italia*, Il Mulino: Bologna.

Pugliese, E. (1993), *Sociologia della disoccupazione*, Il Mulino: Bologna.

Saraceno, C. (1992), *Italy*, Consolidated Report for the Observatory on National Policies to Combat Social Exclusion, European Commission: Brussels.

Saraceno, C. (1994), 'The Ambivalent Familism of the Italian Welfare State', *Social Politics*, No. 1, pp. 60-82.

Saraceno, C. and Negri, N. (1994), 'The Changing Italian Welfare State', *Journal of European Social Policy*, No. 1, pp. 19-34.

Sassen, S. (1991), *Global Cities. London, New York and Tokyo*, Princeton University Press: Princeton, NJ.

Sassen, S. (1996), 'Service Employment Regimes and the New Inequality', in Mingione, E. (ed.), *Urban Poverty and the Underclass. A Reader*, Blackwell: Oxford, pp. 64-82.

Sarpellon, G. (ed.) (1991), *Percorsi di povertà e reti di servizi*, Franco Angeli: Milan.

Scivoletto, A. and Zani, S. (1989), *Malessere nella città ricca. Aspetti della Povertà - antica e nuova - in area parmense*, Franco Angeli: Milan.

Sen, A. K. (1981), *Poverty and Famine*, Clarendon Press: Oxford.

Sen, A. K. (1992), *Inequality re-examined*, Clarendon Press: Oxford.

Sidoti, F. (1989), *Povertà, devianza, criminalità nell'Italia Meridionale*, Franco Angeli: Milan.

Spanò, A. (1992), 'La povertà nel Meridione', *Inchiesta*, Vol. XXII, No. 96, pp. 59-71.

Tosi, A. (1994), *Abitanti. Le nuove strategie dell'azione abitativa*, Il Mulino: Bologna.

Valentine, C. A. (1968), *Culture and Poverty: Critique and Counter-Proposals*, University Press: Chicago.

Wilson, J. W. (1987), *The Truly Disadvantaged*, University of Chicago Press: Chicago.

Wilson, J. W. (1991), 'Studying Inner-City Dislocations', *American Sociological Review*, Vol. 56, pp. 1-14.

Wilson, J. W. (1996), *When Work Disappears. The World of the New Urban Poor*, Alfred A. Knopf: New York.

Zajczyk, F. (1995), 'Gli indicatori della povertà: prospettive macro e micro', *Sociologia e Ricerca Sociale*, No. 47-48, pp. 95-121.

List of contributors

Hans-Jürgen Andreß studied social and political science at the Universities of Frankfurt/Main (Germany) and Ann Arbor (USA). He gained his Dr. phil. at the University of Frankfurt/Main in 1983 and is at present professor for empirical research methods and computer science at the Faculty of Sociology of Bielefeld University (Germany). He has published in the field of multivariate statistical methods, labour market, and poverty research.

Karel Van den Bosch studied sociology at the University of Nijmegen (The Netherlands). He is now working as a researcher at the Centre of Social Policy at the University of Antwerp (Belgium). He has published in the fields of poverty and income distribution. At present he is putting the final touches to his Ph.D. thesis on subjective measures of poverty.

Petra Buhr studied sociology at the University in Bielefeld (Germany) and gained her Dr. rer.pol. at the University of Bremen (Germany) in 1994. At present she is assistant professor in the Special Research Unit 186 'Status Passages and Risks in the Life Course' at the University of Bremen (Germany) where she is working on social policy, poverty, and social assistance.

Henk-Jan Dirven studied sociology at the University of Tilburg (The Netherlands). At present, he is a statistical researcher at Statistics Netherlands. He has published on dynamic aspects of income poverty and relative deprivation. His contributions to this volume are based on research conducted while he was a lecturer in social security studies at Tilburg University. The views expressed in these contributions are his own and do not necessarily reflect the views and policies of Statistics Netherlands.

Didier Fouarge studied economics at the Facultés Universitaires Notre-Dame de la Paix in Namur (Belgium). He is currently working on his Ph.D. thesis on minimum protection in Europe, the principle of subsidiarity, and the role of the European Community in the field of social protection. He did international comparative research in the field of income poverty, relative deprivation, and poverty dynamics using panel data.

Jürgen Friedrichs studied sociology, social psychology, and philosophy at the universities of Berlin and Hamburg (Germany). Her received his Ph.D. in 1968 at the University of Hamburg. He presently has a chair in sociology at the University of Cologne and is director of the Research Institute for Sociology. He has published extensively in the fields of urban socioloyg and research methods.

Björn Halleröd is a Reader in sociology at Umeå University, Sweden. His principal research interests are in the study of distributions of economic resources, standards of living, and poverty. In several works he has discussed different theoretical definitions of poverty and explored how the choice of definition influences the outcomes from empirical analysis. He is currently doing research on consumption patterns among different households and on intra-household distribution of resources.

Bruno Jeandidier gained his Ph.D. in economy at the University of Nancy 2 (France) in 1985. At present he is senior researcher of the Centre National de la Recherche Scientifique (CNRS) and leads the research team of the University of Nancy 2 named Dynamic Analysis of the Effects of Social Policies (ADEPS, Unit associated to CNRS no. 1167). His two principal research interests are the micro-economic analysis of the effects of the family and assistance policies and the methodology of household panel surveys.

Olli Kangas is professor of social policy at the University of Turku (Finland). He works currently as visiting professor at the Swedish Institute for Social Research, University of Stockholm (Sweden). He has worked for many years on comparative analysis of social policy programs in OECD countries with a particular interest in the relationships between politics, social policy programs, and their outcomes in terms of income distribution and poverty.

Yuri Kazepov earned a Ph.D. in sociology and is at present research fellow of the University of Milan (Italy). He teaches economic sociology at the University of Urbino. In 1995/96 he has been Jean Monet Fellow at the Forum on 'Citizenship' of the European University Institute in Florence (Italy). Since 1990 he works on poverty, citizenship, and social policies at the local, national, and international level. He has published extensively on these topics and has been expert of the Poverty Commission of the Italian Government and of the European Commission (DG 22).

Jean-Luc Kop earned a Ph.D. in psychology at the University of Nancy 2 (France) in 1994. He is now assistant professor for methodology of psychology at the University of Nancy 2. Among his principal research interests are psychometry and methodology, measurement of subjective well-being, and relations between objective and subjective measures of poverty.

Martin Kronauer studied sociology, philosophy, and political science at the Universities of Heidelberg and Darmstadt (Germany). He did research in urban studies at the New School for Social Research (New York, USA) and received his Dr. phil. at the Free University of Berlin (Germany). He is currently a research associate at the Sociological Research Institute at the University of Göttingen (Germany). His research and publications are in the field of unemployment, social inequality, and urban studies.

Vladimir Mikhalev studied political science at the Moscow State University and development economics at the Institute of World Economy and International Relations of the Russian Academy of Science in Moscow. He gained his Ph.D. in development economics at the Institute of World Economy and International Relations in Moscow in 1984 and is senior research fellow at that institution. He has been guest professor at the University of Cambridge, Columbia University, Kennan Institute for Advanced Russian Studies (Washington, DC), and at the European University Institute in Florence. He has published in the field of economic and social development of Third World countries, and on income distribution, poverty, and social policy issues in Russia under economic transformation.

Ruud Muffels gained a master's degree in macro-economics at Tilburg University (The Netherlands). He became a lecturer in labour and social security studies in 1990 and got his Ph.D. in 1993. From 1993 on he is professor of socio-economics of ageing and from 1995 a research professor of labour and social security studies at the Work and Organisation Research Centre at Tilburg University. His publications are on labour market, poverty, social security and ageing.

Wim van Oorschot studied sociology at Tilburg University (The Netherlands) and gained his Dr. phil. in Tilburg in 1995. At present he is associate professor for sociology of work and social security and head of the Department of Social Security Studies of Tilburg University. He has published on take-up of social security benefits, poverty and anti-poverty policies, history and legitimacy of the welfare state, social security models, solidarity and privatisation of social policy.

Veli-Matti Ritakallio studied social policy at the University of Turku (Finland). He gained his Ph.D. at the University of Turku in 1994 and is at present associate professor of social policy at Turku University. His main research topic has been cross-national comparisons of sociopolitical institutions in their ability to alleviate poverty.

Katja Schulte studied sociology at the University of Bielefeld (Germany). Since 1996 she has been researcher at the Centre for Social Policy Research at the University of Bremen (Germany). She works on poverty issues and the link between social policy and social exclusion.

Robert Walker was educated as a social geographer at the University of Bristol and the London School of Economics. After working in government he has spent all his university career in research centres at Kent, York and, currently, Loughborough where he is Director of the Social Security Unit in the Centre for Research in Social Policy. He has written or edited more than a dozen books on poverty, social assistance, and social security.

Andreas Weber studied social science at the University of Bremen (Germany). Since 1997, he works at the Centre for Social Policy Research at the University of Bremen. His research interests are in indicators of social change, especially in poverty, migration, and labour market aspects.

For Product Safety Concerns and Information please contact our EU representative GPSR@taylorandfrancis.com Taylor & Francis Verlag GmbH, Kaufingerstraße 24, 80331 München, Germany

Batch number: 10725991

Printed by Printforce, the Netherlands